Feminism Unmodified

Feminism
UNMODIFIED

Discourses on Life and Law

CATHARINE A. MACKINNON

HARVARD UNIVERSITY PRESS
Cambridge, Massachusetts, and London, England

Library of Congress Cataloging-in-Publication Data

MacKinnon, Catharine A.
    Feminism unmodified.

    Bibliography: p.
    Includes index.
    1.   Women—Legal status, laws, etc.—United States.
2.   Feminism—United States.   I. Title.
KF478.M25   1987   346.7301'34   86-25694
ISBN 0-674-29873-X (alk. paper)   (cloth)   347.306134
ISBN 0-674-29874-8   (paper)

For Andrea Dworkin

Contents

INTRODUCTION   The Art of the Impossible   1

I. APPROACHES

1 Not by Law Alone: From a Debate with Phyllis Schlafly   21
2 Difference and Dominance: On Sex Discrimination   32
3 Desire and Power   46
4 Whose Culture? A Case Note on Martinez v. Santa Clara
   Pueblo   63
5 On Exceptionality: Women as Women in Law   70

II. APPLICATIONS

6 A Rally against Rape   81
7 Sex and Violence: A Perspective   85
8 Privacy v. Equality: Beyond Roe v. Wade   93
9 Sexual Harassment: Its First Decade in Court   103
10 Women, Self-Possession, and Sport   117

III. PORNOGRAPHY

11 Linda's Life and Andrea's Work   127
12 "More Than Simply a Magazine": Playboy's Money   134
13 Not a Moral Issue   146
14 Francis Biddle's Sister: Pornography, Civil Rights, and
   Speech   163
15 On Collaboration   198
16 The Sexual Politics of the First Amendment   206

AFTERWORD   215

Notes   231
Acknowledgments   307
Index   309

Feminism Unmodified

The Art of the Impossible

Brian Coyle: It's sometimes said politics is the art of the possible . . .
Sandra Hilary: Sometimes I think it's more the art of the impossible.

Debate on the civil rights law against pornography, Minneapolis City Council,
July 24, 1984

T his is a second look at the second wave of feminism in the
United States, after fifteen years of trying to change the status
of women by law and every other available means. Because I
want you to hear me speaking, rather than read me writing, many of
the texts in this collection appear exactly as they were spoken. The
formality varies with the occasion, but they were all spoken first without a written text, even those that were later revised. These are engaged works, occasioned by the urgency of the problems women
face, not by abstract agendas or academic imperatives. In retrospect,
during the years these speeches encompass, 1981 to 1986, the wom-
en's movement has been moving toward a crossroads.

The Equal Rights Amendment, designed to make sex legally irrelevant, was lost, in part through opposition by women. The abortion
right, framed as a right to privacy rather than a right to sex equality,
was recognized, only to be taken almost immediately from women
who have least access to it.[1] Losing it entirely is an ever-current danger, and its opponents include women. Women are poor, and pay is
at least as far from being sex-equal as it was before the passage of
legislation guaranteeing pay equality by law.[2] Women are more and
more losing custody of their children,[3] in part because of legal re-
forms feminists helped put in place. The rape rate is increasing significantly, while the conviction rate for rape is not,[4] in spite of legal
changes feminists fought for and won over the last decade.[5] We are
headed for another showdown on pregnancy, this time framed as a
debate on whether states that provide maternity benefits are violating the view of sex equality that organized feminism has sought to
institutionalize.[6] In this string of defeats and declines, the law on
sexual harassment[7] and some legal advances against domestic battery
of women and marital rape—the social impact of all of which is as
yet unknown—are among the few exceptions. To this picture, add

1

the feminist attempt to get civil rights for women exploited by pornographers, an attempt that was opposed by some claiming feminist ground for their opposition, and it begins to seem like time for a real reassessment.

Feminism has not changed the status of women. It is not enough to observe that social change is glacial, law is inadequate to move anything basic, and power is powerful. These truisms parade solipsism, the complacency of privilege, and despair as sophistication, critique, even radical politics. And to describe a state of affairs is not to explain it. An explanation of the failure of feminism to change the world for women must be a study *in* that world as well as *of* it.

Because we need to know them, these speeches are looking for answers to the big questions of the subordination of women to men: its roots, damage, pervasiveness, tenacity, enforcement, and capacity for change. We need to know how the inequality of the sexes is lived out, threaded from one moment to the next through millions of lifetimes of habit into individual identities and social relations. We need to know more about how women experience and respond to being second class, from unconsciousness and denial and collaboration to consciousness and resistance and confrontation. We need to know precisely how the benefits and burdens of this system are allocated—including the way showcase indulgences to a few women in a rich liberal state purchase legitimacy for a system that functions nationally and internationally at the expense of all women. We need to know how this system gives each woman a survival stake in the system that is killing her.

We urgently need to comprehend the emerging pattern in which gender, while a distinct inequality, also contributes to the social embodiment and expression of race and class inequalities, at the same time as race and class are deeply imbedded in gender. For example, the sexualization of racial and ethnic attributes like skin color or stereotypes is no less a dynamic within racism for being done through gender. The masculinity of money as a form of power takes nothing from its function as capital, although it does undermine some models of economic rationality, including leftist ones. Women get their class status through their sexual relations with men of particular classes; perhaps their racial status, also no less real for being vicarious, similarly derives from racial hierarchies among men. From these and other examples, gender in this country appears partly to comprise the meaning of, as well as bisect, race and class, even as race and class specificities make up, as well as cross-cut, gender. A

2

general theory of social inequality is prefigured, if inchoately, in these connections.

I am thinking all the time about power: the simplicity of the force and the complexity of the authority that make male supremacy a specific politics, and the changing shades of complicity, its feminine face. Some day, probably a day marked by no one at the time, but some time after the beginning of the end of this system, the questions considered here will simply become part of "the political." How sisterhood became powerful[8] while women were powerless will take its place among the classic alchemies of political history. How *did* they do that? students will be encourged to wonder.

My arguments and meditations to this end provide the themes that unify this volume. The first theme is the analysis that the social relation between the sexes is organized so that men may dominate and women must submit and this relation is sexual—in fact, is sex.[9] Men in particular, if not men alone, sexualize inequality, especially the inequality of the sexes. The second theme is a critique of the notion that gender is basically a difference rather than a hierarchy. To treat gender as a difference (with or without a French accent)[10] means to treat it as a bipolar distinction, each pole of which is defined in contrast to the other by opposed intrinsic attributes.[11] Beloved of left and right alike, construing gender as a difference, termed simply the gender difference, obscures and legitimizes the way gender is imposed by force. It hides that force behind a static description of gender as a biological or social or mythic or semantic partition, engraved or inscribed or inculcated by god, nature, society (agents unspecified), the unconscious, or the cosmos. The idea of gender difference helps keep the reality of male dominance in place.

The third theme identifies pornography in America as a key means of actualizing these two dynamics in life. Pornography turns sex inequality into sexuality and turns male dominance into the sex difference. Put another way, pornography makes inequality into sex, which makes it enjoyable, and into gender, which makes it seem natural. By packaging the resulting product as pictures and words, pornography turns gendered and sexualized inequality into "speech," which has made it a right. Thus does pornography, cloaked as the essence of nature and the index of freedom, turn the inequality between women and men into those twin icons of male supremacy, sex and speech, and a practice of sex discrimination into a legal entitlement.

Confronting pornography through civil rights law[12]—meaning, with a concrete intention of actually doing something about the damage pornography does to women's safety and status—has somewhat illuminated the social meaning of state power. The terms of the pornography debate have been altered through the feminist exposure of pornography as an industry, not just an iconography; as a trade in female flesh, not just imagery or ideas; as more practice than theory; as a means as well as a metaphor for the oppression of women. Liberal convention imagines a state hostile to sexuality and to speech, especially dissident sexuality and dissident speech. The state, in this view, would leap at any opportunity to restrict pornography. The utter failure of this state to do anything effective about it—with the extremely elastic obscenity standard in its hands and all of its power at its disposal—should suggest that this theory of the state is lacking. The hostile, even contemptuous, response of the courts to the first round of women's attempt to gain civil rights against pornographers[13] should suggest that this theory of the state is wrong. At the least, this response implies that the dissident and the conventional have been misdiagnosed. The behavior of the state better supports the view that its interest, expressed through its law, is to guarantee that the pornography stays. Just as aesthetics defines and protects pornography as art, literary criticism defines and protects it as literature, and sexology defines and protects it as sex, the First Amendment defines and protects it as speech. And for the same reasons: political reasons, reasons of sexual politics, reasons of the power of men over women. One wonders which came first, the canon or the pornography.

With few exceptions, feminism applied to law has provided no critique of the state of its own, and little insight into specific legal concepts from the standpoint of women's experience of second-class citizenship. Particularly in its upper reaches, much of what has passed for feminism in law has been the attempt to get for men what little has been reserved for women or to get for some women some of the plunder that some men have previously divided (unequally) among themselves. This is not to argue that women should be excluded from the spoils of dominance on the basis of sex, exactly. Rather, it is to say that it is antithetical to what women have learned and gained, by sacrifice chosen and unchosen, through sheer hanging on by bloody fingernails, to have the equality we fought for turned into equal access to the means of exploitation, equal access to force with impunity, equal access to sex with the less powerful, equal access to the privilege of irrelevance. As male academics have been able to afford to talk in ways that mean nothing, so also women; as male pornographers have been permitted to subordinate women sexually through pictures and words, so also women. In the words of Andrea Dworkin, if this is feminism, it deserves to die.

I think the fatal error of the legal arm of feminism has been its failure to understand that the mainspring of sex inequality is misogyny and the mainspring of misogyny is sexual sadism. The misogyny of liberal legalism included.[14] This, at least, is my understanding of the popular denial that sexual violation is a sexual practice. The determined belief that sex and violence are mutually exclusive is a wish fulfillment that has clouded the theory and confused the activism, including the legal activism, of the movement.[15] Related is the equally popular assumption that the gender inequality we confront is really only a natural biological harmony to be restored, rather than a fundamental social conflict to be resolved. So, too, the alternating and simultaneous rejection and embrace of sex as a difference[16] has evaded the issues of power and left the hierarchy that is gender right in place.

Sexuality

They said, "You are a savage and dangerous woman." [I said] "I am speaking the truth. And the truth is savage and dangerous."

Nawal El Saadawi, *Woman at Point Zero* (1983), the story of a prostitute

Since 1970, feminists have uncovered a vast amount of sexual abuse of women by men. Rape, battery, sexual harassment, sexual abuse of children, prostitution, and pornography, seen for the first time in their true scope and interconnectedness, form a distinctive pattern: the power of men over women in society. These abuses are as allowed de facto as they are prohibited de jure. Formal prohibition has done little to alter their frequency; it has helped make it hard to believe that they are so common. The reports that are believed are treated as if the events and their victims are statistically deviant, because the events they report have been branded as morally and legally deviant. In fact, it is the woman who has not been sexually abused who deviates.

The reason feminism uncovered this reality, its methodological secret, is that feminism is built on believing women's accounts of sexual use and abuse by men.[17] The pervasiveness of male sexual violence against women is therefore not denied, minimized, trivialized, eroticized, or excepted as marginal or episodic or placed to one side while more important matters are discussed. The fact that only 7.8 percent of women in the United States have not been sexually assaulted or harassed in their lifetime[18] is not considered inconsequential or isolated. The fact that sexual violation is a sexual practice is faced. A new paradigm begins here, one that fits the reality of the experience to be explained. All the ways in which women are suppressed and subjected—restricted, intruded on, violated, objectified—are recognized as what sex is for women and as the meaning and content of femininity.

If this is done, sexuality itself is no longer unimplicated in women's second-class status. Sexual violence can no longer be categorized away as violence not sex.[19] Women do not thrive on violation, whether or not it is done through sex. But our rapists,[20] serial murderers ("I killed my mother for the same reason I've killed all those other women. The reason was sex."),[21] and child molesters ("It's as natural for me to have sex with children the way it's natural for some people to have sex with women.")[22] enjoy their acts sexually and as men, to be redundant. It is sex *for them.* What is sex except that which is felt as sexual? When acts of dominance and submission, up to and including acts of violence, are experienced as sexually arousing, as sex itself, that is what they are. The mutual exclusivity of sex and violence is preserved in the face of this evidence by immunizing as "sex" whatever causes a sexual response and by stigmatizing questioning it as repressive, knowing that what is thereby exempted includes humiliation and brutality and molestation and murder as well as rape by any definition. Violence is sex when it is practiced as sex.[23] If violation of the powerless is part of what is sexy about sex, as well as central in the meaning of male and female, the place of sexuality in gender and the place of gender in sexuality need to be looked at together.

When this is done, sexuality appears as the interactive dynamic of gender as an inequality. Stopped as an attribute of a person, sex inequality takes the form of gender; moving as a relation between people, it takes the form of sexuality. Gender emerges as the congealed form of the sexualization of inequality between men and women. So long as this is socially the case, the feelings or acts or desires of particular individuals notwithstanding, gender inequality will divide their society into two communities of interest. The male centrally features hierarchy of control. Aggression against those with less power is experienced as sexual pleasure, an entitlement of masculinity. For the female, subordination is sexualized, in the way that dominance is for the male, as pleasure as well as gender identity, as femininity. Dominance, principally by men, and submission, principally by women, will be the ruling code through which sexual pleasure is experienced. Sexism will be a political inequality that is sexually enjoyed, if unequally so.

Sexual abuse works as a form of terror in creating and maintaining this arrangement. It is a terror so perfectly motivated and systematically concerted that it never need be intentionally organized—an arrangement that, as long as it lasted, would seal the immortality of any totalitarianism. I have come to think that the unique effectiveness of terrorism, like that against Jews in Argentina,[24] is that it is at once absolutely systematic and absolutely random: systematic because one group is its target and lives knowing it; random because there is no way of telling who is next on the list. Just to get through another day, women must spend an incredible amount of time, life, and energy cowed, fearful, and colonized, trying to figure out how not to be next on the list. Learning by osmosis what men want in a woman and trying to give it to them, women hope that being the wanted image will alter their odds. Paying attention to every detail of every incident of a woman's violation they can get their hands on, women attempt not to be her. The problem is, combining even a few circumstances, descriptions, conditions, and details of acts of sexual abuse reveals that no woman has a chance. To be about to be raped is to be gender female in the process of going about life as usual. Some things do increase the odds, like being Black. One cannot live one's life attempting not to be a Black woman. As Black women well know, one cannot save it that way, either.

Because the inequality of the sexes is socially defined as the enjoyment of sexuality itself, gender inequality appears consensual. This helps explain the peculiar durability of male supremacy as a system of hegemony as well as its imperviousness to change once it exists. It also helps explain some of the otherwise more bewildering modes of female collaboration. The belief that whatever is sexually arousing is, ipso facto, empowering for women is revealed as a strategy in male rule. It may be worth considering that heterosexuality, the predominant social arrangement that fuses this sexuality of abuse and objectification with gender in intercourse, with attendant trauma, torture, and dehumanization, organizes women's pleasure so as to give us a stake in our own subordination. It may even be that to be "anti-sex," to be against this sex that is sex, is to refuse to affirm loyalty to this political system of inequality whose dynamic is male control and use and access to women—which would account for the stigma of the epithet.

Gender

I wish I had been born a doormat, or a man.

Jean Harris, headmistress of Madeira School and convicted killer of Herman Tarnower, her former lover. She testified she had intended to kill herself instead.

Gender is an inequality of power, a social status based on who is permitted to do what to whom. Only derivatively is it a difference. Differences between the sexes do descriptively exist; being a doormat is definitely different from being a man. That these are a woman's realistic options, and that they are so limiting, calls into question the explanatory value and political agenda implicit in terming gender a difference. One is not socially permitted to be a woman and neither doormat nor man.

The differences we attribute to sex are lines inequality draws, not any kind of basis for it. Social and political inequality are, I think, basically indifferent to sameness and difference. Differences are inequality's post hoc excuse, its conclusory artifact, its outcome presented as its origin, the damage that is pointed to as the justification for doing the damage after the damage has been done, the distinctions that perception is socially organized to notice because inequality gives them consequences for social power. Distinctions of body or mind or behavior are pointed to as cause rather than effect, without realizing that they are so deeply effect rather than cause that pointing to them at all is an effect.

Inequality comes first; differences come after. Inequality is substantive and identifies a disparity; difference is abstract and falsely symmetrical. If this is so, a discourse of gender difference serves as ideology to neutralize, rationalize, and cover disparities of power, even as it appears to criticize them. Difference is the velvet glove on the iron fist of domination. This is as true when differences are affirmed as when they are denied, when their substance is applauded or when it is disparaged, when women are punished or whey they are protected in their name. A sex inequality is not a difference gone wrong, a lesson the law of sex discrimination has yet to learn.[25] One of the most deceptive antifeminisms in society, scholarship, politics, and law is the persistent treatment of gender as if it truly is a question of

8

difference, rather than treating the gender difference as a construct of the difference gender makes.[26]

Gender inequality pervades the way we think. If a concept like difference is a conceptual tool of gender inequality, it cannot deconstruct the master's house. Especially when it has built it. Difference is what the gender system says gender is; dominance it denies—only this should be a clue. Consider legal reasoning, in which analogy and distinction are methodological.[27] Like and unlike, similar and dissimilar, have been the meta-metaphor through which the law has put its systemic norm of equal treatment into effect: like and unlike are "like" equal and unequal. Like many metaphors, its hold is more tenacious than its applicability often warrants. Why should women have to be "like" men to be treated as equal citizens? Why should sex inequality have to be "like" racial inequality to be treated as an invidious inequality? As Benjamin Cardozo said of metaphor, "[T]he word starts out to free thought and ends by enslaving it."[28] To make a deep change in something that, once it exists, apparently has never not existed—and sex inequality has changed little if sex equality is your standard—requires a new way of thinking, not just thinking about new things.

Try thinking without apology with what you know from being victimized. Give up the Olympian partiality of objectivity and try for a fairness and an authority that neither dominates nor submits to your material or your audience. Keeping time and change moving in your mind, make order intelligible without the crutch of variance. Think the determinism of structural force and the possibility of freedom at the same time. Look for the deepest meanings in the least elevated places. Be more radical than anyone has ever been about the unknown, because what has never been asked is probably what we most need to know. Take the unknowable more seriously than anyone ever has, because most women have died without a trace; but invent the capacity to act, because otherwise women will continue to.

These are largely new conceptual problems, but this is not primarily a conceptual program. This may be what is most new about it. If it does not track bloody footprints across your desk, it is probably not about women. Feminism, the discipline of this reality, refuses to abstract itself in order to be recognized as being a real (that is, axiomatic) theory. In terms of existing theory, the distinctive intellectual challenge of feminism is to retain its specificity without being confined to the parochial; its distinctive practical challenge is to stay concrete without being crushed. In feminist terms, it is difficult to be narrow if you truly are talking about the situation of 53 percent of the population, but it is almost impossible to survive if you do—which makes these one and the same challenge.

Pornography

She gave up, deciding to end this torture once and for all . . . [she] began eagerly to await her death . . . When she had nearly achieved her goal, her Grandmother Clara . . . appeared with the novel idea that the point was not to die, since death came anyway, but to survive, which would be a miracle . . . She suggested that she write a testimony that might one day call attention to the terrible secret she was living through, so that the world would know about this horror that was taking place parallel to the peaceful existence of those who did not want to know, who could afford the illusion of a normal life, and of those who could deny that they were on a raft adrift in a sea of sorrow, ignoring, despite all evidence, that only blocks away from their happy world there were others . . .

Isabel Allende, *The House of the Spirits* (1985), an episode about torture under a Latin American dictatorship

Almost everything that needs to be said about pornography can be said about Linda Marchiano, because everything people think about it, they think about her. As recounted in her book *Ordeal*,[29] Linda Marchiano was coerced by abduction, systematic beatings, surveillance, and torture into the persona of "Linda Lovelace," the centerpiece of the pornographic film *Deep Throat*. During her two and a half years of captivity, she was never out of the sight of the pimp Charles Traynor. When she tried to leave, he threatened her life and the lives of her family. He guarded her with weapons. She had to ask his permission to go to the bathroom, where he watched her through a hole in the wall. He prostituted her; johns who beat her got her for free. He slept on top of her at night. He listened to her telephone calls on an extension. When he recaptured her after escape attempts, he tortured her horribly. He forced her to marry him and, with a gun, to have sex with a dog. These are the conditions under which *Deep Throat*, a paean to women's sexual freedom, was made. In it "Linda Lovelace" finds sexual ecstasy in fellatio because her clitoris is in her throat.

Men. The stunning and durable success of the film suggests that it is enjoyed by many. An equally stunning and durable part of their enjoyment is the belief that *Deep Throat* is true and *Ordeal* is false.

10

Linda was willing; she loved it. Men, the best of them, don't want to believe what she says happened, because they try to think of women as human beings like them, and they just can't believe it would happen to them. Which, for the most part, it wouldn't. So much for humanism. Men, the rest of them, don't want to know that she didn't like it. She loved it, see, she was paid. Never mind that consent in sex—and pornography is a form of sex—is supposed to mean freedom of desire expressed, not compensation for services rendered, which is what it means in commodity exchange. To show she did it for the sex should be to show that she did it for free. Not that Linda saw any of the money.

Maybe because this is a bourgeois culture, which cherishes the belief that individuals freely act, it is important that she personally loved taking a penis to the bottom of her throat, as if women really are like that. To hear that Linda Marchiano had to be hypnotized under threat of death to suppress the normal gag response seems to take something away; it is somehow detumescent. But every actual act of force it took to get her to look as though she was having such a wonderful time would have been completely in context had pornography been made of it. Her screams and cries and terror and inert despair and empty eyes would all have been sex in one of the many pornographic Pygmalions: mere biological female becomes real woman through being raped until she discovers she loves it, that is, she discovers her true self.

Had the slave training of Linda Lovelace been presented in pornography instead of in *Ordeal*, it would have been a sex act. As a sex act, the fact that it happened would have been believed. But even if all the force had been shown, the fact that she was forced would still not have been believed, not even then. Men believe what turns them on. What else can one think about the fact that no one had ever seen a woman deep-throat like that—an act whose verisimilitude approaches absolute zero, especially compared with the violence of pimps, which is known—yet *it* was believed. When a woman becomes the pornographer's "speech," her violation is sex and is therefore the truth. When a woman speaks for herself, her violation becomes an atrocity and is therefore a lie. So *Deep Throat* is protected speech[30] and *Ordeal* is sued for libel.[31]

Women. A lot of women know that what Linda says is true, and some are willing to face it: "I got away and she didn't."[32] A lot of women know that what Linda says is true but are not willing to face it. It means that what happened to her could happen to them at any time, and nothing would be done about it. A very few, who naturally are given the highest visibility, seemingly would rather see Linda being used, or know that they could, than work to keep anyone, even themselves, from being used like her. Perhaps, particularly with some educated women, who have become accustomed to interpolating themselves into culture as a survival and advancement strategy—reading the Nietzschean man and substituting she for he, reading the Freudian man and finding the oedipal problems more personally resonant than the electra ones—it should be no surprise if they relate to the pornography more as for them than as of them. Within the frame of reference they have adopted, everything is supposed to be for them. It is harder to explain why such women have not also learned that most men cannot really tell the difference between them and Linda—men who live out the class definition of women that both the women and the men deny exists. Yet even among the most privileged women, this is an anomalous reaction. Most do not relate to pornography as for them, even if they do not see it as of them. Not yet.

The politics of the pornography issue do remind one that some women, however nominally, are compensated for women's status better than others. This gives the relatively advantaged a stake in the status quo, which they hang on to with all the tenacity of having something to lose. As things stand, all women who are not prostitutes or in pornography get the benefit of not being that class of woman. A precarious status, and a matter of degree, but very real nonetheless. Women who know that men value them in terms of the sexual access they provide as surely as they know the laws of gravity, and who identify and value themselves as the accessed just as the apple values its ability to fall from the tree, see the attack on pornography as an attack on them. The attack is, instead, on the terms by which all women have had no choice but to be identified and limited and used.

Pornography is a complex issue, but on this level it is really simple: if you are a woman, that could have been you, it is you; if you are a man, it is for you, in your name. Most women do not think the woman in the pornography is them, and most men don't, either. The men are mostly right and the women are mostly wrong.

Law. Before working with the pornography issue, I was taught that inalienable rights was a normative principle of natural law that supposedly underlay positive law. Its idea was, individuals were not to be treated in certain ways. Linda Marchiano's numerous and so far unsuccessful attempts to get relief through the legal system and to end the abuse to her person, including stopping *Deep Throat*, reveals the utter sentimentality and deceptiveness of these ideas in law. An individual whose rights are systematically and cumulatively violated—for instance, a woman hurt as a woman, as a member of the gender female—does not seem to be what the law had in mind. Usually, a great deal less happens to people, or they are never heard from again. Lawyers considering whether anything can be done for a woman who is damaged in ways that make her less than the perfect case rarely conclude that they should confront or change the law. They look at cases the way surfers look at waves.

It is apparently difficult to carry on about the ultimate inviolability of the person in the face of a person who has been so ultimately violated. The shame and denial over the term "victim" has the same structure. The embarrassment of Linda's existence in the face of her victimization must be made ideologically comfortable. This is done by turning her into a nonperson and the natural law dogma into a simple empirical tautology: whoever is so cumulatively violated as to be an emblem of collective violation is simply not that bundle of rights termed "the individual." If it happened and it hurt her, she deserved it. If she didn't deserve it, either it didn't happen or it didn't hurt her. If she says it hurt her, she's oversensitive or unliberated. If she says it happened, she's a liar or a natural-born whore. Either it didn't happen or she loved it.

At one American Civil Liberties Union meeting at which I spoke, a woman told me she thought all speech should be protected, including *Deep Throat*. Asked what Ms. Marchiano should do now, she replied, "Deal with whatever in herself allowed her to let this happen to her." Linda's desire not to be dead, is what she was referring to. In this way of thinking, to be a victim, if one is a woman, becomes a statement of status, rather than the noun form of an imposed condition. In this logic, instead of Linda's resilience and dignity being taken as proof that something, unaccountably, is not destroyed, the violations she suffered are taken as the measure of her individual worth. What was done to her is attributed to her. Thus do the women in pornography become, in Andrea Dworkin's words, "the sexual disappeared of this society."[33] When your life is pornography, it's pornograpy for life. On bad days, asking why so much less of it destroys most women looks like a hopeful question.

Even those who believe it did happen and Linda did not love it, don't seem to care. It is this indifference, finally, that gets to you over time. Linda becomes a subject to evade, as if she is not really the issue. *How could she not be the issue?* The erasure and trivialization of what was done to Linda, and to countless other women hurt through pornography in countless ways, is the key to all the opposition to women having civil rights against pornographers. Turning that key could break the lock of liberalism on women's advancement through law. Linda's violation is made insignificant by making it sex.

One of the advantages of male supremacy, along with money and speech and education and respectability, is sexual access to women, of which pornography is one form. Women being the universal sex object under male supremacy, sexual access to women makes you human. It makes you real, like money.[34] The promise that qualified women can have access to whatever men as a gender have had access to, is the promise of liberal equality. Men as a gender have had access to women.

Abstract equality undermines substantive inequality, but it reinforces it at the same time. For example, sexual choice that is abstract as to gender, say men sexually choosing men, can challenge the premises of masculinity. It also, in substance, can affirm male supremacist sexuality: men come first. Similarly, women sexually choosing women can challenge the position of women as the sexually acted-upon. This choice undermines the automatic exclusivity of male sexual access to women. But so long as gender is a system of power, and it is women who have less power, like any other benefit of abstract equality, it can merely extend this choice to those women who can get the power to enforce it. The price of this equal access to sex, which means equal access to those with less power without regard to gender, the price of this so-called abstract equality is loyalty to and defense of the substantive system that delivers up all women as a class to all men.[35] Women who defend this system are, in effect, procuring women for men.

In other words, I think the systemic indifference to Linda's suffering is based on sexual self-interest. It is sexual self-interest whether it is done by women or men, whether by those who gain sexual access through it because they like it or by those who are sexually accessed because of it whether they like it or not, but are trying to make the best of a situation that they think (not without reason) they cannot change. So long as male supremacy exists and is sexual, male identification will exist and be sexual also, and sexuality will be gendered and unequal. Women like Linda will be defined the way women are defined: by what is sexually done to them. And we will be told that no sexuality is safe unless what was done to Linda can be done. And this will mean that no woman is safe so long as what was done to Linda can be done. I hope the substantive misogyny of liberal neutrality requires no further demystification.

Tolerance is the solution liberalism offers. A very substantive sexual blackmail lies at the heart of this liberal tolerance. In order not to criticize anyone's sexuality, it is women, specifically, who are used and abused by men, women who are sacrificed by calling it sex, everyone hoping they will be left alone with theirs. By the same logic, the defense of lesbian sadomasochism would sacrifice all women's ability to walk down the street in safety for the freedom to torture a woman in the privacy of one's basement without fear of intervention, in the name of everyone's freedom of choice. Obscured in this deal is the fact that the status quo has real risks, not just dangerous sexy thrills—real risks run by all women who are targeted for sexual use and abuse on the basis of a condition of birth, such that when that use and abuse is found pleasurable it is called sex and therefore deified, when it is done in private it is called consensual and thereby exonerated, and when it is done through words and pictures it is called speech and thereby constitutionalized.

In this protection racket[37] of tolerance, everybody's sexual bottom line is rhetorically defended as freedom of expression, which has the political genius of making everybody potentially complicit through the stirring between their legs. But anyone with an ounce of political realism knows that the promise is illusory: sexual freedom is not and will not be equally delivered, no matter how many women are sacrificed on its altar. And anyone with an ounce of political analysis should know that freedom before equality, freedom before justice, will only further liberate the power of the powerful and will never free what is most in need of expression. If what turns you on is not your bottom line, and if you understand that pornography literally means what it says, you might conclude that sexuality has become the fascism of contemporary America and we are moving into the last days of Weimar.

• • •

Women have been deprived not only of terms of our own in which to express our lives, but of lives of our own to live. The damage of sexism would be trivial if this were not the case. A feminism that seeks to understand women's situation in order to change it must therefore identify, criticize, and move those forms and forces that have circumscribed women in the world and in the mind. Law, like pornography, inhabits both. To remake society so that women can live here requires a feminism unqualified by preexisting modifiers. Obviously this has not been done, or things would not be as they are. Qualifying feminism by socialism or liberalism, while descriptively accurate to socialist feminism and liberal feminism, signals the limitation of feminism to that province of liberalism where we reason together about women's issues, to that moment on the left when we take up the woman question. Until these theories abandon their gender-neutral absolutes, such as difference and sexuality and speech and the state, they will not only attribute the products of very non-gender-neutral inequality, such as femininity and submission and silence and exclusion, to women as such, as if these are not imposed on us daily, but they will participate in reducing us to them.

Searching for a ground for feminism without giving up its romance with gender, keeping sexuality as modus vivendi and difference as frame, liberal theory looks for the truth of women in the mirror of nature. Left theory looks for the truth of women in the mirror of social materiality. In nature, liberalism discovers the female. In society, the left discovers the feminine. Having located a ground for women's equality within conditions of women's inequality, they speak feminism in the liberal voice, feminism in the left voice. But feminism in its own voice does not speak this way. Feminism has revealed nature and society to be mirrors of each other: the male gender looking at itself looking at itself. Intending to convey something rather different, Norman Mailer deploys the same epistemic convergence to discuss a photograph of Marilyn Monroe. Is a woman nature or society, or do we even exist, when he says, "She is a mirror of the pleasure of those who stare at her"?[38] Suppose this is true and she knew it and killed herself. A feminism that does nothing about that, does nothing for her, does nothing.

Among the accomplishments of this wave of feminism are some voices who, when we say that very little has been done for women, might possibly be heard. Hear this: the abstract equality of liberalism permits most women little more than does the substantive inequality of conservatism. One genius of the system we live under is that the strategies it requires to survive it from day to day are exactly the opposite of what is required to change it. Of women it requires silent sexual submission, just as of workers it requires work. Until the cost of this is collectively experienced as unacceptable by those who have drawn the best of men's options for women, and glimpsed as changeable by those who have drawn the worst, we will continue to live—

if it can be called living—under its aegis. And issues like pornogra-phy and access to abortion, as surely from the left as from the right, will mark the end of the women's movement in this century, rather than what could be its beginning, or its rededication.

I. APPROACHES

[Men] think themselves superior to women, but they mingle that with the notion of equality between men and women. It's very odd.

Jean Paul Sartre, quoted in *Adieux* by Simone de Beauvoir

one

Not by Law Alone:
From a Debate with Phyllis Schlafly
(1982)

I am here to discuss the meaning and future of women's rights. Mrs. Schlafly claims to speak as a woman, to and for all women. So do I. She claims to speak from the woman in all women. So do I. She claims to speak about what women know from our own lives. So do I. And about our deepest fears and aspirations.

We bring you two views on women's situation. The differences between us require asking one of the most important and neglected questions of history: What is it to speak as a woman? Who speaks for women?

I speak as a feminist, although not all feminists agree with everything I say. Mrs. Schlafly speaks as a conservative. She and I see a similar world, but we portray it differently. We see similar facts but have very different explanations and evaluations of those facts.

We both see substantial differences between the situations of women and of men. She interprets the distinctions as natural or individual. I see them as fundamentally social. She sees them as inevitable or just—or perhaps inevitable *therefore* just—either as good and to be accepted or as individually overcomeable with enough will and application. I see women's situation as unjust, contingent, and imposed.

In order to speak of women as a feminist, I need first to correct Mrs. Schlafly's impression of the women's movement. Feminism is not, as she implicitly defines it, liberalism applied to women. Her attack on the women's movement profoundly misconstrues feminism. Her critique of the women's movement is an artifact, an application, of her long-standing critique of liberalism, just as her attack on the ERA is an artifact of her opposition to the federal government.

In the waning days of the last attempt to ratify the Equal Rights Amendment, I twice debated Phyllis Schlafly, a leading conservative opponent. One debate took place at Stanford Law School, Stanford, California, Jan. 26, 1982; the other was at the School of Theology, Claremont, California, Mar. 16, 1982.

Approaches

Women as such are incidental, a subplot, not central, either to liberalism or to her critique.

Liberalism defines equality as sameness. It is comparative. To know if you are equal, you have to be equal to somebody who sets the standard you compare yourself with. According to this approach, gender difference is the evil of women's situation because it enforces the nonsameness of women and men. Feminism—drawing from socialist feminism lessons about class and privilege, from lesbian feminism lessons about sexuality, from the feminism of women of color lessons about racism and self-respecting communities of resistance— does not define equality this way. To feminism, equality means the aspiration to eradicate not gender differentiation, but gender hierarchy.

We stand for an end to enforced subordination, limited options, and social powerlessness—on the basis of sex, among other things. Differentiation, to feminism, is just one strategy in keeping women down. Liberalism has been subversive for us in that it signals that we have the audacity to compare ourselves with men, to measure ourselves by male standards, on male terms. We *do* seek access to the male world. We *do* criticize our exclusion from male pursuits. But liberalism limits us in a way feminism does not. We also *criticize* male pursuits from women's point of view, from the standpoint of our social experience as women.

Feminism seeks to empower women on our own terms. To value what women have always done as well as to allow us to do everything else. We seek not only to be valued as who we are, but to have access to the process of the definition of value itself. In this way, our demand for access becomes also a demand for change.

Put another way, Mrs. Schlafly and I both argue that in a sense "women are not persons," but with very different meanings. When the right affirms women as women, it affirms woman's body as a determinant of woman's existing role, which it sees as her rightful place. Feminists criticize the social disparities between the sexes that not only exclude women from personhood as that has been defined, that not only distort woman's body and mind inseparably, but also define personhood in ways that are repugnant to us. Existing society's image of a person never has represented or encompassed what we, as women, with women's experience, either have had access to or aspire to.

Mrs. Schlafly opposes feminism, the Equal Rights Amendment, and basic change in women's condition, as if the central goal of the women's movement were to impose a gender-free society, as if we defined equality as sameness. This is not accurate. Our issue is not the gender difference but *the difference gender makes*, the *social meaning* imposed upon our bodies—what it means to be a woman or a man is a social process and, as such, is subject to change. Feminists do not seek sameness with men. We more criticize what men have made of themselves and the world that we, too, inhabit. We do not seek dominance over men. To us it is a male notion that power means someone must dominate. We seek a transformation in the terms and conditions of power itself.

I have asserted that women's place is not only different but inferior, that it is not chosen but enforced. To document that, I need to ask: what *is* women's situation? Because it happens to each of us in isolation, one at a time, it looks individual, even chosen. Mrs. Schlafly teaches that if we follow the rules for women's role, are energetic, cheerful, diligent, "positive," and make smart choices, the world is ours. To confront her requires us to ask not only what happens to women who step out of women's place, but also what happens to us *in* that place. What about women who do not seek different bargains with society, but live out society's traditional bargain for women, the bargain she defends?

I want to share with you a body count from women's collective experience in America. We all start as little girls. One of two hundred of us, conservatively estimated, is sexually molested as a child by her father. When brothers, stepfathers, uncles, and friends of the family are included, some estimate that the rates rise to two out of five.[1] As we grow, we are pressured into sex for popularity and out of sex for virtue and are told not to go crazy with this or we will be institutionalized. And we are, for behavior that is not punished, is even encouraged, in little boys. I would like Mrs. Schlafly to explain that.

Any one of us can be raped on the street at any time; conservatively, we are at a rate of one every six minutes. A recent random study in San Francisco showed 44 percent of women have been victims of rape or attempted rape at least once in their lives—including in their marriages. The chances are worse for women of color.[2] What does Mrs. Schlafly propose to do against rape? What is her position on rape in marriage? Is there any such thing, or is it women's duty to submit? Could that be part of why rape is so prevalent? In the same random study, only 7.8 percent of women reported experiencing *no* sexual assault or harassment.[3] How does Mrs. Schlafly's vision of society account for or respond to this?

23

Approaches

Women are systematically beaten in our homes by men with whom we are close. It is estimated that between one quarter and one third of married women experience serious violence in their homes—some studies find as many as 70 percent.[4] Four out of five murdered women are killed by men; between one third and one half are married to their murderers.[5] When you add boyfriends and former spouses, the figures rise. Mrs. Schlafly's defense of the family reinforces the guilt that keeps women in these vicious, emotionally and physically deadly situations. We should stay, stick it out, do more of what he wants, maybe it will get better. Believe him when he repents. But how does she explain men's violence toward us? Will she tell us it is just "some men," they are deviant exceptions? A third to a half of them? Or will she tell us to be grateful—the family civilizes men, think how much worse it could be? I say the family legitimizes violence to women and calls that civilization.

Most women work outside the home as well as inside it—in the female job ghetto, in high-heeled, low-status jobs with low pay. Mrs. Schlafly purports to be for equal pay for equal work, but unequal pay is a function of the traditional male-headed family she defends, in which a man's higher wage is justified because he supports a family. A woman's wages are extra. This is part of why women's work, even when we head families, as increasingly we do, brings home fifty-three to fifty-nine cents to the average male dollar. Even adjusted for education and years worked, women make less.[6] How does Mrs. Schlafly explain this?

Marriage is women's destiny, a destiny she defends and seeks to extend. Now, three of five marriages end in divorce after about five years, leaving the woman with approximately one child, approximately no income, and a standard of living drastically below that of her former husband.[7] Who among us can afford Mrs. Schlafly's "choice" of exclusive home and motherhood? The privileged few, mostly white and upper-class women. Why doesn't she demand a wage for the housework she vaunts—and with it social security, pension rights, and disability insurance for *her* work, not his. Every right she seeks for homemakers is based on the man's work, not the woman's. Doesn't she know that housework *is* work? The government doesn't have to pay for it: private business or families can.

In this context, it is instructive to ask: What is woman's best economic option? In 1981, the average streetwalker in Manhattan earned between $500 and $1,000 a week.[8] Aside from modeling (with which it has much in common), hooking is the only job for which women as a group are paid more than men. Check that out in terms of what we are valued for. A recent study shows that the only difference between hookers and other women with similar class background is that the prostitutes earn twice as much.[9] Thirteen percent of us are or have been prostitutes.[10] She can "reject" it it she wants. But instead of calling us immoral, why doesn't Mrs. Schlafly target the conditions that make prostitution fundamental to women's social status?

Now consider how similar the condition of prostitutes is not only to that of women who make a more permanent sex-for-survival exchange, but to those of us who must make it daily. Sexual harassment on the job amounts to that, except we have to do all that other work too. A study of the federal workplace found that 42 percent of all female employees reported being sexually harassed in the preceding two years, 17 percent severely.[11] Mrs. Schlafly tells us that virtuous women, with rare exceptions, are seldom harassed. In the federal workplace study alone, the women reporting sexual harassment make a group the size of Denver, Colorado. Does she think we ask for rape too?

While all this goes on, poor women suffer botched abortions, and Mrs. Schlafly works to return us to the days before 1973 when illegal abortion was the leading cause of maternal death and mutilation. None of us can afford this risk, but it is disproportionately borne by women of color. In New York in 1970, half of the women who died from abortion-related causes were Black; 44 percent were Puerto Rican.[12] Mrs. Schlafly works to make abortion once again criminal, or as burdened a choice as it can be made, without in any way empowering women to refuse forced sex. Why doesn't she ask whether women really have power over the sex act when she blames *us* for getting pregnant? What is her position on contraception? What is she doing to make abortion unnecessary?

The feminist view of women's situation comes to this: across time and space, there is too much variance in women's status, role, and treatment for it to be biological, and too little variance for it to individual. In this view, women and men appear biologically more alike and socially more different than is generally supposed. Our social *treatment* certainly is different—the difference between power and powerlessness. Woman's commonality, which includes our diversity, comes from our shared social position. This is our explanation of our situation. I want to know: does Mrs. Schlafly think rape, battery, prostitution, incest, sexual harassment, unequal pay, and forced maternity express, to use her phrase, "the differences reasonable people

25

wish to make" between women and men? Are they sex differences? If not, how does she explain them?

Feminists are the first to take women's situation seriously from women's standpoint. We have exposed the outrages of forced sex and forced motherhood. Women respond to feminism: before, I thought it was my fault. Mrs. Schlafly says, it *is* your fault. Women respond to feminism: before, I thought I was alone. Mrs. Schlafly says, you *are* alone.

Now I want to consider with you the role of the law in the future of women's rights. The law alone cannot change our social condition. It can help. So far, it has helped remarkably little. The way the crime of rape is defined and what we have to prove to be believed do not fit our experience of the injury. The reality is that not only married women, but also women men know or live with, can be raped at will. Men know this. Rape is not illegal, it is regulated. When a man assaults his wife, it is still seen as a domestic squabble, as permissible; when she fights back, it is a crime. On the other hand, it has been empowering to women that sexual harassment has become illegal. It has meant that a woman who resists a man's incursions knows she is not alone, that someone besides her thinks that access to her body is not automatically his right. The law has also helped women not to be considered criminals when we need to end a pregnancy. We punish ourselves enough.

I see the ERA in this context. The law—like the hunt, warfare, and religion—has been a male sphere. The values and qualities of these pursuits have defined both the male role and public life. They have defined what power means.

The feminist question for the future of women's rights is: if we acquire and use these forms of power, including economics (the modern equivalent of the hunt), the use of physical force (of which war is a form), and the tools of law (the secular religion), will we use them differently? Will we use them as women, for all women? The final issue is not whether biological males or females hold positions of power, although women must be there. The issue is: what are our identifications? what are our loyalties? to whom are we accountable?

Women who oppose the ERA see it as making them neutered "persons" yet fear they will be treated as women. This is not an illusory fear. Women say to the state: we do not trust you to give as much as you take. Feminists concur. But opposing the ERA on this basis plays on these fears without confronting the fact that it is an unequal society—a society that the ERA in women's hands could improve—which makes these fears rational. I am for the ERA. I think it is progressive if not transformative. It is one of many small initiatives we can use. Whenever I hear the right attack it, I am more for it than I was before, because they think it will be so far-reaching. The reality—and I do not concede that the ERA is dead—is more modest. It would give women a place in the Constitution, strengthen some gains we have made, and provide one basis for going further.

Two of the right's favorite problems with ERA are the draft and gay marriages. ERA would probably compel the military to be gender-neutral on some level. I am against involuntary conscription. I think if a war is truly called for, people will mobilize. I also think a male-only draft is profoundly anti male. Every man drafted would have a 50 percent chance of not being if women were. The male-only draft discriminates against men. It is also profoundly inconsistent for Mrs. Schlafly to be involved in defense policy while maintaining that women have no place in the military. We have had enough of policies made by people who are categorically exempt from the personal consequences of those policies. As to the civilian effects of the military, it trains men in violence. Battered women complain that their husbands learned abusive skills in the military. Don't they want us to learn to kill?

On the issue of gay marriages, I doubt the ERA would be interpreted to legalize them, although I would not be against that. Most marriages would continue to be heterosexual; persons secure in their heterosexuality would not be threatened by the availability of this option. I do wonder, though, why gay men and lesbians would want marriage, even as feminists are exposing some of its problems as a social institution. I understand the desire to legitimate unions, and the legal consequences are not minimal. I do think it might do something amazing to the entire institution of marriage to recognize the unity of two "persons" between whom no superiority or inferiority could be presumed on the basis of gender.

I am clear that everything women need will not be accomplished by the ERA, and not by law alone. To have a future, women's rights will have to mean an end to pornography—not its containment or suppression or regulation, but an end to the demand for eroticizing women's degradation. I mean a world in which men are no longer turned on by putting women down. I would like Mrs. Schlafly to address herself to the question: why do they want it? Until the day women's bodies are not used to sell cars, cosmetics are not a necessity to the success of a woman's image, and we are not humiliated and tortured for male pleasure, women will have no rights.

The ERA is most positive when we remember what it is part of, when we remember what it would be like to have rights worth having. Not only to be allowed to play with the boys, but to question why the point and ethic of sports is competition. Not just to be taken seriously, but to ask why the definition of merit is membership in an elite. Not only to survive, with dignity and sexuality intact, but to be able to measure achievement in other than dollars and to inhabit our bodies and express our sexuality in ways that are not scripted out of scraps of stereotype. We want not only to be able to defend ourselves, but not to have to, every minute of every day, and to change the conditions that have made the test of strength not whether one can bring forth life, but whether one can end it.

So that we remember where we are going—and, in Monique Wittig's words, "failing that, invent,"[13] I propose we ponder a further step. I call it the women's rights amendment. It reads: the subordination of women to men is hereby abolished.

•   •   •

Look: Women resent the society that defines rape as something other than a violation of us, that does not believe us when we protest that violation, that looks to make it all right by asking whether we deserved it or desired it or enjoyed it. We resent the society that protects pornography as freedom of speech without considering that it also terrorizes and silences women, or, as the right would have it, the society that imagines suppressing pornography without addressing why men want it, while defending the social relations that require it. This is a society that turns away from the beating of women in the home, which it calls a haven, and affirms the family to which battery is endemic. It resists paying women for housework, the work most of us do, saying our reward is commendation and appreciation. We would like to be able to eat that. It resists equal jobs for us, and equal pay when we do the same or comparable work, yet refuses to see that our so-called options are connected: work for nothing at home, little in the marketplace, a little more (at least for a while) in the street. We resent having motherhood forced on us by unwanted sex, being deprived of or discouraged from using contraception, having guilt or poverty keep us from abortions, and then being saddled with the entire care of children—alone. We want to be able to *want* our children. We resent being blamed for what men do to us, being told we provoked it when we are raped or sexually harassed, living in constant fear if we face the fact that it could happen to us at any minute, becoming willing, being shrunk to the size of a life trying just not to be next on the list of victims, knowing that most men could probably, statistically, get away with it. We have had enough of the glorification of this heterosexuality, this erotization of dominance and submission,[14] while woman-centered sexual expression is denied and stigmatized.

I would like to return to the issue of who speaks for women and ask a feminist question to answer it. How do our lives express our analysis? Mrs. Schlafly tells us that being a woman has not gotten in her way. That she knows what she is saying because it happened to her. She could be one of the exceptional 7.8 percent, although who's to know? I do submit to you, though, that any man who had a law degree and had done graduate work in political science; had given testimony on a wide range of important subjects for decades; had done effective and brilliant political, policy, and organizational work within the party; had published widely, including nine books; was instrumental in stopping a major social initiative to amend the Constitution just short of victory dead in its tracks; *and* had a beautiful, accomplished family—any man like that would have a place in the current administration. Having raised six children, a qualification not many men can boast of (and if so probably with less good reason) did not make the difference. I would accept correction if I am wrong, and she may yet be appointed. She was widely reported to have wanted such a post, but I don't believe everything I read, especially about women. She certainly deserved a place in the Defense Department. Phyllis Schlafly is a qualified woman.

I charge that the Reagan administration has discriminated against Phyllis Schlafly on the basis of her sex. Not that she's "running with the wrong crowd"—her phrase for women whom men victimize. She has been excluded by the image that women are unfit for the things she is good at, rejected by the men she helped put in power, unfairly presented as shrewish and uncongenial and odd and cold by the press. But like many women, although on a grander scale than most, and taking many of us with her, she has also been enlisted as a participant in her own exclusion. She has actively furthered the image of women as properly outside of official power, as at best volunteers, a role she continues to play—although notice she had to *leave home* to defend its primacy to her as a woman—so that now she has no explanation for her exclusion other than her own less than totally "positive woman" attitude.

For it is the values of the traditionally male spheres that define the underlying continuity, the central coherence, the guiding preoccupations of Mrs. Schlafly's life: the hunt—material success individually, economic policy on the political level; warfare—triumph in competition in her personal life, defense policy on the national level; religion and morality—the virtues of motherhood and family life, and the pursuit of traditional social values on the level of social design, as in her opposition to abortion, and her career in law, the secular religion.

Before she decided that feminists create the problems we fight, back in 1967, she knew sexism when she encountered it. When she was attacked for having six children as a disqualification for a party post, she placed a cartoon in her book *Safe—Not Sorry* showing a door labeled "Republican Party Headquarters," with a sign reading "Conservatives and Women Please Use Servants' Entrance." Now the conservatives are in. Are women still to use the back door?

I am not saying that her finger near the nuclear trigger would make me feel particularly safe—just that by the standards set by the men in the job, she should be there. I privately believe she has been trivialized by her association with women's issues. I'm saying her analysis of her own experience is wrong. Their foot is on her neck, too, and I, for one, am willing to give her this chance to change her mind.

•   •   •

How do you know when a group is on the bottom? It may be some indication when they can be assaulted, and authorities ignore them; physically abused, and people turn away or find it entertaining; economically deprived, and it is seen as all they are worth; made the object of jokes, and few ask what makes the jokes funny; imaged as animallike, confined to a narrow range of tasks and functions, and told it is all harmless or inevitable and even for their benefit as well as the best they can expect, given what they are. These are all true for women. In addition, we are excluded from inner circles and then rejected because we don't know the inside story; told we can't think and had our thoughts appropriated for the advancement of others; told the pedestal is real and called ungrateful and lacking in initiative when we call it a cage; and blamed for creating our conditions when we resist them. When a few of us overcome all this, we are told we show there are no barriers there and are used as examples to put other women down. She made it—why can't you? We are used as tokens while every problem we share is treated as a special case.

"Look around you," as Mrs. Schlafly says. If the fact that women are physically less able than men is proven by our comparative absence in physically demanding roles, why isn't the fact that women are not as smart as men proven by our comparative lack of presence in tenured faculties, Congress, the courts, executive boardrooms, university presidencies, editorships of newspapers and publishing houses?[15] Why don't the few women who achieve athletically prove that *any* woman can, just as Mrs. Schlafly tells you the tokens in the roles I have mentioned prove that we are all capable of such achievements, if only we would try? She says, any woman can. I say, *all* women can't so long as those who make it are the privileged few. The feminist question is not whether you, as an individual woman, can escape women's place, but whether it is socially necessary that there will always be somebody in the position you, however temporarily, escaped from *and that someone will be a woman.* You can't claim to speak for 53 percent of the population and support changes for a few.

Let's return to the question of personhood and rights. Women of the right know that women are socially not persons. Either they acquiesce in this or are fearful of embracing the illusory image of life as "person," knowing they will still be *treated as women.* No wonder they want protection. But male supremacy is a protection racket. It keeps you dependent on the very people who brutalize you so you will keep needing their protection. Feminists know that protection produces the need for more protection—and no rights of your own.[16]

I have often wanted to ask Mrs. Schlafly: why are you so afraid of our freedom? Now I am beginning to see that if you assume, as she does, that sex inequality is inalterable, freedom looks like open season on women. We deserve better, and we will have it. I personally promise you, Mrs. Schlafly, that the only question for the future of women's rights, as with the ERA, is not whether but when.[17]

two

Difference and Dominance:
On Sex Discrimination
(1984)

What is a gender question a question of? What is an inequality question a question of? These two questions underlie applications of the equality principle to issues of gender, but they are seldom explicitly asked. I think it speaks to the way gender has structured thought and perception that mainstream legal and moral theory tacitly gives the same answer to them both: these are questions of sameness and difference. The mainstream doctrine of the law of sex discrimination that results is, in my view, largely responsible for the fact that sex equality law has been so utterly ineffective at getting women what we need and are socially prevented from having on the basis of a condition of birth: a chance at productive lives of reasonable physical security, self-expression, individuation, and minimal respect and dignity. Here I expose the sameness/difference theory of sex equality, briefly show how it dominates sex discrimination law and policy and underlies its discontents, and propose an alternative that might do something.

.   .   .

According to the approach to sex equality that has dominated politics, law, and social perception, equality is an equivalence, not a distinction, and sex is a distinction. The legal mandate of equal treatment—which is both a systemic norm and a specific legal doctrine—becomes a matter of treating likes alike and unlikes unlike; and the sexes are defined as such by their mutual unlikeness. Put another way, gender is socially constructed as difference epistemologically;

The most memorable occasions on which I delivered a version of this speech were: Harvard Law School, Cambridge, Massachusetts, Oct. 24, 1984; Conference on the Moral Foundations of Civil Rights Policy, Center for Philosophy and Public Policy, University of Maryland, College Park, Maryland, Oct. 19, 1984; and the James McCormick Mitchell Lecture, State University of Buffalo Law School, Buffalo, New York, Oct. 19, 1984. I thank the students of Harvard Law School for their response to so many of my initial thoughts.

32

sex discrimination law bounds gender equality by difference doctrin- ally. A built-in tension exists between this concept of equality, which presupposes sameness, and this concept of sex, which presupposes difference. Sex equality thus becomes a contradiction in terms, some- thing of an oxymoron, which may suggest why we are having such a difficult time getting it.

Upon further scrutiny, two alternate paths to equality for women emerge within this dominant approach, paths that roughly follow the lines of this tension. The leading one is: be the same as men. This path is termed gender neutrality doctrinally and the single standard philosophically. It is testimony to how substance gets itself up as form in law that this rule is considered formal equality. Because this ap- proach mirrors the ideology of the social world, it is considered ab- stract, meaning transparent of substance; also for this reason it is con- sidered not only to be *the* standard, but *a* standard at all. It is so far the leading rule that the words "equal to" are code for, equivalent to, the words "the same as"—referent for both unspecified.

To women who want equality yet find that you are different, the doctrine provides an alternate route: be different from men. This equal recognition of difference is termed the special benefit rule or special protection rule legally, the double standard philosophically. It is in rather bad odor. Like pregnancy, which always calls it up, it is something of a doctrinal embarrassment. Considered an exception to true equality and not really a rule of law at all, this is the one place where the law of sex discrimination admits it is recognizing some- thing substantive. Together with the Bona Fide Occupational Quali- fication (BFOQ), the unique physical characteristic exception under ERA policy, compensatory legislation, and sex-conscious relief in par- ticular litigation, affirmative action is thought to live here.[1]

The philosophy underlying the difference approach is that sex *is* a difference, a division, a distinction, beneath which lies a stratum of human commonality, sameness. The moral thrust of the sameness branch of the doctrine is to make normative rules conform to this empirical reality by granting women access to what men have access to: to the extent that women are no different from men, we deserve what they have. The differences branch, which is generally seen as patronizing but necessary to avoid absurdity, exists to value or com- pensate women for what we are or have become distinctively as women (by which is meant, unlike men) under existing conditions.

My concern is not with which of these paths to sex equality is pref- erable in the long run or more appropriate to any particular issue, although most discourse on sex discrimination revolves about these questions as if that were all there is. My point is logically prior: to treat issues of sex equality as issues of sameness and difference *is to take a particular approach.* I call this the difference approach because it is obsessed with the sex difference. The main theme in the fugue is "we're the same, we're the same, we're the same." The counterpoint theme (in a higher register) is "but we're different, but we're different, but we're different." Its underlying story is: on the first day, difference was; on the second day, a division was created upon it; on the third day, irrational instances of dominance arose. Division may be rational or irrational. Dominance either seems or is justified. Difference *is.*

There is a politics to this. Concealed is the substantive way in which man has become the measure of all things. Under the sameness standard, women are measured according to our correspondence with man, our equality judged by our proximity to his measure. Under the difference standard, we are measured according to our lack of correspondence with him, our womanhood judged by our distance from his measure. Gender neutrality is thus simply the male standard, and the special protection rule is simply the female standard, but do not be deceived: masculinity, or maleness, is the referent for both. Think about it like those anatomy models in medical school. A male body is the human body; all those extra things women have are studied in ob/gyn. It truly is a situation in which more is less. Approaching sex discrimination in this way—as if sex questions are difference questions and equality questions are sameness questions—provides two ways for the law to hold women to a male standard and call that sex equality.

•   •   •

Having been very hard on the difference answer to sex equality questions, I should say that it takes up a very important problem: how to get women access to everything we have been excluded from, while also valuing everything that women are or have been allowed to become or have developed as a consequence of our struggle either not to be excluded from most of life's pursuits or to be taken seriously under the terms that have been permitted to be our terms. It negotiates what we have managed in relation to men. Legally articulated as the need to conform normative standards to existing reality, the strongest doctrinal expression of its sameness idea would prohibit taking gender into account in any way.

34

Its guiding impulse is: we're as good as you. Anything you can do, we can do. Just get out of the way. I have to confess a sincere affection for this approach. It has gotten women some access to employment[2] and education,[3] the public pursuits, including academic,[4] professional,[5] and blue-collar work;[6] the military;[7] and more than nominal access to athletics.[8] It has moved to change the dead ends that were all we were seen as good for and has altered what passed for women's lack of physical training, which was really serious training in passivity and enforced weakness. It makes you want to cry sometimes to know that it has had to be a mission for many women just to be permitted to do the work of this society, to have the dignity of doing jobs a lot of other people don't even want to do.

The issue of including women in the military draft[9] has presented the sameness answer to the sex equality question in all its simple dignity and complex equivocality. As a citizen, I should have to risk being killed just like you. The consequences of my resistance to this risk should count like yours. The undercurrent is: what's the matter, don't you want me to learn to kill . . . just like you? Sometimes I see this as a dialogue between women in the afterlife. The feminist says to the soldier, "we fought for your equality." The soldier says to the feminist, "oh, no, *we* fought for *your* equality."

Feminists have this nasty habit of counting bodies and refusing not to notice their gender. As applied, the sameness standard has mostly gotten men the benefit of those few things women have historically had—for all the good they did us. Almost every sex discrimination case that has been won at the Supreme Court level has been brought by a man.[10] Under the rule of gender neutrality, the law of custody and divorce has been transformed, giving men an equal chance at custody of children and at alimony.[11] Men often look like better "parents" under gender-neutral rules like level of income and presence of nuclear family, because men make more money and (as they say) initiate the building of family units.[12] In effect, they get preferred because society advantages them before they get into court, and law is prohibited from taking that preference into account because that would mean taking gender into account. The group realities that make women more in need of alimony are not permitted to matter, because only individual factors, gender-neutrally considered, may matter. So the fact that women will live their lives, as individuals, as members of the group women, with women's chances in a sex-discriminatory society, may not count, or else it is sex discrimination. The equality principle in this guise mobilizes the idea that the way to get things for women is to get them for men. Men have gotten them. Have women? We still have not got equal pay,[13] or equal work,[14] far less equal pay for equal work,[15] and we are close to losing separate enclaves like women's schools through this approach.[16]

Here is why. In reality, which this approach is not long on because it is liberal idealism talking to itself, virtually every quality that distinguishes men from women is already affirmatively compensated in this society. Men's physiology defines most sports,[17] their needs define auto and health insurance coverage, their socially designed biographies define workplace expectations and successful career patterns, their perspectives and concerns define quality in scholarship, their experiences and obsessions define merit, their objectification of life defines art, their military service defines citizenship, their presence defines family, their inability to get along with each other—their wars and rulerships—defines history, their image defines god, and their genitals define sex. For each of their differences from women, what amounts to an affirmative action plan is in effect, otherwise known as the structure and values of American society. But whenever women are, by this standard, "different" from men and insist on not having it held against us, whenever a difference is used to keep us second class and we refuse to smile about it, equality law has a paradigm trauma and it's crisis time for the doctrine.

What this doctrine has apparently meant by sex inequality is not what happens to us. The law of sex discrimination that has resulted seems to be looking only for those ways women are kept down that have *not* wrapped themselves up as a difference—whether original, imposed, or imagined. Start with original: what to do about the fact that women actually have an ability men still lack, gestating children in utero. Pregnancy therefore is a difference. Difference doctrine says it is sex discrimination to give women what we need, because only women need it. It is not sex discrimination not to give women what we need because then only women will not get what we need.[18] Move into imposed: what to do about the fact that most women are segregated into low-paying jobs where there are no men. Suspecting that the structure of the marketplace will be entirely subverted if comparable worth is put into effect, difference doctrine says that because there is no man to set a standard from which women's treatment is a deviation, there is no sex discrimination here, only sex difference. Never mind that there is no man to compare with because no man would do that job if he had a choice, and of course he has because he is a man, so he won't.[19]

Now move into the so-called subtle reaches of the imposed category, the de facto area. Most jobs in fact require that the person, gender neutral, who is qualified for them will be someone who is not the primary caretaker of a preschool child.[20] Pointing out that this raises a concern of sex in a society in which women are expected to care for the children is taken as day one of taking gender into account in the structuring of jobs. To do that would violate the rule against not noticing situated differences based on gender, so it never emerges that day one of taking gender into account was the day the job was structured with the expectation that its occupant would have no child care responsibilities. Imaginary sex differences—such as between male and female applicants to administer estates or between males aging and dying and females aging and dying[21]—I will concede, the doctrine can handle.

I will also concede that there are many differences between women and men. I mean, can you imagine elevating one half of a population and denigrating the other half and producing a population in which everyone is the same? What the sameness standard fails to notice is that men's differences from women are equal to women's differences from men. There is an *equality* there. Yet the sexes are not socially equal. The difference approach misses the fact that hierarchy of power produces real as well as fantasied differences, differences that are also inequalities. What is missing in the difference approach is what Aristotle missed in his empiricist notion that equality means treating likes alike and unlikes unlike, and nobody has questioned it since. Why should you have to be the same as a man to get what a man gets simply because he is one? Why does maleness provide an original entitlement, not questioned on the basis of *its* gender, so that it is women—women who want to make a case of unequal treatment in a world men have made in their image (this is really the part Aristotle missed)—who have to show in effect that they are men in every relevant respect, unfortunately mistaken for women on the basis of an accident of birth?

The women that gender neutrality benefits, and there are some, show the suppositions of this approach in highest relief. They are mostly women who have been able to construct a biography that somewhat approximates the male norm, at least on paper. They are the qualified, the least of sex discrimination's victims. When they are denied a man's chance, it looks the most like sex bias. The more unequal society gets, the fewer such women are permitted to exist. Therefore, the more unequal society gets, the *less* likely the difference doctrine is to be able to do anything about it, because unequal power creates both the appearance and the reality of sex differences along the same lines as it creates its sex inequalities.

The special benefits side of the difference approach has not compensated for the differential of being second class. The special benefits rule is the only place in mainstream equality doctrine where you get to identify as a woman and not have that mean giving up all claim to equal treatment—but it comes close. Under its double standard, women who stand to inherit something when their husbands die have gotten the exclusion of a small percentage of the inheritance tax, to the tune of Justice Douglas waxing eloquent about the difficulties of all women's economic situation.[22] If we're going to be stigmatized as different, it would be nice if the compensation would fit the disparity. Women have also gotten three more years than men get before we have to be advanced or kicked out of the military hierarchy, as compensation for being precluded from combat, the usual way to advance.[23] Women have also gotten excluded from contact jobs in male-only prisons because we might get raped, the Court taking the viewpoint of the reasonable rapist on women's employment opportunities.[24] We also get protected out of jobs because of our fertility. The reason is that the job has health hazards, and somebody who might be a real person some day and therefore could sue—that is, a fetus—might be hurt if women, who apparently are not real persons and therefore can't sue either for the hazard to our health or for the lost employment opportunity, are given jobs that subject our bodies to possible harm.[25] Excluding women is always an option if equality feels in tension with the pursuit itself. They never seem to think of excluding men. Take combat.[26] Somehow it takes the glory out of the foxhole, the buddiness out of the trenches, to imagine us out there. You get the feeling they might rather end the draft, they might even rather not fight wars at all than have to do it with us.

The double standard of these rules doesn't give women the dignity of the single standard; it also does not (as the differences standard does) suppress the gender of its referent, which is, of course, the female gender. I must also confess some affection for this standard. The work of Carol Gilligan on gender differences in moral reasoning[27] gives it a lot of dignity, more than it has ever had, more, frankly, than I thought it ever could have. But she achieves for moral reasoning what the special protection rule achieves in law: the affirmative rather than the negative valuation of that which has accurately distinguished women from men, by making it seem as though those attributes, with their consequences, really are somehow ours, rather than what male supremacy has attributed to us for its own use. For women to affirm difference, when difference means dominance, as it does with gender, means to affirm the qualities and characteristics of powerlessness.

Women have done good things, and it is a good thing to affirm them. I think quilts are art. I think women have a history. I think we create culture. I also know that we have not only been excluded from making what has been considered art; our artifacts have been excluded from setting the standards by which art is art. Women have a history all right, but it is a history both of what was and of what was not allowed to be. So I am critical of affirming what we have been, which necessarily is what we have been permitted, as if it is women's, ours, possessive. As if equality, in spite of everything, already ineluctably exists.

I am getting hard on this and am about to get harder on it. I do not think that the way women reason morally is morality "in a different voice."[28] I think it is morality in a higher register, in the feminine voice. Women value care because men have valued us according to the care we give them, and we could probably use some. Women think in relational terms because our existence is defined in relation to men. Further, when you are powerless, you don't just speak differently. A lot, you don't speak. Your speech is not just differently articulated, it is silenced. Eliminated, gone. You aren't just deprived of a language with which to articulate your distinctiveness, although you are; you are deprived of a life out of which articulation might come. Not being heard is not just a function of lack of recognition, not just that no one knows how to listen to you, although it is that; it is also silence of the deep kind, the silence of being prevented from having anything to say. Sometimes it is permanent. All I am saying is that the damage of sexism is real, and reifying that into differences is an insult to our possibilities.

So long as these issues are framed this way, demands for equality will always appear to be asking to have it both ways: the same when we are the same, different when we are different. But this is the way men have it: equal and different too. They have it the same as women when they are the same and want it, and different from women when they are different and want to be, which usually they do. Equal and different too would only be parity.[29] But under male supremacy, while being told we get it both ways, both the specialness of the pedestal and an even chance at the race, the ability to be a woman and a person, too, few women get much benefit of either.

•   •   •

There is an alternative approach, one that threads its way through existing law and expresses, I think, the reason equality law exists in the first place. It provides a second answer, a dissident answer in law and philosophy, to both the equality question and the gender question. In this approach, an equality question is a question of the distribution of power. Gender is also a question of power, specifically of male supremacy and female subordination. The question of equality, from the standpoint of what it is going to take to get it, is at root a question of hierarchy, which—as power succeeds in constructing social perception and social reality—derivatively becomes a categorical distinction, a difference. Here, on the first day that matters, dominance was achieved, probably by force. By the second day, division along the same lines had to be relatively firmly in place. On the third day, if not sooner, differences were demarcated, together with social systems to exaggerate them in perception and in fact, *because* the systematically differential delivery of benefits and deprivations required making no mistake about who was who. Comparatively speaking, man has been resting ever since. Gender might not even code as difference, might not mean distinction epistemologically, were it not for its consequences for social power.

I call this the dominance approach, and it is the ground I have been standing on in criticizing mainstream law. The goal of this dissident approach is not to make legal categories trace and trap the way things are. It is not to make rules that fit reality. It is critical of reality. Its task is not to formulate abstract standards that will produce determinate outcomes in particular cases. Its project is more substantive, more jurisprudential than formulaic, which is why it is difficult for the mainstream discourse to dignify it as an approach to doctrine or to imagine it as a rule of law at all. It proposes to expose that which women have had little choice but to be confined to, in order to change it.

The dominance approach centers on the most sex-differential abuses of women as a gender, abuses that sex equality law in its difference garb could not confront. It is based on a reality about which little of a systematic nature was known before 1970, a reality that calls for a new conception of the problem of sex inequality. This new in-

formation includes not only the extent and intractability of sex segregation into poverty, which has been known before, but the range
of issues termed violence against women, which has not been. It
combines women's material desperation, through being relegated to
categories of jobs that pay nil, with the massive amount of rape and
attempted rape—44 percent of all women—about which virtually
nothing is done;[30] the sexual assault of children—38 percent of girls
and 10 percent of boys—which is apparently endemic to the patriarchal family;[31] the battery of women that is systematic in one quarter
to one third of our homes;[32] prostitution, women's fundamental economic condition, what we do when all else fails, and for many
women in this country, all else fails often;[33] and pornography, an industry that traffics in female flesh, making sex inequality into sex to
the tune of eight billion dollars a year in profits largely to organized
crime.[34]

These experiences have been silenced out of the difference definition of sex equality largely because they happen almost exclusively
to women. Understand: for this reason, they are considered *not* to
raise sex equality issues. Because this treatment is done almost
uniquely to women, it is implicitly treated as a difference, the sex
difference, when in fact it is the socially situated subjection of
women. The whole point of women's social relegation to inferiority
as a gender is that for the most part these things aren't done to men.
Men are not paid half of what women are paid for doing the same
work on the basis of their equal difference. Everything they touch
does not turn valueless because they touched it. When they are hit,
a person has been assaulted. When they are sexually violated, it is
not simply tolerated or found entertaining or defended as the necessary structure of the family, the price of civilization, or a constitutional right.

Does this differential describe the sex difference? Maybe so. It does
describe the systematic relegation of an entire group of people to a
condition of inferiority and attribute it to their nature. If this differential were biological, maybe biological intervention would have to
be considered. If it were evolutionary, perhaps men would have to
evolve differently. Because I think it is political, I think its politics
construct the deep structure of society. Men who do not rape women
have nothing wrong with their hormones. Men who are made sick
by pornography and do not eroticize their revulsion are not under-
evolved. This social status in which we can be used and abused and
trivialized and humiliated and bought and sold and passed around

41

and patted on the head and put in place and told to smile so that we look as though we're enjoying it all is not what some of us have in mind as sex equality.

This second approach—which is not abstract, which is at odds with socially imposed reality and therefore does not look like a standard according to the standard for standards—became the implicit model for racial justice applied by the courts during the sixties. It has since eroded with the erosion of judicial commitment to racial equality. It was based on the realization that the condition of Blacks in particular was not fundamentally a matter of rational or irrational differentiation on the basis of race but was fundamentally a matter of white supremacy, under which racial differences became invidious as a consequence.[35] To consider gender in this way, observe again that men are as different from women as women are from men, but socially the sexes are not equally powerful. To be on the top of a hierarchy is certainly different from being on the bottom, but that is an obfuscatingly neutralized way of putting it, as a hierarchy is a great deal more than that. If gender were merely a question of difference, sex inequality would be a problem of mere sexism, of mistaken differentiation, of inaccurate categorization of individuals. This is what the difference approach thinks it is and is therefore sensitive to. But if gender is an inequality first, constructed as a socially relevant differentiation in order to keep that inequality in place, then sex inequality questions are questions of systematic dominance, of male supremacy, which is not at all abstract and is anything but a mistake.

If differentiation into classifications, in itself, is discrimination, as it is in difference doctrine, the use of law to change group-based social inequalities becomes problematic, even contradictory. This is because the group whose situation is to be changed must necessarily be legally identified and delineated, yet to do so is considered in fundamental tension with the guarantee against legally sanctioned inequality. If differentiation is discrimination, affirmative action, and any legal change in social inequality, is discrimination—but the existing social differentiations which constitute the inequality are not? This is only to say that, in the view that equates differentiation with discrimination, changing an unequal status quo is discrimination, but allowing it to exist is not.

Looking at the difference approach and the dominance approach from each other's point of view clarifies some otherwise confusing tensions in sex equality debates. From the point of view of the dominance approach, it becomes clear that the difference approach adopts the point of view of male supremacy on the status of the sexes. Simply by treating the status quo as "the standard," it invisibly and uncritically accepts the arrangements under male supremacy. In this sense, the difference approach is masculinist, although it can be expressed in a female voice. The dominance approach, in that it sees the inequalities of the social world from the standpoint of the subordination of women to men, is feminist.

If you look through the lens of the difference approach at the world as the dominance approach imagines it—that is, if you try to see real inequality through a lens that has difficulty seeing an inequality as an inequality if it also appears as a difference—you see demands for change in the distribution of power as demands for special protection. This is because the only tools that the difference paradigm offers to comprehend disparity equate the recognition of a gender line with an admission of lack of entitlement to equality under law. Since equality questions are primarily confronted in this approach as matters of empirical fit[36]—that is, as matters of accurately shaping legal rules (implicitly modeled on the standard men set) to the way the world is (also implicitly modeled on the standard men set)—any existing differences must be negated to merit equal treatment. For ethnicity as well as for gender, it is basic to mainstream discrimination doctrine to preclude any true diversity among equals or true equality within diversity.

To the difference approach, it further follows that any attempt to change the way the world actually is looks like a moral question requiring a separate judgment of how things ought to be. This approach imagines asking the following disinterested question that can be answered neutrally as to groups: against the weight of empirical difference, should we treat some as the equals of others, even when they may not be entitled to it because they are not up to standard? Because this construction of the problem is part of what the dominance approach unmasks, it does not arise with the dominance approach, which therefore does not see its own foundations as moral. If sex inequalities are approached as matters of imposed status, which are in need of change if a legal mandate of equality means anything at all, the question whether women should be treated unequally means simply whether women should be treated as less. When it is exposed as a naked power question, there is no separable question of what ought to be. The only real question is what is and is not a gender question. Once no amount of difference justifies treating women as subhuman, eliminating that is what equality law is for.

In this shift of paradigms, equality propositions become no longer propositions of good and evil, but of power and powerlessness, no more disinterested in their origins or neutral in their arrival at conclusions than are the problems they address.

There came a time in Black people's movement for equality in this country when slavery stopped being a question of how it could be justified and became a question of how it could be ended. Racial disparities surely existed, or racism would have been harmless, but at that point—a point not yet reached for issues of sex—no amount of group difference mattered anymore. This is the same point at which a group's characteristics, including empirical attributes, become constitutive of the fully human, rather than being defined as exceptions to or as distinct from the fully human. To one-sidedly measure one group's differences against a standard set by the other incarnates partial standards. The moment when one's particular qualities become part of the standard by which humanity is measured is a millenial moment.

To summarize the argument: seeing sex equality questions as matters of reasonable or unreasonable classification is part of the way male dominance is expressed in law. If you follow my shift in perspective from gender as difference to gender as dominance, gender changes from a distinction that is presumptively valid to a detriment that is presumptively suspect. The difference approach tries to map reality; the dominance approach tries to challenge and change it. In the dominance approach, sex discrimination stops being a question of morality and starts being a question of politics.

You can tell if sameness is your standard for equality if my critique of hierarchy looks like a request for special protection in disguise. It's not. It envisions a change that would make possible a simple equal chance for the first time. To define the reality of sex as difference and the warrant of equality as sameness is wrong on both counts. Sex, in nature, is not a bipolarity; it is a continuum. In society it is made into a bipolarity. Once this is done, to require that one be the same as those who set the standard—those which one is already socially defined as different from—simply means that sex equality is conceptually designed never to be achieved. Those who most need equal treatment will be the least similar, socially, to those whose situation sets the standard as against which one's entitlement to be equally treated is measured. Doctrinally speaking, the deepest problems of sex inequality will not find women "similarly situated"[37] to men. Far less will practices of sex inequality require that acts be intentionally

44

discriminatory.[38] All that is required is that the status quo be maintained. As a strategy for maintaining social power first structure reality unequally, then require that entitlement to alter it be grounded on a lack of distinction in situation; first structure perception so that different equals inferior, then require that discrimination be activated by evil minds who *know* they are treating equals as less.

I say, give women equal power in social life. Let what we say matter, then we will discourse on questions of morality. Take your foot off our necks, then we will hear in what tongue women speak. So long as sex equality is limited by sex difference, whether you like it or don't like it, whether you value it or seek to negate it, whether you stake it out as a grounds for feminism or occupy it as the terrain of misogyny, women will be born, degraded, and die. We would settle for that equal protection of the laws under which one would be born, live, and die, in a country where protection is not a dirty word and equality is not a special privilege.

three

Desire and Power
(1983)

This conference, however broad its inspiration, sophisticated its conception, competent its organization, and elaborate in what is called here articulation, is not, I've noticed, principally set up to maximize conferring. Conferring happens interstitially. Those of us up here do what are called talks; however, we read them. They are called works in progress; although many of them are quite "done." You then respond with what are called questions, many of which are in the form of statements. This event presents itself as a dialogue but operates through a linear series of speeches. We are presented as being engaged in a process, when in actuality we are here to produce a product. We are in a production-consumption cycle, the product being the book that will come out of all of this. The silence that constitutes your half of the dialogue makes our half sound like the sound of one hand clapping. An ominous sound, I should think, for anyone trained on the left.

In partial, if entirely inadequate, response to these thoughts, I am going to speak rather than read what I have to say. I gather that it will still qualify as a text. At the beginning I will draw on parts of my published work. This will help me be concise in laying out what, I gather from people's responses to that work, is a fairly dense grounding. Things will become a little more open-textured after that, more raw than cooked. I am also now requesting that you interject. I will take your "interruptions" as participation. I've been told that you can, in fact, be heard without those phallic microphones. I say this now because I think that once I get going, it's not going to seem all that clear that there are spaces for you to come in. What I want you to do is wave or say "Give an example" or "Say that again another way" or "Come on, what difference does that make?" I mean this.

Audience: It's not all that easy to do.

C.M.: I know. Thank you. Manners are often taken more seriously than politics. There's a politics to that. I wanted to break into small

This talk was delivered at the Conference on Marxism and the Interpretation of Culture, University of Illinois at Champaign-Urbana, July 11, 1983.

groups after Ellen Willis finished her critique, but I was talked out of it. I will respond to heat on this if you want to do it. I was told that part of the importance of this conference is to make it accessible to people who are not able to be here. I was moved by that. Another way of putting that is that the organizers want our conversations on tape. If we disperse into small places, that won't happen.

Audience: But it won't be the same conversation.

C.M.: That's true; it won't at all. To help in that direction, I am going to attempt, rather than referring to scholarship that has gone on elsewhere, much of which has been adequately covered by people speaking before me, to refer instead to remarks people have made here, as examples for my theoretical points. This conference is an experience I think I can rely on most of us having had. I will include conversations I've had with some of you here, questions you've asked from the floor, and things that have been said from this stage. I will be particularly interested to refer to those anonymous among you who have referred to my work without knowing it was me sitting at the next table or in the row in front of you. These expository choices are an attempt to make this more dialogic and open-textured, even if only marginally so.

One more thing about the politics of this situation and my place in it. We purport to want to change things, but we talk in ways that no one understands. We know that discourses have fashions, that we're in the midst of a certain fashion now, that a few years from now it will be another, that ten years ago it was different. We know better than to think that this is the pure onward progress of knowledge. We participate in these fashions, are swept along in them, but we don't set them. I'm particularly concerned that in talking fashionably about complicated realities—and what we have said here is central to real concerns—we often have highly coded conversations. Not only one-sided, but coded. What conditions create access to the latest code book?

Sometimes I think to myself, MacKinnon, you write. Do you remember that the majority of the world's illiterates are women? *What are you doing?* I feel that powerfully when I think about what brings us all here, which is to make the changes we are talking about. When someone condemns someone else for the use of jargon, they tend to suppose that they themselves speak plain plate glass. I'm not exempting myself from this criticism, I'm saying that I see it as fundamental to developing a politics of language that will be constructive as well as deconstructive.

47

Approaches

This talk is in three parts. The first is in the form of an argument: I will state what I take to be feminism. I will take from and converse around my articles that appeared in *Signs*. I do take it upon myself to define feminism. I challenge everyone to do the same. I would like to open a discourse on what feminism means, rather than on who we think we are to think that we can define what it means. In other words, I'd rather talk substance than relative postures of authority. I undertake this in critical awareness that each of our biographies limits the experience from which we will make such a substantive definition, knowing that none of us individually has the direct experience of all women, but that together we do, so that this theory must be collectively created. We are here to engage that process. Here and now. This is why the hierarchical structure of this conference is such a problem. What kind of theory does one create this way?

In the second part I will attempt to unpack and extend some of the implications from the initial, compressed declarative argument. It will get more discursive. The implications of the initial argument for some central concerns in marxist theory, including the aspiration toward a unified theory of social inequality, will be extended and directed principally to questions of method.

I will end with what I take to be some urgent questions on our agenda. Not that there aren't urgent questions unanswered throughout, but I want to end with some problems I have not yet adequately addressed. The posture of authority I take to speak to you comes because I agree with what I'm saying. Not to shove it down your throats, but to take responsibility for my position.

The first part. In my view, sexuality is to feminism what work is to marxism. (Those of you who know my work will recognize this from the first *Signs* article.)[1] By saying that sexuality is to feminism what work is to marxism, I mean that both sexuality and work focus on that which is most one's own, that which most makes one the being the theory addresses, as that which is most taken away by what the theory criticizes. In each theory you are made who you are by that which is taken away from you by the social relations the theory criticizes. In marxist theory, we see society fundamentally constructed of the relations people form as they do and make those things that are needed to survive humanly. Work is the social process of shaping and transforming the material and social worlds, the process that creates people as social beings, as their interactions create value. Work is that activity by which the theory comprehends people become who they socially are. Class is the social structure of their work, production is its process, capital is one congealed form. Control is its principal issue, that which is contested, that which we care about, the relations of which Marx wrote to attempt to alter.

A parallel argument is implicit in feminism. In my view—you will notice that I equate "in my view" with "feminism"—this argument is that the molding, direction, and expression of sexuality organize society into two sexes, women and men. This division underlies the totality of social relations; it is as structural and pervasive as class is in marxist theory, although of course its structure and quality of pervasion are different. Sexuality is the social process that creates, organizes, expresses, and directs desire. Desire here is parallel to value in marxist theory, not the same, though it occupies an analagous theoretical location. It is taken for a natural essence or presocial impetus but is actually *created by* the social relations, the hierarchical relations, in question. This process creates the social beings we know as women and men, as their relations create society. Sexuality to feminism is, like work to marxism, socially constructed and at the same time constructing. It is universal as activity, yet always historically specific, and jointly comprised of matter and mind. As the organized expropriation of the work of some for the use of others defines the class, workers, the organized expropriation of the sexuality of some for the use of others defines the sex, woman. Heterosexuality is its predominant structure, gender is its social process, the family is a congealed form, sex roles are its qualities generalized to two social personas, and reproduction is a consequence. (Theorists sometimes forget that in order to reproduce one must first, usually, have had sex.) Control is also the issue of gender.

In this analysis, both marxism and feminism are theories of power and of its unequal distribution. They each provide an account of how a systematically unequal social arrangement (by arrangement I don't mean to suggest it's equally chosen by all) is internally coherent and internally rational and pervasive yet unjust. Both theories are total theories. That is, they are both theories of the totality, of the whole thing, theories of a fundamental and critical underpinning of the whole they envision. The problem of the relation between marxism and feminism then becomes how both can be true at the same time. As the focus of my attempt to address this issue, I have taken the relationship between questions of power and questions of knowledge, that is, the relation between the political and the epistemological, as each theory conceives it. I will talk about the feminist theory of power and the feminist theory of knowledge and then move into their implications for an array of marxist methodological issues. I will then say what I think the relationship between marxism and feminism is.

By political, I mean here questions of power. The feminist theory of power is that sexuality is gendered as gender is sexualized. (This comes from the second *Signs* article.)[2] In other words, feminism is a theory of how the erotization of dominance and submission creates gender, creates woman and man in the social form in which we know them. Thus the sex difference and the dominance-submission dynamic define each other. The erotic is what defines sex as an inequality, hence as a meaningful difference. This is, in my view, the social meaning of sexuality and the distinctly feminist account of gender inequality. The feminist theory of knowledge begins with the theory of the point of view of all women on social life. It takes as its point of departure the criticism that the male point of view on social life has constructed both social life and knowledge about it. In other words, the feminist theory of knowledge is inextricable from the feminist critique of male power because the male point of view has forced itself upon the world, and does force itself upon the world, as its way of knowing.

An epistemology is an answer to the question, how do you know? What makes you think you know? Not exactly why should I believe you, but your account of why your account of reality is a true account. The content of the feminist theory of knowledge begins with its criticism of the male point of view by criticizing the posture that has been taken as the stance of "the knower" in Western political thought. That is the stance Stanley Aronowitz previously referred to, the neutral posture, which I will be calling objectivity—that is, the nonsituated, distanced standpoint. I'm claiming that this is the male standpoint socially, and I'm going to try to say why. I will argue that the relationship between objectivity as the stance from which the world is known and the world that is apprehended in this way is the relationship of objectification. Objectivity is the epistemological stance of which objectification is the social process, of which male dominance is the politics, the acted-out social practice. That is, to look at the world objectively is to objectify it. The act of control, of which what I have described is the epistemological level, is itself eroticized under male supremacy. To say women are sex objects is in this way redundant. Sexualized objectification is what defines women as sexual and as women under male supremacy.

I now want to develop some of the implications of this thesis. First, what is gender; then, what is sexuality; then, what kind of analysis this feminism is—in particular, why objectification is specifically male (that's for David Kennedy). I will digress slightly on the subject and object question. Then I will talk about the consequences of setting up a theory this way for questions like falsifiability and uncertainty, and the verb "to be" in feminist discourse.

Gender here is a matter of dominance, not difference. Feminists have noticed that women and men are equally different but not equally powerful. Explaining the subordination of women to men, a political condition, has nothing to do with difference in any fundamental sense. Consequentially, it has a *lot* to do with difference, because the ideology of difference has been so central in its enforcement. Another way to say that is, there would be no such thing as what we know as the sex difference—much less would it be the social issue it is or have the social meaning it has—were it not for male dominance. Sometimes people ask me, "Does that mean you think there's no difference between women and men?" The only way I know how to answer that is: of course there is; the difference is that men have power and women do not. I mean simply that men are not socially supreme and women subordinate by nature; the fact that socially they are, constructs the sex difference as we know it. I mean to suggest that the social meaning of difference—in this I include *différance*—is gender-based.

For those of you who think this is a lot of rhetoric, I want to specify the facts I have in reference. When I speak of male dominance, I mean as its content facts from this culture. The facts have to do with the rate of rape and attempted rape of American women, which is 44 percent. If you ask a random group of women, "Have you ever been raped or been the victim of an attempted rape?" and do not exclude marital rape, that is the figure.[3] Some 4.5 percent of all women are victims of incest by their fathers, an additional 12 percent by other male family members, rising to a total of 43 percent of all girls before they reach the age of eighteen, if sexual abuse within and outside the family is included. These data, by the way, are predicated on believing women, which Freud had a problem with. You know that the theory of the unconscious was devised to explain how women came to invent experiences of childhood sexual abuse, because Freud did not believe, finally, that they could have happened? If you ask women whether they've been sexually harassed in the last two years, about 15 percent report very serious or physical assaults; about 85 percent of all working women report sexual harassment at some time in their working lives. Between a quarter and a third of all women are battered by men in the family. If you look at homicide data, between 60 percent and 70 percent of murdered women have been killed by a husband, lover, or ex-lover. The same is not true for murdered men. (Men also kill each other in great numbers.) About 12 percent of American women are or have been prostitutes. Prostitution, along with modeling, is the only thing for which women as a group are reputed to be paid—by men—more than men. But then, most prostitutes may never get the money; pimps do. The pornography industry, an exemplary synthesis of the erotization of dominance and submission with capitalism's profit motive, is put at eight billion dollars a year, with three to four times as many outlets as McDonald's restaurants.[4] To conceptualize these data as "the sex difference" acquiesces in and obscures the facts of male power they document and suggest are systematic.

By the way, I mean the word male as an adjective. The analysis of sex is social, not biological. This is not to exempt some men or valorize all women; it is to refer to the standpoint from which these acts I have documented are done, that which makes them invisible, glorious, glamorous, and normal. By male, then, I refer to apologists for these data; I refer to the approach that is integral to these acts, to the standard that has normalized these events so that they define masculinity, to the male sex role, and to the way this approach has submerged its gender to become "the" standard. This is what I mean when I speak of the male perspective or male power. Not all men have equal access to male power, nor can men ever fully occupy women's standpoint. If they do, on occasion, they pay for it; and they can always reclaim male power, which is theirs by default unless consciously disavowed. A woman can also take the male point of view or exercise male power, although she remains always a woman. Our access to male power is not automatic as men's is; we're not born and raised to it. We can aspire to it. Me, for instance, standing up here talking to you—socially this is an exercise of male power. It's hierarchical, it's dominant, it's authoritative. You're listening, I'm talking; I'm active, you're passive. I'm expressing myself; you're taking notes. Women are supposed to be seen and not heard.

Audience: Isn't the relationship between mother and child hierarchical and dominant?

C.M.: In a way, but not exactly in the same sense. It comes to have some hierarchical and dominant aspects under male supremacy, which also unites women and children in powerlessness. In short, I disagree with the Chodorow-Dinnerstein analysis[5] that the mother/child relation is an explanation for male dominance. I think it is only within a context where male power already *exists* that the relation between mother and child can be characterized as one in which the mother is seen as powerful in the sense that the relation becomes one of horror, anxiety, betrayal, cruelty, and—crucially—eroticism. I don't think this relation is *why* male supremacy exists.

Audience: But isn't that the situation we are in—male dominance?

C.M.: It is its reality, yes. But I'm attempting to *explain* that reality. The mother/child relation, described as a relation of dominance, is a consequence of male supremacy, not its causal dynamic. Female mothering does not explain to me why hierarchy is eroticized or even why it is gendered. It doesn't explain why girls don't grow up dominating other women, either. If heirarchy were not eroticized in male-dominant sexuality, I do not think hierarchy would mean what it does, exist where it does, much less be attached to gender, hence to "mother," who remains a woman. I don't think female mothering is a *why* of male supremacy; I do think women and children are linked in eroticized powerlessness under male supremacy.

Audience: What about female power?

C.M.: Since I think that is a contradiction in terms, socially speaking, I am going to resume what I had planned to say at this point, because I think it will become clear why I think "female power" is a misnomer. Let me know if it doesn't.

Now I want to speak to the question of what sexuality is in this theory. I do not see sexuality as a transcultural container, as essential, as historically unchanging, or as Eros. I define sexuality as whatever a given society eroticizes. That is, sexual is whatever sexual means in a particular society. Sexuality is what sexuality means. This is a political hermeneutical view. Hermeneutics concerns matters of meaning. If sexuality is seen in this way, it is fundamentally social, fundamentally relational, and it is not a thing—which, by the way, does not mean it is not material, in a feminist sense of materiality. Because sexuality arises in relations under male dominance, women are not the principal authors of its meanings. In the society we currently live in, the content I want to claim for sexuality is the gaze that constructs women as objects for male pleasure. I draw on pornography for its form and content, for the gaze that eroticizes the despised, the demeaned, the accessible, the there-to-be-used, the servile, the child-like, the passive, and the animal. *That* is the content of the sexuality that defines gender female in this culture, and visual thingification is its method.

Michelle Barrett asked earlier, how do women come to want that which is not in our interest? (This is a slight reformulation, but I think it is in the spirit of her question.) I think that sexual desire in women, at least in this culture, is socially constructed as that by which we come to want our own self-annihilation. That is, our subordination is eroticized in and as female; in fact, we get off on it to a degree, if nowhere near as much as men do. This is our stake in this system that is not in our interest, our stake in this system that is killing us. I'm saying femininity as we know it is how we come to want male dominance, which most emphatically is not in our interest. Such a critique of complicity—I say this to Gayatri [Spivak]—does not come from an individualistic theory.

The *kind* of analysis that such a feminism is, and, specifically, the standard by which it is accepted as valid, is largely a matter of the criteria one adopts for adequacy in a theory. If feminism is a critique of the objective standpoint as male, then we also disavow standard scientific norms as the adequacy criteria for our theory, because the objective standpoint we criticize is the posture of science. In other words, our critique of the objective standpoint as male is a critique of science as a specifically male approach to knowledge. With it, we reject male criteria for verification. We're not seeking truth in its female counterpart either, since that, too, is constructed by male power. We do not vaunt the subjective. We begin by seeking the truth of and in that which has constructed all this—that is, in gender.

Why is objectivity as a stance specifically male? First of all, familiar to all of you is the social specificity, the particularity, the social situatedness of thought. Social situation is expressed through the concepts people construct to make sense of their situation. Either gender *is* one such social situation, or it is not. If it is, then theories constructed by those with the social experience of men, most particularly by those who are not conscious that gender is a specific social circumstance, will be, at the least, open to being male theories. It would be difficult, it would take a lot of conscious effort, for them not to be. To repeat myself, it is not that I have a biological theory of gender, so that every utterance out of a biologically gendered person's mouth is socially gendered in the same way. I'm saying it is not foreign to us that social conditions shape thought as well as life. Gender either is or is not such a social condition. I'm claiming that it is.

Objectivity is a stance only a subject can take. This is all very interesting on a verbal plane. Gayatri turned this question around; I'll turn it one more time. It is only a subject who gets to take the objective standpoint, the stance which is transparent to its object, the stance that is no stance. A subject is a self. An object is other to that self. Anyone who is the least bit attentive to gender since reading Simone de Beauvoir knows that it is men socially who are subjects, women socially who are other, objects. Thus the one who has the social access to being that self which takes the stance that is allowed to be objective, that objective person who is a subject, is socially male. When I spoke with David Kennedy about this earlier, he said that the objective subject didn't *have to be* male, so he didn't see how it was gendered. It *could be* any way at all, he said. Well, yes; but my point is that it *isn't* any way at all; it *is* gendered, in fact in the world. If, in order to be gendered, something has to be gendered, those of us in the social change business could pack up and go . . . where? We would give up on changing gender, anyway. Of course it could be any way at all. That it could be and isn't, should be and isn't, is what makes it a political problem.

We notice in language as well as in life that the male occupies both the neutral and the male position. This is another way of saying that the neutrality of objectivity and of maleness are coextensive linguistically, whereas women occupy the marked, the gendered, the different, the forever-female position. Another expression of the sex specificity of objectivity socially is that women have been nature. That is, men have been knowers, mind; women have been "to-be-known," matter, that which is to be controlled and subdued, the acted upon. Of course, this is all a social matter; we live in society, not in the natural world.

Questions of falsifiability look different in this context. One consequence of women's rejection of science in its positivistic form is that we reject the head-counting theory of verification. Structural truths about the meaning of gender may or may not produce big numbers. For example, to say "not only women experience that" in reply to a statement characterizing women's experience, is to suggest that to be properly sex-specific, something must be unique to one sex. Similarly, to say "not all women experience that," as if that contraindicates sex specificity (this point is to Larry Grossberg), is to suggest that to be sex-specific, something must be true of 100 percent of the sex affected. Both of those are implicitly biological criteria for sex: unique and exclusive. Never mind that the biology of sex is not bipolar or

55

exclusive. This is the way the biology of gender is ideologically conceived.

Methodological assumptions have political consequences. One result of this implicitly biological notion of sex specificity is that differences *among* women (notice differences again), such as, crucially, race and class, are seen to undercut the meaningfulness or even the reality of gender. If I say such and so is true of women, and someone responds, but it's not the same for all women, that is supposed to undercut the statement, rather than to point out features that make up the sex specificity of the thing. If gender is a social category, gender is whatever it socially means. All women either will or will not be hit in particular ways by the reality of gender, the totality of which will then comprise the meaning of gender as a social category. In other words, to show that an observation or experience is not the same for all women proves only that it is not biological, not that it is not gendered. Similarly, to say that not only women experience something—for example, to suggest that because some men are raped rape is not an act of male dominance—only suggests that the status of women is not biological. Men can be feminized too, and they know they are when they are raped. The fact that sometimes whites have been slaves does not make Black slavery not racist. That some non-Jews, such as gypsies and gays, were victims of the Holocaust does not mean the Holocaust was not, or was less, anti-Semitic. We know something about the content of Black slavery—that is, of white racism—and about the content of the Holocaust, I trust, that makes it impossible to present isolated if significant counterexamples as if they undercut the specific meaning of the atrocities for the groups who were *defined* by their subjection to them. The fact that lots of white people are poor does not mean that the poverty of Blacks has nothing to do with white racism. It just means that social relations cannot be understood by analogy to machines or bodies or thermodynamics or even quantum mechanics.

It has been suggested that men who experience feelings similar to those women articulate as women may be expressing ways in which being on the bottom of hierarchies can produce similar feelings in people. The declassed status of student, for example, however temporary, makes a lot of men feel the way most women feel most of the time—except that the men tend to *feel* it, because they've fallen from something. There is nothing like femininity to dignify one's indignity as one's identity. Nor do women and men come to the status of "student" the same. Women have been silenced as women: we have been

56

told we are stupid because we are women, told that our thoughts are trivial because we are women, told that our experiences as women are unspeakable, told that women can't speak the language of significance, had our ideas appropriated by men, only to find those ideas have suddenly become worthy, even creative. Women have been excluded from education as women. This isn't to say we're the only ones who have been excluded from education, but rather that the specific history of that for us *as women* brings us to a structure like that of this conference—in which there's authoritative discourse emanating from the podium and silent receptivity in a mass—in a way that specifically intimidates and has specific exclusionary resonances for us. To those of you who denied this yesterday, I claim the sex specificity of that aspect of this experience.

The next thing I want to address is the methodological question of uncertainty. I want your thoughts on all of this, but in particular on this. I'm coming to think that because men have power over women, women come to epistemological issues situated in a way that sheds a rather distinct light on the indeterminacy/determinacy question as men have agonized over it. Take the problem of "is there a reality and how do I know I'm right about it?" The "is there a there there?" business. How do we deal in the face of Cartesian—updated as existential—doubt? Women know the world is out there. Women know the world is out there because it hits us in the face. Literally. We are raped, battered, pornographed, defined by force, by a world that begins, at least, entirely outside us. No matter what we think about it, how we try to think it out of existence or into a different shape for us to inhabit, the world remains real. Try some time. It exists independent of our will. We can tell that it is there, because no matter what we do, we can't get out of it. Male power is for us—therefore *is*—this kind of fact.

The point of science, as I get it, has been to replace opinion with certainty, to replace religion and faith with the empirical hard stuff. Social science does this by analogy to the physical world: as things move, so society moves. Its laws of motion make society predictable and controllable, or try to. By the way, this analogy, between the social and physical worlds, which underlies the whole "science of society" project, which I'm here calling a specifically male project, has not been very deeply looked into to see whether it applies. Women's situation with respect to that project is that we have *been* "world" for an implicitly male-centered social science. We come to this project as the to-be-known-about, as part of that world to be transformed and controlled. Cartesian doubt—this anxiety about whether the world is really there independent of our will or of our representations, if I can doubt it, maybe it doesn't exist—comes from the luxury of a position of power that entails the possibility of making the world as one thinks or wants it to be. Which is exactly the male standpoint. You can't tell the difference between what you think and the way the world is—or which came first—if your standpoint for thinking and being is one of social power.

Consider the example of faking orgasms, which Gayatri brought up. Men have anxiety that women fake orgasms. Take women's orgasms as an example of something about which one can have Cartesian doubt. "How do I know" she's satisfied, right? Now consider *why* women fake orgasms, rather than how too bad it is that men can't, so that therefore they're unequal to us. I would bet that if we had the power men have, they would *learn*. What I'm saying is, men's power to *make* the world here is their power to make us make the world of their sexual interaction with us the way they want it. They want us to have orgasms; that proves they're virile, potent, effective. We provide them that appearance, whether it's real for us or not. We even get into it. Our reality is, it is far less damaging and dangerous for us to do this, to accept a lifetime of simulated satisfaction, than to hold out for the real thing from them. For them, we are "world" to their knowledge of world. Their Cartesian doubt is entirely justified: their power to force the world to be their way means that they're forever wondering what's really going on out there.

Heisenberg's uncertainty principle comes close to this awareness. If the way you know the world is this intervention, piercing the veil, making penetrating observations, incisive analyses . . . well, women's social powerlessness gives us the opposite problem. We're forever wondering whether there's anything *other* than the reality of the world men make. Whether there is *any* sphere of the world that responds to our will, our thought. Women are awash in doubt, but ours has never had the credibility of Descartes'. It is our *reality*, even before our knowledge, that is in doubt. Thus I think that the indeterminacy that arises in discourse theory, and in the social text, describes something that, as genders, we are unequally situated in. If you don't determine reality, its indeterminacy—its *un*fixity—is a good deal less apparent to you. Your world is *very determinate*; it is *all too fixed*. It *can't* just be any way at all.

Now I want to say something about the use of the verb "to be" in feminist theory. If the analysis I have given is right, to be realistic about sexuality socially is to see it from the male point of view. To be feminist is to do that with a critical awareness that that is what you are doing. This explains why feminist insights are often criticized for replicating male ideology, why feminists are called "condescending to women," when what we are doing is expressing and exposing how women are condescended to. Because male power has created in reality the world to which feminist insights, when they are accurate, refer, many of our statements will capture that reality, simply exposing it as specifically male for the first time. For example, men say all women are whores. We say men have the power to make this our fundamental condition. So feminism stresses the indistinguishability of prostitution, marriage, and sexual harassment. See: what a woman "is" is what you have *made* women "be." That "is" women, as men make women mean. They have the power to; they *do*—otherwise power means nothing. It's a very empirical "is." Men define women as sexual beings; feminism comprehends that femininity "is" sexual. Men see rape as intercourse; feminists say much intercourse "is" rape. Men say women desire degradation; feminists see female masochism as the ultimate success of male supremacy and marvel at its failures.

If male power makes the world as it "is," theorizing this reality requires capturing it in order to subject it to critique, hence to change. Feminists say women are not individuals. To retort that we "are" will not make it so; it will obscure the need to *make change so that it can be so*. To retort to the feminist charge that women "are" not equal, "Oh, you think women aren't equal to men" is to act as though *saying* we "are" will make it so. What it will do instead, what it has done and is doing, is legitimize the vision that we already "are" equal. That *this* life as we live it now is equality for us. It acts as if the purpose of speech is to say what we want reality to be like, as if it already is that way, as if that will help move reality to that place. This may work in fiction, but it won't work in theory. Rather, if this is reality, nothing needs changing: *this* is freedom; we choose *this*. To me, this answer is about denial and is the opposite of change.

Stanley Aronowitz talked pretty extensively about marxist method. I see two strains in marxist method; it is not monolithic. One is the more objectivist strain, which purports to take the neutral position. The other, which I draw on, is more critical of the necessary situatedness of its own standpoint. This strain purports to capture as thought the flux of history, and it understands itself—more in Lukacs' mode—as reflexive, as participating in an ongoing situation, trapped in it in a way, needing to be self-critical and also having, by virtue of that involvement, some access to the truth of the situation.

Feminism has widely been thought to contain tendencies of liberal feminism, radical feminism, and socialist feminism. Too often, socialist or marxist feminism has applied the objectivist strain in marxism to women and called that marxist feminism. Liberal feminism has applied to women the same objectivism that marxism shares with liberalism, resulting in liberalism applied to women. This, especially on questions of sexuality, is markedly similar to the left view, because of the common maleness of the epistemological posture. What I am calling feminism includes at least some versions of radical feminism, not the biological determinist, but the socially based ones. This feminism is methodologically postmarxist. It is a move to resolve the relationship between marxism and feminism on the level of method. Methodologically, a post-marxist analysis treats women as a social group, not in individualist, naturalist, idealist, moralist, voluntarist, or harmonist terms. (In those terms, we're all really equal, and socially we have a naturally harmonious relation between the genders, which needs, at most, marginal reequilibration). I've noticed that for many people liberal views of sexuality—treating it in terms that are individual, natural, ideal, moral, and voluntarist—seem to coexist remarkably well with otherwise marxist views. In my opinion, no feminism worthy of the name is *not* methodologically post-marxist.

As an example of post-marxist feminism, I want to consider the often-raised question of whether "all women" are oppressed by heterosexuality. The question is posed as if sexual practice were a matter of unconstructed choice. If heterosexuality is the dominant gendered form of sexuality in a society where gender oppresses women through sex, sexuality and heterosexuality are essentially the same thing. This does not erase homosexuality, it merely means that sexuality in that form may be no less gendered. Either heterosexuality is the structure of the oppression of women or it is not. Most people see sexuality as individual and biological and voluntary; that is, they see it in terms of the politically and formally liberal myth structure. If you applied such an analysis to the issue of work—anyone who thinks this is not a valid parallel should target this peculiarly sensitive example—would you agree, as people say about heterosexuality, that a worker chooses to work? Does a worker even meaningfully choose his or her specific line or place of work? If working conditions improve, would you call that worker not oppressed? If you have comparatively good or easy or satisfying or well-paying work, if you even like your work, or have a good day at work, does that mean, from a marxist perspective, your work is not exploited? Those who think that one chooses heterosexuality under conditions that make it compulsory should either explain why it is not compulsory or explain why the word choice can be meaningful here. And I would like you to address a question that I think few here would apply to the workplace, to work, or to workers: whether a good fuck is any compensation for getting fucked. And why everyone knows what that means.

.   .   .

How to make change. Marxism teaches that exploitation and degradation somehow produce resistance and revolution. It's been hard to say why. What I've learned from women's experience with sexuality is that exploitation and degradation produce grateful complicity in exchange for survival. They produce self-loathing to the point of extinction of self, and it is respect for self that makes resistance conceivable. The issue is not why women acquiesce but why we ever do anything but. I would like us to see this as a particular question for explanation and for organizing. My second urgent question has to do with class and with race. I would like to see some consideration of the connections between the theory of sexuality I have outlined and the forms of property possession and ownership *and* the erotization of racial degradation and money. A third urgent issue is the relation between everything I've said and all forms of inequality. Am I describing only one form within a larger system, or is this *the* system, or is this too abstract a question?

I do believe that none of our work can be done the way it has been done if what I am saying is taken seriously. We cannot address aesthetics without considering pornography. We cannot think about sexuality and desire without considering the normalization of rape, and I do not mean rape as surplus repression. We cannot do or criticize science without talking about the masculinity of its premises. We cannot talk about everyday life without understanding its division by gender, or about hegemony without understanding male dominance as a form of it. We cannot talk about production without pointing out that its sex division, as well as sexual harassment and prostitution (and housework), underpins and constitutes the labor market. We cannot talk about the phallus in a way that obscures the penis, and we cannot talk about woman as signifier in a way that loses sight of woman the signified. We need to systematically understand in order

61

to criticize and change, rather than reproduce, the connection between the fact that the few have ruled and used the many in their
own interest and for their own pleasure as well as profit and the fact
that those few have been men.

four

Whose Culture? A Case Note on Martinez v. Santa Clara Pueblo (1983)

We made the fires. We are the fire-tenders. We are the ones who do not allow anyone to speak for us *but* us.

Beth Brant, *Sinister Wisdom* (1983)

T he white man's law, recognizing what he calls equality, has since the late 1950s prohibited discrimination. Under this law, equal treatment, without regard to race, ethnicity, and sex (among other characteristics) is thought to be secured in many areas of social life. The idea is that people should be free from arbitrary and unreasonable treatment on the basis of qualities that have no fair or reasonable or just relation to the purpose for which they are being used. People shouldn't encounter built-in bias everywhere they go. In this idea of equality, group characteristics have no necessary relation to one's ability to perform tasks, to merit, to potential contributions to society, or to needs for particular benefits.

I am sure it will surprise no one at the Survival School when I say that the white man has kept the meaning of this principle in his own hands. Or, he has placed it in the hands of people who may not be white or male but adopt and agree with the point of view of the white man's culture, which is the dominant culture. This has tended to mean that the principle of equality has been interpreted to affirm specific white and male cultural values as "the standard." Arbitrariness is measured as deviance from this standard. Equality has come to mean a right to be treated like the white man when you can show you *are* like him. Other rules for interpreting the equality principle include the intent requirement: something is discriminatory only if the person doing it meant it to be.[1] The white man has to know what

This talk was given at the request of Native American women at the North American Survival School, Red Earth, St. Paul, Minnesota, March 12, 1983. It grew considerably from the dialogue that followed the presentation. I dedicate these thoughts to Glenn Morris.

63

he's doing. That certainly keeps the definition of victimization in the victimizer's hands. If a whole set of people who, as they put it, "just happen to be" women or "just happen to be" Black or Chicano or Native are hurt, if it wasn't intentional or can't be proved to be intentional then it's just too bad. It doesn't count as discrimination. Given such notions, it makes sense that to date most of the cases that have shaped the highest law against sex discrimination have been brought and won by white men.[2]

Also consistent with this is that laws guaranteeing equality tend not to apply to some of the most extreme instances of enforced inequality. For example, most women work in jobs that mostly women work in.[3] If there is no man around who is being treated better than you to compare yourself with, to set the standard, the fact that you're segregated into an entire category of occupation, and that the whole occupation pays very little, has not been seen as a problem to be addressed by the law against sex inequality. You're just in a "different" situation, even though what makes it different is segregation.

There has been a similar circularity to the way the laws against racial and ethnic discrimination have been applied in the white man's courts. When discrimination in one area of society creates inequality in other areas, that has often been seen as just the way it happens to be, as just *facts*, not as discrimination.[4] The courts limit the scope of the issues they are willing to recognize in each case; in this way segregation in housing can become a reason that schools are not found to be segregated. It's just that only certain people live in these communities, so the fact that the schools are segregated just reflects the local community. The school boards are not segregating anyone. Why is the housing segregated? It just happens that some folks who just happen not to be white don't happen to make so much money, so they can't afford this housing, so they don't live here. Why don't these folks happen to make enough money to live here? That is not really discrimination, it's just that the jobs they do just happen to pay a lot less than other jobs because those people don't happen to have the educational qualifications that would enable them to get the higher-paying jobs. Why don't they have the educational qualifications? They just didn't happen to go to such good schools. Why? Because they live in poor communities that tend to have the less good schools. Everything is seen as if it were happenstance, at each step. Nobody discriminates, everybody just takes things as they really are, as they just happen to be. Whenever it's real, whenever it's a trap, whenever it's a closed system, it isn't discrimination. The more un-equal it is in life, the less discriminatory it looks to the law.

In a society that is anything but sex-blind and color-blind, courts insist on color blindness and sex blindness as the rule for discerning inequality and enforcing equality.[5] The moment you complain in court about discrimination is probably the first moment in your life when your color, your race, your ethnicity, or your sex becomes "ir-relevant." This is supposed to be a principled and neutral stance. But the white man's standard for equality is: are you equal *to him?* That is hardly a neutral standard. It is a racist, sexist standard. If you can prove that you have what are socially white and male qualifications— money, education, credibility—and that you are basically white and male in every cultural way but were oddly mistaken for, say, a Third World woman and so were turned down for some benefit, at that moment the white man may see that you have not been treated equally. But if you present yourself as affirmatively and self-respectingly a member of your own culture or sex, deprived or dam-aged or contributing as such, if you insist that *your* cultural diversity be affirmatively accommodated and recognized in ways equal to the ways *theirs* has been, that's not seen to be an equality challenge at all. If you say: I am a woman; I insist that what it is and what it means to be a woman—for example, the fact that I am pregnant or the fact that I need an abortion—shall not be a reason to deny employment or health benefits when you cover all the employment or health needs that men have, they say: that's not an equality right. You're *different.* You're asking for special treatment for your differences. The white man's meaning of equality is being equal to him, which is the same as being the same as him. This meaning of equality has not valued any cultural or sexual distinctiveness except his own.

In this context, I want to raise and consider, far from resolve, some of the issues from the case of Julia Martinez against the Santa Clara Pueblo,[6] a lawsuit a Native American woman brought against her tribe. This case is important not because the most pressing inequali-ties involve discriminations against Native women by Native tribes. Genocide in all its forms is a massive imposition of inequality on Na-tive peoples and Native cultures by white people and white culture. I raise this case because its poses difficult tensions, even conflicts, between equality of the sexes, on the one hand, and the need to ap-proach those questions within their particular cultural meanings, in an awareness of history and out of respect for cultural diversity and the need for cultural survival, on the other. If questions of sex and sexism are not to be separated from questions of race and racism under the specific cultural and historical conditions in which both arise, as I think they cannot be, we need to ask: who will define what equality means? White man's equality law has largely defined it the way I have sketched. The issue I want to raise, which the *Martinez* case in the end leaves open, is how Native people will define it.

Julia Martinez sued her tribe in United States federal court over a tribal rule. The rule said that if Native women married outside the tribe, the children of that union were not full tribal members; if Native men married out, there were no such consequences. Julia Martinez married a Navaho man. Her children, who sued with her, could therefore not be full members of her Santa Clara tribe. They could not vote or inherit her rights in communal land, for example. Children of men who married non–Santa Clara women remained full members of the tribe and succeeded to all their rights. When men marry outside the tribe, the families they create become families of the tribe; when women marry outside the tribe, the families they create are not families of the tribe. Julia Martinez apparently tried to get the tribe to change this rule. When she was unsuccessful, she went to federal court—the white man's court—and argued that this was discrimination under the Indian Civil Rights Act, which has a provision against denying equal protection of the laws.

The United States Supreme Court, in a departure from its more common posture toward Indian tribal rights, said that this was a question of Indian sovereignty to be resolved by the tribe.[7] In this, the United States Supreme Court will respect tribal sovereignty. Perhaps the control of Indian women matters less to the United States than does the control of land, fish, minerals, and foreign relations, as to which tribes are not as sovereign.[8] Whatever you think of the reasons, the result is that the tribes will define what equality of the sexes is going to mean, at least on the question of who is an Indian.

I find *Martinez* a difficult case on a lot of levels, and I don't usually find cases difficult. Missing from the Supreme Court's account of the case is the history of the tribal rule. I am told that the rule was made in 1939 after the General Allotment Act[9] divided up communal lands into individually held parcels, in something like an attempt to make Indians into proper agrarians. Although this law did not apply to the Pueblos, they recognized that Congress could apply it to them at any time. In the experience of tribes it did apply to, lands were being taken away by white men marrying Native women. The Santa Clara rule was passed to prevent women who married out from passing land out, in an attempt to secure the survival of a culture for which land is life. Without knowing this, which I have by word of mouth, it is hard to understand what the Supreme Court meant when it said that this rule was "'no more or less than a mechanism of social . . . self-definition,' and as such [was] basic to the tribes' survival as a cultural and economic entity."[10] The rule was seen as basic to survival because it discouraged Native women from marrying white men—or white men from marrying Native women, depending on how you see who does what—because that was taking away Native land. When Native men married white women, the experience apparently had been that white women more often integrated with the tribe.

Given this history, which the tribe did not choose or make, I imagine the tribe saying, we need this rule. I imagine Julia Martinez replying: I understand that history, it is also my history, but this is a male supremacist solution to a problem male supremacy created. The rule keeps Indian women for Indian men at the price of loss of tribal rights, from a time when Native women did not have formal power in rule-making. What would be wrong with preventing *any* child from inheriting land from parents who were not both tribal members? Whose system is it that ties ownership of land to ownership of women? Is that *our* tradition? Why is it seen as a matter of cultural survival when men guarantee exclusive access to Indian women as a requirement of tribal membership, but when an Indian woman attempts to claim that her family is an Indian family, to choose who to make a family with, it's called a *threat* to cultural survival? Whose culture is this culture? Is male supremacy sacred because it has become a tribal tradition? Under what conditions?

The tribe says: how can you apply the white cultural idea of equality to take us into this foreign court that has historically justified the atrocities that have subjected our people? Julia Martinez responds, how can you say that my desire for equality is not an Indian idea? When I say I am the equal of an Indian man, why do you say that I do not speak as an Indian woman? Why do you make me choose between my equality as woman and my cultural identity? The tribe says: because of the white man's history of racism and genocide, this is not an issue of sex discrimination. Your claim cannot be separated from either our history or your forum. How can you go to them for justice? Julia Martinez replies, how could the tribe make this rule?

Approaches

Why have you made me go to them for justice? Directly to me, I hear her say: since when is the way a woman is treated *anywhere* strictly an internal or national matter for you? If your country treated *you* this way, wouldn't you want somewhere else to go for justice?

As I said, the Supreme Court decided to stay out of this. I want to suggest that cultural survival is as contingent upon equality between women and men as it is upon equality among peoples. The sex division in this case undermined the ability of Native Americans to survive as autonomous cultures. It was certainly not a means of promoting that survival. This is not the case because Julia Martinez fought over it, and not because she fought it in the white man's court, but because the tribe was willing to sacrifice *her tribal connection*, her full membership in the tribal community, in the face of a white male supremacist threat. Their rule did nothing to address or counteract the reasons why Native women were vulnerable to white male land imperialism through marriage—it gave in to them, by punishing the *woman*, the Native person. Sex inequality, looked at close up, may threaten the cultural survival of Native peoples just as going outside the culture to resolve it threatens tribal sovereignty. But this only appears if one recognizes that the systematic vulnerability of Native women to marriages that can destroy the tribe indicates the *tribe* has a problem—and not a problem to be solved by punishing Native women through their children to provide a disincentive. Why is excluding women always an option for solving problems men create between men? Maybe women's loyalty would be more reliable if their communities were more equitable.

In the *Martinez* case, the Supreme Court allowed the tribe to make its own rules, allowing—even if for some reasons I might criticize—that the most important meanings of equality are the meanings communities make for themselves. The question now is, what will the tribes make equality mean, and whose voice will speak for them? When I discuss this issue, I find that some people consider equality to be a white idea. If you think equality means what the white man has made it mean—being the same as him—it definitely is a white idea. But the aspiration of women to be no less than men—not to be punished where a man is glorified, not to be considered damaged or disloyal where a man is rewarded or left in peace, not to lead a derivative life, but to do everything and be anybody at all—is an aspiration indigenous to women across place and across time. I think the tribal rule in the *Martinez* case is male supremacist, not just sex differentiated. Since when is male supremacy a tribal tradition? For at least some tribes, since *contact* with European whites.[11] At that point, it looks more like *in*equality is the white idea. And what women like Julia Martinez might make equality mean, no white man invented.

five

On Exceptionality: Women as Women in Law (1982)

S isters and friends. I speak tonight to celebrate the victory, for them and for all women, of the ascension of Rosalie and Mary Jean to the Supreme Court of the state of Minnesota. I plan to be critical and inspirational. When I told Rosalie that I planned to be inspirational, she said, "Oh, really? not controversial?" I said, "Rosalie, you can't be inspirational in speaking about women and not be controversial." I particularly plan not to be instrumental. You may think that I'm not being very practical. I have learned that practical means something that can be done while keeping everything else the same. In that sense, the analysis and vision that I'm giving you tonight is not practical. It is, however, a form of practice.

Dean Bob Stein said that this subject had everyone intrigued. I think it has everyone's teeth on edge. From one traditional perspective (particularly given my reputation which seems, as people tactfully put it, to have preceded me) you expect a feminist diatribe. You want to know why we can't all relax and just be persons. Why does she have to say it twice, women as women, to get it across? Feminists, hearing this subject, wonder whether I'm going to glorify our oppression and embrace it as identity. Will she shove the female stereotype down our throats in the name of the eternal female and call that feminism? Finally, successful women, whether traditional or feminist— that is, women who have succeeded in a system that is not built for women to be successful—feel a trash coming on. When a feminist speaks about women as women in law, such a woman braces for a critique of women who have succeeded for having succeeded. On the assumption that they must have sold out, therefore are not real women, because real women fail or die trying.

Instead I am going to do something that, at least in my experience,

This address was given in honor of Rosalie Wahl, Associate Justice, Minnesota Supreme Court, and Mary Jean Coyne, Associate Justice, Minnesota Supreme Court, at the University of Minnesota Law School, Minneapolis, Minnesota, Oct. 4, 1982.

has never been done. I will talk in a way that doesn't fall into any of these categories that might have set your teeth on edge in anticipation. I will speak—and this is where we'll run into trouble with the more concretely inclined among us—about something that has not been allowed to exist, but also somehow nevertheless does. I will make one argument: that the definition of women in law and in life is *not ours*. There will be two parts: the law part and the life part. I will argue that women, in sex discrimination law and in the experience of lawyering, do not exist as we, as women, see ourselves. In these spheres we do not find women from women's point of view. We do not have women for ourselves, women for all women, women as members of a community of interest of women, women measured by standards that reflect the experience and aspirations of women as such. We are not allowed to be women on our own terms. Justice Holmes (without quoting whom no discussion on law seems complete) said in 1881, "The life of the law has not been logic: it has been experience."[1] As I think about law and life, the life of the law and a life in law, I wonder, *whose* experience?

Now I will make some broad and sweeping generalizations about sex discrimination doctrine. On my reading, sex discrimination—this law under which we are offered a chance to assert equality with men—offers women two routes to sex equality. The primary avenue views women as if we were men. It measures our similarity with men to see if we are or can be men's equals. This standard is called the equality rule. It is considered gender-neutral, abstract, neutral, principled, essentially procedural and objective. I will argue that it substantively embraces masculinity, the male standard for men, and applies it to women. The second approach available under sex discrimination doctrine views women as men view women: in need of special protection, help, or indulgence. To make out a case, complainants have to meet the male standard for women: femininity. It is openly, if uncomfortably, recognized as substantive, not objective or abstract. It is considered compensatory and sex-specific. This so-called "benign discrimination" is considered the *only* way to analyze women substantively as women for legal purposes. In other words, for purposes of sex discrimination law, to be a woman means either to be like a man or to be like a lady. We have to meet either the male standard for males or the male standard for females.

The first approach, considered the gender-neutral equality rule, ignores the fact that the indices and injuries of sex or sexism often make certain that simply being a woman may mean seldom being in a position sufficiently similar to that of a man to have different treatment which hurts us be a matter of sex bias. This approach reinforces our social disadvantages whenever it finds sex differences—which, given sex inequality, is often. The second approach reflects rather than alters the substance of women's inferior status. It presents as equal protection what looks more like a protection racket: you get so little out of this that you are going to keep needing a lot more of it, but you wouldn't even need it at all if they would stop keeping you down with it. In these two ways, the legal forms for arguing the injuries of sex inequality obscure the gender of equality's reference point while effectively contradicting, not changing, and hardly compensating for, the content of women's sex-specific grievances.

We are living out the combined consequences of both rules. At the same time that very few women are gaining access to the preconditions for being able to effectively assert equality on male terms under the first standard, women created in the image of society's traditional role are losing the guarantees of those roles—very often to men asserting sex equality under the first rule. Women who ask courts to enforce the guarantees that have been an ideological part of the bargain of women's roles are getting very little—and less and less—while also not receiving the benefits of the social change that would qualify them to assert rights on the same terms as men. Women who wish to step out of women's traditional relations with men and become abstract persons, to be exceptional to women's condition rather than to receive the protections of it, are treated as if we are seeking to be like men, without any realization that that concedes the gender of the standard. Women who seek to meet this standard under sex discrimination doctrine are served equality with a vengeance. To win sex discrimination cases under the equality rubric, athletes, academic women, professional women, blue-collar women, and military women, for instance, have to meet the male standard: the standard that men are trained and prepared for socially as men. They tell us no, it's not a male standard, it is just *the* standard. If you protest that, they say measure up or get out. Women in these roles are then required to pay the price of admission, to meet these socially stacked standards—standards men are supposed to meet but very often do not.

Women who assert sex discrimination claims in terms of traditional roles, meaning in terms of women's traditional relations with men, such as widows, mothers, wives, have to present ourselves as in need of their protection. If we don't present that image, we are evaluated like men, rather than according to the specific vulnerabilities of all women's current situation. For example, to apply this critique to a case you may be familiar with, *Dothard v. Rawlinson*, women were excluded from guard jobs in contact positions in male prisons because of what the court called "their very womanhood," meaning their capacity to be raped.[2] The plaintiffs were protected out of a job they wanted while the conditions that create women's rapeability as the definition of womanhood were not even seen as susceptible to change. When courts learn that sexual harassment is as vicious and pervasive and damaging to women in workplaces everywhere as rape is to women guards in male prisons, and as disruptive to production as rape is to prison security, will women be excluded from the workplace altogether?

Now we will do a sex comparison. You're supposed to do that in sex discrimination law. Apply everything just said about women to men. From the list of women who receive the protections or compensatory benefits of women's situation, I'm granting that there are undoubtedly many widowers who are in the situation of most widows—poor. A few husbands are like most wives—financially dependent on their spouse. It is also true that a few fathers, like most mothers, are primary parents, to invoke another case.[3] My point, though, is that occupying those particular positions is consistent with the norms for gender female. To be poor, financially dependent, and a primary parent constitutes part of what being a woman means. Most of those who are in those circumstances are women. A gender-neutral approach to those circumstances obscures, while the protectionist approach declines to change, the fact that women's poverty, financial dependency, motherhood, and sexual accessibility (our targeted-for-sexual-violation status) substantively make up women's status *as women*. It describes what it is to be most women. That some men find themselves in a similar situation doesn't mean that they occupy that status *as men*, as members of their gender. They do so as exceptions, both in norms and numbers.

Women, to claim being similarly situated with men in the sense sex discrimination law demands, also have to be exceptions. Specifically, they must be able to claim everything that gender inequality has in general systematically denied to women as a sex: financial independence, job qualifications, business experience, leadership capacities, assertiveness and confidence, the esteem of your peers, physical stature, strength or prowess, combat skill, sexual inviolability, and at all stages of legal proceedings, credibility. Taking the sexes as individuals, meaning one at a time as if they did not belong to a gender, perfectly obscures these collective realities behind the mask of recognition of individual rights. Given that women are *not* situated similarly to men, but rather are socially unequal, looking at women one at a time rather than as women ensures that it is only the exceptional woman who escapes gender inequality enough to be able to claim she is injured by it. It seems that we already have to be equal before we can complain of inequality.

Nor have women as such, women as women in the sense I'm trying to develop, under any doctrinal guise, defined the terms of discourse or the standards of judgment from women's standpoint. Women athletes or academics or military women may be allowed to play with the boys, but we are not allowed to criticize competition or strength or profitability as the standard for athletics, to question objectivity as a measure of intellectual excellence or abstraction as the point of scholarship, nor are we allowed to reject combat as a peculiarly ejaculatory means of conflict resolution.

Now I want to talk about life in a different mode: in the practice of law. Available to women in the practice of law are the same two roles as those in standards of sex discrimination law, except that women lawyers are held to both at once. I call them the man standard and the lady standard. I think it will be apparent to most of us that a successful lawyer is a man, in the sense that the role of a successful lawyer is a male role regardless of the biology of its occupant. No man is made to feel like less of a man for being a good lawyer, regardless of his particular style. Being a lawyer is also substantially more consistent with the content of the male role, with what men are taught to be in this society: ambitious, upwardly striving, capable of hostility, aggressive not just assertive, not particularly receptive or set off from the track of an argument by what someone else might be saying or, god forbid, feeling. It also requires one to be unserious. By this I mean what I think Virginia Woolf meant when she spoke of "unreal loyalties."[4] Not being present in what you say in a way that might make you vulnerable, skilled at false and manipulative passion and manufactured intensity. The lawyer role has as its implicit norms the same qualities that are the explicit norms of masculinity as it is socially defined. It is a power role.

A successful lady, by contrast, is deferential, considerate, at most assertive, receptive, and overly sincere, emotional. Emotional is the word we get, not just when we are told we are being hysterical, but when we *really mean* what we say and don't want to say things as if we mean them that we not only don't mean but oppose. I'm not saying women have a corner on being principled. I'm saying that part of a lawyer's role includes the ability not to care which side of the argument you are on, and women are regularly faulted for failing at that. Now, given that you are a woman lawyer, are you feeling a little schizoid?

The cardinal quality of the ability to successfully negotiate this particular schism, this demand to be professionally masculine and personally feminine at the same time at all times, is that you *not identify as a woman*. I'm going to read a short excerpt from a statement an attorney recently made at a placement seminar here. He was asked, "Do you take sex into account in hiring?" His answer was:

As long as I've recruited I've kept records, talked to other attorneys, there is a recruiters' network. Everyone gets together around now and violates the Robinson-Patman Act on how much we are going to offer in terms of salaries and so forth. [Laughter.] But one generalized comment about women in particular is that one reason that recruiting now of females is from a recruiter's standpoint a lot easier is that there are more mainstream women going into law school. You know where you were in 1970 or 1971 it was very often almost a suffragette, very activist sort of person, and indeed it had to be to break down some of the existing barriers in the private practice or in the corporate area. People who were really willing to come out swinging that made at least some of the initial assimilation process [this is a dramatic reading] in some of the more silk-stocking law firms a bit more difficult at first, but I think those are really old issues because the women who are going to law school now for the most part and men too, for that matter, we're just seeing a more mainstream type of candidate than we did in the very turbulent period of the seventies.

Men who come out swinging are perhaps seen as lawyers that they want, law being a form of combat. It also seems clear that their idea is for women to assimilate to a standard men set, and that that is contradicted by identifying with the interests of all women, in particular, to be activist, a suffragette sort. Women are supposed to take on this male context and integrate—in his word, assimilate. To qualify, interviewers want to know: are you man and lady enough for this job?

So what do *I* mean by women? When I think about what women as women see, about the point of view from the situation of all women, I think about the fact that between 7 and 8 percent of us have never been sexually assaulted or harassed.[5] That we make half a man's income and that the only occupations this society, as a structural matter, pays women as a group more than men are prostitution and modeling. The destiny of all of us is marriage. To those of you who think that marriage is an equal bargain, I would suggest, just to begin with, that in any place where one cannot prosecute for marital rape, the woman's obligation to sexually deliver is effectively enforced by the state. The support obligation that men supposedly provide overwhelmingly is not.

Next, it is important to my comprehension of the situation of all women that all women are not the same. That's what *they* think—all women are the same. That does not mean we have nothing in common. The specificity of each woman's situation, all of our particularities, to frame a dialectical sentence, makes up our commonality. For example, the statement, woman's place is in the home. Stereotypes become standards; people try to measure up to them. That's how they work, that's what they're for; that's why they are so often true. So is this stereotype in some way true of the situation of all women? It strikes me that it is as a standard, as what we are measured against, but as a description, it needs particularity. For instance, not all women have had a choice of a home to be in, or had a choice to stay in it all day. So if you say a woman's place is in the home, as if that describes the generic situation of women, it is not true. Unless Black women's place is in other people's homes. Which is *not the same.* My suggestion is that what we have in common is not that our conditions have no particularity in ways that matter. But we are all measured by a male standard for women, a standard that is not ours.

This includes women lawyers. In addition to sharing the conditions that I have described, of sexual assault and economics and marriage and the definition of all women set by those circumstances, women lawyers have found ourselves excluded from inner circles and then rejected because we don't know the inside story or don't play by the real rules of the game, the rules in the tacit curriculum. We are told we can't think, while our thoughts are appropriated for the advancement of others. We are told that the pedestal is real and called ungrateful or lacking in initiative or in the ability to use the power we have as women when we call it a cage, and then told by people like Phyllis Schlafly that we have created these conditions when we resist them. When a few of us, the exceptions, overcome all this, we are told we prove that there are no barriers there and are used as examples to put other women down. She made it, why can't you? We are used as tokens, vaunted as exceptions, while every problem that we share is treated as itself an exception, as a special case. So to those who say, "Any woman can," as if there were no such thing as discrimination, as if *that* were exceptional, I say this, and I say it as a woman: *all women can't*. And that will be true so long as those who do make it are the privileged few. Until all women can, none of us succeed as women, but as exceptions. When we fail, we fail with 53 percent of the population; when we succeed, we succeed alone. So the feminist issue for me is not whether one of us, as an individual woman, can escape some of the burdens of the condition of all women, but whether it remains socially necessary that someone will remain in the position we have temporarily escaped from, and that someone will be a woman. To speak as a woman in this sense is to speak from the perspective and in the interest of 53 percent of the population, a community of interest based on a common reality of treatment. I'm not saying that the meaning of this is easy or obvious in every case, but it certainly is not a perspective of exceptionality.

When I think about Rosalie and Mary Jean on this Court, I ask myself: will they use the tools of law as women, for all women? I think that the real feminist issue is not whether biological males or biological females hold positions of power, although it is utterly essential that women be there. And I am not saying that viewpoints have genitals. My issue is what our identifications are, what our loyalties are, who our community is, to whom we are accountable. If it seems as if this is not very concrete, I think it is because we have no idea what women as women would have to say. I'm evoking for women a role that we have yet to make, in the name of a voice that, unsilenced, might say something that has never been heard. I will hazard a little bit about its content. In the legal world of win and lose, where success is measured by other people's failures, in this world of kicking or getting kicked, I want to say: there is another way. Women who refuse to forget the way women everywhere are treated every day, who refuse to forget that *that* is the meaning of being a woman, no matter how secure we may feel in having temporarily escaped it, women as women will find that way.

II. APPLICATIONS

If you're living with a man, what are you doing running around the streets getting raped?

Edward Harrington, defense attorney in New Bedford gang rape case.

Romance was her suicidal substitute for action; fantasy her suicidal substitute for a real world, a wide world. And intercourse was her suicidal substitute for freedom.

Andrea Dworkin, *Intercourse* (1987), discussing Emma Bovary

six

A Rally against Rape
(1981)

Whun the wind blows, I hear the pitchforks rumbling in the
background over this P.A. system.
    I want to speak with you about rape as a problem of
sexism, a problem of the inequality between women and men. We
are not in the midst of an epidemic of rape; we are in the midst of a
short flurry of rape reporting and rape publicity. Why are these rapes
being reported and, in particular, why are they being publicized? If
for every reported rape there are between two and ten unreported
rapes (a conservative estimate), it is extremely important to ask not
only why the ones that are reported are, but why the ones that are
not reported are not.

I think women report rapes when we feel we will be believed. The
rapes that have been reported, as they have been reported, are the
kinds of rapes women think will be believed when we report them.
They have two qualities: they are by a stranger, and they are by a
Black man. These two elements give you the white male archetype of
rape. When the newspaper says that these rapes are unusual, they
are right in a way. They are right because rapes by strangers are the
least common rapes women experience. And to the extent that these
are interracial, they are also the least common rapes women experience. Most rapes are by a man of the woman's race[1] and by a man
she knows: her husband, her boss, an acquaintance, or a date.[2]

In considering the element of racism in this particular publicity and
the nerve that this rape reporting seems to hit, I think it is important
to tell you what I have been told. That is, that two of the victims of
this current rapist are women of color. I think that the nonreporting
of this aspect, although it may have been requested initially by the
women victims and may be an attempt to preserve confidentiality,
also plays into the racist image that what rape is about is Black men
defiling "our white womanhood." The invisibility of women of color

This talk was given at White Plaza, Stanford University, Stanford, California, Nov. 16,
1981, where several hundred students gathered to grieve and protest a series of rapes
reported on campus.

is such that if you do not say that a woman is of color, it is assumed that her race is nonexistent—therefore, oddly, white. It's also important for us to be aware that women of color (this is specifically a statistic about Black women) are raped four times as often as white women.[3]

Of the reasons raped women give for not reporting rape, the most common[4] is fear of retribution. The retaliation they usually have in mind is that the rapist will come back after them, which he often says he will do during the rape. Or they fear that their boyfriends or husbands will beat them or reject them. Very young women, and also older women, are often afraid that they will be kicked out of the house. Women who have been victims of incest are particularly likely to feel this. Women also feel fear and despair of police, hospitals, and the legal system. Women believe that not only will we not be believed by the police, not only will the doctors treat us in degrading ways, but when we go to court, the incident will not be seen from our point of view. It is unfortunate that these fears have, on the whole, proved accurate. The fear of being treated poorly is not an invention of women's imaginations. It is the result of the way we have been treated. I'm hoping that responsible officials at Stanford are taking notice of the interest and the anger that women are expressing now to realize that they are seeing only the tip of the iceberg and that they are part of the reason why.

Women who do not report rape also say that we want to forget about it; that we feel embarrassed and humiliated by it and that just talking to someone else adds to that sense of exposure, the sense of utter loss of privacy. The very loss we felt when we were raped is compounded by complaining about the rape. That says something about the receptiveness of the context we're in when we try to talk about it. Our protest and resistance are turned into a continuation of the violation. Women also blame ourselves. We fear being blamed by other people, and they do blame us.

In what I've said so far, I've had in mind an entire range of rape experiences. Politically, I call it rape whenever a woman has sex and feels violated. You might think that's too broad. I'm not talking about sending all of you men to jail for that. I'm talking about attempting to change the nature of the relations between women and men by having women ask ourselves, "Did I feel violated?" To me, part of the culture of sexual inequality that makes women not report rape is that the definition of rape is not based on our sense of our violation.

I think it's fairly common, and is increasingly known to be common, for men to seek sexual access to women in ways that we find coercive and unwanted. On those occasions the amount and kind of force are only matters of degree. The problem is that rapes do not tend to be reported or prosecuted or sanctioned based on the force that was used; not based on how coercive it was and not based on how violated the woman feels; instead they are based on how intimate she is with the person who did it. This is why most women think we won't be believed in reporting the most common rapes, that is, rapes by people we know. As a result, I agree with what people have been saying, that rape is everyone's problem. But that doesn't mean that it's men's problem and women's problem in the same way.

To men I want to say: have you ever had sex with a woman when she didn't want it? Were you and are you really careful to find out? Is it enough that you say to yourself now, "I don't know"? Are you really afraid that nothing will happen between you and a woman if you don't make it happen? Are you afraid of our rage today? That we will turn it against you? Is there perhaps a reason for your fear? I think you need to remember that we love you. And that as a result it's often very unclear to us why you are so urgent. It's unclear to us why you are so pressured in seeking sexual access to us. We want you not to denigrate us if we refuse. We want you to support us, to listen to us, and to back off a little. Maybe to back off a lot. And we also want you to realize that supporting us is not the same as taking over either our injuries or our pleasure.

To women I want to say: what do you really want? Do you feel that you have the conditions under which you can ask yourself that question? If you feel that you are going to be raped when you say no, how do you know that you really want sex when you say yes? Do you feel responsible for men's sexual feelings about you? What about their responsibility for yours, including your lack of them? I also want to say that women need self-protection; we do not need more paranoia. The Stanford police tell us, "A little fear is a good thing right now." I think we do not need more fear. We need to make fear unnecessary.

On an individual basis the only thing that I know that begins to address this is something we have access to here: real training in self-defense. Martial arts is not just physical preparation for a one-time shot or a quick fix or a bag of tricks. It is a spiritual, integrated way of relating to one's body as one's own, in which one acts and lives and embodies oneself in the world. Not something that exists only

Applications

for carrying your head about or to be looked at by other people. Self-defense, if it's done right, can begin to give us back a sense that we have a self worth defending.

I have spoken with you about what holds women back from reporting rape in the context of what I think rape is. The only way for us to have this episode not just blow over, as such episodes have for centuries, is to use this occasion seriously to question and to change our lives and to support all sisters who resist.

seven

Sex and Violence:
A Perspective
(1981)

I want to raise some questions about the concept of this panel's title, "Violence against Women," as a concept that may coopt us as we attempt to formulate our own truths. I want to speak specifically about four issues: rape, sexual harassment, pornography, and battery. I think one of the reasons we say that each of these issues is an example of violence against women is to reunify them. To say that aggression against women has this unity is to criticize the divisions that have been imposed on that aggression by the legal system. What I see to be the danger of the analysis, what makes it potentially cooptive, is formulating it—and it *is* formulated this way—these are issues of violence, *not* sex: rape is a crime of violence, not sexuality; sexual harassment is an abuse of power, not sexuality; pornography is violence against women, it is not erotic. Although battering is not categorized so explicitly, it is usually treated as though there is nothing sexual about a man beating up a woman so long as it is with his fist. I'd like to raise some questions about that as well.

I hear in the formulation that these issues are violence against women, not sex, that we are in the shadow of Freud, intimidated at being called repressive Victorians. We're saying we're *op*pressed and they say we're *re*pressed. That is, when we say we're against rape, the immediate response is, "Does that mean you're against sex?" "Are you attempting to impose neo-Victorian prudery on sexual expression?" This comes up with sexual harassment as well. When we say we're against sexual harassment, the first thing people want to know is, "What's the difference between that and ordinary male-to-female sexual initiation?" That's a good question . . . The same is also true of criticizing pornography. "You can't be against erotica?" It's the latest version of the accusation that feminists are anti-male.

This early synthesis was framed in part to respond to panel members' concerns with cooptation at the National Conference on Women and the Law, Boston, Massachusetts, Apr. 5, 1981.

Applications

To distinguish ourselves from this, and in reaction to it, we call these abuses violence. The attempt is to avoid the critique—we're not against sex—and at the same time retain our criticism of these practices. So we rename as violent those abuses that have been seen to be sexual, without saying that we have a very different perspective on violence and on sexuality and their relationship. I also think a reason we call these experiences violence is to avoid being called lesbians, which for some reason is equated with being against sex. In order to avoid that, yet retain our opposition to sexual violation, we put this neutral, objective, abstract word *violence* on it all.

To me this is an attempt to have our own perspective on these outrages without owning up to having one. To have our point of view but present it as *not* a particular point of view. Our problem has been to label something as rape, as sexual harassment, as pornography in the face of a suspicion that it might be intercourse, it might be ordinary sexual initiation, it might be erotic. To say that these purportedly sexual events violate us, to be against them, we call them not sexual. But the attempt to be objective and neutral avoids owning up to the fact that women do have a specific point of view on these events. It avoids saying that from women's point of view, intercourse, sex roles, and eroticism can be and at times are violent to us as women.

My approach would claim our perspective; we are not attempting to be objective about it, we're attempting to represent the point of view of women. The point of view of men up to this time, called objective, has been to distinguish sharply between rape on the one hand and intercourse on the other; sexual harassment on the one hand and normal, ordinary sexual initiation on the other; pornography or obscenity on the one hand and eroticism on the other. The male point of view defines them by distinction. What women experience does not so clearly distinguish the normal, everyday things from those abuses from which they have been defined by distinction. Not just "Now we're going to take what *you* say is rape and call it violence"; "Now we're going to take what *you* say is sexual harassment and call it violence"; "Now we're going to take what *you* say is pornography and call it violence." We have a deeper critique of what has been done to women's sexuality and who controls access to it. What we are saying is that sexuality in exactly these normal forms often *does* violate us. So long as we say that those things are abuses of violence, not sex, we fail to criticize what has been made of *sex*,

86

what has been done to us *through* sex, because we leave the line between rape and intercourse, sexual harassment and sex roles, pornography and eroticism, right where it is.

I think it is useful to inquire how women and men (I don't use the term *persons*, I guess, because I haven't seen many lately) live through the meaning of their experience with these issues. When we ask whether rape, sexual harassment, and pornography are questions of violence or questions of sexuality, it helps to ask, to whom? What is the perspective of those who are involved, whose experience it is—to rape or to have been raped, to consume pornography or to be consumed through it. As to what these things *mean* socially, it is important whether they are about sexuality to women and men or whether they are instead about "violence,"—or whether violence and sexuality can be distinguished in that way, as they are lived out.

The crime of rape—this is a legal and observed, not a subjective, individual, or feminist definition—is defined around penetration. That seems to me a very male point of view on what it means to be sexually violated. And it is exactly what heterosexuality as a social institution is fixated around, the penetration of the penis into the vagina. Rape is defined according to what men think violates women, and that is the same as what they think of as the *sine qua non* of sex. What women experience as degrading and defiling when we are raped includes as much that is distinctive to us as is our experience of sex. Someone once termed penetration a "peculiarly resented aspect" of rape—I don't know whether that meant it was peculiar that it was resented or that it was resented with heightened peculiarity. Women who have been raped often do resent having been penetrated. But that is not all there is to what was intrusive or expropriative of a woman's sexual wholeness.

I do think the crime of rape focuses more centrally on what men define as sexuality than on women's experience of our sexual being, hence its violation. A common experience of rape victims is to be unable to feel good about anything heterosexual thereafter—or anything sexual at all, or men at all. The minute they start to have sexual feelings or feel sexually touched by a man, or even a woman, they start to relive the rape. I had a client who came in with her husband. She was a rape victim, a woman we had represented as a witness. Her husband sat the whole time and sobbed. They couldn't have sex anymore because every time he started to touch her, she would flash to the rape scene and see his face change into the face of the man who had raped her. That, to me, is sexual. When a woman has been raped, and it is sex that she then cannot experience without connecting it to that, it was her sexuality that was violated.

Similarly, men who are in prison for rape think it's the dumbest thing that ever happened . . . It isn't just a miscarriage of justice; they were put in jail for something very little different from what most men do most of the time and call it sex. The only difference is they got caught. That view is nonremorseful and not rehabilitative. It may also be true. It seems to me we have here a convergence between the rapist's view of what he has done and the victim's perspective on what was done to her. That is, for both, their ordinary experiences of heterosexual intercourse and the act of rape have something in common. Now this gets us into intense trouble, because that's exactly how judges and juries see it who refuse to convict men accused of rape. A rape victim has to prove that it was not intercourse. She has to show that there was force and she resisted, because if there was sex, consent is inferred. Finders of fact look for "more force than usual during the preliminaries." Rape is defined by distinction from intercourse—not nonviolence, intercourse. They ask, does this event look more like fucking or like rape? But what is their standard for sex, and is this question asked from the *woman's point of view?* The level of force is not adjudicated at her point of violation; it is adjudicated at the standard of the normal level of force. Who sets this standard?

In the criminal law, we can't put everybody in jail who does an ordinary act, right? Crime is supposed to be deviant, not normal. Women continue not to report rape, and a reason is that they believe, and they are right, that the legal system will not see it from their point of view. We get very low conviction rates for rape.[1] We also get many women who believe they have never been raped, although a lot of force was involved. They mean that they were not raped in a way that is legally provable. In other words, in all these situations, there was not *enough* violence against them to take it beyond the category of "sex"; they were not coerced enough. Maybe they were forced-fucked for years and put up with it, maybe they tried to get it over with, maybe they were coerced by something other than battery, something like economics, maybe even something like love.

What I am saying is that unless you make the point that there is much violence in intercourse, as a usual matter, none of that is changed. Also we continue to stigmatize the women who claim rape as having experienced a deviant violation and allow the rest of us to go through life feeling violated but thinking we've never been raped, when there were a great many times when we, too, have had sex and didn't want it. What this critique does that is different from the "violence, not sex" critique is ask a series of questions about normal, heterosexual intercourse and attempt to move the line between heterosexuality on the one hand—intercourse—and rape on the other, rather than allow it to stay where it is.

Having done that so extensively with rape, I can consider sexual harassment more briefly. The way the analysis of sexual harassment is sometimes expressed now (and it bothers me) is that it is an abuse of power, not sexuality. That does not allow us to pursue whether sexuality, as socially constructed in our society through gender roles, is *itself* a power structure. If you look at sexual harassment as power, not sex, what is power supposed to be? Power is employer/employee, not because courts are marxist but because this is a recognized hierarchy. Among men. Power is teacher/student, because courts recognize a hierarchy there. Power is on one side and sexuality on the other. Sexuality is ordinary affection, everyday flirtation. Only when ordinary, everyday affection and flirtation and "I was just trying to be friendly" come into the context of *another* hierarchy is it considered potentially an abuse of power. What is not considered to be a hierarchy is women and men—men on top and women on the bottom. That is not considered to be a question of power or social hierarchy, legally or politically. A feminist perspective suggests that it is.

When we have examples of coequal sexual harassment (within these other hierarchies), worker to worker on the same level, involving women and men, we have a lot of very interesting, difficult questions about sex discrimination, which is supposed to be about gender difference, but does not conceive of gender as a social hierarchy. I think that implicit in race discrimination cases for a brief moment of light was the notion that there is a social hierarchy between Blacks and whites. So that presumptively it's an exercise of power for a white person to do something egregious to a Black person or for a white institution to do something egregious systematically to many Black people. Situations of coequal power—among coworkers or students or teachers—are difficult to see as examples of sexual harassment unless you have a notion of male power. I think we lie to women when we call it not power when a woman is come onto by a man who is not her employer, not her teacher. What do we labor under, what do we feel, when a man—any man—comes and hits on us? I think we require women to feel fine about turning down male-initiated sex so long as the man doesn't have some *other* form of power over us. Whenever—every and any time—a woman feels conflicted and wonders what's wrong with her that she can't decline although she has no inclination, and she feels open to male accusations, whether they come from women or men, of "why didn't you just tell him to buzz off?" we have sold her out, not named her experience. We are taught that we exist for men. We should be flattered or at least act as if we are—be careful about a man's ego because you never know what he can do to you. To flat out say to him, "You?" or "I don't want to" is not *in* most women's sex-role learning. To say it is, is bravado. And that's because he's a man, not just because you never know what he can do to you because he's your boss (that's two things—he's a man and he's the boss) or your teacher or in some other hierarchy. It seems to me that we haven't talked very much about gender *as* a hierarchy, as a division of power, in the way that's expressed and acted out, primarily I think sexually. And therefore we haven't expanded the definition according to women's experience of sexuality, including our own sexual intimidation, of what things are sexual in this world. So men have also defined what can be called sexual about us. They say, "I was just trying to be affectionate, flirtatious and friendly," and we were just all felt up. We criticize the idea that rape comes down to her word against his—but it really *is* her perspective against his perspective, and the law has been written from *his* perspective. If he didn't mean it to be sexual, it's not sexual. If he didn't see it as forced, it wasn't forced.[2] Which is to say, only male sexual violations, that is, only male ideas of what sexually violates us as women, are illegal. We buy into this when we say our sexual violations are abuses of power, not sex.

Just as rape is supposed to have nothing against intercourse, just as sexual harassment is supposed to have nothing against normal sexual initiation (men initiate, women consent—that's mutual?), the idea that pornography is violence against women, not sex, seems to distinguish artistic creation on the one hand from what is degrading to women on the other. It is candid and true but not enough to say of pornography, as Justice Stewart said, "I know it when I see it."[3] *He* knows what he thinks it is when he sees it—but is that what *I* know? Is that the same "it"? Is he going to know what I know when I see it? I think pretty much not, given what's on the newsstand, given what is not considered hard-core pornography. Sometimes I think what is obscene is what does *not* turn on the Supreme Court—or what revolts them more. Which is uncommon, since revulsion is eroticized.

We have to admit that pornography turns men on; it is therefore erotic. It is a lie to say that pornography is not erotic. When we say it is violence, not sex, we are saying, there is this degrading to women, over here, and this erotic, over there, without saying to whom. It is overwhelmingly disproportionately men to whom pornography is erotic. It is women, on the whole, to whom it is violent, among other things. And this is not just a matter of perspective, but a matter of reality.

Pornography turns primarily men on. Certainly they are getting something out of it. They pay incredible amounts of money for it; it's one of the largest industries in the country. If women got as much out of it as men do, we would buy it instead of cosmetics. It's a massive industry, cosmetics. We are poor but we have *some* money; we are some market. We spend our money to set ourselves up as the objects that emulate those images that are sold as erotic to men. What pornography says about us is that we enjoy degradation, that we are sexually turned on by being degraded. For me that obliterates the line, as a line at all, between pornography on one hand and erotica on the other, if what turns men on, what men find beautiful, is what degrades women. It is pervasively present in art, also, and advertising. But it is definitely present in eroticism, if that is what it is. It makes me think that women's sexuality as such is a stigma. We also sometimes have an experience of sexuality authentic somehow in all this. We are not allowed to have it; we are not allowed to talk about it; we are not allowed to speak of it or image it as from our own point of view. And, to the extent we try to assert that we are beings equal with men, we have to be either asexual or virgins.

To worry about cooptation is to realize that lies make bad politics. It is ironic that cooptation often results from an attempt to be "credible," to be strategically smart, to be "effective" on existing terms. Sometimes you become what you're fighting. Thinking about issues of sexual violation as issues of violence not sex could, if pursued legally, lead to opposing sexual harassment and pornography through morals legislation and obscenity laws. It is actually interesting that this theoretical stance has been widely embraced but these legal strategies have not been. Perhaps women realize that these legal approaches would not address the subordination of women to men, specifically and substantively. These approaches are legally as abstract as the "violence not sex" critique is politically abstract. They are both not enough and too much of the wrong thing. They deflect us from criticizing everyday behavior that is pervasive and normal and concrete and fuses sexuality with gender in violation and is not amenable to existing legal approaches. I think we need to think more radically in our legal work here.

Battering is called violence, rather than something sex-specific: this is done to women. I also think it is sexually done to women. Not only in where it is done—over half of the incidents are in the bedroom.[4] Or the surrounding events—precipitating sexual jealousy. But when violence against women is eroticized as it is in this culture, it is very difficult to say that there is a major distinction in the level of sex involved between being assaulted by a penis and being assaulted by a fist, especially when the perpetrator is a man. If women as gender female are defined as sexual beings, and violence is eroticized, then men violating women has a sexual component. I think men rape women because they get off on it in a way that fuses dominance with sexuality. (This is different in emphasis from what Susan Brownmiller says.)[5] I think that when men sexually harass women it expresses male control over sexual access to us. It doesn't mean they all want to fuck us, they just want to hurt us, dominate us, and control us, and that *is* fucking us. They want to be able to have that and to be able to say when they can have it, to *know* that. That is in itself erotic. The idea that opposing battering is about saving the family is, similarly, abstracted, gender-neutral. There are gender-neutral formulations of all these issues: law and order as opposed to derepression, Victorian morality as opposed to permissiveness, obscenity as opposed to art and freedom of expression. Gender-neutral, objective formulations like these avoid asking *whose* expression, from whose point of view? Whose law and whose order? It's not just a question of who is free to express ourselves; it's not just that there is almost no, if any, self-respecting women's eroticism. The fact is that what we do see, what we are allowed to experience, even in our own suffering, even in what we are allowed to complain about, is overwhelmingly constructed from the male point of view. Laws against sexual violation express what men see and do when they engage in sex with women; laws against obscenity center on the display of women's bodies in ways that men are turned on by viewing. To me, it not only makes us cooptable to define such abuses in gender-neutral terms like violence; when we fail to assert that we are fighting for the affirmative definition and control of our own sexuality, of our own lives as women, and that these experiences violate *that*, we have already been bought.

eight

Privacy v. Equality:
Beyond Roe v. Wade
(1983)

In a society where women entered sexual intercourse willingly, where adequate contraception was a genuine social priority, there would be no "abortion issue" . . . Abortion is violence . . . It is the offspring, and will continue
to be the accuser of a more pervasive and prevalent violence, the violence of
rapism.

Adrienne Rich, *Of Woman Born* (1976)

R*oe v. Wade*[1] guaranteed the right to choose abortion, subject
to some countervailing considerations, by conceiving it as a
private choice, included in the constitutional right to privacy.
In this critique of that decision, I first situate abortion and the abortion right in the experience of women. The argument is that abortion
is inextricable from sexuality, assuming that the feminist analysis of
sexuality is our analysis of gender inequality. I then criticize the doctrinal choice to pursue the abortion right under the law of privacy.
The argument is that privacy doctrine reaffirms and reinforces what
the feminist critique of sexuality criticizes: the public/private split.
The political and ideological meaning of privacy as a legal doctrine is
connected with the concrete consequences of the public/private split
for the lives of women. This analysis makes *Harris v. McRae*,[2] in
which public funding for abortions was held not to be required, appear consistent with the larger meaning of *Roe.*

I will neglect two important explorations, which I bracket now. The
first is: what are babies to men? On one level, men respond to wom-
en's rights to abort as if confronting the possibility of their own potential nonexistence—at *women's* hands, no less. On another level,
men's issues of potency, of continuity as a compensation for mortality,
of the thrust to embody themselves or their own image in the world,
underlie their relation to babies (as well as to most else). To overlook

I discussed these ideas at the Conference on Persons, Morality, and Abortion, Hampshire College, Amherst, Massachusetts, Jan. 21, 1983, and at the Planned Parenthood
Conference, "Who Governs Reproduction?" New Haven, Connecticut, Nov. 2, 1985.

these meanings of abortion to men as men is to overlook political and strategic as well as fundamental theoretical issues and to misassess where much of the opposition to abortion is coming from. The second issue I bracket is one that, unlike the first, has been discussed extensively in the abortion debate: the moral rightness of abortion itself. My stance is that the abortion choice must be legally available and must be *women's*, but not because the fetus is not a form of life. In the usual argument, the abortion decision is made contingent on whether the fetus is a form of life. I cannot follow that. Why should women not make life or death decisions? This returns us to the first bracketed issue.

The issues I will explore have largely not been discussed in the terms I will use. Instead, I think, women's embattled need to survive in a world hostile to our survival has precluded our exploring these issues as I am about to. That is, the perspective from which we have addressed abortion has been shaped and constrained by the very situation that the abortion issue puts us in and requires us to address. We have not been able to risk thinking about these issues on our own terms because the terms have not been ours. The attempt to grasp women's situation on our own terms, from our own point of view, defines the feminist impulse. If doing that is risky, our situation also makes it risky not to. So, first feminism, then law.

Most women who seek abortions became pregnant while having sexual intercourse with men. Most did not mean or wish to conceive. In contrast to this fact of women's experience, which converges sexuality with reproduction with gender, the abortion debate has centered on separating control over sexuality from control over reproduction, and on separating both from gender and the life options of the sexes. Liberals have supported the availability of the abortion choice as if the woman just happened on the fetus.[3] The political right, imagining that the intercourse preceding conception is usually voluntary, urges abstinence, as if sex were up to women, while defending male authority, specifically including a wife's duty to submit to sex. Continuing with this logic, many opponents of state funding of abortions, such as supporters of some versions of the Hyde Amendment, would permit funding of abortions when pregnancy results from rape or incest.[4] They make *exceptions* for those special occasions during which they presume women did *not* control sex. From all this I deduce that abortion's proponents and opponents share a tacit assumption that women significantly do control sex.

Feminist investigations suggest otherwise. Sexual intercourse, still the most common cause of pregnancy, cannot simply be presumed coequally determined. Feminism has found that women feel compelled to preserve the appearance—which, acted upon, becomes the reality—of male direction of sexual expression, as if male initiative itself were what we want, as if it were that which turns us on. Men enforce this. It is much of what men want in a woman. It is what pornography eroticizes and prostitutes provide. Rape—that is, intercourse with force that is recognized as force—is adjudicated not according to the power or force that the man wields, but according to indices of intimacy between the parties. The more intimate you are with your accused rapist, the less likely a court is to find that what happened to you was rape. Often indices of intimacy include intercourse itself. If "no" can be taken as "yes," how free can "yes" be?

Under these conditions, women often do not use birth control because of its social meaning, a meaning we did not create. Using contraception means acknowledging and planning the possibility of intercourse, accepting one's sexual availability, and appearing nonspontaneous. It means appearing available to male incursions. A good user of contraception can be presumed sexually available and, among other consequences, raped with relative impunity. (If you think this isn't true, you should consider rape cases in which the fact that a woman had a diaphragm in is taken as an indication that what happened to her was intercourse, not rape. "Why did you have your diaphragm in?") From studies of abortion clinics, women who repeatedly seek abortions (and now I'm looking at the repeat offenders high on the list of the right's villains, their best case for opposing abortion as female irresponsibility), when asked why, say something like, "The sex just happened." Like every night for two and a half years.[5] I wonder if a woman can be presumed to control access to her sexuality if she feels unable to interrupt intercourse to insert a diaphragm; or worse, cannot even want to, aware that she risks a pregnancy she knows she does not want. Do you think she would stop the man for any other reason, such as, for instance, the real taboo—lack of desire? If she would not, how is sex, hence its consequences, meaningfully voluntary for women? Norms of sexual rhythm and romance that are felt interrupted by women's needs are constructed against women's interests. Sex doesn't look a whole lot like freedom when it appears normatively less costly for women to risk an undesired, often painful, traumatic, dangerous, sometimes illegal, and potentially life-threatening procedure than to protect themselves in advance. Yet abortion policy has never been explicitly approached in the context of how women get pregnant, that is, as a consequence of intercourse under conditions of gender inequality; that is, as an issue of forced sex.

Now, law. In 1973 *Roe v. Wade* found that a statute that made criminal all abortions except those to save the life of the mother violated the constitutional right to privacy.[6] The privacy right had been previously created as a constitutional principle in a case that decriminalized the prescription and use of contraceptives.[7] Note that courts use the privacy rubric to connect contraception with abortion through privacy in the same way that I just did through sexuality. In *Roe* that right to privacy was found "broad enough to encompass a woman's decision whether or not to terminate her pregnancy." In 1977 three justices observed, "In the abortion context, we have held that the right to privacy shields the woman from undue state intrusion in and external scrutiny of her very personal choice."[8]

In 1981 the Supreme Court in *Harris v. McRae* decided that this right to privacy did not mean that federal Medicaid programs had to fund medically necessary abortions. Privacy, the Court had said, was guaranteed for "a woman's *decision* whether or not to terminate her pregnancy." The Court then permitted the government to support one decision and not another: to fund continuing conceptions and not to fund discontinuing them. Asserting that decisional privacy was nevertheless constitutionally intact, the Court stated that "although the government may not place obstacles in the path of a woman's exercise of her freedom of choice, it need not remove those not of its own creation."[9] It is apparently a very short step from that which the government has a duty *not* to intervene in to that which it has *no* duty to intervene in.

The idea of privacy, if regarded as the outer edge of the limitations on government, embodies, I think, a tension between the preclusion of public exposure or governmental intrusion, on the one hand, and autonomy in the sense of protecting personal self-action on the other. This is a tension, not just two facets of one whole right. In the liberal state this tension is resolved by demarking the threshold of the state at its permissible extent of penetration into a domain that is considered free by definition: the private sphere. It is by this move that the state secures to individuals what has been termed "an inviolable personality" by ensuring what has been called "autonomy or control over the intimacies of personal identity."[10] The state does this by centering its self-restraint on body and home, especially bedroom. By staying out of marriage and the family, prominently meaning sexuality—that is to say, heterosexuality—from contraception through pornography to the abortion decision, the law of privacy proposes to guarantee individual bodily integrity, personal exercise of moral intelligence, and freedom of intimacy.[11] But if one asks whether *women's* rights to these values have been guaranteed, it appears that the law of privacy works to translate traditional social values into the rhetoric of individual rights as a means of subordinating those rights to specific social imperatives.[12] In feminist terms, I am arguing that the logic of *Roe* consummated in *Harris* translates the ideology of the private sphere into the individual woman's legal right to privacy as a means of subordinating women's collective needs to the imperatives of male supremacy.

This is my retrospective on *Roe v. Wade.* Reproduction is sexual, men control sexuality, and the state supports the interest of men as a group. *Roe* does not contradict this. So why was abortion legalized? Why were women even imagined to have such a right as privacy? It is not an accusation of bad faith to answer that the interests of men as a social group converged with the definition of justice embodied in law in what I call the male point of view. The way the male point of view constructs a social event or legal need will be the way that social event or legal need is framed by state policy. For example, to the extent that possession is the point of sex, illegal rape will be sex with a woman who is not yours unless the act makes her yours. If part of the kick of pornography involves eroticizing the putatively prohibited, illegal pornography—obscenity—will be prohibited enough to keep pornography desirable without ever making it truly illegitimate or unavailable. If, from the male standpoint, male is the implicit definition of human, maleness will be the implicit standard by which sex equality is measured in discrimination law. In parallel terms, abortion's availability frames, and is framed by, the conditions men work out among themselves to grant legitimacy to women to control the reproductive consequences of intercourse.

Since Freud, the social problem posed by sexuality has been perceived as the problem of the innate desire for sexual pleasure being repressed by the constraints of civilization. In this context, the inequality of the sexes arises as an issue only in women's repressive socialization to passivity and coolness (so-called frigidity), in women's so-called desexualization, and in the disparate consequences of biology, that is, pregnancy. Who defines what is sexual, what sexuality therefore is, to whom what stimuli are erotic and why, and who defines the conditions under which sexuality is expressed—these issues are not even available to be considered. "Civilization's" answer to these questions fuses women's reproductivity with our attributed sexuality in its definition of what a woman is. We are defined as women by the uses to which men put us. In this context it becomes clear why the struggle for reproductive freedom has never included a woman's right to refuse sex. In this notion of sexual liberation, the equality issue has been framed as a struggle for women to have sex with men on the same terms as men: "without consequences." In this sense the abortion right has been sought as freedom from the reproductive consequences of sexual expression, with sexuality defined as centered on heterosexual genital intercourse. It is as if biological organisms, rather than social relations, reproduced the species. But if your concern is not how more people can get more sex, but who defines sexuality—pleasure and violation both—then the abortion right is situated within a very different problematic: the social and political problematic of the inequality of the sexes. As Susan Sontag said, "Sex itself is not liberating for women. Neither is more sex . . . The question is, what sexuality shall women be liberated to enjoy?"[13] To address this requires reformulating the problem of sexuality from the repression of drives by civilization to the oppression of women by men.

Arguments for abortion under the rubric of feminism have rested upon the right to control one's own body—gender neutral. I think that argument has been appealing for the same reasons it is inadequate: socially, women's bodies have not been ours; we have not controlled their meanings and destinies. Feminists tried to assert that control without risking pursuit of the idea that something more might be at stake than our bodies, something closer to a net of relations in which we are (at present unescapably) gendered.[14] Some feminists have noticed that our right to decide has become merged with the right of an overwhelmingly male profession's right not to have its professional judgment second-guessed by the government.[15] But most abortion advocates argue in rigidly and rigorously gender-neutral terms.

Thus, for instance, Judith Jarvis Thomson's argument that an abducted woman had no obligation to be a celebrated violinist's life support system meant that women have no obligation to support a fetus.[16] The parallel seems misframed. No woman who needs an abortion—no woman, period—is valued, no potential a woman's life might hold is cherished, like a gender-neutral famous violinist's unencumbered possibilities. The problems of gender are thus underlined here rather than solved, or even addressed. Too, the underlying recognition in the parallel of the origin of the problem in rape—the origin in force, in abduction, that gives the hypothetical much of its moral weight—would confine abortions to instances in which force is recognized as force, like rape or incest. The applicability of this to the normal case of abortion is neither embraced nor disavowed, although the parallel was meant to apply to the normal case, as is abortion policy, usually. This parable is constructed precisely to begin the debate after sex occurred, yet even it requires discussion of intercourse in relation to rape in relation to conception, in order to make sense. Because this issue has been studiously avoided in the abortion context, the unequal basis on which woman's personhood is being constructed is obscured.

In the context of a sexual critique of gender inequality, abortion promises to women sex with men on the same reproductive terms as men have sex with women. So long as women do not control access to our sexuality, abortion facilitates women's heterosexual availability. In other words, under conditions of gender inequality, sexual liberation in this sense does not free women; it frees male sexual aggression. The availability of abortion removes the one remaining legitimized reason that women have had for refusing sex besides the headache. As Andrea Dworkin put it, analyzing male ideology on abortion, "Getting laid was at stake." [17] The Playboy Foundation has supported abortion rights from day one; it continues to, even with shrinking disposable funds, on a level of priority comparable to that of its opposition to censorship.

Privacy doctrine is an ideal vehicle for this process. The liberal ideal of the private—and privacy as an ideal has been formulated in liberal terms—holds that, so long as the public does not interfere, autonomous individuals interact freely and equally. Conceptually, this private is hermetic. It *means* that which is inaccessible to, unaccountable to, unconstructed by anything beyond itself. By definition, it is not part of or conditioned by anything systematic or outside of it. It is personal, intimate, autonomous, particular, individual, the original source and final outpost of the self, gender neutral. It is, in short, defined by everything that feminism reveals women have never been allowed to be or to have, and everything that women have been equated with and defined in terms of *men's* ability to have. To complain in public of inequality within it contradicts the liberal definition of the private. In this view, no act of the state contributes to—hence should properly participate in—shaping the internal alignments of the private or distributing its internal forces. Its inviolability by the state, framed as an individual right, presupposes that the private is not already an arm of the state. In this scheme, intimacy is implicitly thought to guarantee symmetry of power. Injuries arise in violating the private sphere, not within and by and because of it.

In private, consent tends to be presumed. It is true that a showing of coercion voids this presumption. But the problem is getting anything private to be perceived as coercive. Why one would allow force in private—the "why doesn't she leave" question asked of battered women—is a question given its urgency by the social meaning of the private as a sphere of choice. But for women the measure of the intimacy has been the measure of the oppression. This is why feminism has had to explode the private. This is why feminism has seen the personal as the political. The private is the public for those for whom the personal is the political. In this sense, there is no private, either normatively or empirically. Feminism confronts the fact that women have no privacy to lose or to guarantee. We are not inviolable. Our sexuality is not only violable, it is—hence, we are—seen *in* and *as* our violation. To confront the fact that we have no privacy is to confront the intimate degradation of women as the public order.

In this light, a right to privacy looks like an injury got up as a gift. Freedom from public intervention coexists uneasily with any right that requires social preconditions to be meaningfully delivered. For example, if inequality is socially pervasive and enforced, equality will require intervention, not abdication, to be meaningful. But the right to privacy is not thought to require social change. It is not even thought to require any social preconditions, other than nonintervention by the public. The point of this for the abortion cases is not that indigency—which was the specific barrier to effective choice in *Harris*—is well within the public power to remedy, nor that the state is exempt in issues of the distribution of wealth. The point is rather that *Roe v. Wade* presumes that government nonintervention into the private sphere promotes a woman's freedom of choice. When the alternative is jail, there is much to be said for this argument. But the *Harris* result sustains the ultimate meaning of privacy in *Roe:* women are guaranteed by the public no more than what we can get in private—that is, what we can extract through our intimate associations with men. Women with privileges get rights.

So women got abortion as a private privilege, not as a public right. We got control over reproduction that is controlled by "a man or The Man," an individual man or the doctors or the government. Abortion was not decriminalized; it was legalized. In *Roe* the government set the stage for the conditions under which women gain access to this right. Virtually every ounce of control that women won out of this legalization has gone directly into the hands of men—husbands, doctors, or fathers—or is now in the process of attempts to reclaim it through regulation.[18] This, surely, must be what is meant by reform.

It is not inconsistent, then, that framed as a privacy right, a woman's decision to abort would have no claim on public support and would genuinely not be seen as burdened by that deprivation. Privacy conceived as a right against public intervention and disclosure is the opposite of the relief that *Harris* sought for welfare women. State intervention would have provided a choice women did *not* have in private. The women in *Harris*, women whose sexual refusal has counted for particularly little, needed something to make their privacy effective.[19] The logic of the Court's response resembles the logic by which women are supposed to consent to sex. Preclude the alternatives, then call the sole remaining option "her choice." The point is that the alternatives are precluded *prior to* the reach of the chosen legal doctrine. They are precluded by conditions of sex, race, and class—the very conditions the privacy frame not only leaves tacit but exists to *guarantee*.

When the law of privacy restricts intrusions into intimacy, it bars change in control over that intimacy. The existing distribution of power and resources within the private sphere will be precisely what the law of privacy exists to protect. It is probably not coincidence that the very things feminism regards as central to the subjection of women—the very place, the body; the very relations, heterosexual; the very activities, intercourse and reproduction; and the very feelings, intimate—form the core of what is covered by privacy doctrine. From this perspective, the legal concept of privacy can and has shielded the place of battery, marital rape, and women's exploited labor; has preserved the central institutions whereby women are *deprived* of identity, autonomy, control and self-definition; and has protected the primary activity through which male supremacy is expressed and enforced. Just as pornography is legally protected as individual freedom of expression—without questioning whose freedom and whose expression and at whose expense—abstract privacy protects abstract autonomy, without inquiring into whose freedom of action is being sanctioned at whose expense.

To fail to recognize the meaning of the private in the ideology and reality of women's subordination by seeking protection behind a right *to* that privacy is to cut women off from collective verification and state support in the same act. I think this has a lot to do with why we can't organize women on the abortion issue. When women are segregated in private, separated from each other, one at a time, a right to that privacy isolates us at once from each other and from public recourse. This right to privacy is a right of men "to be let alone"[20] to oppress women one at a time. It embodies and reflects the private sphere's existing definition of womanhood. This is an instance of liberalism called feminism, liberalism applied to women as if we *are* persons, gender neutral. It reinforces the division between public and private that is *not* gender neutral. It is at once an ideological division that lies about women's shared experience and that mystifies the unity among the spheres of women's violation. It is a very material division that keeps the private beyond public redress and depoliticizes women's subjection within it. It keeps some men out of the bedrooms of other men.[21]

nine

Sexual Harassment:
Its First Decade in Court
(1986)

S exual harassment, the event, is not new to women. It is the law of injuries that it is new to. Sexual pressure imposed on someone who is not in an economic position to refuse it became sex discrimination in the midseventies,[1] and in education soon afterward.[2] It became possible to do something legal about sexual harassment because some women took women's experience of violation seriously enough to design a law around it, as if what happens to women matters. This was apparently such a startling way of proceeding that sexual harassment was protested as a feminist invention. Sexual harassment, the event, was not invented by feminists; the perpetrators did that with no help from us. Sexual harassment, the legal claim—the idea that the law should see it the way its victims see it—is definitely a feminist invention. Feminists first took women's experience seriously enough to uncover this problem and conceptualize it and pursue it legally. That legal claim is just beginning to produce more than a handful of reported cases. Ten years later, "[i]t may well be that sex harassment is the hottest present day Title VII issue."[3] It is time for a down-the-road assessment of this departure.

The law against sexual harassment is a practical attempt to stop a form of exploitation. It is also one test of sexual politics as feminist jurisprudence, of possibilities for social change for women through law. The existence of a law against sexual harassment has affected both the context of meaning within which social life is lived and the concrete delivery of rights through the legal system. The sexually

The original version of this speech was part of a panel on sexual harassment shared with Karen Haney, Pamela Price, and Peggy McGuiness at Stanford University, Stanford, California, Apr. 12, 1983. It thereafter became an address to the Equal Employment Opportunities Section of the American Bar Association, New Orleans, Louisiana, May 3, 1984 and to a workshop for the national conference of the National Organization for Women, Denver, Colorado, June 14, 1986. The ideas developed further when I represented Mechelle Vinson as co-counsel in her U.S. Supreme Court case in the spring of 1986. I owe a great deal to my conversations with Valerie Heller.

harassed have been given a name for their suffering and an analysis that connects it with gender. They have been given a forum, legitimacy to speak, authority to make claims, and an avenue for possible relief. Before, what happened to them was all right. Now it is not.

This matters. Sexual abuse mutes victims socially through the violation itself. Often the abuser enforces secrecy and silence; secrecy and silence may be part of what is so sexy about sexual abuse. When the state also forecloses a validated space for denouncing and rectifying the victimization, it seals this secrecy and reenforces this silence. The harm of this process, a process that utterly precludes speech, then becomes all of a piece. If there is no right place to go to say, this hurt me, then a woman is simply the one who can be treated this way, and no harm, as they say, is done.

In point of fact, I would prefer not to have to spend all this energy getting the law to recognize wrongs to women as wrong. But it seems to be necessary to legitimize our injuries as injuries in order to delegitimize our victimization by them, without which it is difficult to move in more positive ways. The legal claim for sexual harassment made the events of sexual harassment illegitimate socially as well as legally for the first time. Let me know if you figure out a better way to do that.

At this interface between law and society, we need to remember that the legitimacy courts give they can also take. Compared with a possibility of relief where no possibility of relief existed, since women started out with nothing in this area, this worry seems a bit fancy. Whether the possibility of relief alters the terms of power that gives rise to sexual harassment itself, which makes getting away with it possible, is a different problem. Sexual harassment, the legal claim, is a demand that state authority stand behind women's refusal of sexual access in certain situations that previously were a masculine prerogative. With sexism, there is always a risk that our demand for self-determination will be taken as a demand for paternal protection and will therefore strengthen male power rather than undermine it. This seems a particularly valid concern because the law of sexual harassment began as case law, without legislative guidance or definition.

Institutional support for sexual self-determination is a victory; institutional paternalism reinforces our lack of self-determination. The problem is, the state has never in fact protected women's dignity or bodily integrity. It just says it does. Its protections have been both condescending *and* unreal, in effect strengthening the protector's choice to violate the protected at will, whether the protector is the individual perpetrator or the state. This does not seem to me a reason not to have a law against sexual harassment. It is a reason to demand that the promise of "equal protection of the laws" be *delivered upon* for us, as it is when real people are violated. It is also part of a larger political struggle to value women more than the male pleasure of using us is valued. Ultimately, though, the question of whether the use of the state for women helps or hurts can be answered only in practice, because so little real protection of the laws has ever been delivered.

The legal claim for sexual harassment marks the first time in history, to my knowledge, that women have defined women's injuries in a law. Consider what has happened with rape. We have never defined the injury of rape; men define it. The men who define it, define what they take to be this violation of women according to, among other things, what they think they don't do. In this way rape becomes an act of a stranger (they mean Black) committed upon a woman (white) whom he has never seen before. Most rapes are intraracial and are committed by men the women know.[4] Ask a woman if she has ever been raped, and often she says, "Well . . . not really." In that silence between the well and the not really, she just measured what happened to her against every rape case she ever heard about and decided she would lose in court. Especially when you are part of a subordinated group, your own definition of your injuries is powerfully shaped by your assessment of whether you could get anyone to do anything about it, including anything official. You are realistic by necessity, and the voice of law is the voice in power. When the design of a legal wrong does not fit the wrong as it happens to you, as is the case with rape, that law can undermine your social and political as well as legal legitimacy in saying that what happened was an injury at all—even to yourself.

It is never too soon to worry about this, but it may be too soon to know whether the law against sexual harassment will be taken away from us or turn into nothing or turn ugly in our hands. The fact is, this law is working surprisingly well for women by any standards, particularly when compared with the rest of sex discrimination law. If the question is whether a law designed from women's standpoint and administered through this legal system can do anything for women—which always seems to me to be a good question—this experience so far gives a qualified and limited yes.

It is hard to unthink what you know, but there was a time when the facts that amount to sexual harassment did not amount to sexual harassment. It is a bit like the injuries of pornography until recently. The facts amounting to the harm did not socially "exist," had no shape, no cognitive coherence; far less did they state a legal claim. It just happened to you. To the women to whom it happened, it wasn't part of anything, much less something big or shared like gender. It fit no known pattern. It was neither a regularity nor an irregularity. Even social scientists didn't study it, and they study anything that moves. When law recognized sexual harassment as a practice of sex discrimination, it moved it from the realm of "and then he . . . and then he . . . ," the primitive language in which sexual abuse lives inside a woman, into an experience with a form, an etiology, a cumulativeness—as well as a club.

The shape, the positioning, and the club—each is equally crucial politically. Once it became possible to do something about sexual harassment, it became possible to know more about it, because it became possible for its victims to speak about it. Now we know, as we did not when it first became illegal, that this problem is commonplace. We know this not just because it has to be true, but as documented fact. Between a quarter and a third of women in the federal workforce report having been sexually harassed, many physically, at least once in the last two years.[5] Projected, that becomes 85 percent of all women at some point in their working lives. This figure is based on asking women "Have you ever been sexually harassed?"—the conclusion—not "has this fact happened? has that fact happened?" which usually produces more. The figures for sexual harassment of students are comparable.[6]

When faced with individual incidents of sexual harassment, the legal system's first question was, is it a personal episode? Legally, this was a way the courts inquired into whether the incidents were based on sex, as they had to be to be sex discrimination. Politically, it was a move to isolate victims by stigmatizing them as deviant. It also seemed odd to me that a relationship was either personal or gendered, meaning that one is not a woman personally. Statistical frequency alone does not make an event not personal, of course, but the presumption that sexual pressure in contexts of unequal power is an isolated idiosyncrasy to unique individual victims has been undermined both by the numbers and by their division by gender. Overwhelmingly, it is men who sexually harass women, a lot of them. Actually, it is even more accurate to say that men do this than to say

106

that women have this done to them. This is a description of the per-petrators' behavior, not of the statisticians' feminism.

Sexual harassment has also emerged as a creature of hierarchy. It inhabits what I call hierarchies among men: arrangements in which some men are below other men, as in employer/employee and teacher/student. In workplaces, sexual harassment by supervisors of subordinates is common; in education, by administrators of lower-level administrators, by faculty of students. But it also happens among coworkers, from third parties, even by subordinates in the workplace, men who are women's hierarchical inferiors or peers. Ba-sically, it is done by men to women regardless of relative position on the formal hierarchy. I believe that the reason sexual harassment was first established as an injury of the systematic abuse of power in hier-archies among men is that this is power men recognize. They com-prehend from ·personal experience that something is held over your head if you do not comply. The lateral or reverse hierarchical ex-amples[7] suggest something beyond this, something men don't under-stand from personal experience because they take its advantages for granted: gender is also a hierarchy. The courts do not use this anal-ysis, but some act as though they understand it.[8]

Sex discrimination law had to adjust a bit to accommodate the re-alities of sexual harassment. Like many other injuries of gender, it wasn't written for this. For something to be based on gender in the legal sense means it happens to a woman as a woman, not as an individual. Membership in a gender is understood as the opposite of, rather than part of, individuality. Clearly, sexual harassment is one of the last situations in which a woman is treated without regard to her sex; it is because of her sex that it happens. But the social meaning attributed to women as a class, in which women are defined as gen-der female by sexual accessibility to men, is not what courts have considered before when they have determined whether a given in-cident occurred because of sex.

Sex discrimination law typically conceives that something happens because of sex when it happens to one sex but not the other. The initial procedure is arithmetic: draw a gender line and count how many of each are on each side in the context at issue, or, alternatively, take the line drawn by the practice or policy and see if it also divides the sexes. One by-product of this head-counting method is what I call the bisexual defense.[9] Say a man is accused of sexually harassing a woman. He can argue that the harassment is not sex-based because he harasses both sexes equally, indiscriminately as it were. Originally it was argued that sexual harassment was not a proper gender claim because someone could harass both sexes. We argued that this was an issue of fact to be pleaded and proven, an issue of did he do this, rather than an issue of law, of whether he could have. The courts accepted that, creating this kamikaze defense. To my knowledge, no one has used the bisexual defense since.[10] As this example suggests, head counting can provide a quick topography of the terrain, but it has proved too blunt to distinguish treatment whose meaning is based on gender from treatment that has other social hermeneutics, especially when only two individuals are involved.

Once sexual harassment was established as bigger than personal, the courts' next legal question was whether it was smaller than biological. To say that sexual harassment was biological seemed to me a very negative thing to say about men, but defendants seemed to think it precluded liability. Plaintiffs argued that sexual harassment is not biological in that men who don't do it have nothing wrong with their testosterone levels. Besides, if murder were found to have biological correlates, it would still be a crime. Thus, although the question purported to be whether the acts were based on sex, the implicit issue seemed to be whether the source of the impetus for doing the acts was relevant to their harmfulness.

Similarly structured was the charge that women who resented sexual harassment were oversensitive. Not that the acts did not occur, but rather that it was unreasonable to experience them as harmful. Such a harm would be based not on sex but on individual hysteria. Again shifting the inquiry away from whether the acts are based on sex in the guise of pursuing it, away from whether they occurred to whether it should matter if they did, the question became whether the acts were properly harmful. Only this time it was not the perpetrator's drives that made him not liable but the target's sensitivity that made the acts not a harm at all. It was pointed out that too many people are victimized by sexual harassment to consider them all hysterics. Besides, in other individual injury law, victims are not blamed; perpetrators are required to take victims as they find them, so long as they are not supposed to be doing what they are doing.

Once these excuses were rejected, then it was said that sexual harassment was not really an employment-related problem. That became hard to maintain when it was her job the woman lost. If it was, in fact, a personal relationship, it apparently did not start and stop there, although this is also a question of proof, leaving the true meaning of the events to trial. The perpetrator may have thought it was all affectionate or friendly or fun, but the victim experienced it as hateful, dangerous, and damaging. Results in such cases have been mixed. Some judges have accepted the perpetrator's view; for instance, one judge held queries by the defendant such as "What am I going to get for this?" and repeated importunings to "go out" to be "susceptible of innocent interpretation."[11] Other judges, on virtually identical facts, for example, "When are you going to do something nice for me?"[12] have held for the plaintiff. For what it's worth, the judge in the first case was a man, in the second a woman.

That sexual harassment is sex-based discrimination seems to be legally established, at least for now.[13] In one of the few recent cases that reported litigating the issue of sex basis, defendants argued that a sex-based claim was not stated when a woman worker complained of terms of abuse directed at her at work such as "slut," "bitch," and "fucking cunt" and "many sexually oriented drawings posted on pillars and at other conspicuous places around the warehouse" with plaintiffs' initials on them, presenting her having sex with an animal.[14] The court said: "[T]he sexually offensive conduct and language used would have been almost irrelevant and would have failed entirely in its crude purpose had the plaintiff been a man. I do not hesitate to find that but for her sex, the plaintiff would not have been subjected to the harassment she suffered."[15] "Obvious" or "patently obvious" they often call it.[16] I guess this is what it looks like to have proven a point.

Sexual harassment was first recognized as an injury of gender in what I called incidents of quid pro quo. Sometimes people think that harassment has to be constant. It doesn't; it's a term of art in which once can be enough. Typically, an advance is made, rejected, and a loss follows.[17] For a while it looked as if this three-step occurrence was in danger of going from one form in which sexual harassment can occur into a series of required hurdles. In many situations the woman is forced to submit instead of being able to reject the advance. The problem has become whether, say, being forced into intercourse at work will be seen as a failed quid pro quo or as an instance of sexual harassment in which the forced sex constitutes the injury.

I know of one reported case in employment and one in education in which women who were forced to submit to the sex brought a sexual harassment claim against the perpetrator; so far only the education case has won on the facts.[18] The employment case that lost on the facts was reversed on appeal. The pressures for sex were seen to state a claim without respect to the fact that the woman was not able to avoid complying.[19] It is unclear if the unwanted advances constitute a claim, separate and apart from whether or not they are able to be resisted, which they should; or if the acts of forced sex would also constitute an environmental claim separate from any quid pro quo, as it seems to me they also should. In the education case, the case of Paul Mann, the students were allowed to recover punitive damages for the forced sex.[20] If sexual harassment is not to be defined only as sexual attention imposed upon someone who is not in a position to refuse it, who refuses it, women who are forced to submit to sex must be understood as harmed not less, but as much or more, than those who are able to make their refusals effective.

Getting recoveries for women who have actually been sexually violated by the defendant will probably be a major battle. Women being compensated in money for sex they *had* violates male metaphysics because in that system sex is what a woman is for. As one judge concluded, "[T]here does not seem to be any issue that the plaintiff did not desire to have relations with [the defendant], but it is also altogether apparent that she willingly had sex with him."[21] Now what do you make of that? The woman was not physically forced at the moment of penetration, and since it is sex she must have willed it, is about all you can make of it. The sexual politics of the situation is that men do not see a woman who has had sex as victimized, whatever the conditions. One dimension of this problem involves whether a woman who has been violated through sex has any credibility. Credibility is difficult to separate from the definition of the injury, since an injury in which the victim is not believed to have been injured *because she has been injured* is not a real injury, legally speaking.

The question seems to be whether a woman is valuable enough to hurt, so that what is done to her is a harm. Once a woman has had sex, voluntarily or by force—it doesn't matter—she is regarded as too damaged to be further damageable, or something. Many women who have been raped in the course of sexual harassment have been advised by their lawyers not to mention the rape because it would destroy their credibility! The fact that abuse is long term has suggested to some finders of fact that it must have been tolerated or even wanted, although sexual harassment that becomes a condition of work has also been established as a legal claim in its own right.[22] I once was talking with a judge about a case he was sitting on in which Black teenage girls alleged that some procedures at their school violated their privacy. He told me that with their sexual habits they had

110

no privacy to lose. It seemed he knew what their sexual habits were from evidence in the case, examples of the privacy violations.

The more aggravated an injury becomes, the more it ceases to exist. Why is incomprehensible to me, but how it functions is not. Our most powerful moment is on paper, in complaints we frame, and our worst is in the flesh in court. Although it isn't much, we have the most credibility when we are only the idea of us and our violation in their minds. In our allegations we construct reality to some extent; face to face, their angle of vision frames us irrevocably. In court we have breasts, we are Black, we are (in a word) women. Not that we are ever free of that, but the moment we physically embody our complaint, and they can see us, the pornography of the process starts in earnest.

I have begun to think that a major reason that many women do not bring sexual harassment complaints is that they know this. They cannot bear to have their personal account of sexual abuse reduced to a fantasy they invented, used to define them and to pleasure the finders of fact and the public. I think they have a very real sense that their accounts are enjoyed, that others are getting pleasure from the first-person recounting of their pain, and that is the content of their humiliation at these rituals. When rape victims say they feel raped again on the stand, and victims of sexual harassment say they feel sexually harassed in the adjudication, it is not exactly metaphor. I hear that they—in being publicly sexually humiliated by the legal system, as by the perpetrator—are pornography. The first time it happens, it is called freedom; the second time, it is called justice.

If a woman is sexually defined—meaning all women fundamentally, intensified by previous sexual abuse or identification as lesbian, indelible if a prostitute—her chances of recovery for sexual abuse are correspondingly reduced. I'm still waiting for a woman to win at trial against a man who forced her to comply with the sex. Suppose the male plaintiff in one sexual harassment case who rented the motel room in which the single sexual encounter took place had been a woman, and the perpetrator had been a man. When the relationship later went bad, it was apparently not a credibility problem for *him* at trial that he had rented the motel room. Nor was *his* sexual history apparently an issue. Nor, apparently, was it said when he complained he was fired because the relationship went bad, that he had "asked for" the relationship. That case was reversed on appeal on legal grounds, but he did win at trial.[23] The best one can say about women in such cases is that women who have had sex but not with the accused may have some chance. In one case the judge did not believe the plaintiff's denial of an affair with another coworker, but did believe that she had been sexually harassed by the defendant.[24] In another, the woman plaintiff actually had "linguistic intimacy" with another man at work, yet when she said that what happened to her with the defendant was sexual harassment, she was believed.[25] These are miraculous. A woman's word on these matters is usually indivisible. In another case a woman accused two men of sexual harassment. She had resisted and refused one man to whom she had previously submitted under pressure for a long time. He was in the process of eliminating her from her job when the second man raped her. The first man's defense was that it went on so long, she must have liked it. The second man's defense was that he had heard that she had had sexual relations with the first man, so he felt this was something she was open to.[26] This piggyback defense is premised on the class definition of woman as whore, by which I mean what men mean: one who exists to be sexually done to, to be sexually available on men's terms, that is, a woman. If this definition of women is accepted, it means that if a woman has ever had sex, forced or voluntary, she can't be sexually violated.

A woman can be seen in these terms by being a former rape victim or by the way she uses language. One case holds that the evidence shows "the allegedly harassing conduct was substantially welcomed and encouraged by plaintiff. She actively contributed to the distasteful working environment by her own profane and sexually suggestive conduct."[27] She swore, apparently, and participated in conversations about sex. This effectively made her harassment-proof. Many women joke about sex to try to defuse men's sexual aggression, to try to be one of the boys in hopes they will be treated like one. This is to discourage sexual advances, not to encourage them. In other cases, judges have understood that "the plaintiffs did not appreciate the remarks and . . . many of the other women did not either."[28]

The extent to which a woman's job is sexualized is also a factor. If a woman's work is not to sell sex, and her employer requires her to wear a sexually suggestive uniform, if she is repeatedly sexually harassed by the clientele, she may have a claim against her employer.[29] Similarly, although "there may well be a limited category of jobs (such as adult entertainment) in which sexual harassment may be a rational consequence of such employment," one court was "simply not prepared to say that a female who goes to work in what is apparently a predominantly male workplace should reasonably expect sexual harassment as part of her job."[30] There may be trouble at some point over what jobs are selling sex, given the sexualization of anything a woman does.

Sexual credibility, that strange amalgam of whether your word counts with whether or how much you were hurt, also comes packaged in a variety of technical rules in the sexual harassment cases: evidence, discovery, and burden of proof. In 1982 the EEOC held that if a victim was sexually harassed without a corroborating witness, proof was inadequate as a matter of law.[31] (Those of you who wonder about the relevance of pornography, get this: if nobody watched, it didn't happen.) A woman's word, even if believed, was legally insufficient, even if the man had nothing to put against it other than his word and the plaintiff's burden of proof. Much like women who have been raped, women who have experienced sexual harassment say, "But I couldn't prove it." They mean they have nothing but their word. Proof is when what you say counts against what someone else says—for which it must first be believed. To say as a matter of law that the woman's word is per se legally insufficient is to assume that, with sexual violations uniquely, the defendant's denial is dispositive, is proof. To say a woman's word is no proof amounts to saying a woman's word is worthless. Usually all the man has is his denial. In 1983 the EEOC found sexual harassment on a woman's word alone. It said it was enough, without distinguishing or overruling the prior case.[32] Perhaps they recognized that women don't choose to be sexually harassed in the presence of witnesses.

The question of prior sexual history is one area in which the issue of sexual credibility is directly posed. Evidence of the defendant's sexual harassment of other women in the same institutional relation or setting is increasingly being considered admissible, and it should be.[33] The other side of the question is whether evidence of a victim's prior sexual history should be discoverable or admissible, and it seems to me it should not be. Perpetrators often seek out victims with common qualities or circumstances or situations—we are fungible to them so long as we are similarly accessible—but victims do not seek out victimization at all, and their nonvictimized sexual behavior is no more relevant to an allegation of sexual force than is the perpetrator's consensual sex life, such as it may be.

So far the leading case, consistent with the direction of rape law,[34] has found that the victim's sexual history with other individuals is not relevant, although consensual history with the individual perpetrator may be. With sexual harassment law, we are having to deinstitutionalize sexual misogyny step by step. Some defendants' counsel have even demanded that plaintiffs submit to an unlimited psychiatric examination,[35] which could have a major practical impact on victims' effective access to relief. How much sexual denigration will victims have to face to secure their right to be free from sexual denigration? A major part of the harm of sexual harassment is the public and private sexualization of a woman against her will. Forcing her to speak about her sexuality is a common part of this process, subjection to which leads women to seek relief through the courts. Victims who choose to complain know they will have to endure repeated verbalizations of the specific sexual abuse they complain about. They undertake this even though most experience it as an exacerbation, however unavoidable, of the original abuse. For others, the necessity to repeat over and over the verbal insults, innuendos, and propositions to which they have been subjected leads them to decide that justice is not worth such indignity.

Most victims of sexual harassment, if the incidence data are correct, never file complaints. Many who are viciously violated are so ashamed to make that violation public that they submit in silence, although it devastates their self-respect and often their health, or they leave the job without complaint, although it threatens their survival and that of their families. If, on top of the cost of making the violation known, which is painful enough, they know that the entire range of their sexual experiences, attitudes, preferences, and practices are to be discoverable, few such actions will be brought, no matter how badly the victims are hurt. Faced with a choice between forced sex in their jobs or schools on the one hand and forced sexual disclosure for the public record on the other, few will choose the latter. This cruel paradox would effectively eliminate much progress in this area.[36]

Put another way, part of the power held by perpetrators of sexual harassment is the threat of making the sexual abuse public knowledge. This functions like blackmail in silencing the victim and allowing the abuse to continue. It is a fact that public knowledge of sexual abuse is often worse for the abused than the abuser, and victims who choose to complain have the courage to take that on. To add to their burden the potential of making public their entire personal life, information that has no relation to the fact or severity of the incidents complained of, is to make the law of this area implicitly complicit in the blackmail that keeps victims from exercising their rights and to enhance the impunity of perpetrators. In effect, it means open season on anyone who does not want her entire intimate life available to public scrutiny. In other contexts such private information has been found intrusive, irrelevant, and more prejudicial than probative.[37] To allow it to be discovered in the sexual harassment area amounts to a requirement that women be further violated in order to be permitted to seek relief for having been violated. I also will never understand why a violation's severity, or even its likelihood of occurrence, is measured according to the character of the violated, rather than by what was done to them.

In most reported sexual harassment cases, especially rulings on law more than on facts, the trend is almost uniformly favorable to the development of this claim. At least, so far. This almost certainly does not represent social reality. It may not even reflect most cases in litigation.[38] And there may be conflicts building, for example, between those who value speech in the abstract more than they value people in the concrete. Much of sexual harassment is words. Women are called "cunt," "pussy," "tits";[39] they are invited to a company party with "bring your own bathing suits (women, either half)";[40] they confront their tormenter in front of their manager with, "You have called me a fucking bitch," only to be answered, "No, I didn't. I called you a fucking cunt."[41] One court issued an injunction against inquiries such as "Did you get any over the weekend?"[42] One case holds that where "a person in a position to grant or withhold employment opportunities uses that authority to attempt to induce workers and job seekers to submit to sexual advances, prostitution, and pornographic entertainment, and boasts of an ability to intimidate those who displease him," sexual harassment (and intentional infliction of emotional distress) are pleaded.[43] Sexual harassment can also include pictures; visual as well as verbal pornography is commonly used as part of the abuse. Yet one judge found, apparently as a matter of law, that the pervasive presence of pornography in the workplace did not constitute an unreasonable work environment because, "For better or worse, modern America features open displays of written and pictorial erotica. Shopping centers, candy stores and prime time television regularly display naked bodies and erotic real or simulated sex acts. Living in this milieu, the average American should not be legally offended by sexually explicit posters."[44] She did not say she was offended, she said she was discriminated against based on her sex. If the pervasiveness of an abuse makes it nonactionable, no inequality sufficiently institutionalized to merit a law against it would be actionable.

Applications

Further examples of this internecine conflict have arisen in education. At the Massachusetts Institute of Technology pornography used to be shown every year during registration.[45] Is this *not* sexual harassment in education, as a group of women complained it was, because attendance is voluntary, both sexes go, it is screened in groups rather than individually, nobody is directly propositioned, and it is pictures and words? Or is it sexual harassment because the status and treatment of women, supposedly secured from sex-differential harm, are damaged, including that of those who do not attend, which harms individuals and undermines sex equality; therefore pictures and words are the media through which the sex discrimination is accomplished?

For feminist jurisprudence, the sexual harassment attempt suggests that if a legal initiative is set up right from the beginning, meaning if it is designed from women's real experience of violation, it can make some difference. To a degree women's experience can be written into law, even in some tension with the current doctrinal framework. Women who want to resist their victimization with legal terms that imagine it is not inevitable can be given some chance, which is more than they had before. Law is not everything in this respect, but it is not nothing either.[46] Perhaps the most important lesson is that the mountain can be moved. When we started, there was absolutely no judicial precedent for allowing a sex discrimination suit for sexual harassment. Sometimes even the law does something for the first time.

ten

Women, Self-Possession, and Sport
(1982)

S ince I grew up in pre–Title IX America, the first time it ever occurred to me to identify as an athlete was when I was being given a blood pressure test after a training accident. The nurse put the sleeve on me, made a reading, paused, took it off, put it back on, made more readings, and stopped and looked at me. Is anything wrong? I asked. Well, she said, either you're a football player or you have some exotic disease. Since only men played football then, to my knowledge, it seemed as though this was not my first chance—and probably not my last—to choose whether I was a man or whether I was sick. I mean, she said, are you an *athlete?* I contemplated the five years I had spent two hours a night, five nights a week, at martial arts as a physical, spiritual, and political activity. I told her yes.

The issues of sexual politics in this story are new to none of you. They raise a series of feminist questions on athletic planning, policy, and institution creation, and also connect to women's presence and possibilities in other areas of life, such as the law.

As context for pursuing these issues, I propose for your consideration two different strands of feminist theory. Most work on women in sport (most work on women in anything) comes from the first approach. In this approach the problem of the inequality of the sexes revolves around gender differentiation. The view is that there are real differences between the sexes, usually biological or natural. Upon these differences, society has created some distorted, inaccurate, irrational, and arbitrary distinctions: sex stereotypes or sex roles. To eliminate sex inequality, in this view, is to eliminate these wrong and irrational distinctions. The evil and dynamic of sexism here is the twisting of biological males and females into masculine and feminine sex roles. These roles are thought to shape men in one way and women in another way, but each sex equally. Implicit here is the view

---

This was the keynote address at the Conference on Feminism and Sport, University of Iowa, Iowa City, Iowa, June 18, 1982. I thank Lyn LeMaire for her contribution to these thoughts.

that initiatives toward sex equality are limited to or constrained by real underlying differences. "Arbitrariness" of treatment in social life is measured by implicit reference to these differences. This is liberal feminism's diagnosis of the condition of women. The solution that responds to this diagnosis is that we need to ignore or eliminate these distortions so that people can realize their potential as individuals. Liberal feminism does not usually purport to be sure what the real underlying differences are, but its idea is that they are there. The way you know the wrong of stereotyping is distortion is that there is something preexisting to distort. Liberal feminist strategies for change correspond to its critique: ignore or eliminate irrational differences. To the extent that differentiation is irrational, assimilation or integration is recommended. Those things that men have been, psychologically and physically, so also women should be allowed to become. Androgyny as a solution, free choice of qualities of both roles, is also consistent with these politics.

I want to contrast a second view with this. This view doubts that differences or differentiation have much to do with inequality. Sexism is a problem not of gender differentiation, but of gender hierarchy, in which gender differentiation is only one strategy. Nor is sexism gender neutral in the sense that it hurts men and women equally; the problem is instead male supremacy and female subjection. From this second point of view, issues like rape, incest, sexual harassment, prostitution, pornography—issues of the violation of women, in particular of women's sexuality—connect directly with issues of athletics. The systematic maiming of women's physicality that marks those athletic and physical pursuits that women have been forced or pressured or encouraged to do, on the one hand, connect with those we have been excluded from doing, on the other. If you ask, not why do women and men do different physical activities, but why has femininity *meant* physical weakness, you notice that someone who is physically weak is more easily able to be raped, available to be molested, open to sexual harassment. Feminine means violable.

This critique of gender hierarchy, which I identify as the radical feminist analysis, is developing a theory beyond stereotyping, beyond the dynamics of differentiation but including them. It is developing a theory that objectification is the dynamic of the subordination of women. Objectification is different from stereotyping, which acts as though it's all in the head. Stereotyping, as critique, proceeds as though what we need to change so that women will no longer be

118

kept down is women's images of ourselves as victims and men's mistaken views of us as second class. It's not that that wouldn't help. It's
just that the problem goes a great deal deeper than illusion or delusion. Masks become personas become people, socially, especially
when they are enforced. The history of women's athletics should
prove that, if nothing else does. The notion that women cannot do
certain things, cannot break certain records, cannot engage in certain
physical pursuits has been part of preventing women from doing
those things. It isn't only that women are excluded, it's that even
women who do sport are limited. This isn't just ideas or images—or
just women, for that matter. When you think, for instance, about the
relationship between the scientific discovery of the physical possibility of running a mile in less than x time and people actually running
the mile in less than x time, you see a real relationship between images of the possibility of a particular achievement and the actual
physical ability to do it. Anyone who trains seriously understands
this on some level.

What I'm suggesting is that the sexual, by which I mean the
gender, objectification of women that has distinguished between
women, on the one hand, and the successful athlete, on the other,
has reached deeper than just mistaken ideas about what women can
and cannot do, notions that can be thought out of existence by the
insightful or the exceptionally ambitious. It is not only ideas in the
head that have excluded us from resources and most everything else.
It is also the social meaning of female identity that has restricted and
contained us. If a woman is defined hierarchically so that the male
idea of a woman defines womanhood, and if men have power, this
idea becomes reality. It is therefore real. It is not just an illusion or a
fantasy or a mistake. It becomes *embodied* because it is enforced.

Radical feminism is not satisfied with women emulating the existing image of the athlete, which has been a male image. Neither with
that, nor with the separate and vicarious role of cheerleader, nor with
other feminine physical pursuits that have been left to us. Instead,
feminism moves to transform the meaning of athletics, of sport itself.
I am going to talk about what it would look like to transform sport
from a feminist perspective. To do this, I need finally to distinguish
this feminist perspective from what I have characterized as the aspiration to the genderless point of view that characterizes liberal feminism. The idea of liberal feminism is that because society and thought
are so twisted by sexism, we have to somehow transcend all that in

order to have a nonsexist perspective from which to view social life. I think the radical feminist move is exactly the opposite. It says that we need a women's point of view that criticizes all the ways we have been created by being excluded and kept down but that also claims the validity of our own experience. This is not a transcendence operation, whereby we get to act as though we don't have any particular perspective, but instead an embrace of what we have become with a criticism of the process of having been forced to become it, together with a similar dual take on everything we've never been allowed to be.

In the context of liberal feminism, when one asks why don't women participate in athletics or why haven't they participated in athletics, the answer looks like: illusions about women's weakness, notions about femininity, stereotypes. These are all part of it, to be sure. The corresponding solution reveals the limitations on the underlying account, though: challenge wrong ideas so that women can play with the boys. From a radical feminist perspective, if you ask why women have not participated in athletics, you get a much more complicated picture. Women have learned a lot all these years on the sidelines, watching. Not only have we been excluded from resources, excluded from participation, we have learned actual disability, enforced weakness, lack of spirit/body connection in being and in motion. It is not that men are trained to be strong and women are just not trained. Men are trained to be strong and women are trained to be weak. It's not *not* learned; it's very specifically learned. Also, observing athletics as pursuits, we notice that most athletics, particularly the most lucrative of them, have been internally designed to maximize attributes that are identical with what the male sex role values in men. In other words, men, simply learning to be men, learn not only sports but learn those things that become elevated, extended, measured, valued, and organized *in and as sport itself.* Women, simply learning to be women, do not learn those things, do learn the opposite of those things. So it's no news to any of you that being female and being athletic have been socially contradictory and that being male and being athletic have been more or less socially synonymous. Femininity has contradicted, masculinity has been consistent with, being athletic. Women get to choose between being a successful girl and being a successful athlete.

Now I want to extend and deepen the feminist analysis of athletics from this second perspective, which I will call simply feminist. When you look at athletics from the feminist standpoint, the question becomes: what is athletics *for?* Once, when I asked a class of Harvard law students this question, one woman answered: what is *education* for without athletics? Which I thought was very much the point. It was not just that without basketball, she would have had no interest whatever in school, but that physical education was central to becoming an educated person. Keeping this in mind, and keeping in mind that the standard for personhood, in athletics as elsewhere, has substantively, socially, been a male standard, I want to answer the question "what is athletics for?" in two parts: what has it meant to men? and what can it mean to women?

From a feminist perspective, athletics to men is a form of combat. It is a sphere in which one asserts oneself against an object, a person, or a standard. It is a form of coming against and subduing someone who is on the other side, vanquishing enemies. It's competitive. From women's point of view, some rather major elements of the experience appear to be left out, both for men and for women. These include things that men occasionally experience, but that on the whole are not allowed to be the central purpose of male athletics, such as kinesthesis, pleasure in motion, cooperation (and by this I do not mean the male bond), physical self-respect, self-possession, and fun. Because of the history of women's subjection, physicality for women has a different meaning from physicality for men. Physicality for men has meant male dominance; it has meant force, coercion, and the ability to subdue and subject the natural world, one central part of which has been us.

For women, when we have engaged in sport, when we have been physical, it has meant claiming and possessing a physicality that is our own. We have had something to fight and therefore something to gain here, and that is a different relation to our bodies than women are allowed to have in this society. We have had to gain a relation to our bodies *as if they are our own.* This physical self-respect and physical presence that women can get from sport is antithetical to femininity. It is our bodies as acting rather than as acted upon. It is our bodies as being and presence, our bodies that *we* do things with, that we in fact are and identify with as ourselves, rather than our bodies as things to be looked at or for us to look at in preparation for the crucialness of how we will appear, or even to carry our heads around in the world. In other words, athletics can give us our bodies as a form of being rather than as a form of appearance, or death-likeness.

Applications

In particular, I think, athletics can give us a sense of an actuality of our bodies as our own rather than primarily as an instrument to communicate sexual availability.

If you doubt that we are not allowed to have what I am saying athletics gives us, I suggest that we can tell we've broken some rules when people start calling us what they consider epithets. We all know that women athletes are considered unfeminine. This is integrally related to the fact that women athletes are experienced as having physical self-respect. We also know that women athletes are routinely accused, explicitly or implicitly, of being lesbian. I think that this is directly related to the sense women athletes have of body as self, as acting, as opposed to body as something that conveys sexual accessibility to men, as there to be acted upon. I often find that the allegedly nasty words people use to describe us have truth in them, in that if one asks why they see us this way, we learn some real things. On the equation of woman athlete with unfeminine with lesbian, I wonder: why does women's self-respect and conveyed capacity to act *mean* that we reject male sexual access? *They're* the ones who are telling us that's what it means. What does it say about the relation between sexuality and physicality, what does it tell us in particular about the content of heterosexuality, that when a woman comes to own her own body, that makes her heterosexuality problematic? I think it tells us that the image and in large part the reality we have of female sexuality is equated with and defined as availability to being taken by a man. It's threatening to one's takeability, one's rapeability, one's femininity, to be strong and physically self-possessed. To be able to resist rape, not to communicate rapeability with one's body, to hold one's body for uses and meanings other than that can transform what *being a woman means*.

Some of you may be thinking that what I have described as the image of weakness, pregnability, vulnerability, passivity, the feminine stereotype, the eternal female, and the ways in which those are antithetical to the image of the athlete, is outdated. You may be thinking that since the passage of Title IX and the new improved image of the woman athlete, it has become more acceptable, hence less stigmatic, for women to be physical. Title IX has been extremely important. But the minute women claim something for ourselves and it is seen as powerful and important, especially if it becomes profitable, it immediately gets claimed and taken over by men. I mean to include everything from the eroticization of the female athlete in *Playboy* to the recent moves by the NCAA.[1]

122

That comment suggests some institutional consequences, not all of which I have resolved in my own mind. Given what I have said about women's physicality, women's point of view on athletics, and its connections with sexuality and the subordination of women generally, *now* let's ask, what about separate teams? what about separate programs? what about separate institutions? If women/men is a distinction not just of difference, but of power and powerlessness, if power/powerlessness *is* the sex difference, those questions need to be asked very differently than they have been. For instance, if not participating in male-defined sport does not mean fear or rejection of failure or success, but the creation of a new standard, of a new vision of sport, the problem of pursuing a feminist perspective in an institutional context is not solved, but it is differently posed.

This attempt at a new perspective, in other words, does not simply justify separatism.[2] It is an argument that women as women in a feminist sense have a distinctive contribution to make to sport that is neither a sentimentalization of our oppression as women nor an embrace of the model of the oppressor. As feminists, we are critical of both femininity and masculinity as serving the interest of men, as furthering male power, and as instrumental to male dominance. We are attempting to create a social reality, a social identity, that is bound up with neither. A vision of sport from this standpoint finds ritualized violence alien and dangerous as well as faintly ridiculous, every bit as much as it finds sex-scripted cheering from the sidelines demeaning and vicarious and silly. The place of women's athletics in a larger feminist analysis is that women *as women* have a survival stake in reclaiming our bodies in our physical relations with other people. We need to do this in a way that claims our bodies as ourselves, rather than as an eager embrace of our bodies as nature, or abdication of them to other people as something to be resisted or overcome or subdued.

I hope that what I'm about to say won't get sentimentalized. It is part of a critical analysis of art as well as of sport. I have said that I think women's physicality, or what it could be, has a distinct meaning, a meaning that comes from women's oppression through our bodies, but that means we have something to offer the world of athletics, much as it has something to offer us. I do mean to include men who have been excluded from sports by their rejection of the masculine ideal. But it is not only men who can't make it, and not only women who can, who stand to benefit from a revaluation of sport. Women have a contribution of perspective to make here that is a lot

123

Applications

more powerful than either playing with the boys or allowing the boys to play with us. Once when I was talking about this with the same student I mentioned earlier, she reminded me that both men and women have climbed Mount Everest. When asked why, the man said, because it is there. The woman said, because it is beautiful.

III. PORNOGRAPHY

I describe life with Chuck as twisted and brutal, demented and violent, insane and sadistic; he describes it as normal—believe it or not, we're both telling the truth.

Linda Lovelace, *Out of Bondage* (1986)

A life is such a fragile thing. It can be snuffed out . . . like a candle. Go beyond the limits of realism . . . to reality.

Promotional copy for *Snuff* [ellipses in original]

You could run a daily newspaper committed to a conspiracy, not of silence, but of speech.

Virginia Woolf, *Three Guineas* (1938)

eleven

Linda's Life and Andrea's Work (1982)

What you are hearing tonight from Andrea Dworkin and from Linda Marchiano and now from me, unless you have previously spoken with us or have read our work or some of the very small amount of work that is part of what we are trying to do, you have never heard before. Although it may be unnecessary to say this, I do so in order to try to avoid misunderstandings caused by your translating what we say into things that you think are said by people who you think think like we do. For example, I heard Burton Joseph say, in relation to the Comstock law, as he moved into discussing the evil forces at work in this country to restrict existing freedoms he supposes we all have, that "these people's justifications for their arguments are always the same." Our arguments are not the same as the arguments he refers to. What you are hearing tonight is not only something you have not heard before, it is something he has not heard before, because it is something that has not been said before. He is speaking from and about the language, the noise, of an apparatus that, along with protecting many values all of us share, exists to protect male supremacy as a system. This is the system Andrea discussed, of which Linda was a specific victim and of which we all, as women, are survivors.

I want to speak with you, first, about the meaning of Linda's experience for all women and, second, about the meaning of Andrea's analysis for the law of the First Amendment; third, I want to engage in an act of political speech on behalf of the three of us. When I mentioned to Andrea what I was going to do in my twenty-five minutes, she said, it will be twenty-five more minutes than has ever gone into any of that. I say this to underline the point that you have not heard any of this before.

As to the meaning of Linda's experience for all women, I do not mean to take away whatever meaning it has to you or to change it or

At Stanford University, Stanford, California, Apr. 2, 1982, Linda Marchiano, Andrea Dworkin, Burton Joseph (chairman of the board, Playboy Foundation), and I presented a panel on pornography, which the intrepid Sharon Dyer organized.

127

make my own meaning out of the meaning that she gives it or that she communicates by her presence. I do think that her experience is on the one hand individually extreme, specifically horrible and unusually brutal, and is on the other hand a very common, everywoman kind of experience. I want to talk about the connection between those two aspects.

The film *Deep Throat*, in which Linda was pornographed, became a chic success. It was a turning point in legitimizing pornography in this country. Lots of rising young executives, as well as the usual middle-aged settled ones, took their respectively appropriately annexed women to see it. The film is often defended in courts as well as in the press as nonobscene because, they say, it is sexually liberating. People report feeling sexually more free to engage in oral sex as a result of having seen Linda deep-throat in the film. Linda spoke to you about her alienation. That word abstracts her experience but begins to convey the out-of-it-ness that one needs to survive torture.[1] Accounts of torture show that it is a common survival strategy to remove oneself from the situation, to split away, to say this body that is being abused is not my body. I believe this reality is the key to the success of *Deep Throat* as a sex film. I'm saying Linda's out-of-it-ness is the key to what is *sexual* about the film.

On one level, this quality is part of her projection of the image of the sweet young porn star who liked sex but wasn't a slut. She didn't come off as a whore, but it was clear she was one. A whore is not out of it, a whore is (supposedly) into it. Simultaneously Linda conveyed that she was having a good time. Her apparent enjoyment is crucial. As she says, what people remember is the smile on my face. The purported plot of *Deep Throat* is premised upon rearranging the woman by putting a clitoris in her throat, so that she gets sexual pleasure out of giving oral sex to men. Chic, rising young executive men who took their women to this film came out saying, if you love me you'll do that too. The superficial lie, that we get pleasure in ways we do not, is the central conceit. The deeper lie is that Linda enjoyed it. That is the lie she was forced to act out. That she was there for the sex would have been a lie even if she was there more voluntarily. That is, even if she had done it for money, it would have been a lie that she was doing the sex for her own pleasure; that she was voluntarily enjoying it is the *role* she was there to *portray*.

But here, put a gun to someone's head and say, act like you're enjoying it. If you have any kind of acting ability, as well as respect for your life, a desire to live, maybe you want to do it well once so you won't have to do a retake—you do it. You do it relatively convincingly. Linda's apparent enjoyment, which was a well-done charade, is the charade women learn in order to survive: to project sexual enjoyment whether we feel it or not. Underlying this is that out-of-it-ness, that same above-it-all quality, that not-really-into-it-ness of a lot of women under a lot of different conditions. This is what she conveyed, and the film was a success because it felt *real* to men. It's the same reality Jane Fonda exposed in that second of complete brilliance in *Klute.* Remember the part where she's playing the prostitute having a wonderful time having sex, making orgiastic sounds, and then she checks her watch? That. Linda projected in *Deep Throat* what women learn in order to get by as women. It is a major part of our self-presentation. It is what men experience *as* our sexuality. What connects Linda's ordeal and the success of *Deep Throat* with the situation of all women is the force they are based on.

Now I want to talk about the meaning of Andrea's analysis of pornography for the law. It's a testament to what I call the hegemony of legalism—by which I mean the ability of the legal system to assign the categories within which people then conceive their lives—that when we come here to speak about the feminist critique of pornography, Burton Joseph stands up and addresses a whole series of issues premised on the view that anyone who is against pornography is promoting state censorship of free expression. What I learn from reading Andrea's book and listening to her tonight is that what Burton Joseph defends as his free speech is premised on what Linda describes as her life. *Deep Throat* is protected speech.[2] The *film* apparently cannot be reached *by her* any more than by anyone else, no matter what was done to her in making it. The fact that Linda was coerced makes the film no less protected as speech, even though the publication of *Ordeal*[3] makes clear that the film documents crimes, acts that violate laws in all fifty states.

From thinking further about Linda's relation to that film in the context of Andrea's analysis, I learned that the social preconditions, the presumptions, that underlie the First Amendment do not apply to women. The First Amendment essentially presumes some level of social equality among people and hence essentially equal social access to the means of expression. In a context of inequality between the sexes, we cannot presume that that is accurate. The First Amendment also presumes that for the mind to be free to fulfill itself, speech must be free and open. Andrea's work shows that pornography contributes to enslaving women's minds and bodies. As a social process and as a form of "speech," pornography amounts to terrorism and promotes not freedom but silence. Rather, it promotes freedom for men and enslavement and silence for women.

Burton Joseph repeatedly separates conduct from speech. Speech he's for; acts he can be against. The distinction has been heavily fought over. It is unclear what's conduct and what's speech at many points, but this separation is thought to exist. Mr. Joseph then goes on to discuss data about how irrelevant speech is to action. In my view, none of these studies has yet asked the right questions about pornography. They don't ask whether sexuality is itself violating or even whether it is itself violent; they are premised instead on the view that sexuality and violence are distinct; hence pornography is distinct from erotica. The subjects of the studies are typically exposed to so-called erotic films, meaning that the films produce erections in men and (when they use women) vaginal secretions in women. Then they try to measure whether the subjects will do violent acts, such as administering electric shocks. Sometimes they find that they do. But they don't test for whether sexual excitement means they will express violent *sex*, although there is some evidence that pornography makes men more tolerant of rape. The work is premised on a clear split between sex and violence. The studies of the speech/action connection do not look for the right acts. When Andrea speaks of the penis as a weapon, violence and sexuality are not so separable.

In Andrea's work, expression is not just talk. Pornography not only teaches the reality of male dominance. It is one way its reality is imposed as well as experienced. It is a way of seeing and using women. Male power makes authoritative a way of seeing and treating women, so that when a man looks at a pornographic picture—pornographic meaning that the woman is defined as to be acted upon, a sexual object, a sexual thing—the *viewing* is an *act*, an act of male supremacy. It also takes a lot of acts to make it, as Linda makes clear. An additional assumption underlying the First Amendment is that free speech is necessary to discern truth, that the partiality produced by supression distorts truth. What I hear Andrea saying is that under conditions of sexual dominance, pornography hides and distorts truth while at the same time enforcing itself, imprinting itself on the world, making itself real. That's another way in which pornography *is* a kind of act.

Another notion underlying the First Amendment is that free speech promotes consensus by allowing unorthodox expression. Pornography is thought to be a divergent and unorthodox view. Andrea's analysis reveals that the views in pornography are conventional; they *are* the consensus. This is why legal line-drawing is so difficult in this area. That difficulty was implicit in all Mr. Joseph said to make us afraid of the consequences of trying to do anything about pornography: the inability to draw a line between pornography and everything else. To me that exposes the pervasiveness of the value system Andrea analyzes, its presence in literature, in advertising, in daily life. If I have any difficulty distinguishing those areas from pornography, it is not because I don't think some things are worse than others, because they are, but because the same values pervade them all.

Now I want to engage in an act of political speech. The three of us are in some ways unique, but as women we are not alone. The existence of Linda and Andrea and me, according to the system we have described to you, is impossible. It is impossible for Linda to exist as who she is, having been through what she's been through. Usually, what happened to Linda would make it impossible for you ever to hear about her. Once these things happen, the women are silenced forever, so it's impossible to be both a victim and a survivor. The deepest victims of sexism are the ones you never hear from again. What's so amazing about Linda is that she is one of its deepest victims and you have heard from her. In this she is like Andrea, who has survived the streets of this country and writes. Her uncompromised advocacy for women has been vilified, denigrated, and ignored—as well as read and understood and recognized and respected and acted upon. By the values of most of what is published and taken seriously, there is no way to account for her existence or her voice. We cannot explain the fact that you have heard from her.

Women have also been systematically excluded from access to the tools of the law and from the possession and legitimacy of a legal and political education. To the extent we are granted that access, we are not allowed to identify as women. I have survived that, among other things. Nor are we allowed to make women the center of our work, so that essentially there is no feminist critique of law. The price of getting the tools to do it seems to include being trained out of wanting to.

If all this fails to silence us, the success of our survival is used to delegitimize what we have survived to say, our critique. Do you realize that part of people's difficulty believing Linda is *because* she survived? It couldn't have been that bad; other women can't be in her situation. *She* escaped; why can't they? Similarly with Andrea. See, the First Amendment works, you got published. I am told, see, a feminist can teach at Harvard, Yale, and Stanford law schools. How can academia, legal education, law be antiwoman?

This ignores the precariousness and threat of our situations, as well as what we have been through. It ignores the pornography of our daily lives, as well as deprives us of whatever victories we have achieved over it. As to the precariousness and threat, because Linda has refused to lie down, roll over, be silent, play dead, her survival as a woman with self-respect is turned into yet one more way that she can be used. The men she wrote about in *Ordeal* continue to come after her for any money she makes on the book. Saying that Andrea's success vindicates the First Amendment ignores the way Andrea has to live from article to article, book to book, day to day, sustaining continual assaults to her dignity and worth; it ignores what all of us have been through financially, living below the poverty line year after year. It's not just a question of how life is hard all over, but of how once you have identified as a woman, which Linda did by being violated and surviving as one, which we all do by speaking as one, you have no credibility. For Linda it looks like she's a whore. People do not believe this woman because what happened to her, happened. It proved who she really is. Andrea is depicted through all the usual slanders against effective women. The attacks on her appearance, her sexuality, her relationships, her heritage, and her ideas are on a level of viciousness that is almost impossible to characterize. My work is considered not law by lawyers, not scholarship by academics, too practical by intellectuals, too intellectual by practitioners, and neither politics nor science by political scientists.

When I ask myself what could make us credible, I realize that for Linda it would help if she were dead. Then they might believe she didn't want it. Maybe. Short of that, maybe it takes more women's bodies. How many women has Chuck Traynor done this to? Maybe if we have two or three or maybe four more, people will start to believe Linda? Just the doubt that this one man can raise by saying, when I met her she was a whore, she's still a whore. She's just going around selling herself, you know. Now she's selling her story about how her story was sold. How many women's bodies do we have to stack up just to begin to have something to stand on to question that credibility? As for Andrea, I think that the women who have the credibility she doesn't have are the feminists who do not criticize male supremacy, specifically male sexuality. And as for me, I notice that law gives me some credibility, but that being woman-identified takes it away. The law gives male credibility; female identification erases it. In that connection and context, you should all know that this event tonight would not have been allowed to occur had there not been a representative from what is regarded as the other side. For how long have these issues been discussed without our side? Have you *ever* heard what we are saying before? I haven't. When world hunger is discussed, is it necessary to have the pro-hunger side presented?

Linda, Andrea, and I would not have been allowed by Stanford to give this panel unless we also provided this forum to Burton Joseph, the chairman of the board of the Playboy Foundation. Is it a coincidence that each of us also represents a pornographic stereotype? Linda is the whore, Andrea is the feminist bitch, and I am the liberated lady lawyer. Check us out in *Playboy* some time. Do they give what we are saying here tonight equal time?

The point is, because we all identify as women, but also because, like all women, we inescapably *are* identified as women, the values of pornography are the values that rule our lives. But each day I have students and clients, Andrea has readers, and Linda, as herself, has an audience. And every day there are more of us.

twelve

"More Than Simply a Magazine":
Playboy's Money
(1982)

They are able to distort the pictures or do anything that they want to with them . . . for example, I was a puzzle. I was a deck of playing cards. This is what they call Playboy products . . . By the way, a Playmate is a product. The term "Playmate" is a trademark of Playboy.

Miki Garcia ("Miss January 1973"), Hearings of the National Commission on Pornography, Los Angeles, October 17, 1985

Playboy, the magazine, sells women's sexuality as "entertainment for men."[1] It is socially accepted. Playboy, the foundation, gives a fair amount of the money the magazine makes this way to some kinds of feminist work[2] and brags about it more than a fair amount. I want to think through the connections between these facts, focusing on how feminists' acceptance of money from Playboy, the foundation, helps make acceptable what *Playboy*, the magazine, does to women. This is a preliminary report on some research. I am just beginning to get a handle on what I think Playboy is, what they are doing, what their views of themselves are, and how they are socially regarded.

Among feminists I see two views of Playboy's money. One is that it is really our money. Playboy took and sold women's sexuality to make it in the first place, so we should use it in the interests of women to cushion or change the system that extracts it from us. If feminism is at all about transforming the sexuality-for-survival dynamic, this reparations theory could make Playboy's money look like part of a feminist strategy for change.

This speech was originally part of a panel Pauline Bart organized at the National Women's Studies Association meetings, Humboldt, California, June 19, 1982. Jeanne M. Barkey did much of the research on Playboy that made the analysis possible. In "The Playboy Philosophy," *Playboy*, February 1963, at 48, Hugh Hefner said that Playboy was becoming "more than simply a magazine." He was right. I dedicate this speech to Dorchen Leidholdt.

The other view is not that Playboy's money is dirty money; the objection is not a moral one, that Playboy is dirty in some sense in which other things are clean. The objection is not from the standpoint of any kind of purity. It is a political objection. By this I mean it is not about good and evil or virtue and perversity but about power and powerlessness. From this standpoint, the argument against taking Playboy's money is: if we think we are going to use their money to undercut the system of power that extracts it, we think we are more powerful than we are and Playboy is less powerful than it is, which is a dangerous delusion. Even more, if much of *Playboy*'s power against women derives from its legitimacy, and what its legitimacy in turn makes legitimate, we become part of their legitimacy support system when we accept their financial help. Taking their money, in this view, digs us deeper into the system we are fighting. The issue then becomes not whether we are pure, or even whether we can afford not to take their money and still survive, but whether taking their money hurts us more than the money helps us, although it comes as an influx of often desperately needed resources. Can feminists survive *taking* their money? What do we survive *as*?

Those are the positions in their most difficult postures, for me. If their analysis of women's situation is not identical, at least their senses of feminist goals overlap. On one level of theory, the question of Playboy's money can be seen as an example of the marxism-feminism problematic, because it connects materiality in the money sense with male power in the sexual sense. What follows is one attempt to work through that tension, understanding that money and sexuality are *both* material and gendered.

Playboy's money, considered from a feminist perspective, requires answering three questions: what is feminism? what is Playboy? what is money? I will bring in facts about who Playboy gives money to and, to the extent we have been able to determine empirically, how much is involved, under what conditions it is given, and with what results.

Playboy asserts it is a feminist publication; at least both Hugh Hefner and Christie Hefner say that they are feminists and that the magazine liberates women.[3] I am less interested in what is utterly ludicrous about this claim than in the sense in which it might have some truth. If you ask, is there anything that goes around calling itself feminist that *Playboy* has anything in common with, the answer is yes. For that reason I need to discuss what feminism is before I can evaluate Playboy in its terms. I will also say I am real tired of people calling things feminist that come from quite other traditions. Applying other traditions to women doesn't make them feminist.

I believe that thought is systematic, socially speaking, even when it is not particularly consistent or coherent, logically or philosophically speaking. It always occupies a place in society's material/consciousness context, which is a context that gives some people power over other people. When Playboy says it is feminist, the substance of the positions it refers to is systematically—formally, historically, and philosophically—liberal, period.

Liberalism applied to the sex question provides a critique of gender differentiation in which the sexes are imagined as fundamentally different, so inequality means inaccurate or irrational differentiation. Why inequality happens is never very clear. No one is ever actively doing it, everybody has it done to them, and no one benefits from it. It sort of just comes from the stork. Liberal feminism seeks to solve this version of the sex problem, which is this imperfect fit between gender differentiation—social sex—and sexual dimorphism—biological sex. The resulting liberal feminist position on sexuality, like its position on most else, is that women should be able to get what men have had access to, so long as biological differentiation is not altered as a bottom line. On this view of equality, what you get is the sixties' "liberated woman," that is, the woman who initiates sex with lots of men ("partners") and regards it as an indoor or spectator sport (like men have) and has lots of (biologically female) orgasms.

Playboy certainly presents the biological differences between the sexes on its pages, if a difference can be shown by displaying only half of it. What are thought of as women's *gender* characteristics are what the magazine sells as *sexuality*. To say that *Playboy* presents the natural beauty of women's bodies and promotes the sexual liberation of women—here I draw on *Playboy* itself, which says it does these things—reveals a liberal concept of the relation between nature and freedom. It starts with the idea that people, even people who as a group are poor and powerless, do what they do voluntarily, so that women who pose for *Playboy* are there by their own free will. Forget the realities of womens' sexual/economic situation. When women express our free will, we spread our legs for a camera.

Implicit here, too, is the idea that a natural physical body exists, prior to its social construction through being viewed, which can be captured and photographed, even, or especially, when "attractively posed"—that's a quote from the Playboy Philosophy.[4] Then we are

136

told that to *criticize* this is to criticize "ideas," not what is being *done* either to the women in the magazine or to women in society as a whole. Any critique of what is done is then cast as a moral critique, which, as liberals know, can involve only opinions or ideas, not facts about life. This entire defensive edifice, illogical as it may seem, relies utterly coherently on the five cardinal dimensions of liberalism: individualism, naturalism, voluntarism, idealism, and moralism. I mean: members of groups who have no choice but to live life *as* members of groups are taken as if they are unique individuals; their social characteristics are then reduced to natural characteristics; preclusion of choices becomes free will; material reality is turned into "ideas about" reality; and concrete positions of power and powerlessness are transformed into relative value judgments, as to which reasonable people can form different but equally valid preferences.

What I have just described is the ideological defense of pornography. Given the consequences for women of this formal theoretical structure, consequences that we live out daily as social inequality (not to mention its *inherent* blame-the-victim posture), I do not think it can be said that liberal feminism is feminist. What it is, is liberalism applied to women. If the sexes are equally different but not equally socially powerful, "differences" in the liberal sense are irrelevant to the politics of our situation, which is one of inequality. Radical feminism, as I understand it, is against gender hierarchy. Since such a critique *does* address the situation of women as I understand it, I term it simply feminism.

One's position, then, on whether feminists should accept Playboy's money depends on one's analysis of the situation of women: where it comes from, what makes it move, how to change it. It means one thing to take their money if the situation of women is forced—specifically, if the situation is one of forced sex—and quite another if women's problem is, say, that selling our sexuality is illegal. I think that gender defines the status of women, that forced sex defines gender, that pornography eroticizes and thereby legitimizes forced sex, and that *Playboy* is pornography and makes pornography legitimate. Playboy is, in part and in turn, legitimized through its articles, which include some by putative feminists, and its intensive and very successful public relations, of which its financial contributions to the women's movement are a real part. Playboy uses its contributions to our work (among other things) to transform its position as active oppressors of women into the appearance of being standard bearers of women's equality.

137

Pornography

Playboy's legitimacy I term "the *Playboy* standard." The way it works is that anything that might hurt *Playboy*, meaning anything real addressing pornography, can't be done. According to this standard, *Playboy* isn't "really" pornography, but it is indistinguishable from it; since nothing can be done about pornography that wouldn't also hurt *Playboy*, nothing can be done about pornography. *Playboy* is so much a standard that people may even be against what they call the violence in pornography yet think *Playboy* is fine. Either they miss or don't mind the force in and behind *Playboy*; or if they do see it, they don't feel they can take a stand even against the more expressly violent pornography, because that might do something to *Playboy*. I'm saying, the first premise is "*Playboy* is OK"; everything else, including what *Playboy* does to women, has to be measured against the standard *Playboy* sets, rather than measuring *Playboy* by some other standard of how women should be treated.

From a feminist perspective, what exactly does *Playboy* do? It takes a woman and makes her sexuality into something any man who wants to can buy and hold in his hand for three dollars and fifty cents. His access to her sexuality is called freedom—his *and hers*. She becomes something to be used by him, specifically, an object for his sexual use. Think of it this way. A cup is part of the object world, valued according to its looks and for how it can be used. If someone breaks it, maybe that is considered an abuse, or maybe it is briefly mourned and then replaced. But using it does not violate anything, because that is what it is for. *Playboy* as a standard means that to use a woman sexually does not violate her nature because it expresses her nature; it is what she is *for*. To criticize *Playboy* as a standard for how a woman should be treated is to say something very simple: a woman is not a cup, and her sexuality isn't, either.

What *Playboy* does to women is very carefully legitimized, both inside and outside the magazine. *Playboy*'s articles push their views, including their views of the First Amendment, in an expressly sexualized context, and at the same time those articles serve to legitimize what their pictures do to women. Masturbating over the positions taken by the women's bodies associates male orgasm with the positions expressed in the articles. Ever wonder why men are so passionate about the First Amendment? At the same time the articles help make it seem legitimate to treat women the way *Playboy* does, because the articles are so legitimate. The sex contextualizes the articles and the articles contextualize the sex.

Playboy defends itself against the charge of being merely a skin

138

magazine by pointing to having published many people it calls feminists, some we might call feminists, women like Gloria Emerson, Susan Sontag, Doris Lessing, Joyce Carol Oates, Pearl Buck, and Mary McCarthy. And interviews with Germaine Greer, Jane Fonda, Betty Friedan, Mary Calderone, Bernadette Devlin, Shere Hite, and Virginia Johnson. Under the legal doctrine of obscenity, courts may not take materials apart. They have to take them "as a whole."[5] *Playboy*'s format, like that of much pornography, is designed around obscenity law so that its sexual objectification of women is legalized as well as legitimized through being surrounded by legitimate articles. In one recent case the Supreme Court said that people who are having sex on a street corner cannot protect that as speech even if they are at the same time engaging in valid political dialogue.[6] On the level of publications, this is what *Playboy* does. It gets itself off the hook for pimping women under the "taken as a whole" rule by simultaneously publishing works that are unquestionably protected speech.[7]

Another way Playboy legitimizes itself is by its research grants. Playboy has funded particular research items; say you need a videotape machine to do an experiment on pornography, they'll send you a check for $2,500.[8] What do we make of this? Perhaps Playboy *is* interested in figuring out if there is a relation between explicit sex, their version, and rape or force or violence and all those things they say they are so much against and don't do. Maybe Playboy wants the people who are asking these questions to be friendly to them. When people claim that the brutalization of women is a recurring theme and reality of and in *Playboy* and its imitators, *Playboy* responds, "We can infer that they are referring to psychological or social brutalizations because we never lay a hand on a female except in passion or self-defense."[9] As if passion is never violent, as if women can't wait to jump on playboys. Psychic or social brutality they own up to only to trivialize. How sincere or cynical their rejection of rape is, I don't know. I do know that breaking a cup, accidentally or on purpose, is made less wrenching by the availability of glue and replacements and that the line between use and abuse of women, a line *Playboy* insists on to defend itself, does not exist in practice.[10]

As I see it, the cornerstone of *Playboy*'s principled civil libertarianism comes from the bedrock of their material self-interest: "publishing sex." Forget for the moment that what they "publish" is women; that *is* sex. The freer the access to sex in print, the more freedom there is, the sexier the sex is, and the more money they make. Any critique of this is seen as the forces of darkness moving in to have the government restrict existing freedom. The term freedom in the phrase "freedom of speech" here means free sexual access to women. Freedom is freedom of *access* to us. Listen, I want to increase women's power over sexuality, hence over our social definition and treatment. I think that means decreasing the pornographers' power over it. I have no particular interest in increasing the power of the *state* over sexuality or speech. I do not have that kind of faith in the government. It has largely operated from the same perspective that Playboy does—that is, the male point of view. At least, no one has yet convinced me that extending the obscenity prohibition, liberalizing its application, would do anything but further eroticize pornography. Suppressing obscenity criminally has enhanced its value, made it more attractive and more expensive and a violation to get, therefore more valuable and more sexually exciting. Censoring pornography has not delegitimized it; I want to delegitimize it. What would do that is unclear to me at this time. Maybe there is a way. There needs to be. It is not that I think the state can't do anything for women in this area. I think making sexual harassment sex discrimination has helped delegitimize sexual harassment. That is as far as I have gotten with the problem at this time.

The First Amendment absolutist position is very different from this position. Absolutism supposes that we all have an equal interest in the marketplace of ideas[11] it supposedly guarantees. This is not the case for women. First of all, the marketplace of ideas is literal: those with the most money can buy the most speech, and women are poor. Second, protecting pornographers, as the First Amendment now does, does not promote the freedom of speech of women. It *has* not done so. Pornography terrorizes women into silence. Pornography is therefore not in the interest of our speech. We do not, as women, have the stake in the existing system we have been said to have. The First Amendment has also been interpreted to support the speech of Nazis, as if that would promote the rights of Jews.[12] I doubt that, too, although the issues are specific to each case. Jews are not lying down for anti-Semitism any more than women are lying down for misogyny. But that isn't a victory for the First Amendment; it's a victory for Jews and women against odds that the First Amendment has been used to stack. What I think is that people who are absolutely interested in the First Amendment should turn their efforts to getting speech for people, like women, who have been denied that speech almost entirely, who have not been able to speak or to get themselves heard. Understanding free speech as an abstract system is a liberal position. Understanding how speech also exists within a substantive system of power relations is a feminist position.

On the basis of the First Amendment values I have just criticized, Playboy selects people who epitomize them, people who will also give Playboy legitimacy, and calls them First Amendment Awards judges and gives them First Amendment Awards. They make a major public event of it. In one situation some students objected to the participation of one of their professors as a judge.[13] Discussing this issue with the students, the professor said that his association with Playboy went back to 1971, when it was the only organization willing to fund his draft counseling activities. He was very impressed with it—as many people who deal with only the foundation often are, by the way. They feel that the foundation is socially concerned, that it funds many highly important activities, and that it is, as they put it, "totally unrelated to the magazine." (When asked where they think it gets its money, they demur.) The students asked the professor whether he really understood their concern with lending his name to legitimizing the use of women's bodies to make money. He assured them that he did understand but did not agree that that was what was going on. They spoke about laundering money and pointed out that he could object strongly to that laundering, and especially to the exploitation that originally made that money, without denigrating the worth of the projects the money was spent on. His bottom line was that he had taken lots of Hefner's money for lots of very good causes and was not about to turn on him now. Soon after, however, he withdrew.[14]

I learned a lot from this, because it never would have occurred to me that the professor's original position was a takeable one, even in the abstract. What does money buy? I mean, if someone gives you ten dollars to do something good, does that mean you are loyal to that person for life? If someone who helped you when you were a starving student rapes a child, are you obligated to defend him in court? Is there nothing that breaks the loyalty of money, or is it only an issue of what does or how much money? I had imagined that one could take the money—for draft counseling if it is needed and no one else would pay for it—and that would be that. We have found projects in which people said that no one other than Playboy would pay for the work, like rape victim assistance kits, for instance.[15] So you take the money and you use it in good ways, in ways that support your opposition to sexism, knowing *Playboy* is sexist and that other women paid for that money. Then I come across someone who took such money and felt that it bought extended loyalty, that is, *he* was bought, not just his project. There is something about money as a social relation that I was not taking seriously enough when I thought that people could take the money and do good things with it and then have no further ties with or loyalty to Playboy.

Audience: Why can't we take the money and continue to say *Playboy* is not okay without delegitimizing our work?

C. M.: In theory, we could take the money and continue to say, "*Playboy*'s not okay." But even if we do, *Playboy* uses us to make themselves appear okay to the world, by saying that they fund us. This legitimizes *them* and everything they do, which undermines our work. We legitimize them more than our delegitimizing of them ever takes away—which is part of what powerlessness means. The dilemma, of course, is that it is also delegitimizing not to be able to do feminist work.

To think about whether the question you just asked is a hypothetical one or a question in the real world, I want to ask about the feminism of the projects and the funding relations that are said *not* to be undermined when Playboy says they funded it. The pattern of who Playboy funds and how they do it makes my analysis of their funding consistent with Playboy's real function in male supremacy. Playboy's contributions seem typically to be not especially large but very well targeted. Often they are absolutely crucial to small projects. The amounts are $1,000, $2,000, $5,000,[16] which is a lot to us, but in the foundation world it is not a lot. A contribution often goes to a group that is midstream in a project when it is hit by a postage increase or needs a printed document or pilot leaflet or mailing, or if they can get this document out maybe other people will give them more money, or an ongoing community organization suddenly needs to do a single event. Discrete, crucial events that begin and end, Playboy tends to fund: little newsletters, documents to get conferences off the ground, things like that. A lot of them. The Playboy Foundation gives money to feminists the way a pimp does a prostitute: at desperate moments, just enough to keep you hooked and in line, never enough so you don't need to crawl back for more, never enough so you don't have to worry all the time about how he will see who you are and what you do, buying gratitude and loyalty way out of proportion to the amount of money, in part *because* so little is involved that the relation that money maintains is dependence. You are doing the work, and he isn't, but you never get enough money not to need him anymore.

This parallel raises the question of whether the specific *work* Playboy funds is in their interest in any way. What Playboy has funded is a little different from what they will fund in the immediate future, because they don't have as much money as they have had.[17] But their history with sexology research and the abortion movement is revealing. Playboy funds Masters and Johnson.[18] This makes sense. Not that Masters and Johnson have not discovered some truth. But their research, like *Playboy,* revolves around the search for the perfect fuck, the modern equivalent of the holy grail. It is about the science, the technology, of how to produce the same sexuality the pornography eroticizes without facing the fact that women's unequal social status is the precondition for their definition of sexual adjustment. Playboy funded Masters and Johnson's sex therapist training. This is so perfect for *Playboy's* "achiever" philosophy. There is a way to fuck right, and if you can't manage it, Playboy is there to help you. Beneath this "how to" is a sexual politics. Technique is never pure means.

Some say that sexology has been monopolized or taken over by Playboy funding.[19] To ask what it means to take something over is to need to ask whether the sexologists' sexuality is all that different from *Playboy's* sexuality in the first place.[20] *Playboy's* operative definition of sexuality, like that of most sexology, essentially derives from neo-Freudian derepression theory, even when Freud is superficially repudiated as inadequately empirically based. (The same basic view of sexuality can be found in most marxist feminism and in liberalism, as well as in a lot of behavioral work, such as the 1970 President's Commission report on obscenity.) This view underlies what has been called the movement for sexual liberation. A feminist critique of it suggests that this definition of sexuality frees male sexual aggression. Making the penis work and getting women to go with that is what sex research perfects. In other words, saying that *Playboy* is feminist means that *Playboy* furthers the sexual liberation of women, meaning it frees women for sexual access by men. That *is* female sexuality, hence freedom for women, according to them. They will take away whatever inhibitions we "frigid" ones have had when we say we are not moved, we don't want "it," *you* we don't want. Our resistance is taken as our repression, something we need sex therapy and pornography for.

It is interesting that censorship of speech is discussed in the same terms that this purported sexual restriction is discussed: as "suppression." Censorship excites men a lot. It is as if they make an analogy from the Freudian view of the individual experience of sexual intercourse to the public experience of sex in words and pictures, so that censorship is a form of sexual repression. It seems that what they *do* to us sexually is their speech. Freedom of sexual explicitness de-represses the public in the same way that an individual's freedom is actuated by more intercourse. In other words, the more sex an individual or a society has, in print or in life interchangeably, the more sexually free and healthy he/she/it is.

Without launching into a full critique of Freudian derepression theory, I will say that I think feminism is developing a non-Freudian theory of sexuality. Repressed in the Freudian sense is not exactly what has been done to women's sexuality. We *have* experienced deadening and silence and subordination. Male sexuality has not exactly been repressed either. Men have eroticized the idea that their sexuality has been denied, but their sexuality has been nothing but expressed and expressed and expressed. Sexual liberation, from this perspective, looks like a male rationalization for forcing sex on women. Intellectually, it derives from Freud, including Freud's (in the end) disbelief of women's accounts of victimization through sexual abuse as children. When women reported what had happened to them, Freud couldn't finally believe it was real, so he invented fantasy to explain the inexplicable and put it in the unconscious. That's where you keep things you repress; repression is how you keep them there. All this presupposes that what women said happened *didn't*. Check it out: these parts of Freud's *formal* theory are based on his substantive belief that women who told him about childhood sexual abuse were lying.

That Playboy would fund abortion rights—which, as they never tire of pointing out, they have done from its beginning[21]—also makes sense in this context. Abortion allows women to have sex on the same terms as men have had it: "no consequences."[22] The entire right wing, and men in general, know that abortion has been fought as an issue of sexual liberation in the sense I mentioned. When women need abortion, it is often so that, since we cannot stop the sex being forced on us, we can at least stop being stuck with the reproductive consequences for the rest of our lives. If women's sexuality means our being able to have sex initiated by men, or our initiating sex with men when men want us to, then freeing *that* sexuality includes separating it from reproduction, so that we don't have to stay pregnant as a result of it. *That* is the liberation of women: women equaling heterosexual intercourse, liberation equaling lack of restraints on men getting it. Abortion offers women the liberal feminist dream of

144

being real women—that is, available to be freely fucked—while still being able to live out a socially male biography—not having to be responsible for children. This is the "equality" it offers us. I hope this makes clear why liberal so-called feminists and the pornographers wind up on the same side of things.

What I really want to know is how much of the women's movement the pornographers own. I wonder if there is a relationship between the money Playboy gives the women's movement and the fact that we have not yet been able to establish—or as a movement even to begin—a real critique of pornography.[23] It is very difficult to think certain thoughts, to get beyond certain ways of thinking, if you have a material investment in not letting your thinking lead in certain directions. Playboy funded one sexual harassment conference proposal that did not even mention sexuality as part of the problem—it was entirely an economic analysis.[24] *Playboy* regularly celebrates what is essentially sexual harassment in its pages, but it's presented as fun, as consensual, as sex. Maybe the conference organizers would have had the same analysis of sexual harassment whether or not they were looking to Playboy for funding. But I doubt that Playboy would have funded a conference to explore sexual harassment as integral to male supremacist *sexuality*.

Some might see feminists' material interest in pornography as similar to our material interest in the family or the workplace, like prostitutes' interest in pimps: we can't afford to destroy them, we need them, we are dependent on them, they help us get from one day to the next. But they also destroy us. Any system of power gives an interest in the status quo to those it keeps powerless. Our stake in *this* family structure, *this* workplace organization, *this* sexuality, *this* protection racket. This makes me wonder, if taking Playboy's money is okay, is anybody's money too damaging to take? How about directly from Hefner? What about Larry Flynt? Al Goldstein? La Cosa Nostra? If we refuse Playboy's money, is there anyone's money we will take? How about cosmetic companies? Is there a difference—say, the famous difference between cause and effect—between those who create the system and those who pander to it? Or is it just two ways of getting through another day?

I know it matters how much room we have, but how can a feminism worthy of the name live off something women are paying for?[25] If it is Playboy's money that is allowing us to survive, and *Playboy* is what I have said it is, is this survival killing us?

thirteen

Not a Moral Issue
(1983)

Pornosec, the subsection of the Fiction Department which turned out cheap
pornography for distribution among the proles . . . nicknamed Muck House
by the people who worked in it . . . produce[d] booklets in sealed packets
with titles like *Spanking Stories* or *One Night in a Girls' School*, to be bought
furtively by proletarian youths who were under the impression that they
were buying something illegal.

George Orwell, *Nineteen Eighty-four* (1949)

A critique of pornography[1] is to feminism what its defense is
to male supremacy. Central to the institutionalization of
male dominance, pornography cannot be reformed or suppressed or banned. It can only be changed. The legal doctrine of obscenity, the state's closest approximation to addressing the pornography question, has made the First Amendment[2] into a barrier to this
process. This is partly because the pornographers' lawyers have per-
suasively presented First Amendment absolutism,[3] their advocacy
position, as a legal fact, which it never has been. But they have gotten
away with this (to the extent they have) in part because the abstractness of obscenity as a concept, situated within an equally abstract
approach to freedom of speech embodied in First Amendment doctrine, has made the indistinguishability of the pornographers' speech
from everyone else's speech, their freedom from our freedom, appear
credible, appealing, necessary, inevitable, *principled*.[4] To expose the
absence of a critique of gender[5] in this area of law is to expose both
the enforced silence of women and the limits of liberalism.

This brief preliminary commentary focuses on the obscenity standard in order to explore some of the larger implications of a feminist
critique of pornography for First Amendment theory. This is the ar-

This speech was originally delivered to the Morality Colloquium, University of Minnesota, Feb. 23, 1983. These ideas were also discussed at the National Conference on
Women and the Law, Apr. 4, 1983, and at the Conference on Media Violence and Pornography, Ontario Institute for Studies in Education, Feb. 4, 1984. The title is a play
on "Not a Love Story," a 1983 anti-pornography film by the Canadian Film Board.

gument. Obscenity law is concerned with morality, specifically morals from the male point of view, meaning the standpoint of male dominance. The feminist critique of pornography is a politics, specifically politics from women's point of view, meaning the standpoint of the subordination of women to men.[6] Morality here means good and evil; politics means power and powerlessness. Obscenity is a moral idea; pornography is a political practice. Obscenity is abstract; pornography is concrete. The two concepts represent two entirely different things. Nudity, explicitness, excess of candor, arousal or excitement, prurience, unnaturalness—these qualities bother obscenity law when sex is depicted or portrayed. Abortion, birth control information, and treatments for "restoring sexual virility" (whose, do you suppose?) have also been included.[7] Sex forced on real women so that it can be sold at a profit to be forced on other real women; women's bodies trussed and maimed and raped and made into things to be hurt and obtained and accessed, and this presented as the nature of women; the coercion that is visible and the coercion that has become invisible—this and more bothers feminists about pornography. Obscenity as such probably does little harm;[8] pornography causes attitudes and behaviors of violence and discrimination that define the treatment and status of half of the population.[9] To make the legal and philosophical consequences of this distinction clear, I will describe the feminist critique of pornography, criticize the law of obscenity in terms of it, then discuss the criticism that pornography "dehumanizes" women to distinguish the male morality of liberalism and obscenity law from a feminist political critique of pornography.[10]

This inquiry is part of a larger project that attempts to account for gender inequality in the socially constructed relationship between power—the political—on the one hand and the knowledge of truth and reality—the epistemological—on the other.[11] For example, the candid description Justice Stewart once offered of his obscenity standard, "I know it when I see it,"[12] becomes even more revealing than it is usually understood to be if taken as a statement that connects epistemology with power. If I ask, from the point of view of women's experience, does he know what I know when I see what I see, I find that I doubt it, given what's on the newsstands. How does his point of view keep what is there, there? To liberal critics, his admission exposed the obscenity standard's relativity, its partiality, its insufficient abstractness. Not to be emptily universal, to leave your concreteness showing, is a sin among men. Their problem with Justice Stewart's formulation is that it implies that anything, capriciously, could be suppressed. They are only right by half. My problem is more the other half: the meaning of what his view permits, which, as it turns out, is anything but capricious. In fact, it is entirely systematic and determinate. To me, his statement is precisely descriptively accurate; its candor is why it has drawn so much criticism.[13] Justice Stewart got in so much trouble because he said out loud what is actually done all the time; in so doing, he both *did it* and gave it the stature of doctrine, even if only dictum. That is, the obscenity standard—in this it is not unique—*is* built on what the male standpoint sees. My point is: *so is pornography.* In this way the law of obscenity reproduces the pornographic point of view on women on the level of Constitutional jurisprudence.

• • •

Pornography, in the feminist view, is a form of forced sex, a practice of sexual politics, an institution of gender inequality. In this perspective, pornography is not harmless fantasy or a corrupt and confused misrepresentation of an otherwise natural and healthy sexuality. Along with the rape and prostitution in which it participates, pornography institutionalizes the sexuality of male supremacy, which fuses the erotization of dominance and submission with the social construction of male and female.[14] Gender is sexual. Pornography constitutes the meaning of that sexuality. Men treat women as who they see women as being. Pornography constructs who that is. Men's power over women means that the way men see women defines who women can be. Pornography is that way.

In pornography, women desire dispossession and cruelty. Men, permitted to put words (and other things) in women's mouths, create scenes in which women desperately want to be bound, battered, tortured, humiliated, and killed. Or merely taken and used. This is erotic to the male point of view. Subjection itself, with self-determination ecstatically relinquished, is the content of women's sexual desire and desirability. Women are there to be violated and possessed, men to violate and possess them, either on screen or by camera or pen, on behalf of the viewer.

One can be for or against this pornography without getting beyond liberalism. The critical yet formally liberal view of Susan Griffin, for example, conceptualizes eroticism as natural and healthy but corrupted and confused by "the pornographic mind."[15] Pornography distorts Eros, which preexists and persists, despite male culture's pornographic "revenge" upon it. Eros is, unaccountably, *still there.*

Pornography mis-takes it, mis-images it, mis-represents it. There is no critique of *reality* here, only objections to how it is seen; no critique of that reality that pornography imposes on women's real lives, those lives that are so seamlessly *consistent* with the pornography that pornography can be credibly defended by saying it is only a mirror of reality.

Contrast this view with the feminist analysis of Andrea Dworkin, in which sexuality itself is a social construct, gendered to the ground. Male dominance here is not an artificial overlay upon an underlying inalterable substratum of uncorrupted essential sexual being. Sexuality free of male dominance will require *change*, not reconceptualization, transcendence, or excavation. Pornography is not imagery in some relation to a reality elsewhere constructed. It is not a distortion, reflection, projection, expression, fantasy, representation, or symbol either. It is sexual reality. Dworkin's *Pornography: Men Possessing Women*[16] presents a sexual theory of gender inequality of which pornography is a core constitutive practice. The way pornography produces its meaning constructs and defines men and women as such. Gender is what gender means.[17] It has no basis in anything other than the social reality its hegemony constructs. The process that gives sexuality its male supremacist meaning is therefore the process through which gender inequality becomes socially real.

In this analysis the liberal defense of pornography as human sexual liberation, as derepression—whether by feminists, lawyers, or neo-Freudians[18]—is a defense not only of force and sexual terrorism, but of the subordination of women. Sexual liberation in the liberal sense frees male sexual aggression in the feminist sense. What looks like love and romance in the liberal view looks a lot like hatred and torture in the feminist view. Pleasure and eroticism become violation. Desire appears as lust for dominance and submission. The vulnerability of women's projected sexual availability—that acting we are allowed: asking to be acted upon—is victimization. Play conforms to scripted roles, fantasy expresses ideology—is not exempt from it—and admiration of natural physical beauty becomes objectification.

The experience of the (overwhelmingly) male audiences who consume pornography[19] is therefore not fantasy or simulation or catharsis[20] but sexual reality: the level of reality on which sex itself largely operates. To understand this, one does not have to notice that pornography models are real women to whom something real is being done,[21] nor does one have to inquire into the systematic infliction of pornographic sexuality upon women,[22] although it helps.

149

Pornography

The aesthetic of pornography itself, the *way* it provides what those who consume it want, is itself the evidence. When uncensored explicit—that is, the most pornographic—pornography tells all, all means what a distanced detached observer would report about who did what to whom. This is the turn-on. Why does observing sex objectively presented cause the male viewer to experience his own sexuality? Because his eroticism is, socially, a watched thing.

If objectivity is the epistemological stance of which objectification is the social process,[23] the way a perceptual posture is embodied as a social form of power, the most sexually potent depictions and descriptions *would* be the most objective blow-by-blow re-presentations. Pornography participates in its audience's eroticism because it creates an accessible sexual object, the possession and consumption of which *is* male sexuality, to be consumed and possessed as which *is* female sexuality. In this sense, sex in life is no less mediated than it is in art. Men *have sex* with their *image* of a woman. Escalating explicitness, "exceeding the bounds of candor,"[24] is the aesthetic of pornography not because the materials depict objectified sex but because they create the experience of a sexuality that is itself objectified. It is not that life and art imitate each other; in sexuality, they *are* each other.

•   •   •

The law of obscenity,[25] the state's primary approach[26] to its version of the pornography question, has literally nothing in common with this feminist critique. Their obscenity is not our pornography. One commentator has said, "Obscenity is not suppressed primarily for the protection of others. Much of it is suppressed for the purity of the 'community.' Obscenity, at bottom, is not a crime. Obscenity is a sin."[27] This is, on one level, literally accurate. Men are turned on by obscenity, including its suppression, the same way they are by sin. Animated by morality from the male standpoint, in which violation—of women and rules—is eroticized, obscenity law can be seen to proceed according to the interest of male power, robed in gender-neutral good and evil.

Morality in its specifically liberal form (although, as with most dimensions of male dominance, the distinction between left and right is more formal than substantive) revolves around a set of parallel distinctions that can be consistently traced through obscenity law. Even though the approach this law takes to the problem it envisions has shifted over time, its fundamental norms remain consistent: public is

150

opposed to private, in parallel with ethics and morality, and factual is opposed to valued determinations. Under male supremacy, these distinctions are gender-based: female is private, moral, valued, subjective; male is public, ethical, factual, objective.[28] If such gendered concepts are constructs of the male experience, imposed from the male standpoint on society as a whole, liberal morality expresses male supremacist politics. That is, discourse conducted in terms of good and evil that does not expose the gendered foundations of these concepts proceeds oblivious to—and serves to disguise—the position of power that underlies, and is furthered by, that discourse.

For example, obscenity law proposes to control what and how sex can be publicly shown. In practice, its standard centers upon the same features feminism identifies as key to male sexuality: the erect penis and penetration.[29] Historically, obscenity law was vexed by restricting such portrayals while protecting great literature. (Nobody considered protecting women.) Having solved this by exempting works of perceived value from obscenity restrictions,[30] the subsequent relaxation—some might say collapse—of obscenity restrictions in the last decade reveals a significant shift. The old private rules have become the new public rules. The old law governing pornography was that it would be publicly repudiated while being privately consumed and actualized: do anything to women with impunity in private behind a veil of public denial and civility. Now pornography is publicly celebrated.[31] This victory for Freudian derepression theory probably did not alter the actual treatment of women all that much. Women were sex and still are sex. Greater efforts of brutality have become necessary to eroticize the tabooed—each taboo being a hierarchy in disguise—since the frontier of the tabooed keeps vanishing as one crosses it. Put another way, more and more violence has become necessary to keep the progressively desensitized consumer aroused to the illusion that sex is (and he is) daring and dangerous. Making sex with the powerless "not allowed" is a way of defining "getting it" as an act of power, an assertion of hierarchy. In addition, pornography has become ubiquitous. Sexual terrorism has become democratized. Crucially, pornography has become truly available to women for the first time in history. Show me an atrocity to women, I'll show it to you eroticized in the pornography. This central mechanism of sexual subordination, this means of systematizing the definition of women as a sexual class, has now become available to its victims for scrutiny and analysis as an open public system, not just as a private secret abuse.[32] Hopefully, this was a mistake.

Pornography

Reexamining the law of obscenity in light of the feminist critique of pornography that has become possible, it becomes clear that male morality sees as good that which maintains its power and sees as evil that which undermines or qualifies it or questions its absoluteness. Differences in the law over time—such as the liberalization of obscenity doctrine—reflect either changes in the group of men in power or shifts in their perceptions of the best strategy for maintaining male supremacy—probably some of both. But it must be made to work. The outcome, descriptively analyzed, is that obscenity law prohibits what it sees as immoral, which from a feminist standpoint tends to be relatively harmless, while protecting what it sees as moral, which from a feminist standpoint is often that which is damaging to women. So it, too, is a politics, only covertly so. What male morality finds evil, meaning threatening to its power, feminist politics tends to find comparatively harmless. What feminist politics identifies as central in our subordination—the erotization of dominance and submission—male morality tends to find comparatively harmless or defends as affirmatively valuable, hence protected speech.

In 1973 obscenity under law came to mean that which "'the average person applying contemporary community standards' would find that, . . . taken as a whole, appeals to the prurient interest . . . [which] depicts or describes, in a patently offensive way, sexual conduct specifically defined by the applicable state law; and [which], taken as a whole, lacks serious literary, artistic, political, or scientific value."[33] Feminism doubts whether the average person, gender neutral, exists; has more questions about the content and process of definition of community standards than about deviations from them; wonders why prurience counts but powerlessness doesn't; why sensibilities are better protected from offense than women are from exploitation; defines sexuality, hence its violation and expropriation, more broadly than does any state law and wonders why a body of law that can't in practice tell rape from intercourse should be entrusted with telling pornography from anything less. The law of obscenity says that intercourse on street corners is not legitimized by the fact that the persons are "simultaneously engaged in a valid political dialogue."[34] But, in a feminist light, one sees that the requirement that a work be considered "as a whole" legitimizes something very like that on the level of publications like *Playboy*.[35] Experimental evidence is beginning to support what victims have long known: legitimate settings diminish the injury perceived as done to the women whose trivialization and objectification it contextualizes.[36] Besides, if

152

a woman is subjected, why should it matter that the work has other value?[37] Perhaps what redeems a work's value among men *enhances* its injury to women. Existing standards of literature, art, science, and politics are, in feminist light, remarkably consonant with pornography's mode, meaning, and message. Finally and foremost, a feminist approach reveals that although the content and dynamic of pornography are about women—about the sexuality of women, about women as sexuality—in the same way that the vast majority of "obscenities" refer specifically to women's bodies, our invisibility has been such that the law of obscenity has *never even considered pornography a women's issue.*[38]

To appeal to "prurient interest"[39] means, I believe, to give a man an erection. Men are scared to make it possible for some men to tell other men what they can and cannot have sexual access to because men have power. If you don't let them have theirs, they might not let you have yours. This is why the *indefinability* of pornography, all the "one man's this is another man's that,"[40] is so central to pornography's *definition*. It is not because they are such great liberals, but because some men might be able to do to them whatever they can do to those other men, and this is more why the liberal principle is what it is. Because the fought-over are invisible in this, it obscures the fact that the fight over a definition of obscenity is a fight among men over the best means to guarantee male power as a system. The question is, whose sexual practices threaten this system that can afford to be sacrificed to its maintenance for the rest? Public sexual access by men to anything other than women is less likely to be protected speech. This is not to say that male sexual access to anything—children, other men, women with women, objects, animals—is not the real system. The issue is *how public* that system will be; the obscenity laws, their definition and patterns of enforcement, have a major role in regulating that. The bind of the "prurient interest" standard here is that, to find it as a fact, someone has to admit that they are sexually aroused by the materials,[41] but male sexual arousal signals the importance of protecting them. They put themselves in this bind and then wonder why they cannot agree. Sometimes I think that what is ultimately found obscene is what does *not* turn on the Supreme Court, or what revolts them more, which is rare, since revulsion is eroticized; sometimes I think that what is obscene is what turns on those men the men in power think they can afford to ignore; sometimes I think that part of it is that what looks obscene to them is what makes them see themselves as potential targets of male sexual aggression, even if only momentarily; sometimes I think that the real issue is how male sexuality is presented, so that anything can be done to a woman, but obscenity is sex that makes male sexuality look bad.[42]

The difficulties courts have in framing workable standards to separate "prurient" from other sexual interest, commercial exploitation from art or advertising, sexual speech from sexual conduct, and obscenity from great literature make the feminist point. These lines have proven elusive in law because they do not exist in life. Commercial sex resembles art because both exploit women's sexuality. The liberal's slippery slope is the feminist totality. Whatever obscenity may do, pornography converges with more conventionally acceptable depictions and descriptions just as rape converges with intercourse because both express the same power relation. Just as it is difficult to distinguish literature or art against a background, a standard, of objectification, it is difficult to discern sexual freedom against a background, a standard, of sexual coercion. This does not mean it cannot be done. It means that legal standards will be practically unenforceable, will reproduce this problem rather than solve it, until they address its fundamental issue—gender inequality—directly.

To define the pornographic as the "patently offensive" further misconstrues its harm. Pornography is not bad manners or poor choice of audience; obscenity is. Pornography is also not an idea; obscenity is. The legal fiction whereby the obscene is "not speech"[43] has deceived few; it *has* effectively avoided the need to adjudicate pornography's social etiology. But obscenity law got one thing right: pornography is more actlike than thoughtlike. The fact that pornography, in a feminist view, furthers the idea of the sexual inferiority of women, a political idea, does not make the pornography itself a political idea. That one can express the idea a practice embodies does not make that practice into an idea. Pornography is not an idea any more than segregation is an idea, although both institutionalize the idea of the inferiority of one group to another. The law considers obscenity deviant, antisocial. If it causes harm, it causes antisocial acts, acts against the social order.[44] In a feminist perspective, pornography is the essence of a sexist social order, its quintessential social act.

If pornography is an act of male supremacy, its harm is the harm of male supremacy made difficult to see because of its pervasiveness, potency, and success in making the world a pornographic place. Specifically, the harm cannot be discerned from the objective standpoint because it *is* so much of "what is." Women live in the world pornography creates. We live its lie as reality. As Naomi Scheman has said,

154

"Lies are what we have lived, not just what we have told, and no story about correspondence to what is real will enable us to distinguish the truth from the lie."[45] So the issue is not whether pornography is harmful, but how the harm of pornography is to become visible. As compared with what? To the extent pornography succeeds in constructing social reality, it becomes *invisible as harm*. Any perception of the success, therefore the harm, of pornography, I will argue, is precluded by liberalism and so has been defined out of the customary approach taken to, and dominant values underlying, the First Amendment.

The theory of the First Amendment under which most pornography is protected from governmental restriction proceeds from liberal assumptions[46] that do not apply to the situation of women. First Amendment theory, like virtually all liberal legal theory, presumes the validity of the distinction between public and private: the "role of law [is] to mark and guard the line between the sphere of social power, organized in the form of the state, and the area of private right."[47] On this basis, courts distinguish between obscenity in public (which can be regulated, even if some attempts founder, seemingly in part *because* the presentations are public)[48] and the private possession of obscenity in the home.[49] The problem is that not only the public but also the private *is* a "sphere of social power" of sexism. On paper and in life pornography is thrust upon unwilling women in their homes.[50] The distinction between public and private does not cut the same for women as for men.[51] It is men's right to inflict pornography upon women in private that is protected.

The liberal theory underlying First Amendment law further believes that free speech, including pornography, helps discover truth. Censorship restricts society to partial truths. So why are we now—with more pornography available than ever before—buried in all these lies? Laissez faire might be an adequate theory of the social preconditions for knowledge in a nonhierarchical society. But in a society of gender inequality, the speech of the powerful impresses its view upon the world, concealing the truth of powerlessness under that despairing acquiescence that provides the appearance of consent and makes protest inaudible as well as rare. Pornography can invent women because it has the power to make its vision into reality, which then passes, objectively, for truth. So while the First Amendment supports pornography, believing that consensus and progress are facilitated by allowing all views, however divergent and unorthodox, it fails to notice that pornography (like the racism, in which I include

155

anti-Semitism, of the Nazis and the Klan) is not at all divergent or unorthodox. It is the ruling ideology. Feminism, the dissenting view, is suppressed by pornography. Thus, while defenders of pornography argue that allowing all speech, including pornography, frees the mind to fulfill itself, pornography freely enslaves women's minds and bodies inseparably, normalizing the terror that enforces silence from women's point of view.

To liberals, speech must never be sacrificed for other social goals.[52] But liberalism has never understood that the free speech of men silences the free speech of women. It is the same social goal, just other *people*. This is what a real inequality, a real conflict, a real disparity in social power looks like. The law of the First Amendment comprehends that freedom of expression, in the abstract, is a system, but it fails to comprehend that sexism (and racism), *in the concrete*, are also systems. That pornography chills women's expression is difficult to demonstrate empirically because silence is not eloquent. Yet on no more of the same kind of evidence, the argument that suppressing pornography might chill legitimate speech has supported its protection.

First Amendment logic, like nearly all legal reasoning, has difficulty grasping harm that is not linearly caused in the "John hit Mary" sense. The idea is that words or pictures can be harmful only if they produce harm in a form that is considered an action. Words work in the province of attitudes, actions in the realm of behavior. Words cannot constitute harm in themselves—never mind libel, invasion of privacy, blackmail, bribery, conspiracy or most sexual harassment. But which is saying "kill" to a trained guard dog, a word or an act? Which is its training? How about a sign that reads "Whites only"? Is that the idea or the practice of segregation? Is a woman raped by an attitude or a behavior? Which is sexual arousal? Notice that the specific idea of causality used in obscenity law dates from around the time that it was first "proved" that it is impossible to prove that pornography causes harm.[53] Instead of the more complex causality implicit in the above examples, the view became that pornography must cause harm the way negligence causes car accidents or its effects are not cognizable as harm. The trouble with this individuated, atomistic, linear, isolated, tortlike—in a word, positivistic—conception of injury is that the way pornography targets and defines women for abuse and discrimination does not work like this. It does hurt individuals, not *as* individuals in a one-at-a-time sense, but as members of the group "women." Harm is caused to one individual woman rather than another essentially the way one number rather than another is caused in roulette. But on a group basis, as women, the selection process is absolutely selective and systematic. Its causality is essentially collective and totalistic and contextual. To reassert atomistic linear causality as a sine qua non of injury—you cannot be harmed unless you are harmed through this etiology—is to refuse to respond to the true nature of this specific kind of harm. Such a refusal calls for explanation. Morton Horowitz says that the issue of causality in tort law is "one of the pivotal ideas in a system of legal thought that sought to separate private law from politics and to insulate the legal system from the threat of redistribution."[54] Perhaps causality in the pornography issue is an attempt to privatize the injury pornography does to women in order to insulate the same system from the threat of gender equality, also a form of redistribution.

Women are known to be brutally coerced into pornographic performances.[55] But so far it is only with children, usually male children, that courts consider that the speech of pornographers was once someone else's *life*.[56] Courts and commissions and legislatures and researchers have searched and re-searched, largely in vain, for the injury of pornography in the mind of the (male) consumer or in "society," or in empirical correlations between variations in levels of "antisocial" acts and liberalization in obscenity laws.[57] Speech can be regulated "in the interests of unwilling viewers, captive audiences, young children, and beleaguered neighborhoods,"[58] but the normal level of sexual force—force that is not seen as force because it is inflicted on women and called sex—has never been a policy issue. Until the last few years experimental research never approached the question of whether pornographic stimuli might support *sexual* aggression against women[59] or whether violence might be sexually stimulating or have sexual sequelae.[60] Only in the last few months have laboratory researchers begun to learn the consequences for women of so-called consensual sexual depictions that show normal dominance and submission.[61] We still don't have this kind of data on the impact of female-only nudity or of depictions of specific acts like penetration or even of mutual sex in a social context of gender inequality.

The most basic assumption underlying First Amendment adjudication is that, socially, speech is free. The First Amendment says, "Congress shall not abridge *the freedom of speech*." Free speech exists. The problem for government is to avoid constraining that which, if unconstrained by government, *is* free. This tends to presuppose that whole segments of the population are not systematically silenced so-

cially, prior to government action. The place of pornography in the inequality of the sexes makes such a presupposition untenable and makes any approach to *our* freedom of expression so based worse than useless. For women, the urgent issue of freedom of speech is not primarily the avoidance of state intervention as such, but finding an affirmative means to get access to speech for those to whom it has been denied.

•   •   •

Beyond offensiveness or prurience, to say that pornography is "dehumanizing" is an attempt to articulate its harm. But "human being" is a social concept with many possible meanings. Here I will criticize some liberal moral meanings of personhood through a feminist political analysis of what pornography does to women, showing how the inadequacy of the liberal dehumanization critique reflects the inadequacy of its concept of person. In a feminist perspective, pornography dehumanizes women in a culturally specific and empirically descriptive—not liberal moral—sense. Pornography dispossesses women of the power of which, in the same act, it possesses men: the power of sexual, hence gender, definition. Perhaps a human being, for gender purposes, is someone who controls the social definition of sexuality.

A person, in one Kantian view, is a free and rational agent whose existence is an end in itself, as opposed to instrumental.[62] In pornography women exist to the *end* of male pleasure. Kant sees human as characterized by universal abstract rationality, with no component of individual or group differences, and as a "bundle of rights."[63] Pornography purports to define what a woman *is.* It does this on a group basis, including when it raises individual qualities to sexual stereotypes, as in the strategy of *Playboy's* "Playmate of the Month." I also think that pornography derives much of its sexual power, as well as part of its justification, from the implicit assumption that the Kantian notion of person actually describes the condition of women in this society. According to that assumption, if we are there, we are freely and rationally there, when the fact is that women—in pornography and in part because of pornography—have no such rights.

Other views of the person include one of Wittgenstein's, who says that the best picture of the human soul is the human body.[64] I guess this depends upon what picture of the human body you have in mind. Marx's work offers various concepts of personhood deducible from his critique of various forms of productive organization. A person is defined by whatever material conditions the society values; in a bourgeois society, a person might be a property owner.[65] The problem here is that women *are* the property that constitutes the personhood, the masculinity, of men under capitalism. Thinking further in marxian theoretical terms, I have wondered whether women in pornography are more properly conceived as fetishes or objects. Does pornography more attribute lifelikeness to that which is dead—as in fetishism—or make deathlike that which is alive—as in objectification? I guess it depends upon whether, socially speaking, women are more alive than dead.

In Hume's concept of a person as a bundle or collection of sense perceptions, such that the feeling of self-identity over time is a persistent illusion,[66] we finally have a view of the human that coincides with the view of women in pornography. That is, the empiricist view of person is the pornographic view of women. No critique of dominance or subjection, certainly not of objectification, can be grounded in a vision of reality in which all sense perceptions are just sense perceptions. This is one way an objectivist epistemology supports the unequal holding and wielding of power in a society in which the persistent illusion of selfhood of one half of the population is materially supported and maintained at the expense of the other half. What I'm saying is that those who are socially allowed a self are also allowed the luxury of postulating its illusoriness and having that called a philosophical position. Whatever self they ineluctably have, they don't lose by saying it is an illusion. Even if it is not particularly explanatory, such male ideology, if taken as such, is often highly descriptive. Thus Hume defines the human in the same terms feminism uses to define women's dehumanization: for women in pornography, the self is, precisely, a persistent illusion.

Contemporary ordinary language philosopher Bernard Williams says "person" ordinarily means things like valuing self-respect and feeling pain.[67] How self is defined, what respect attaches to, stimuli of pleasure and to an extent stimuli and thresholds of pain, are cultural variables. Women in pornography are turned on by being put down and feel pain as pleasure. We want it; we beg for it; we get it. To argue that this is dehumanizing need not mean to take respect as an ahistorical absolute or to treat the social meaning of pain as invariant or uniformly negative. Rather, it is to argue that it is the acceptance of the social definition of these values—the acceptance of self-respect and the avoidance of pain as values—that permits the erotization of their negative—debasement and torture—in pornography. It is only to the extent that each of these values is *accepted as human* that their negation becomes a quality of, and is eroticized in and as, woman. Only when self-respect is accepted as human does debasement become sexy and female; only when the avoidance of pain is accepted as human does torture become sexy and female. In this way, women's sexuality as expressed in pornography precisely negates her status as human. But there is more: exactly what is defined as degrading to a human being, *however* that is socially defined, is exactly what is sexually arousing to the male point of view in pornography, just as the one to whom it is done is the girl regardless of sex. In this way, it is specifically women whom pornography identifies with and by sexuality, as the erotic is equated with the dehumanizing.

To define the pornographic as that which is violent, not sexual, as liberal moral analyses tend to, is to trivialize and evade the essence of this critique, while seeming to express it. As with rape, where the issue is not the presence or absence of force but what sex *is* as distinct from coercion,[68] the question for pornography is what eroticism *is* as distinct from the subordination of women. This is not a rhetorical question. Under male dominance, whatever sexually arouses a man is sex. In pornography the violence *is* the sex. The inequality is the sex. Pornography does not work sexually without hierarchy. If there is no inequality, no violation, no dominance, no force, there is no sexual arousal.[69] Obscenity law does the pornographers a real favor by clouding this, pornography's central dynamic, under the coy gender-neutral abstraction of "prurient interest." Obscenity law also adds the attraction of state prohibition, a tool of dominance, to whatever the law of obscenity is seen to encompass.

Calling rape and pornography violent, not sexual, the banner of much antirape and antipornography organizing,[70] is an attempt to protest that women do not find rape pleasurable or pornography stimulating while avoiding claiming this rejection as *women's* point of view. The concession to the objective stance, the attempt to achieve credibility by covering up the specificity of one's viewpoint, not only abstracts from our experience, it lies about it. Women and men know men find rape sexual and pornography erotic. It therefore *is*. We also know that sexuality is commonly violent without being any the less sexual. To deny this sets up the situation so that when women are aroused by sexual violation, meaning we experience it *as* our sexuality, the feminist analysis is seen to be contradicted. But it is not contradicted, it is *proved*. The male supremacist definition of female sexuality as lust for self-annihilation has won. It would be surprising, feminist analysis would be wrong, and sexism would be trivial, if this were merely exceptional. (One might ask at this point, not why some women embrace explicit sadomasochism, but why any women do not.) To reject forced sex in the name of women's point of view requires an account of women's experience of being violated by the same acts both sexes have learned as natural and fulfilling and erotic, since no critique, no alternatives, and few transgressions have been permitted.

The depersonalization critique, with the "violence not sex" critique, exposes pornography's double standard but does not attack the masculinity of the standards for personhood and for sex that pornography sets. The critiques are thus useful, to some extent deconstructive, but beg the deeper questions of the place of pornography in sexuality and of sexuality in the construction of women's definition and status, because they act as if women can be "persons" by interpretation, as if the concept is not, in every socially real way, defined by and in terms of and reserved for men and as if sexuality is not itself a construct of male power. To do this is to act as if pornography did not exist or were impotent. Deeper than the personhood question or the violence question is the question of the mechanism of social causation by which pornography *constructs* women and sex, defines what "woman" means and what sexuality is, in terms of each other.

The law of obscenity at times says that sexual expression is only talk, therefore cannot be intrinsically harmful. Yet somehow pornographic talk is vital to protect. If pornography is a practice of the ideology[71] of gender inequality, and gender *is an ideology,* if pornography is sex and gender is sexual, the question of the relation between pornography and life is nothing less than the question of the dynamic of the subordination of women to men. If "objectification . . . is never trivial,"[72] girls *are* ruined by books.[73] To comprehend this process will require an entirely new theory of social causality—of ideology in life, of the dynamic of mind and body in social power—that connects point of view with politics. The development of such an analysis has been stymied equally by fear of repressive state use of any critique of any form of expression, by the power of pornography to create women in its image of use, and by the power of pornographers to create a climate hostile to inquiry into their power and profits.

·   ·   ·

I said all that in order to say this: the law of obscenity has the same surface theme and the same underlying theme as pornography itself. Superficially both involve morality: rules made and transgressed for purposes of sexual arousal. Actually, both are about power, about the equation between the erotic and the control of women by men: *women* made and transgressed for purposes of sexual arousal. It seems essential to the kick of pornography that it be to some degree against the rules, but it is never truly unavailable or truly illegitimate. Thus obscenity law, like the law of rape, preserves the value of, without restricting the ability to get, that which it purports to both devalue and to prohibit. Obscenity law helps keep pornography sexy by putting state power—force, hierarchy—behind its purported prohibition on what men can have sexual access to. The law of obscenity is to pornography as pornography is to sex: a map that purports to be a mirror, a legitimization and authorization and set of directions and guiding controls that project themselves onto social reality while claiming merely to reflect the image of what is already there. Pornography presents itself as fantasy or illusion or idea, which can be good or bad as it is accurate or inaccurate, while it actually, *hence accurately,* distributes power. Liberal morality cannot deal with illusions that *constitute* reality because its theory of reality, lacking a substantive critique of the distribution of social power, cannot get behind the empirical world, truth by correspondence. On the surface, both pornography and the law of obscenity are about sex. In fact, it is the status of women that is at stake.

fourteen

Francis Biddle's Sister: Pornography, Civil Rights, and Speech (1984)

I thank the committee that selected me for this lectureship, the Harvard faculty, Dean Vorenburg, and the Biddles for this thrill, this honor, and this forum. I am also existentially amazed to be here.

Topically, in order, I will first situate a critique of pornography within a feminist analysis of the condition of women. I will speak of what pornography means for the social status and treatment of women. I will briefly contrast that with the obscenity approach, the closest this government has come to addressing pornography. Next I will outline an argument for the constitutionality of the ordinance Andrea Dworkin and I conceived, in which we define pornography as a civil rights violation.[1] Here I will address what pornography *does* as a practice of sex discrimination, and the vision of the First Amendment with which our law is consistent. Evidence, much of it drawn from hearings on the ordinance in Minneapolis,[2] supports this argument. The Supreme Court has never considered this legal injury before, nor the factual support we bring to it. They have allowed the recognition of similar injuries to other people, consistent with their interpretation of the First Amendment. More drastic steps have been taken on a showing of a great deal less harm, and the courts have allowed it. The question is: Will they do it for women?

To get ahead of my story intellectually, this is the horizontal structure of this talk, the threads I will pull through it, the themes that underlie it. I don't expect you to be persuaded by these arguments now, but I am going to tell you what they are. My formal agenda has three parts. The first treats pornography by connecting epistemology—which I understand to be about theories of knowing—with politics—which I will take to be about theories of power.[3] For instance, Justice Stewart said of obscenity, "I know it when I see it."[4] I see this

---

The 1984 Francis Biddle Memorial Lecture, Harvard Law School, Cambridge, Massachusetts, Apr. 5, 1984. Some themes from "Not a Moral Issue" are expanded here.

as a statement connecting epistemology—what he knows through his way of knowing, in this case, seeing—with the fact that his seeing determines what obscenity *is* in terms of what he sees it to be, because of his position of power. To wonder if he and I know the same things from what we see, given what's on the newsstand, is not a personal query about him.

Another example of the same conceptual connection is this. Having power means, among other things, that when someone says, "This is how it is," it is taken as being that way. When this happens in law, such a person is accorded what is called credibility. When that person is believed over another speaker, what was said becomes proof. Speaking socially, the beliefs of the powerful become proof, in part because the world actually arranges itself to affirm what the powerful want to see. If you perceive this as a process, you might call it force, or at least pressure or socialization or what money can buy. If it is imperceptible as a process, you may consider it voluntary or consensual or free will or human nature, or just the way things are. Beneath this, though, the world is not entirely the way the powerful say it is or want to believe it is. If it appears to be, it is because power constructs the appearance of reality by silencing the voices of the powerless, by excluding them from access to authoritative discourse. Powerlessness means that when you say "This is how it is," it is *not* taken as being that way. This makes articulating silence, perceiving the presence of absence, believing those who have been socially stripped of credibility, critically contextualizing what passes for simple fact, necessary to the epistemology of a politics of the powerless.

My second thematic concern is jurisprudential. It is directed toward identifying, in order to change, one dimension of liberalism as it is embodied in law: the definition of justice as neutrality between abstract categories. The liberal view is that abstract categories—like speech or equality—define systems. Every time you strengthen free speech in one place, you strengthen it everywhere. Strengthening the free speech of the Klan strengthens the free speech of Blacks.[5] Getting things for men strengthens equality for women. Getting men access to women's schools strengthens women's access to education. What I will be exploring is the way in which substantive systems, made up of real people with social labels attached, are *also systems*. You can reverse racism abstractly, but white supremacy is unfudgeably substantive. Sexism can be an equal abstraction, but male supremacy says who is where. Substantive systems like white supremacy do substantively different things to people of color than they do to white people. To say they are *also systems* is to say that every time you score one for white supremacy in one place, it is strengthened every place else.

In this view, the problem with neutrality as the definition of principle in constitutional adjudication[6] is that it equates substantive powerlessness with substantive power and calls treating these the same, "equality." The neutrality approach understands that abstract systems are systems, but it seems not to understand that substantive systems are also systems. This criticism frames a problem that is the same for equal protection law under the sex-blind/color-blind rubric[7] as it is for the First Amendment under the absolutist rubric—the systematic defense of those who own the speech because they can buy it or have speech to lose because they have the power to articulate in a way that counts.[8] Although absolutism has never been the law of the First Amendment, it has left its impression upon it. Its contributions include helping to make the marketplace of ideas, the original metaphor for how the First Amendment was supposed to work,[9] rather more literal than figurative.

If this argument is right, it makes sense that Professor Wechsler's seminal exposition of the neutral principles approach[10] would be couched as an abstract defense of *Plessy v. Ferguson*[11]—in which separate but equal in the racial context was found equal—and an abstract attack on *Brown v. Board of Education,*[12] which recognized the inequality in racial separation in a racially hierarchical society. *Plessy* was neutral toward racism; *Brown* recognized its substantivity, therefore its inequality. Similarly, noticing the substantive context within which many of the big systemic constitutional debates have been carried out reveals that much of the legal tradition on the evils of substantivity as such—*Lochner* and so on[13]—revolves around cases that substantively concern the treatment of women. Yet nobody talks about these as cases about women. Women are substantively absent.[14] Just as the struggle of Blacks for an education was a vehicle for Wechsler's exposition of the virtues of neutrality, women's lives provide the occasion for confronting the issues the legal system regards as the real issues, the abstract issues, to which the treatment of women is as invisible in law—just as essential and just as marginalized—as women's substantive framing of social existence is invisible in life.

The *Lochner* line of cases created concern about the evils of their substance, which, as women were erased, came to stand for the evils of substantivity *as such*. There has been correspondingly little discus-

165

sion, with the partial exception of the debate on affirmative action,[15] on the drawbacks of abstraction as such. Granted, trying to do anything on a substantive basis is a real problem in a legal system that immediately turns everything into an abstraction. I do hope to identify this as something of a syndrome, as a risk of abuse. Considering it the definition of principle itself ensures that nothing will ever basically change, at least not by law.

When these two frames converge—epistemology and politics on the one hand with the critique of neutrality on the other—they form a third frame: one of political philosophy. Here is how they converge. Once power constructs social reality, as I will show pornography constructs the social reality of gender, the force behind sexism, the subordination in gender inequality, is made invisible; dissent from it becomes inaudible as well as rare. What a woman is, is defined in pornographic terms; this is what pornography *does*. If the law then looks neutrally on the reality of gender so produced, the harm that has been done *will not be perceptible as harm*. It becomes just the way things are. Refusing to look at what has been done substantively institutionalizes inequality in law and makes it look just like principle.

In the philosophical terms of classical liberalism, an equality–freedom dilemma is produced: freedom to make or consume pornography weighs against the equality of the sexes. Some people's freedom hurts other people's equality. There is something to this, but my formulation, as you might guess, comes out a little differently. If one asks whose freedom pornography represents, a tension emerges that is not a dilemma among abstractions so much as it is a conflict between groups. Substantive interests are at stake on *both* sides of the abstract issues, and women are allowed to matter in neither. If women's freedom is as incompatible with pornography's construction of our freedom as our equality is incompatible with pornography's construction of our equality, we get neither freedom nor equality under the liberal calculus. Equality for women is incompatible with a definition of men's freedom that is at our expense. What can freedom for women mean, so long as we remain unequal? Why should men's freedom to use us in this way be purchased with our second-class civil status?

·　　　　　　　　·　　　　　　　　·

Substantively considered, the situation of women is *not really like anything else*. Its specificity is not just the result of our numbers—we are half the human race—and our diversity, which at times has obscured that we are a group with an interest at all. It is, in part, that our status as a group relative to men has almost never, if ever, been much changed from what it is. Women's roles do vary enough that gender, the social form sex takes, cannot be said to be biologically determined. Different things are valued in different cultures, but whatever is valued, women are not that. If bottom is bottom, look across time and space, and women are who you will find there. Together with this, you will find, in as varied forms as there are cultures, the belief that women's social inferiority to men is not that at all but is merely the sex difference.

Doing something legal about a situation that is not really like anything else is hard enough in a legal system that prides itself methodologically on reasoning by analogy.[16] Add to this the specific exclusion or absence of women and women's concerns from the definition and design of this legal system since its founding, combined with its determined adherence to precedent, and you have a problem of systemic dimension. The best attempt at grasping women's situation in order to change it by law has centered on an analogy between sex and race in the discrimination context. This gets a lot, since inequalities are alike on some levels, but it also misses a lot. It gets the stigmatization and exploitation and denigration of a group of people on the basis of a condition of birth. It gets that difference, made an issue of, is an excuse for dominance, and that if forced separation is allowed to mean equality in a society where the line of separation also divides top from bottom in a hierarchy, the harm of that separation is thereby made invisible. It also gets that defining neutrality as principle, when reality is not neutral, prevents change in the guise of promoting it. But segregation is not the central practice of the inequality of the sexes. Women are as often forcibly integrated with men, if not on an equal basis. And it did help the struggle against white supremacy that Blacks had not always been in bondage to white people.

Most important, I think it never was a central part of the ideology of racism that the system of chattel slavery of Africans really was designed for their enjoyment and benefit. The system *was* defended as an expression of their true nature and worth. They *were* told to be grateful for good treatment and kind masters. Their successful struggle to organize resistance and avoid complicity while still surviving is instructive to all of us. But although racism *has* been defended by institutionalizing it in law, and then calling that legal; although it *has* been cherished not just as a system of exploitation of labor but as a way of life; and although it *is* based on force, changes in its practices are opposed by implying that they are really only a matter of choice of personal values. For instance: "You can't legislate morality."[17] And slave owners *did* say they couldn't be racist—they loved their slaves. Nonetheless, few people pretended that the entire system existed *because* of its basis in love and mutual respect and veneration, that white supremacy really treated Blacks in many cases *better* than whites, and that the primary intent and effect of their special status was and is their protection, pleasure, fulfillment, and liberation. Crucially, many have believed, and some actually still do, that Black people were not the equals of whites. But at least since *Brown v. Board of Education*,[18] few have pretended, much less authoritatively, that the social system, as it was, *was equality for them.*

There is a belief that this is a society in which women and men are basically equals. Room for marginal corrections is conceded, flaws are known to exist, attempts are made to correct what are conceived as occasional lapses from the basic condition of sex equality. Sex discrimination law has concentrated most of its focus on these occasional lapses.[19] It is difficult to overestimate the extent to which this belief in equality is an article of faith for most people, including most women, who wish to live in self-respect in an internal universe, even (perhaps especially) if not in the world. It is also partly an expression of natural law thinking: if we are inalienably equal, we can't "really" be degraded.

This is a world in which it is worth trying. In this world of presumptive equality, people make money based on their training or abilities or diligence or qualifications. They are employed and advanced on the basis of merit. In this world of just deserts, if someone is abused, it is thought to violate the basic rules of the community. If it doesn't, victims are seen to have done something they could have chosen to do differently, by exercise of will or better judgment. Maybe such people have placed themselves in a situation of vulnerability to physical abuse. Maybe they have done something provocative. Or maybe they were just unusually unlucky. In such a world, if such a person has an experience, there are words for it. When they speak and say it, they are listened to. If they write about it, they will be published. If certain experiences are never spoken about, if certain people or issues are seldom heard from, it is supposed that silence has been chosen. The law, including much of the law of sex discrimination and the First Amendment, operates largely within the realm of these beliefs.

Feminism is the discovery that women do not live in this world, that the person occupying this realm is a man, so much more a man if he is white and wealthy. This world of potential credibility, authority, security, and just rewards, recognition of one's identity and capacity, is a world that some people do inhabit as a condition of birth, with variations among them. It is not a basic condition accorded humanity in this society, but a prerogative of status, a privilege, among other things, of gender.

I call this a discovery because it has not been an assumption. Feminism is the first theory, the first practice, the first movement, to take seriously the situation of all women from the point of view of all women, both on our situation and on social life as a whole. The discovery has therefore been made that the implicit social content of humanism, as well as the standpoint from which legal method has been designed and injuries have been defined, has not been women's standpoint. Defining feminism in a way that connects epistemology with power as the politics of women's point of view, this discovery can be summed up by saying that women live in another world: specifically, a world of *not* equality, a world of inequality.

Looking at the world from this point of view, a whole shadow world of previously invisible silent abuse has been discerned. Rape, battery, sexual harassment, forced prostitution, and the sexual abuse of children emerge as common and systematic.[20] We find that rape happens to women in all contexts, from the family, including rape of girls and babies, to students and women in the workplace, on the streets, at home, in their own bedrooms by men they do not know and by men they do know, by men they are married to, men they have had a social conversation with, and, least often, men they have never seen before.[21] Overwhelmingly, rape is something that men do or attempt to do to women (44 percent of American women according to a recent study)[22] at some point in our lives. Sexual harassment of women by men is common in workplaces and educational institutions.[23] Based on reports in one study of the federal workforce, up to 85 percent of women will experience it, many in physical forms.[24] Between a quarter and a third of women are battered in their homes by men.[25] Thirty-eight percent of little girls are sexually molested inside or outside the family.[26] Until women listened to women, this world of sexual abuse was *not spoken* of. It was the unspeakable. What I am saying is, if you *are* the tree falling in the epistemological forest, your demise doesn't make a sound if no one is listening. Women did not "report" these events, and overwhelmingly do not today, because

169

no one is listening, because no one believes us. This silence does not mean nothing happened, and it does not mean consent. It is the silence of women of which Adrienne Rich has written, "Do not confuse it with any kind of absence."[27]

Believing women who say we are sexually violated has been a radical departure, both methodologically and legally. The extent and nature of rape, marital rape, and sexual harassment itself, were discovered in this way. Domestic battery as a syndrome, almost a habit, was discovered through refusing to believe that when a woman is assaulted by a man to whom she is connected, that it is not an assault. The sexual abuse of children was uncovered, Freud notwithstanding, by believing that children were not making up all this sexual abuse.[28] Now what is striking is that when each discovery is made, and somehow made real in the world, the response has been: it happens to men too. If women are hurt, men are hurt. If women are raped, men are raped. If women are sexually harassed, men are sexually harassed. If women are battered, men are battered. Symmetry must be reasserted. Neutrality must be reclaimed. Equality must be re-established.

The only areas where the available evidence supports this, where anything like what happens to women also happens to men, involve children—little boys are sexually abused—and prison.[29] The liberty of prisoners is restricted, their freedom restrained, their humanity systematically diminished, their bodies and emotions confined, defined, and regulated. If paid at all, they are paid starvation wages. They can be tortured at will, and it is passed off as discipline or as means to a just end. They become compliant. They can be raped at will, at any moment, and nothing will be done about it. When they scream, nobody hears. To be a prisoner means to be defined as a member of a group for whom the rules of what can be done to you, of what is seen as abuse of you, are reduced as part of the definition of your status. To be a woman is that kind of definition and has that kind of meaning.

Men *are* damaged by sexism. (By men I mean the status of masculinity that is accorded to males on the basis of their biology but is not itself biological.) But whatever the damage of sexism to men, the condition of being a man is not defined as subordinate to women by force. Looking at the facts of the abuses of women all at once, you see that a woman is socially defined as a person who, whether or not she is or has been, can be treated in these ways by men at any time, and little, if anything, will be done about it. This is what it means when feminists say that maleness is a form of power and femaleness is a form of powerlessness.

In this context, all of this "men too" stuff means that people don't really believe that the things I have just said are true, though there really is little question about their empirical accuracy. The data are extremely simple, like women's pay figure of fifty-nine cents on the dollar.[30] People don't really seem to believe that either. Yet there is no question of its empirical validity. This is the workplace story: what women do is seen as not worth much, or what is not worth much is seen as something for women to do. *Women* are seen as not worth much, is the thing. Now why are these basic realities of the subordination of women to men, for example, that only 7.8 percent of women have never been sexually assaulted,[31] not effectively believed, not perceived as real in the face of all this evidence? Why don't *women* believe our own experiences? In the face of all this evidence, especially of systematic sexual abuse—subjection to violence with impunity is one extreme expression, although not the only expression, of a degraded status—the view that basically the sexes are equal in this society remains unchallenged and unchanged. The day I got this was the day I understood its real message, its real coherence: *This is equality for us.*

I could describe this, but I couldn't explain it until I started studying a lot of pornography. In pornography, there it is, in one place, all of the abuses that women had to struggle so long even to begin to articulate, all the *unspeakable* abuse: the rape, the battery, the sexual harassment, the prostitution, and the sexual abuse of children. Only in the pornography it is called something else: sex, sex, sex, sex, and sex, respectively. Pornography sexualizes rape, battery, sexual harassment, prostitution, and child sexual abuse; it thereby celebrates, promotes, authorizes, and legitimizes them. More generally, it eroticizes the dominance and submission that is the dynamic common to them all. It makes hierarchy sexy and calls that "the truth about sex"[32] or just a mirror of reality. Through this process pornography constructs what a woman is as what men want from sex. This is what the pornography means.

Pornography constructs what a woman is in terms of its view of what men want sexually, such that acts of rape, battery, sexual harassment, prostitution, and sexual abuse of children become acts of sexual equality. Pornography's world of equality is a harmonious and balanced place.[33] Men and women are perfectly complementary and perfectly bipolar. Women's desire to be fucked by men is equal to men's desire to fuck women. All the ways men love to take and violate women, women love to be taken and violated. The women who most love this are most men's equals, the most liberated; the most participatory child is the most grown-up, the most equal to an adult. Their consent merely expresses or ratifies these preexisting facts.

The content of pornography is one thing. There, women substantively desire dispossession and cruelty. We desperately want to be bound, battered, tortured, humiliated, and killed. Or, to be fair to the soft core, merely taken and used. This is erotic to the male point of view. Subjection itself, with self-determination ecstatically relinquished, is the content of women's sexual desire and desirability. Women are there to be violated and possessed, men to violate and possess us, either on screen or by camera or pen on behalf of the consumer. On a simple descriptive level, the inequality of hierarchy, of which gender is the primary one, seems necessary for sexual arousal to work. Other added inequalities identify various pornographic genres or subthemes, although they are always added through gender: age, disability, homosexuality, animals, objects, race (including anti-Semitism), and so on. Gender is never irrelevant.

What pornography *does* goes beyond its content: it eroticizes hierarchy, it sexualizes inequality. It makes dominance and submission into sex. Inequality is its central dynamic; the illusion of freedom coming together with the reality of force is central to its working. Perhaps because this is a bourgeois culture, the victim must look free, appear to be freely acting. Choice is how she got there. Willing is what she is when she is being equal. It seems equally important that then and there she actually be forced and that forcing be communicated on some level, even if only through still photos of her in postures of receptivity and access, available for penetration. Pornography in this view is a form of forced sex, a practice of sexual politics, an institution of gender inequality.

From this perspective, pornography is neither harmless fantasy nor a corrupt and confused misrepresentation of an otherwise natural and healthy sexual situation. It institutionalizes the sexuality of male supremacy, fusing the erotization of dominance and submission with the social construction of male and female. To the extent that gender is sexual, pornography is part of constituting the meaning of that sexuality. Men treat women as who they see women as being. Pornography constructs who that is. Men's power over women means that the way men see women defines who women can be. Pornography is that way. Pornography is not imagery in some relation to a reality elsewhere constructed. It is not a distortion, reflection, projection, expression, fantasy, representation, or symbol either. It is a sexual reality.

In Andrea Dworkin's definitive work, *Pornography: Men Possessing Women*,[34] sexuality itself is a social construct gendered to the ground. Male dominance here is not an artificial overlay upon an underlying inalterable substratum of uncorrupted essential sexual being. Dworkin presents a sexual theory of gender inequality of which pornography is a constitutive practice. The way pornography produces its meaning constructs and defines men and women as such. Gender has no basis in anything other than the social reality its hegemony constructs. Gender is what gender means. The process that gives sexuality its male supremacist meaning is the same process through which gender inequality becomes socially real.

In this approach, the experience of the (overwhelmingly) male audiences who consume pornography is therefore not fantasy or simulation or catharsis but sexual reality, the level of reality on which sex itself largely operates. Understanding this dimension of the problem does not require noticing that pornography models are real women to whom, in most cases, something real is being done; nor does it even require inquiring into the systematic infliction of pornography and its sexuality upon women, although it helps. What matters is the way in which the pornography itself provides what those who consume it want. Pornography *participates* in its audience's eroticism through creating an accessible sexual object, the possession and consumption of which *is* male sexuality, as socially constructed; to be consumed and possessed as which, *is* female sexuality, as socially constructed; pornography is a process that constructs it that way.

The object world is constructed according to how it looks with respect to its possible uses. Pornography defines women by how we look according to how we can be sexually used. Pornography codes how to look at women, so you know what you can do with one when you see one. Gender is an assignment made visually, both originally and in everyday life. A sex object is defined on the basis of its looks, in terms of its usability for sexual pleasure, such that both the looking—the quality of the gaze, including its point of view—and the definition according to use become eroticized as part of the sex itself. This is what the feminist concept "sex object" means. In this sense, sex in life is no less mediated than it is in art. Men have sex with their image of a woman. It is not that life and art imitate each other; in this sexuality, they *are* each other.

173

Pornography

To give a set of rough epistemological translations, to defend pornography as consistent with the equality of the sexes is to defend the subordination of women to men as sexual equality. What in the pornographic view is love and romance looks a great deal like hatred and torture to the feminist. Pleasure and eroticism become violation. Desire appears as lust for dominance and submission. The vulnerability of women's projected sexual availability, that acting we are allowed (that is, asking to be acted upon), is victimization. Play conforms to scripted roles. Fantasy expresses ideology, is not exempt from it. Admiration of natural physical beauty becomes objectification. Harmlessness becomes harm. Pornography is a harm of male supremacy made difficult to see because of its pervasiveness, potency, and, principally, because of its success in making the world a pornographic place. Specifically, its harm cannot be discerned, and will not be addressed, if viewed and approached neutrally, because it *is* so much of "what is." In other words, to the extent pornography succeeds in constructing social reality, it becomes invisible as harm. If we live in a world that pornography creates through the power of men in a male-dominated situation, the issue is not what the harm of pornography is, but how that harm is to become visible.

•   •   •

Obscenity law provides a very different analysis and conception of the problem of pornography.[35] In 1973 the legal definition of obscenity became that which the average person, applying contemporary community standards, would find that, taken as a whole, appeals to the prurient interest; that which depicts or describes in a patently offensive way—you feel like you're a cop reading someone's *Miranda* rights—sexual conduct specifically defined by the applicable state law; and that which, taken as a whole, lacks serious literary, artistic, political or scientific value.[36] Feminism doubts whether the average person gender-neutral exists; has more questions about the content and process of defining what community standards are than it does about deviations from them; wonders why prurience counts but powerlessness does not and why sensibilities are better protected from offense than women are from exploitation; defines sexuality, and thus its violation and expropriation, more broadly than does state law; and questions why a body of law that has not in practice been able to tell rape from intercourse should, without further guidance, be entrusted with telling pornography from anything less. Taking the work "as a whole" ignores that which the victims of pornography have long known: legitimate settings diminish the perception of injury done to those whose trivialization and objectification they contextualize. Besides, and this is a heavy one, if a woman is subjected, why should it matter that the work has other value? Maybe what redeems the work's value is what enhances its injury to women, not to mention that existing standards of literature, art, science, and politics, examined in a feminist light, are remarkably consonant with pornography's mode, meaning, and message. And finally—first and foremost, actually—although the subject of these materials is overwhelmingly women, their contents almost entirely made up of women's bodies, our invisibility has been such, our equation as a sex *with* sex has been such, that the law of obscenity has never even considered pornography a women's issue.

Obscenity, in this light, is a moral idea, an idea about judgments of good and bad. Pornography, by contrast, is a political practice, a practice of power and powerlessness. Obscenity is ideational and abstract; pornography is concrete and substantive. The two concepts represent two entirely different things. Nudity, excess of candor, arousal or excitement, prurient appeal, illegality of the acts depicted, and unnaturalness or perversion are all qualities that bother obscenity law when sex is depicted or portrayed. Sex forced on real women so that it can be sold at a profit and forced on other real women; women's bodies trussed and maimed and raped and made into things to be hurt and obtained and accessed, and this presented as the nature of women in a way that is acted on and acted out, over and over; the coercion that is visible and the coercion that has become invisible—this and more bothers feminists about pornography. Obscenity as such probably does little harm.[37] Pornography is integral to attitudes and behaviors of violence and discrimination that define the the treatment and status of half the population.

• • •

At the request of the city of Minneapolis, Andrea Dworkin and I conceived and designed a local human rights ordinance in accordance with our approach to the pornography issue. We define pornography as a practice of sex discrimination, a violation of women's civil rights, the opposite of sexual equality. Its point is to hold those who profit from and benefit from that injury accountable to those who are injured. It means that women's injury—our damage, our pain, our enforced inferiority—should outweigh their pleasure and their profits, or sex equality is meaningless.

175

Pornography

We define pornography as the graphic sexually explicit subordination of women through pictures or words that also includes women dehumanized as sexual objects, things, or commodities; enjoying pain or humiliation or rape; being tied up, cut up, mutilated, bruised, or physically hurt; in postures of sexual submission or servility or display; reduced to body parts, penetrated by objects or animals, or presented in scenarios of degradation, injury, torture; shown as filthy or inferior; bleeding, bruised, or hurt in a context that makes these conditions sexual.[38] Erotica, defined by distinction as not this, might be sexually explicit materials premised on equality.[39] We also provide that the use of men, children, or transsexuals in the place of women is pornography.[40] The definition is substantive in that it is sex-specific, but it covers everyone in a sex-specific way, so is gender neutral in overall design.

There is a buried issue within sex discrimination law about what sex, meaning gender, is. If sex is a *difference,* social or biological, one looks to see if a challenged practice occurs along the same lines; if it does, or if it is done to both sexes, the practice is not discrimination, not inequality. If, by contrast, sex has been a matter of *dominance,* the issue is not the gender difference but the difference gender makes. In this more substantive, less abstract approach, the concern with inequality is whether a practice *subordinates* on the basis of sex. The first approach implies that marginal correction is needed; the second requires social change. Equality, in the first view, centers on abstract symmetry between equivalent categories; the asymmetry that occurs when categories are not equivalent is not inequality, it is treating unlikes differently. In the second approach, inequality centers on the substantive, cumulative disadvantagement of social hierarchy. Equality for the first is nondifferentiation; for the second, nonsubordination.[41] Although it is consonant with both approaches, our antipornography statute emerges largely from an analysis of the problem under the second approach.

To define pornography as a practice of sex discrimination combines a mode of portrayal that has a legal history—the sexually explicit—with an active term that is central to the inequality of the sexes—subordination. Among other things, subordination means to be in a position of inferiority or loss of power, or to be demeaned or denigrated.[42] To be someone's subordinate is the opposite of being their equal. The definition does not include all sexually explicit depictions *of* the subordination of women. That is not what it says. It says, this which *does* that: the sexually explicit that subordinates women. To these active terms to capture what the pornography *does,* the definition adds a list of what it must also contain. This list, from our analysis, is an exhaustive description of what must be in the pornography for it to do what it does behaviorally. Each item in the definition is supported by experimental, testimonial, social, and clinical evidence. We made a legislative choice to be exhaustive and specific and concrete rather than conceptual and general, to minimize problems of chilling effect, making it hard to guess wrong, thus making self-censorship less likely, but encouraging (to use a phrase from discrimination law) voluntary compliance, knowing that if something turns up that is not on the list, the law will not be expansively interpreted.

The list in the definition, by itself, would be a content regulation.[43] But together with the first part, the definition is not simply a content regulation. It is a medium-message combination that resembles many other such exceptions to First Amendment guarantees.[44]

To focus what our law is, I will say what it is not. It is not a prior restraint. It does not go to possession. It does not turn on offensiveness. It is not a ban, unless relief for a proven injury is a "ban" on doing that injury again. Its principal enforcement mechanism is the civil rights commission, although it contains an option for direct access to court as well as de novo judicial review of administrative determinations, to ensure that no case will escape full judicial scrutiny and full due process. I will also not discuss various threshold issues, such as the sources of municipal authority, preemption, or abstention, or even issues of overbreadth or vagueness, nor will I defend the ordinance from views that never have been law, such as First Amendment absolutism. I will discuss the merits: how pornography by this definition is a harm, specifically how it is a harm of gender inequality, and how that harm outweighs any social interest in its protection by recognized First Amendment standards.[45]

This law aspires to guarantee women's rights consistent with the First Amendment by making visible a conflict of rights between the equality guaranteed to all women and what, in some legal sense, is now the freedom of the pornographers to make and sell, and their consumers to have access to, the materials this ordinance defines. Judicial resolution of this conflict, if the judges do for women what they have done for others, is likely to entail a balancing of the rights of women arguing that our lives and opportunities, including our freedom of speech and action, are constrained by—and in many cases flatly precluded by, in, and through—pornography, against those who argue that the pornography is harmless, or harmful only

177

in part but not in the whole of the definition; or that it is more important to preserve the pornography than it is to prevent or remedy whatever harm it does.

In predicting how a court would balance these interests, it is important to understand that this ordinance cannot now be said to be either conclusively legal or illegal under existing law or precedent,[46] although I think the weight of authority is on our side. This ordinance enunciates a new form of the previously recognized governmental interest in sex equality. Many laws make sex equality a governmental interest.[47] Our law is designed to further the equality of the sexes, to help make sex equality real. Pornography is a practice of discrimination on the basis of sex, on one level because of its role in creating and maintaining sex as a basis for discrimination. It harms many women one at a time and helps keep all women in an inferior status by defining our subordination as our sexuality and equating that with our gender. It is also sex discrimination because its victims, including men, are selected for victimization on the basis of their gender. But for their sex, they would not be so treated.[48]

The harm of pornography, broadly speaking, is the harm of the civil inequality of the sexes made invisible as harm because it has become accepted as the sex difference. Consider this analogy with race: if you see Black people as different, there is no harm to segregation; it is merely a recognition of that difference. To neutral principles, separate but equal was equal. The injury of racial separation to Blacks arises "solely because [they] choose to put that construction upon it."[49] Epistemologically translated: how you see it is not the way it is. Similarly, if you see women as just different, even or especially if you don't know that you do, subordination will not look like subordination at all, much less like harm. It will merely look like an appropriate recognition of the sex difference.

Pornography does treat the sexes differently, so the case for sex differentiation can be made here. But men as a group do not tend to be (although some individuals may be) treated the way women are treated in pornography. As a social group, men are not hurt by pornography the way women as a social group are. Their social status is not defined as *less* by it. So the major argument does not turn on mistaken differentiation, particularly since the treatment of women according to pornography's dictates makes it all too often accurate. The salient quality of a distinction between the top and the bottom in a hierarchy is not difference, although top is certainly different

178

from bottom; it is power. So the major argument is: subordinate but equal is not equal.

Particularly since this is a new legal theory, a new law, and "new" facts, perhaps the situation of women it newly exposes deserves to be considered on its own terms. Why do the problems of 53 percent of the population have to look like somebody else's problems before they can be recognized as existing? Then, too, they can't be addressed if they do look like other people's problems, about which something might have to be done if something is done about these. This construction of the situation truly deserves inquiry. Limiting the justification for this law to the situation of the sexes would serve to limit the precedential value of a favorable ruling.

Its particularity to one side, the *approach* to the injury is supported by a whole array of prior decisions that have justified exceptions to First Amendment guarantees when something that matters is seen to be directly at stake. What unites many cases in which speech interests are raised and implicated but not, on balance, protected, is harm,[50] harm that counts. In some existing exceptions, the definitions are much more open-ended than ours.[51] In some the sanctions are more severe, or potentially more so. For instance, ours is a civil law; most others, although not all, are criminal.[52] Almost no other exceptions show as many people directly affected. Evidence of harm in other cases tends to be vastly less concrete and more conjectural, which is not to say that there is necessarily less of it.[53] None of the previous cases addresses a problem of this scope or magnitude—for instance, an eight-billion-dollar-a-year industry.[54] Nor do other cases address an abuse that has such widespread legitimacy. Courts have seen harm in other cases. The question is, will they see it here, especially given that the pornographers got there first. I will confine myself here to arguing from cases on harm to people, on the supposition that, the pornographers notwithstanding, women are not flags.[55]

I will discuss the four injuries we make actionable with as much evidence as time permits. I want you to hear the voices of the women and men who spoke at our hearing.

.   .   .

The first victims of pornography are the ones in it. To date, it has only been with children, and male children at that, that the Supreme Court has understood that before the pornography became the pornographer's speech, it was somebody's life.[56] This is particularly true in visual media, where it takes a real person doing each act to make what you see. This is the double meaning in a statement one ex-prostitute made at our hearing: "[E]very single thing you see in pornography is happening to a real woman right now."[57] Linda Marchiano, in her book *Ordeal*,[58] recounts being coerced as "Linda Lovelace" into performing for *Deep Throat*, a fabulously profitable film,[59] by being abducted, systematically beaten, kept prisoner, watched every minute, threatened with her life and the lives of her family if she left, tortured, and kept under constant psychological intimidation and duress. Not all pornography models are, to our knowledge, coerced so expressly, but the fact that some are not does not mean that those who are, aren't. It only means that coercion into pornography cannot be said to be biologically female. The further fact that prostitution and modeling are structurally women's best economic options should give pause to those who would consider women's presence there a true act of free choice. In the case of other inequalities, it is sometimes understood that people do degrading work out of a lack of options caused by, say, poverty. The work is not seen as *not* degrading "for them" because they do it. With women, it just proves that this is what we are really for, this is our true nature. I will leave you wondering, with me, why it is that when a woman spreads her legs for a camera, she is assumed to be exercising free will. Women's freedom is rather substantively defined here. And as you think about the assumption of consent that follows women into pornography, look closely sometime for the skinned knees, the bruises, the welts from the whippings, the scratches, the gashes. Many of them are not simulated. One relatively soft-core pornography model said, "I knew the pose was right when it hurt."[60] It certainly seems important to the audiences that the events in the pornography be real. For this reason pornography becomes a motive for murder, as in "snuff" films, in which someone is tortured to death to make a sex film. They exist.[61]

Coerced pornography models encounter devastating problems of lack of credibility because of a cycle of forced acts in which coercion into pornography is central. For example, children are typically forced to perform the acts in the pornography that is forced on them; photographs are taken of these rapes, and the photographs are used to coerce the children into prostitution or into staying in prostitution. They are told that if they try to leave, the pictures will be shown to the authorities, their parents, their teachers (whoever is *not* coercing them at the time), and no one will believe them. This gets them into prostitution and keeps them there.[62] Understand, the documentation of the harm as it is being done is taken as evidence that no harm was done. In part, the victim's desire for the abuse is attributed to the victim's nature from the fact of the abuse: she's a natural-born whore; see, there she is chained to a bed. Too, the victims are often forced to act as though they are enjoying the abuse. One pornographer said to a woman he abducted and was photographing while bound: "Smile or I'll kill you. I can get lots of money for pictures of women who smile when they're tied up like you."[63] When women say they were forced, they are not believed, in part because, as Linda Marchiano says, "What people remember is the smile on my face."[64]

Pornography defines what a woman is through conditioning the male sexual response to that definition, to the unilateral sexuality pornography is part of and provides. Its power can be illustrated by considering the credibility problems Linda Marchiano encounters when she says that the presentation of her in *Deep Throat* is not true, in the sense that she does not and did not feel or enjoy what the character she was forced to portray felt and enjoyed. Most concretely, before "Linda Lovelace" was seen performing deep throat, no one had ever seen it being done in that way, largely because it cannot be done without hypnosis to repress the natural gag response. *Yet it was believed.* Men proceeded to demand it of women, causing the distress of many and the death of some.[65] Yet when Linda Marchiano now tells that it took kidnapping and death threats and hypnosis to put her there, that is found *difficult to believe.*[66]

The point is not only that when women can be coerced with impunity the results, when mass-produced, set standards that are devastating and dangerous for all women. The point is also that the assumptions the law of the First Amendment makes about adults—that adults are autonomous, self-defining, freely acting, *equal* individuals—are exactly those qualities that pornography systematically denies and undermines for women.[67] Some of the same reasons children are granted some specific legal avenues for redress—relative lack of power, inability to command respect for their consent and self-determination, in some cases less physical strength or lowered legitimacy in using it, specific credibility problems, and lack of access to resources for meaningful self-expression—also hold true for the social position of women compared to men. It is therefore vicious to suggest, as many have, that women like Linda Marchiano should remedy their situations through the exercise of more speech. Pornography makes their speech impossible, and where possible, worthless.

181

Pornography

Pornography makes women into objects. Objects do not speak. When they do, they are by then regarded as objects, not as humans, which is what it means to have no credibility. Besides, it is unclear how Ms. Marchiano's speech is supposed to redress her injury, except by producing this legal remedy, since no amount of saying anything remedies what is being *done* to her in theaters and on home videos all over the world, where she is repeatedly raped for public entertainment and private profit.

What would justice look like for these women?[68] Linda Marchiano said, "Virtually every time someone watches that film, they are watching me being raped."[69] Nancy Holmes, who was forced to perform for pornography by her father and who, like many such victims, has been searching for the film for years, says,

You wonder who might have seen the film. In some back-alley adult book shop someone has dropped a quarter and maybe it might be you they are looking at. You would not ordinarily mix company with this person under these circumstances . . . [b]ut in some back alley, in someone's dark mind you are worth 25 cents. Someone has just paid 25 cents to see you being brutally raped and beaten. And some total stranger gets to gain sadistic and voyeuristic pleasure from your pain. It costs you your sanity and years of suffering and psychological turmoil. It cost him only a quarter, and he gained tremendous pleasure. It robbed you of your childhood; it gave him satisfaction.[70]

Now think about his freedom and her powerlessness, and think about what it means to call that "just the construction she chooses to put upon it."

As part of the relief for people who can prove this was done to them, our law provides an injunction to remove these materials from public view. The best authority we have for this is the *Ferber* case, which permits criminal prohibitions on child pornography.[71] That case recognized that child pornography need not be obscene to be child abuse. The Court found such pornography harmful in part because it constituted "a permanent record of children's participation and the harm to the child is exacerbated by circulation."[72] This was a film, by the way, largely of two boys masturbating.[73] The sensitivities of obscenity law, the Court noted, were inapt because "a work which, taken on the whole, contains value may nevertheless embody the hardest core of child pornography."[74] Whether a work appeals to the prurient interest is not the same as whether a child is physically or psychologically harmed to make it.[75]

Both of these reasons apply to coerced women. Women are not

182

children, but coerced women are effectively deprived of power over the expressive products of their coercion. Coerced pornography should meet the test that "the evil to be restricted . . . overwhelmingly outweighs the expressive interests, if any, at stake."[76] Unless one wishes to retain the incentive structure that has introduced a profit motive into rape, pornography made this way should be able to be eliminated.[77]

.   .   .

We also make it actionable to force pornography on a person in employment, education, in a home, or in any public place.[78] Persons who are forced cannot, under this part of the law, reach the pornography, but they can reach the perpetrator or institution that does the forcing. In our hearings we heard the ways in which pornography is forced on people. It is used to show children how to perform sex acts, to duplicate exactly these so-called natural childish acts;[79] on men's jobs, it is used to intimidate women into leaving;[80] in women's jobs, to have or set up a sexual encounter;[81] it is used to show prostitutes or wives what a "natural woman" is supposed to do.[82] In therapy, it is seen as aiding in transference, meaning submitting to the therapist;[83] in medical school, it desensitizes doctors so that when patients say they are masturbating with a chicken or wondering if intercourse with a cow will give them exotic diseases, the doctor does not react.[84] In language classes, it becomes material to be worked over meticulously for translation.[85] It is used to terrorize children in homes, so they will keep still about its use in the rape of their mothers and sisters: look at this; if you tell, here's what I'll do to you.[86] Sometimes it ends there; some children "only" have the pornography forced on them. Some of them later develop psychological difficulties that are identical to those of children who had the *acts* forced on them.[87] Do a thought-act distinction on that one.

Women who live in neighborhoods where pornography is concentrated, much of it through state and local legal action called "zoning," report similar effects on a broad scale.[88] Because prostitutes know what others seem to have a lot staked on denying, which is that pornography makes men want the real thing, they sometimes locate around it. This means that any woman there may be considered a prostitute, which is dangerous enough if you are one, but becomes particularly dangerous if you are not. The threat of sexual harassment is constant. The presence of the pornography conditions women's physical environment. Women have no place to go to avoid it, no place to avert their eyes *to*.[89] Certainly not home, where the presence of pornography is so sanctified[90] we don't even challenge it in this law. One woman who as a child was a victim of incest and now lives in a community saturated with pornography, relates a Skokie-type injury.[91] She relives the incest every time she walks by the pornography she cannot avoid. "[L]ooking at the women in those pictures, I saw myself at 14, at 15, at 16. I felt the weight of that man's body, the pain, the disgust . . . I don't need studies and statistics to tell me that there is a relationship between pornography and real violence against women. My body remembers."[92] Now recall that more than a third of all women are victims of child sexual abuse; about the same proportion are victims of domestic battery; just under half are victims of rape or attempted rape. I am not saying that every such presence of the pornography is legally force, but what does it mean for targeted survivors to live in a society in which the rehearsal and celebration and ritual reenactment of our victimization is enjoyed, is an entertainment industry, is arguably a constitutional right?

.   .   .

Specific pornography does directly cause some assaults.[93] Some rapes *are* performed by men with paperback books in their pockets.[94] One young woman testified in our hearings about walking through a forest at thirteen and coming across a group of armed hunters reading pornography. As they looked up and saw her, one said, "There is a live one."[95] They gang-raped her at gunpoint for several hours. One Native American woman told us about being gang-raped in a reenactment of a video game on her. "[T]hat's what they screamed in my face as they threw me to the ground. 'This is more fun than Custer's Last Stand.' They held me down and as one was running the tip of his knife across my face and throat he said, 'Do you want to play Custer's Last Stand? It's great, you lose but you don't care, do you? You like a little pain, don't you, squaw? . . . Maybe we will tie you to a tree and start a fire around you."[96]

Received wisdom seems to be that because there is so little difference between convicted rapists and the rest of the male population in levels and patterns of exposure, response to, and consumption of pornography, the role of pornography in rape is insignificant.[97] A more parsimonious explanation of this data is that knowing patterns of exposure to, response to, or consumption of pornography will not tell you who will be reported, apprehended, and convicted for rape. But the commonalities such data reveal between convicted rapists and other men are certainly consistent with the fact that only a tiny fraction of rapes ever come to the attention of authorities.[98] It does

184

not make sense to assume that pornography has no role in rape simply because little about its use or effects distinguishes convicted rapists from other men, when we know that a lot of those other men *do* rape women; they just never get caught. In other words, the significance of pornography in acts of forced sex is one thing if sex offenders are considered deviants and another if they are considered relatively nonexceptional except for the fact of their apprehension and incarceration. Professionals who work with that tiny percentage of men who get reported and convicted for such offenses, a group made special only by our ability to assume that they once had sex by force in a way that someone (in addition to their victim) eventually regarded as serious, made the following observations about the population they work with. "Pornography is the permission and direction and rehearsal for sexual violence."[99] "[P]ornography is often used by sex offenders as a stimulus to their sexually acting out." It is the "tools of sexual assault,"[100] "a way in which they practice" their crimes, "like a loaded gun,"[101] "like drinking salt water,"[102] "the chemical of sexual addiction."[103] They hypothesize that pornography leads some men to abusiveness out of fear of loss of the control that has come to mean masculinity when real women won't accept sex on the one-sided terms that pornography gives and from which they have learned what sex is. Because pornography is reinforcing, and leads to sexual release, it "leads men to want the experience which they have in photographic fantasy to happen in 'real' life."[104] "They live vicariously through the pictures. Eventually, that is not satisfying enough and they end up acting out sexually."[105] "[S]exual fantasy represents the hope for reality."[106] These professionals are referring to what others are fond of terming "just an idea."

Although police have known it for years, reported cases are increasingly noting the causal role of pornography in some sexual abuse.[107] In a recent Minnesota case, a fourteen-year-old girl on a bicycle was stopped with a knife and forced into a car. Her hands were tied with a belt, she was pushed to the floor and covered with a blanket. The knife was then used to cut off her clothes, and fingers and a knife were inserted into her vagina. Then the man had her dress, drove her to a gravel pit, ordered her to stick a safety pin into the nipple of her left breast, and forced her to ask him to hit her. After hitting her, he forced her to commit fellatio and to submit to anal penetration, and made her use a cigarette to burn herself on her breast and near her pubic area. Then he defecated and urinated on her face, forced her to ingest some of the excrement and urine and made her urinate into a cup and drink it. He took a string from her blouse and choked her to the point of unconsciousness, leaving burn marks on her neck, and after cutting her with his knife in a couple of places, drove her back to where he had gotten her and let her go. The books that were found with this man were: *Violent Stories of Kinky Humiliation, Violent Stories of Dominance and Submission*—you think feminists made up these words?—*Bizarre Sex Crimes, Shamed Victims,* and *Water Sports Fetish, Enemas and Golden Showers.* The Minnesota Supreme Court said "It appears that in committing these various acts, the defendant was giving life to some stories he had read in various pornographic books."[108]

To reach the magnitude of this problem on the scale it exists, our law makes trafficking in pornography—production, sale, exhibition, or distribution—actionable.[109] Under the obscenity rubric, much legal and psychological scholarship has centered on a search for the elusive link between harm and pornography defined as obscenity.[110] Although they were not very clear on what obscenity was, it was its harm they truly could not find. They looked high and low—in the mind of the male consumer,[111] in society or in its "moral fabric,"[112] in correlations between variations in levels of antisocial acts and liberalization of obscenity laws.[113] The only harm they have found has been harm to "the social interest in order and morality."[114] Until recently, no one looked very persistently for harm to women, particularly harm to women through men. The rather obvious fact that the sexes *relate* has been overlooked in the inquiry into the male consumer and his mind. The pornography doesn't just drop out of the sky, go into his head, and stop there. Specifically, men rape, batter, prostitute, molest, and sexually harass women. Under conditions of inequality, they also hire, fire, promote, and grade women, decide how much or whether we are worth paying and for what, define and approve and disapprove of women in ways that count, that determine our lives.

If women are not just born to be sexually used, the fact that we are seen and treated as though that is what we are born for becomes something in need of explanation. If we see that men relate to women in a pattern of who they see women as being, and that forms a pattern of inequality, it becomes important to ask where that view came from or, minimally, how it is perpetuated or escalated. Asking this requires asking different questions about pornography than the ones obscenity law made salient.

Now I'm going to talk about causality in its narrowest sense.[115] Recent experimental research on pornography[116] shows that the materials covered by our definition cause measurable harm to women through increasing men's attitudes and behaviors of discrimination in both violent and nonviolent forms. Exposure to some of the pornography in our definition increases the immediately subsequent willingness of normal men to aggress against women under laboratory conditions.[117] It makes normal men more closely resemble convicted rapists attitudinally, although as a group they don't look all that different from them to start with.[118] Exposure to pornography also significantly increases attitudinal measures known to correlate with rape and self-reports of aggressive acts, measures such as hostility toward women, propensity to rape, condoning rape, and predicting that one would rape or force sex on a woman if one knew one would not get caught.[119] On this latter measure, by the way, about a third of all men predict that they would rape, and half would force sex on a woman.[120]

As to that pornography covered by our definition in which normal research subjects seldom perceive violence, long-term exposure still makes them see women as more worthless, trivial, nonhuman, and objectlike,[121] that is, the way those who are discriminated against are seen by those who discriminate against them. Crucially, all pornography by our definition acts dynamically over time to diminish the consumer's ability to distinguish sex from violence. The materials work behaviorally to diminish the capacity of men (but not women) to perceive that an account of a rape is an account of a rape.[122] The so-called sex-only materials, those in which subjects perceive no force, also increase perceptions that a rape victim is worthless and decrease the perception that she was harmed.[123] The overall direction of current research suggests that the more expressly violent materials accomplish with less exposure what the less overtly violent—that is, the so-called sex-only materials—accomplish over the longer term. Women are rendered fit for use and targeted for abuse. The only thing that the research cannot document is which individual women will be next on the list. (This cannot be documented experimentally because of ethics constraints on the researchers—constraints that do not operate in life.) Although the targeting is systematic on the basis of sex, for individuals it is random. They are selected on a roulette basis. Pornography can no longer be said to be just a mirror. It does not just reflect the world or some people's perceptions. It *moves* them. It increases attitudes that are lived out, circumscribing the status of half the population.

What the experimental data predict will happen actually does happen in women's real lives. You know, it's fairly frustrating that women have known for some time that these things do happen. As Ed Donnerstein, an experimental researcher in this area, often puts it, "We just quantify the obvious."[124] It is women, primarily, to whom the research results have been the obvious, because we live them. But not until a laboratory study predicts that these things *will* happen do people begin to believe you when you say they *did* happen to you. There is no—*not any*—inconsistency between the patterns the laboratory studies predict and the data on what actually happens to real women. Show me an abuse of women in society, I'll show it to you made sex in the pornography. If you want to know who is being hurt in this society, go see what is being done and to whom in pornography and then go look for them other places in the world. You will find them being hurt in just that way. We did in our hearings.

In our hearings women spoke, to my knowledge for the first time in history in public, about the damage pornography does to them. We learned that pornography is used to break women, to train women to sexual submission, to season women, to terrorize women, and to silence their dissent. It is this that has previously been termed "having no effect." The way men inflict on women the sex they experience through the pornography gives women no choice about seeing the pornography or doing the sex. Asked if anyone ever tried to inflict unwanted sex acts on them that they knew came from pornography, 10 percent of women in a recent random study said yes.[125] Among married women, 24 percent said yes.[126] That is a lot of women. A lot more don't know. Some of those who do testified in Minneapolis. One wife said of her ex-husband, "He would read from the pornography like a textbook, like a journal. In fact when he asked me to be bound, when he finally convinced me to do it, he read in the magazine how to tie the knots."[127] Another woman said of her boyfriend, "[H]e went to this party, saw pornography, got an erection, got me . . . to inflict his erection on . . . There is a direct causal relationship there."[128] One woman, who said her husband had rape and bondage magazines all over the house, discovered two suitcases full of Barbie dolls with rope tied on their arms and legs and with tape across their mouths.[129] Now think about the silence of women.

She said, "He used to tie me up and he tried those things on me."[130] A therapist in private practice reported:

Presently or recently I have worked with clients who have been sodomized by broom handles, forced to have sex with over 20 dogs in the back seat of their car, tied up and then electrocuted on their genitals. These are children, [all] in the ages of 14 to 18, all of whom [have been directly affected by pornography,] [e]ither where the perpetrator has read the manuals and manuscripts at night and used these as recipe books by day or had the pornography present at the time of the sexual violence.[131]

One woman, testifying that all the women in a group of ex-prostitutes were brought into prostitution as children through pornography, characterized their collective experience: "[I]n my experience there was not one situation where a client was not using pornography while he was using me or that he had not just watched pornography or that it was verbally referred to and directed me to pornography."[132] "Men," she continued, "witness the abuse of women in pornography constantly and if they can't engage in that behavior with their wives, girl friends or children, they force a whore to do it."[133]

Men also testified about how pornography hurts them. One young gay man who had seen *Playboy* and *Penthouse* as a child said of such heterosexual pornography: "It was one of the places I learned about sex and it showed me that sex was violence. What I saw there was a specific relationship between men and women . . . [T]he woman was to be used, objectified, humiliated and hurt; the man was in a superior position, a position to be violent. In pornography I learned that what it meant to be sexual with a man or to be loved by a man was to accept his violence."[134] For this reason, when he was battered by his first lover, which he described as "one of the most profoundly destructive experiences of my life,"[135] he accepted it.

Pornography also hurts men's capacity to relate to women. One young man spoke about this in a way that connects pornography— not the prohibition on pornography—with fascism. He spoke of his struggle to repudiate the thrill of dominance, of his difficulty finding connection with a woman to whom he is close. He said: "My point is that if women in a society filled by pornography must be wary for their physical selves, a man, even a man of good intentions, must be wary for his mind . . . I do not want to be a mechanical, goose-stepping follower of the Playboy bunny, because that is what I think it is . . .[T]hese are the experiments a master race perpetuates on those slated for extinction."[136] The woman he lives with is Jewish. There was a very brutal rape near their house. She was afraid; she tried to joke. It didn't work. "She was still afraid. And just as a well-meaning German was afraid in 1933, I am also very much afraid."[137]

Pornography stimulates and reinforces, it does not cathect or mirror, the connection between one-sided freely available sexual access to women and masculine sexual excitement and sexual satisfaction. The catharsis hypothesis is fantasy. The fantasy theory is fantasy. Reality is: pornography conditions male orgasm to female subordination. It tells men what sex means, what a real woman is, and codes them together in a way that is behaviorally reinforcing. This is a real five-dollar sentence, but I'm going to say it anyway: pornography is a set of hermeneutical equivalences that work on the epistemological level. Substantively, pornography defines the meaning of what a woman is seen to be by connecting access to her sexuality with masculinity through orgasm. What pornography means *is* what it does.

So far, opposition to our ordinance centers on the trafficking provision. This means not only that it is difficult to comprehend a group injury in a liberal culture—that what it *means* to be a woman is defined by this and that it is an injury for all women, even if not for all women equally. It is not only that the pornography has got to be accessible, which is the bottom line of virtually every objection to this law. It is also that power, as I said, is when you say something, it is taken for reality.[138] If you talk about rape, it will be agreed that rape is awful. But rape is a conclusion. If a victim describes the facts of a rape, maybe she was asking for it or enjoyed it or at least consented to it, or the man might have thought she did, or maybe she had had sex before. It is now agreed that there is something wrong with sexual harassment. But describe what happened to you, and it may be trivial or personal or paranoid, or maybe you should have worn a bra that day. People are against discrimination. But describe the situation of a real woman, and they are not so sure she wasn't just unqualified. In law, all these disjunctions between women's perspective on our injuries and the standards we have to meet go under dignified legal rubrics like burden of proof, credibility, defenses, elements of the crime, and so on. These standards all contain a definition of what a woman is in terms of what sex is and the low value placed on us through it. They reduce injuries done to us to authentic expressions of who we are. Our silence is written all over them. So is the pornography.

190

We have as yet encountered comparatively little objection to the coercion, force, or assault provisions of our ordinance. I think that's partly because the people who make and approve laws may not yet see what they do as that. They *know* they use the pornography as we have described it in this law, and our law defines that, the reality of pornography, as a harm to women. If they suspect that they might on occasion engage in or benefit from coercion or force or assault, they may think that the victims won't be able to prove it—and they're right. Women who charge men with sexual abuse are not believed. The pornographic view of them is: they want it; they all want it.[139] When women bring charges of sexual assault, motives such as veniality or sexual repression must be invented, because we cannot really have been hurt. Under the trafficking provision, women's lack of credibility cannot be relied upon to negate the harm. There's no woman's story to destroy,[140] no credibility-based decision on what happened. The hearings establish the harm. The definition sets the standard. The grounds of reality definition are authoritatively shifted. Pornography is bigotry, *period.* We are now—*in* the world pornography has decisively defined—having to meet the burden of proving, once and for all, for all of the rape and torture and battery, all of the sexual harassment, all of the child sexual abuse, all of the forced prostitution, *all* of it that the pornography is part of and that is part of the pornography, that the harm *does happen* and that when it happens it looks like this. Which may be why all this evidence never seems to be enough.

.   .   .

It is worth considering what evidence has been enough when other harms involving other purported speech interests have been allowed to be legislated against. By comparison to our trafficking provision, analytically similar restrictions have been allowed under the First Amendment, with a legislative basis far less massive, detailed, concrete, and conclusive. Our statutory language is more ordinary, objective, and precise and covers a harm far narrower than the legislative record substantiates. Under *Miller,* obscenity was allowed to be made criminal in the name of the "danger of offending the sensibilities of unwilling recipients, or exposure to juveniles."[141] Under our law, we have direct evidence of harm, not just a conjectural danger, that unwilling women in considerable numbers are not simply offended in their sensibilities, but are violated in their persons and restricted in their options. Obscenity law also suggests that the applicable standard for legal adequacy in measuring such connections

191

may not be statistical certainty. The Supreme Court has said that it is not their job to resolve empirical uncertainties that underlie state obscenity legislation.[142] Rather, it is for them to determine whether a legislature could reasonably have determined that a connection might exist between the prohibited material and harm of a kind in which the state has legitimate interest. Equality should be such an area. The Supreme Court recently recognized that prevention of sexual exploitation and abuse of children is, in their words, "a governmental objective of surpassing importance."[143] This might also be the case for sexual exploitation and abuse of women, although I think a civil remedy is initially more appropriate to the goal of empowering adult women than a criminal prohibition would be.[144]

Other rubrics provide further support for the argument that this law is narrowly tailored to further a legitimate governmental interest consistent with the goals underlying the First Amendment. Exceptions to the First Amendment—you may have gathered from this—exist. The reason they exist is that the harm done by some speech outweighs its expressive value, if any. In our law a legislature recognizes that pornography, as defined and made actionable, undermines sex equality. One can say—and I have—that pornography is a causal factor in violations of women; one can also say that women will be violated so long as pornography exists; but one can also say simply that pornography violates women. Perhaps this is what the woman had in mind who testified at our hearings that for her the question is not just whether pornography causes violent acts to be perpetrated against some women. "Porn is already a violent act against women. It is our mothers, our daughters, our sisters, and our wives that are for sale for pocket change at the newsstands in this country."[145] *Chaplinsky v. New Hampshire* recognized the ability to restrict as "fighting words" speech which, "by [its] very utterance inflicts injury."[146] Perhaps the only reason that pornography has not been "fighting words"—in the sense of words that by their utterance tend to incite immediate breach of the peace—is that women have seldom fought back, yet.[147]

Some concerns that are close to those of this ordinance underlie group libel laws, although the differences are equally important. In group libel law, as Justice Frankfurter's opinion in *Beauharnais* illustrates, it has been understood that an individual's treatment and alternatives in life may depend as much on the reputation of the group to which that person belongs as on their own merit.[148] Not even a partial analogy can be made to group libel doctrine without examining the point made by Justice Brandeis[149] and recently underlined by Larry Tribe:[150] would more speech, rather than less, remedy the harm? In the end, the answer may be yes, but not under the abstract system of free speech, which only enhances the power of the pornographers while doing nothing substantively to guarantee the free speech of women, for which we need civil equality. The situation in which women presently find ourselves with respect to the pornography is one in which more *pornography* is inconsistent with rectifying or even counterbalancing its damage through speech, because so long as the pornography exists in the way it does there *will not be more speech by women.* Pornography strips and devastates women of credibility, from our accounts of sexual assault to our everyday reality of sexual subordination. We are stripped of authority and reduced and devalidated and silenced. Silenced here means that the purposes of the First Amendment, premised upon conditions presumed and promoted by protecting free speech, do not pertain to women because they are not our conditions. Consider them: individual self-fulfillment[151]—how does pornography promote our individual self-fulfillment? How does sexual inequality even permit it? Even if she can form words, who listens to a woman with a penis in her mouth? Facilitating consensus—to the extent pornography does so, it does so one-sidedly by silencing protest over the injustice of sexual subordination. Participation in civic life—central to Professor Meiklejohn's theory[152]—how does pornography enhance women's participation in civic life? Anyone who cannot walk down the street or even lie down in her own bed without keeping her eyes cast down and her body clenched against assault is unlikely to have much to say about the issues of the day, still less will she become Tolstoy. Facilitating change[153]—*this law* facilitates the change that existing First Amendment theory had been used to throttle. Any system of freedom of expression that does not address a problem where the free speech of men silences the free speech of women, a real conflict between speech interests as well as between people, is not serious about securing freedom of expression in this country.[154]

For those of you who still think pornography is only an idea, consider the possibility that obscenity law got one thing right. Pornography is more actlike than thoughtlike. The fact that pornography, in a feminist view, furthers the idea of the sexual inferiority of women, which is a political idea, doesn't make the pornography itself into a political idea. One can express the idea a practice embodies. That does not make that practice into an idea. Segregation expresses the idea of the inferiority of one group to another on the basis of race. That does not make segregation an idea. A sign that says "Whites Only" is only words. Is it therefore protected by the First Amendment? Is it not an act, a practice, of segregation because what it means is inseparable from what it does?[155] *Law* is only words.

The issue here is whether the fact that words and pictures are the central link in the cycle of abuse will immunize that entire cycle, about which we cannot do anything without doing something about the pornography. As Justice Stewart said in *Ginsburg*, "When expression occurs in a setting where the capacity to make a choice is absent, government regulation of that expression may coexist with and *even implement* First Amendment guarantees."[156] I would even go so far as to say that the pattern of evidence we have closely approaches Justice Douglas' requirement that "freedom of expression can be suppressed if, and to the extent that, it is so closely brigaded with illegal action as to be an inseparable part of it."[157] Those of you who have been trying to separate the acts from the speech—that's an act, that's an act, there's a law against that act, regulate that act, don't touch the speech—notice here that the illegality of the acts involved doesn't mean that the speech that is "brigaded with" it *cannot* be regulated. This is when it *can* be.[158]

I take one of two penultimate points from Andrea Dworkin, who has often said that pornography is not speech for women, it is the silence of women.[159] Remember the mouth taped, the woman gagged, "Smile, I can get a lot of money for that." The smile is not her expression, it is her silence. It is not her expression not because it didn't happen, but because it *did* happen. The screams of the women in pornography are silence, like the screams of Kitty Genovese, whose plight was misinterpreted by some onlookers as a lovers' quarrel. The flat expressionless voice of the woman in the New Bedford gang rape, testifying, is silence. She was raped as men cheered and watched, as they do in and with the pornography. When women resist and men say, "Like this, you stupid bitch, here is how to do it" and shove their faces into the pornography,[160] this "truth of sex"[161] is the silence of women. When they say, "If you love me, you'll try,"[162] the enjoyment we fake, the enjoyment we learn is silence. Women who submit because there is more dignity in it than in losing the fight over and over[163] live in silence. Having to sleep with your publisher or director to get access to what men call speech is silence. Being humiliated on the basis of your appearance, whether by approval or disapproval, because you have to look a certain way for a certain job, whether you get the job or not, is silence. The absence of a woman's voice, everywhere that it cannot be heard, is silence. And anyone who thinks that what women say in pornography is women's speech—the "Fuck me, do it to me, harder," all of that—has never heard the sound of a woman's voice.[164]

The most basic assumption underlying First Amendment adjudication is that, socially, speech is free. The First Amendment says Congress shall not abridge the freedom of speech.[165] Free speech, get it, *exists*. Those who wrote the First Amendment *had* speech—they wrote the Constitution. *Their* problem was to keep it free from the only power that realistically threatened it: the federal government. They designed the First Amendment to prevent government from constraining that which, if unconstrained by government, was free, meaning *accessible to them*. At the same time, we can't tell much about the intent of the framers with regard to the question of women's speech, because I don't think we crossed their minds. It is consistent with this analysis that their posture toward freedom of speech tends to presuppose that whole segments of the population are not systematically silenced socially, prior to government action. If everyone's power were equal to theirs, if this were a nonhierarchical society, that might make sense. But the place of pornography in the inequality of the sexes makes the assumption of equal power untrue.

This is a hard question. It involves risks. Classically, opposition to censorship has involved keeping government off the backs of people. Our law is about getting some people off the backs of other people. The risks that it will be misused have to be measured against the risks of the status quo. Women will never have that dignity, security, compensation that is the promise of equality so long as the pornography exists as it does now. The situation of women suggests that the urgent issue of our freedom of speech is not primarily the avoidance of state intervention as such, but getting affirmative access to speech for those to whom it has been denied.

•   •   •

While I was thinking about all of this, I had an imagination. I was haunted by an entirely imaginary person: Francis Biddle had a sister. Do not look for her story in the diplomatic or legal sections of the library. She wrote no autobiography, much less two.[166] No legal footnotes embellish her life story. No one endowed a lecture series in

195

recognition of her exemplary life of accomplishment. When she confronted people directly, it was not said, as Dean Fisher gracefully said of her brother, that she was "anti-tact";[167] they simply said she was tactless. People do not recall her elegance or grace on ceremonial occasions. Her compassion, her recognition that torture is real even when planned and systematic and carried out against targets defined as appropriate at the time, did not lead, as her brother's did, to sitting in judgment at Nuremburg. Her passion for justice did not express itself in the interstices of procedure. She never acted for her government for well or ill, regretting it or recalling it in pride in later years. Fact is, we don't know a thing Francis Biddle's sister said, much less in her own words. Maybe she spent her life changing typewriter ribbons or diapers or bedpans or beds. If she was lucky, she was well treated, at least most of the time while she was being used. If she was not, meaning that no man ever chose her for more than one night at a time or approved of her for whatever reasons are within their power to bestow or withhold, maybe she ended up walking the streets, talking out loud to no one in particular, until someone locked her up. Maybe, if she could manage it, she retreated to the home, in Andrea Dworkin's words, "that open grave where so many women lie waiting to die."[168] Maybe she hit bottom of women's options. Maybe she did well, carrying around the most whole self any woman can have in a society in which the degradation of her body is enjoyed. Some days she tried. Some days she gave up. In large part because of the society in which she lived, when she died it all came to about the same. Nothing much. Which, especially if you applied the standards her brother lived up to, is about what she was seen as good for.

You may be thinking that there isn't much we can do about this. I think there is something, as Virginia Woolf once wrote about a similar sister she invented for Shakespeare, that is in our power to give her.[169] Those of us who are as much her descendants as Francis Biddle's would apply his passion, his developed skills, his talents, if only some of his commitments, to her life. We would have this law I have been urging tonight. We would have this recognition and institutional support for our equality. If this proposal were to become law and if it were to be used, if it were to be given the life in women's hands for which it is designed, there could come a day when she would speak in her own voice and you would hear her. And I think only then would we understand how unimaginable what she would say is for us now. She would write, she would lecture, she would carry on in public, she would make policy. From that day forward, neutrality might make some sense. Sexual equality would not be an empty standard, a taunting aspiration, or a vicious illusion. And silence would be a choice.

fifteen

On Collaboration
(1985)

I am here because I really wanted to talk with you about something.

Over the history of this conference, legal initiatives against rape and battery have been discussed—for instance, the spousal exclusion and the corroboration requirement and the question of disclosure of the victim's sexual history. It was not thought necessary to have someone—a woman, a feminist—represent the rapist or the batterer, although major issues of racism, due process, the horrors of incarceration, police discretion, and the intrusion of the state into the privacy of the bedroom were involved.

Legal initiatives have been taken here to secure equal pay for work of comparable worth, and it was not thought necessary to make sure there was someone—a woman, a feminist—to defend the existing economic distribution of value under the capitalist system because some women have been able to get something out of it, although (to credit the commentators) the entire structure of the American economy is at stake. Legal initiatives against sexual harassment have been discussed at this conference, and those arguing that the sex-for-survival dynamic was *not* the model of women's liberation did not have to be opposed by defenders of men's right to sexual access, calling it "pro-sex," even though serious issues of privacy and even speech are involved. Nor did women lawyers who identify as feminists worry about how women were ever going to get over, if sleeping our way to the top became legally actionable as sex discrimination. Nor were they concerned that we would lose the source of our power.

Pornography is an eight-billion-dollar-a-year industry of rape and battery and sexual harassment, an industry that both performs these abuses for the production of pornography and targets women for them societywide. Rape is involved when women are coerced into pornography with "Smile, or I'll kill you." Sexual harassment is in-

---

This speech was part of a debate at the National Conference on Women and the Law in New York, Mar. 24, 1985. The struggle against pornography has freed many to express themselves in ways that were previously silenced. It freed me to say this.

volved when pornography is forced on women with "Here, you stupid bitch, this is what I want you to do." Assault and battery are involved when a woman is gang-raped to the tune of "This is more fun than Custer's Last Stand." This is also an industry that sets women's value in terms of our sexual accessibility and use. But it took months of argument for me to get even this much access to you, and it was granted only on the condition that someone—a woman, a feminist—be here to speak for the pornographers, although that will not be what she will say she is doing.

I want to speak about the civil rights law Andrea Dworkin and I wrote, making pornography actionable as sex discrimination. I have two goals. It is my view that you are being largely lied to; I want you to hear the truth straight, just one time. I also want to consider what it means that women lawyers who identify as feminists oppose this initiative for sex equality.

I have never done anything like this in public before. I also realize that I have been wanting to say it for a very long time.

Women in pornography are bound, battered, tortured, humiliated, and killed. Or, to be fair to the soft core, merely taken and used. This is being done to real women now. It is being done for a reason: it gives sexual pleasure to its consumers and therefore profits to its providers. But to the women and children who are the victims of its making or use, it means being bound, battered, tortured, humiliated, and killed—or merely taken and used, until they are used up or can get out. It is done for a reason: because someone with more power than they have gets pleasure from seeing it, or doing it, or seeing it as a form of doing it.

In the hundreds of magazines and pictures and films and so-called books now available in this country, new ones every month, women's legs are splayed, bodies presented in postures of sexual submission, display, and access. We are pussy, beaver, bitch, chick, cunt—named after parts of our bodies or after animals interchangeably. We are cut up into parts of our bodies or mated with animals interchangeably. We are told this is a natural woman's sexuality, but it is elaborately contrived. The photographs may not be retouched, but the poses are, the bodies are. Children are presented as adult women; adult women are presented as children. Pregnant women are accessible, displayed. Lesbian is a pervasive theme. Lesbian sex is shown as men imagine women touch each other.

Pornography is a major medium for the sexualization of racial hatred. Every racial stereotype is used: Black women presented as vio-

199

lent bitches, struggling against their bonds, bruised and bleeding. The pornography of Asian women is almost entirely one of torture. The women are presented so passive they cannot be said to be alive, so bound they are not recognizably human, hanging from light fixtures and clothes pegs and trees. There are amputees, their stumps and prostheses presented as sexual fetishes. Retarded girls are gratifyingly compliant. In some pornography called "snuff" films women or children are tortured to death to make a sex film. They exist.

Why do women lawyers who identify as feminists ignore, gloss over, shrug this off? Why do some refuse to discuss the issue of pornography when the pornography is in the room, making it as invisible and nonexistent as its victims have been? How can they ignore even, say, the racism?

You may think snuff is one thing, *Playboy* another. Our law says something very simple: a woman is not a thing to be used, any more than to be abused, and her sexuality isn't either. Why do women lawyers who identify as feminists buy and defend the pornographers' view of what a woman is for, what a woman's sexuality is? Why, when they look in the mirror, do they see the image of themselves the pornographers put there?

Because the medium of pornography is words and pictures, it has been considered speech, even by women lawyers, feminists. Because of the pleasure pornography gives, they have also considered it exempt from scrutiny, repressive to question. This misses what they know best: because pornography is sexual, it is not like the literatures of other inequalities. It is a specific and compelling behavioral stimulus, conditioner, and reinforcer. The way it works is unique: it makes orgasm a response to bigotry. It is a major way that dominance and submission—a daily dynamic of social hierarchy, particularly of gender inequality—are enjoyed and practiced and reinforced and experienced. And fused with male and female. Pornography makes sexism sexy. We live in a society in which intrusion on women is the definition of sex, and the pornographers practice and promote it. Why are there women lawyers, feminists, who defend this, telling us everything is just fine, and the only problem is that "we" don't have enough of it?

Based on the observation and analysis that everything is not just fine, Andrea Dworkin and I have considered pornography to be a violation of civil rights—the civil rights of women and children primarily, but of everyone who is hurt by it on the basis of their sex. In our view, pornography is a major social force for institutionalizing a subhuman, victimized, and second-class status for women in this country. This is inconsistent with any serious vision or legal mandate of equality and with the reasons speech is protected. Why do women lawyers who identify as feminists not see the insult in a law of the First Amendment that is outweighed by so many other considerations but has looked at pornography for decades, looking for the harm in it, and has never seen anything except sex that men don't want to say they want to see?

Our law defines pornography as the sexually explicit subordination of women through pictures or words that also includes women presented dehumanized as sexual objects who enjoy pain, humiliation, or rape; women bound, mutilated, dismembered, or tortured; women in postures of servility or submission or display; women being penetrated by objects or animals. Men, children, and transsexuals, all of whom are sometimes violated like women through and in pornography, can sue for similar treatment. The term "sexually explicit" is an existing term with a legal meaning. It has never before, to my knowledge or the knowledge of LEXIS,[1] been considered unclear; it is often used to clarify the meaning of other terms. It refers to something objective in the world, unlike obscenity law's "prurient interest," yet it captures the active sexual dynamic of the materials. The term "subordination" refers to materials that, in one way or another, are active in placing women in an unequal position. Presumably, people know that if you are someone's subordinate, you are not their equal. Why do women lawyers seem unable to comprehend the simple statutory requirement that all these elements must be there? Why do they distort the law ludicrously? Can't they get it right and still oppose it? Why do they, feminists, insist that they have no idea what subordination means, what being put down is about or looks like? Why do they say that at most equality in this area should mean that sexual dominance and submission be made available on a gender-neutral basis?

Our civil rights law allows victims of four activities, and four activities only—coercion, force, assault, and trafficking—to sue civilly those who hurt them through pornography. Coercion, force, assault, and trafficking are not ideas; they are not fantasies; they are not, in themselves, speech. Why, when women's agony and pain becomes what pornographers want to say, when our bodies are their media of expression, are women lawyers, feminists, among those who tell us it is only an idea, information, symbolic, a fantasy, just representation? Aren't these women real to them either?

Pornography

Trafficking in female sexual slavery does not become speech because it is a business, any more than any form of discrimination becomes legalized when it is bought and sold. Nor does it become protected simply because it is only words. A sign that says "Whites Only" is only words, but it is still an integral act in a system of segregation, which is a system of force. Should it become more protected if it is done on an eight-billion-dollar-a-year scale? Why do women lawyers, feminists, want to require that we reach the acts, not the "speech," when these acts are done to make the "speech" or because of the "speech"? Why can there be a law for every other abuse, but when harmed women want to move against pornographers, women lawyers, calling it feminist, say this is something there should be no law on?

Our hearings in Minneapolis produced overwhelming evidence of the damage done by pornography. Researchers and clinicians documented what women know from life: that pornography increases attitudes and behaviors of aggression and other discrimination, principally by men against women. The relation is causal. It is better than the smoking/cancer correlation and at least as good as the data on drinking and driving. Social studies and other expert and personal testimony documented that the laboratory predictions of increased aggression toward women do occur in real life. There are no contradictions in this evidence. You know, it is fairly frustrating that it takes studies by men of men in laboratories to predict that viewing pornography makes men be sexually more violent and makes them believe we are sexual things, before women are believed when we say that this does happen, and did happen, to us. It's even more frustrating to have women lawyers, feminists, say or act as though it doesn't happen—or, if it does, that it is not as important as the pleasure to be gotten from it.

In *Brown v. Board of Education*, it took one study to show that the harm of segregation was that it affected the hearts and minds of Black children, gave them a sense of their inferiority, and affected their feeling of status in the community in a way that was unlikely ever to be undone.[2] How do you suppose it affects the hearts and minds of women, what does it tell us about our status in the community, that when a woman is hung on a meat hook, a study has to be done to see if there is harm, and then that harm remains constitutionally protected as entertainment and inflicting it is a civil liberty that the ACLU and a woman judge[3] and some women lawyers, identifying as feminists, defend?

202

Women in our hearings testified to the use of pornography to break their self-esteem, to train them to sexual submission, to season them to forced sex, to intimidate them out of job opportunities, to blackmail them into prostitution and keep them there, to terrorize and humiliate them into sexual compliance, and to silence their dissent. We heard testimony that it takes coercion to make pornography. We heard how pornography is forced on women and children in ways that give them no choice about viewing the pornography or performing the sex. We heard how pornography stimulates and condones rape, battery, sexual harassment, sexual abuse of children, and forced prostitution—all presented in the pornography as sex, sex, sex, sex, and more sex, respectively. Almost none of this had been reported. The most astounding event of all: they were believed. Why don't women lawyers, feminists, believe them? Or, if they do, why don't they act as though they give a goddamn? Why do they tell us it is doing something about pornography that is so risky and endangers our freedom, and talk about *this* status quo as if it has no risks and *is* that freedom?

Under current law, the First Amendment, which guarantees speech against abridgment by government, recognizes exceptions. It is also at times outweighed by other interests. The most common reason is harm: the harm done by the materials outweighs their expressive value, if any. Harm to someone who matters. Why are there women lawyers, feminists, trying to make sure that women don't matter enough?

Our law is not criminal. It places enforcement in the hands of the victim, not the state. It is not protective unless suing organized crime is a form of protection. It does not provide for a ban unless relief for a proven injury is a ban. Its trafficking provision is not a "prior restraint"—the one thing Judge Barker in Indianapolis, a woman lawyer, not a feminist—got right. The harm is not triggered by any kind of offensiveness. Why do even feminist lawyers repeatedly make this law into what it is not in order to attack it?

Speech interests have been outweighed to some degree when materials are false, obscene, indecent, racist, coercive, threatening, intrusive, inconvenient, commercial, or inaesthetic. Why can't they be civilly actionable if they are coerced? If they are sex discriminatory? What or who are women lawyers who oppose this possibility protecting—and why are they calling their opposition feminism?

The most attacked provision of the ordinance is the trafficking cause of action, which reaches production, sale, exhibition, and distribution. We know that pornography targets women, meaning that so long as the pornography is actively purveyed, saturating our communities, as it does now, women and children will be used and abused to make it, as they are now, and it will be used to abuse them, as it is now. When women lawyers, feminists, tell us to enforce existing law, the question is: why do we have to wait for each act of victimization to occur, confining the work of our lives to cleaning up after the pornographers one body at a time, never noticing that the bodies have a gender, never noticing that the victimization is centrally actualized through words and pictures, never noticing that we encounter the pornography in the laws, in the courts every time we try to prove we are hurt? The pornography sets the real rules of our lives. If we can't reach the traffic, this source of our condition is exempt, off limits, a base of operations outside direct attack through some laws of war we never agreed to. Why do women lawyers, feminists, oppose any avenue of change that might mean we don't have to spend our lives in this mop-up operation?

Pornography is historically defended in the name of freedom of speech. I am here to speak for those, particularly women and children, upon whose silence the law, including the law of the First Amendment, has been built. Their social inequality, which is not just fine, has never been taken into account in its jurisprudence. The First Amendment was written by those who already had the speech; they also had slaves, many of them, and owned women. They made sure to keep their speech safe from what threatened it: the federal government. You have to already have speech before the First Amendment, preventing government from taking it away from you, does you any good. Now the pornographers, who have the so-called speech, with women lawyers, feminists, fronting for them, take as a principled position that what the pornographers do is indistinguishable from what anyone else does, even in the face of our exact description of what they do, which is utterly unlike what anyone else does. Our definition of pornography is, in fact, the pornographers' definition: pornography is created by formula, it does not vary. No pornographer has any trouble knowing what to make. No adult bookstore or theater has any trouble knowing what to stock. No consumer has any trouble knowing what to buy. We only described what they all already know and do. Yet, knowing this, they and their supporters, including feminist lawyers, who have the speech, have taken the position that the pornographers are the rebels, the disenfranchised, and the hated, rather than the bearers and defenders of a ruling ideology of misogyny and racism and sexualized bigotry—hated to the tune of eight billion dollars a year, some of which they give to the ACLU and some women lawyers who identify as feminists and this conference.

Claiming to represent women, these people have in effect decided that there will continue to exist an entire class of women who will be treated in these ways so that they can have what they call freedom of speech. Freedom meaning their free access to women. Speech meaning women's bodies saying what they want them to say.

Why are women lawyers, feminists, siding with the pornographers? To be a lawyer orients you to power, probably sexually as well as in every other way. The law has a historical hostility to new ideas, hurt women, and social change. But more than that, we were let into this profession on the implicit condition that we would enforce the real rules: women kept out and down, sexual access to women enforced. These remain the rules whether you are in and up, and whether you practice it or have it practiced on you. It keeps the value of the most exceptional women high to keep other women out and down and on their backs with their legs spread. I may be missing something, but I don't see a lot of women lawyers, feminist or otherwise, selling their asses on the street or looking for a pornographer with a camera in order to fulfill their sexual agency and I don't think it is because they are sexually repressed. What law school does for you is this: it tells you that to become a lawyer means to forget your feelings, forget your community, most of all, if you are a woman, forget your experience. Become a maze-bright rat. Women lawyers as a group have not been much of an exception to this, except that they go dead in the eyes like ghetto children, unlike the men, who come out of law school glowing in the dark. Women who defend the pornographers are defending a source of their relatively high position among women under male supremacy, keeping all women, including them, an inferior class on the basis of sex, enforced by sexual force.

I really want you to stop your lies and misrepresentations of our position. I want you to do something about your thundering ignorance about the way women are treated. I want you to remember your own lives. I also really want you on our side. But, failing that, I want you to stop claiming that your liberalism, with its elitism, and your Freudianism, with its sexualized misogyny, has anything in common with feminism.

sixteen

The Sexual Politics of the First Amendment (1986)

[The Dred Scott case] was a law to be cited, a lesson to be learned, judicial vigor to be emulated, political imprudence to be regretted, but most of all, as time passed, it was an embarrassment—the Court's highly visible skeleton in a transparent closet.

Don E. Ferrenbacher, *The Dred Scott Case: Its Significance in American Law and Politics*

Frankfurter is said to have remarked that Dred Scott was never mentioned by the Supreme Court any more than ropes and scaffolds were mentioned by a family that had lost one of its number to the hangman.

Bruce Catton, in John A. Garraty, ed., *Quarrels That Have Shaped the Constitution*

The Constitution of the United States, contrary to any impression you may have received, is a piece of paper with words written on it. Because it is old, it is considered a document. When it is interpreted by particular people under particular conditions, it becomes a text. Because it is backed up by the power of the state, it is a law.

Feminism, by contrast, springs from the impulse to self-respect in every woman. From this have come some fairly elegant things: a metaphysics of mind, a theory of knowledge, an approach to ethics, and a concept of social action. Aspiring to the point of view of all women on social life as a whole, feminism has expressed itself as a political movement for civil equality.

Looking at the Constitution through the lens of feminism, initially one sees exclusion of women from the Constitution. This is simply to say that we had no voice in the constituting document of this state. From that one can suppose that those who did constitute it may not have had the realities of our situation in mind.

This speech was delivered at the Seventeenth Annual Conference on Women and the Law, panel on Feminist Ethical Approaches to the First Amendment, organized by Lorelei Pettigrew, Chicago, Illinois, Mar. 23, 1986.

Next one notices that the Constitution as interpreted is structured around what can generically be called the public, or state action. This constituting document pervasively assumes that those guarantees of freedoms that must be secured to citizens begin where law begins, with the public order. This posture is exalted as "negative liberty"[1] and is a cornerstone of the liberal state. You notice this from the feminist standpoint because women are oppressed socially, prior to law, without express state acts, often in intimate contexts. For women this structure means that those domains in which women are distinctively subordinated are assumed by the Constitution to be the domain of freedom.

Finally, combining these first two observations, one sees that women are not given affirmative access to those rights we need most. Equality, for example. Equality, in the words of Andrea Dworkin, was tacked on to the Constitution with spit and a prayer. And, let me also say, late.

If we apply these observations to the First Amendment, our exclusion means that the First Amendment was conceived by white men from the point of view of their social position. Some of them owned slaves; most of them owned women.[2] They wrote it to guarantee their freedom to keep something they felt at risk of losing.[3] Namely—and this gets to my next point—speech which they did not want lost through state action. They wrote the First Amendment so their speech would not be threatened by this powerful instrument they were creating, the federal government. You recall that it reads, "Congress shall make no law abridging . . . the freedom of speech." They were *creating* that body. They were worried that it would abridge something they *did have.* You can tell that they had speech, because what they said was written down: it became a document, it has been interpreted, it is the law of the state.[4]

By contrast with those who wrote the First Amendment so they could keep what they had, those who didn't have it didn't get it. Those whose speech was silenced prior to law, prior to any operation of the state's prohibition of it, were not secured freedom of speech. Their speech was not regarded as something that had to be—and this gets to my next point—affirmatively guaranteed. Looking at the history of the First Amendment from this perspective, reprehensible examples of state attempts to suppress speech exist. But they constitute a history of comparative privilege in contrast with the history of silence of those whose speech has never been able to exist for the state even to contemplate abridging it.

207

Pornography

A few affirmative guarantees of access to speech do exist. The *Red Lion* decision is one, although it may be slated for extinction.[5] Because certain avenues of speech are inherently restricted—for instance, there are only so many broadcast frequencies—according to the *Red Lion* doctrine of fairness in access to broadcast media, some people's access has to be restricted in the interest of providing access to all. In other words, the speech of those who could buy up all the speech there is, is restricted. Conceptually, this doctrine works exactly like affirmative action. The speech of those who might be the only ones there, is not there, so that others' can be.

With a few exceptions like that[6] we find no guarantees of access to speech. Take, for example, literacy. Even after it became clear that the Constitution applied to the states, nobody argued that the segregation of schools that created inferior conditions of access to literacy for Blacks violated their First Amendment rights. Or the slave codes that made it a crime to teach a slave to read and write or to advocate their freedom.[7] Some of those folks who struggled for civil rights for Black people must have thought of this, but I never heard their lawyers argue it. If access to the means of speech is effectively socially precluded on the basis of race or class or gender, freedom from state burdens on speech does not meaningfully guarantee the freedom to speak.

First Amendment absolutism, the view that speech must be absolutely protected, is not the law of the First Amendment. It is the conscience, the superego of the First Amendment, the implicit standard from which all deviations must be justified. It is also an advocacy position typically presented in debate as if it were legal fact. Consider for example that First Amendment bog, the distinction between speech and conduct. Most conduct is expressive as well as active; words are as often tantamount to acts as they are vehicles for removed cerebration. Case law knows this.[8] But the first question, the great divide, the beginning and the end, is still the absolutist question, "Is it speech or isn't it?"

First Amendment absolutism was forged in the crucible of obscenity litigation. Probably its most inspired expositions, its most passionate defenses, are to be found in Justice Douglas's dissents in obscenity cases.[9] This is no coincidence. Believe him when he says that pornography is at the core of the First Amendment. Absolutism has developed through obscenity litigation, I think, because pornography's protection fits perfectly with the power relations embedded in First Amendment structure and jurisprudence from the start. Pornography is exactly that speech of men that silences the speech of women. I take it seriously when Justice Douglas speaking on pornography and others preaching absolutism say that pornography has to be protected speech or else free expression will not mean what it has always meant in this country.

I must also say that the First Amendment has become a sexual fetish through years of absolutist writing in the melodrama mode in *Playboy* in particular. You know those superheated articles where freedom of speech is extolled and its imminent repression is invoked. Behaviorally, *Playboy*'s consumers are reading about the First Amendment, masturbating to the women, reading about the First Amendment, masturbating to the women, reading about the First Amendment, masturbating to the women. It makes subliminal seduction look subtle. What is conveyed is not only that using women is as legitimate as thinking about the Constitution, but also that if you don't support these views about the Constitution, you won't be able to use these women.

This general approach affects even religious groups. I love to go speaking against pornography when the sponsors dig up some religious types, thinking they will make me look bad because they will agree with me. Then the ministers come on and say, "This is the first time we've ever agreed with the ACLU about anything . . . why, what she's advocating would *violate the First Amendment.*" This isn't their view universally, I guess, but it has been my experience repeatedly, and I have personally never had a minister support me on the air. One of them finally explained it. The First Amendment, he said, also guarantees the freedom of religion. So this is not only what we already know: regardless of one's politics and one's moral views, one is into using women largely. It is also that, consistent with this, First Amendment absolutism resonates historically in the context of the long-term collaboration in misogyny between church and state. Don't let them tell you they're "separate" in that.

In pursuit of absolute freedom of speech, the ACLU has been a major institution in defending, and now I describe their behavior, the Nazis, the Klan, and the pornographers. I am waiting for them to add the antiabortionists, including the expressive conduct of their violence. Think about one of their favorite metaphors, a capitalist metaphor, the marketplace of ideas. Think about whether the speech of the Nazis has historically enhanced the speech of the Jews. Has the speech of the Klan expanded the speech of Blacks? Has the so-called speech of the pornographers enlarged the speech of women?

209

Pornography

In this context, apply to what they call the marketplace of ideas the question we were asked to consider in the keynote speech by Winona LaDuke: Is there a relationship between our poverty in speech and their wealth?

As many of you may know, Andrea Dworkin and I, with a lot of others, have been working to establish a law that recognizes pornography as a violation of the civil rights of women in particular. It recognizes that pornography is a form of sex discrimination. Recently, in a fairly unprecedented display of contempt, the U.S. Supreme Court found that the Indianapolis version of our law violates the First Amendment.[10] On a direct appeal, the Supreme Court invalidated a local ordinance by summary affirmance—no arguments, no briefs on the merits, no victims, no opinion, not so much as a single line of citation to controlling precedent. One is entitled to think that they would have put one there if they had had one.

The Court of Appeals opinion they affirmed[11] expressly concedes that pornography violates women in all the ways Indianapolis found it did. The opinion never questioned that pornography is sex discrimination. Interesting enough, the Seventh Circuit, in an opinion by Judge Frank Easterbrook, conceded the issue of objective causation. The only problem was, the harm didn't matter as much as the materials mattered. They are valuable. So the law that prohibited the harm the materials caused was held to be content-based and impermissible discrimination on the basis of viewpoint.

This is a law that gives victims a civil action when they are coerced into pornography, when pornography is forced on them, when they are assaulted because of specific pornography, and when they are subordinated through the trafficking in pornography. Some of us thought that sex discrimination and sexual abuse were against public policy. We defined pornography as the sexually explicit subordination of women through pictures or words that also includes presentations of women being sexually abused. There is a list of the specific acts of sexual abuse. The law covers men, too. We were so careful that practices whose abusiveness some people publicly question—for example, submission, servility, and display—are not covered by the trafficking provision. So we're talking rape, torture, pain, humiliation: we're talking violence against women turned into sex.

Now we are told that pornography, which, granted, does the harm we say it does, this pornography as we define it is protected speech. It has speech value. You can tell it has value as speech because it is so effective in doing the harm that it does.[12] (The passion of this rendition is mine, but the opinion really does say this.) The more harm, the more protection. This is now apparently the law of the First Amendment, at least where harm to women is the rationale. Judge LaDoris Cordell spoke earlier about the different legal standards for high-value and low-value speech, a doctrine that feminists who oppose pornography have always been averse to. But at least it is now clear that whatever the value of pornography is—and it is universally conceded to be low—the value of women is lower.

It is a matter of real interest to me exactly what the viewpoint element in our law is, according to Easterbrook's opinion. My best guess is that our law takes the point of view that women do not enjoy and deserve rape, and he saw that as just one point of view among many. Where do you suppose he got that idea? Another possible rendering is that our law takes the position that women should not be subordinated to men on the basis of sex, that women are or should be equal, and he regards relief to that end as the enforcement of a prohibited viewpoint.

Just what is and is not valuable, is and is not a viewpoint, is and is not against public policy was made even clearer the day after the summary affirmance. In the *Renton* case the Supreme Court revealed the conditions under which pornography can be restricted: it can be zoned beyond the city limits.[13] It can be regulated this way on the basis of its "secondary effects"—which are, guess what, property values. But it cannot be regulated on the basis of its primary effects on the bodies of the women who had to be ground up to make it.

Do you think it makes any difference to the woman who is coerced into pornography or who has just hit the end of this society's chances for women that the product of her exploitation is sold on the other side of the tracks? Does it matter to the molested child or the rape victim that the offender who used the pornography to get himself up or to plan what he would do or to decide what "type" to do it to had to drive across town to get it? It *does* matter to the women who live or work in the neighborhoods into which the pornography is zoned. They pay in increased street harassment, in an atmosphere of terror and contempt for what other neighborhoods gain in keeping their property values up.

Reading the two decisions together, you see the Court doing what it has always done with pornography: making it available in private while decrying it in public. Pretending to be tough on pornography's effects, the *Renton* case still *gives it a place to exist*. Although obscenity is supposed to have such little value that it is not considered speech at all, *Renton* exposes the real bottom line of the First Amendment: the pornography stays. Anyone who doesn't think absolutism has made any progress, check that.

Why is it that obscenity law can exist and our trafficking provision cannot? Why can the law against child pornography exist and not our law against coercion? Why aren't obscenity[14] and child pornography[15] laws viewpoint laws? Obscenity, as Justice Brennan pointed out in his dissent in *Renton*, expresses a viewpoint: sexual mores should be more relaxed, and if they were, sex would look like pornography.[16] Child pornography also presents a viewpoint: sex between adults and children is liberating, fulfilling, fun, and natural for the child. If one is concerned about the government taking a point of view through law, the laws against these things express the state's opposition to these viewpoints, to the extent of making them crimes to express. Why is a time-place-manner distinction all right in *Renton*, and not our forcing provision, which is kind of time-and-place-like and does not provide for actions against the pornographers at all? Why is it all right to make across-the-board, content-based distinctions like obscenity and child pornography, but not our trafficking provision, not our coercion provision?

When do you see a viewpoint as a viewpoint? When you don't agree with it. When is a viewpoint not a viewpoint? When it's yours.[17] What is and is not a viewpoint, much less a prohibited one, is a matter of individual values and social consensus. The reason Judge Easterbrook saw a viewpoint in our law was because he disagrees with it. (I don't mean to personify it, because it isn't at all personal; I mean, it *is* him, personally, but it isn't him only or only him, as a person.) There is real social disagreement as to whether women are or should be subordinated to men. Especially in sex.

His approach obscured the fact that our law is not content-based at all; it is harm-based. A harm is an act, an activity. It is not just a mental event. Coercion is not an image. Force is not a representation. Assault is not a symbol. Trafficking is not simply advocacy. Subordination is an activity, not just a point of view. The problem is, pornography is both theory and practice, both a metaphor for and a means of the subordination of women. The Seventh Circuit allowed the fact that pornography has a theory to obscure the fact that it is a practice, the fact that it is a metaphor to obscure the fact that it is also a means.

I don't want you to misunderstand what I am about to say. Our law comes nowhere near anybody's speech rights,[18] and the literatures of other inequalities do not relate to those inequalities in the same way pornography relates to sexism. But I risk your misunderstanding on both of these points in order to say that there have been serious movements for liberation in this world. This is by contrast with liberal movements. In serious movements for human freedom, speech is serious, both the attempt to get some for those who do not have any and the recognition that the so-called speech of the other side is a form of the practice of the other side. In union struggles, yellow-dog presses are attacked.[19] Abolitionists attacked slave presses.[20] The monarchist press was not tolerated by the revolutionaries who founded this country.[21] When the White Circle League published a racist pamphlet, it was found to violate a criminal law against libeling groups.[22] After World War II the Nazi press was restricted in Germany by law under the aegis of the Allies.[23] Nicaragua considers it "immoral" and contrary to the progress of education and the cultural development of the people to publish, distribute, circulate, exhibit, transmit, or sell materials that, among other things, "stimulate viciousness," "lower human dignity," or to "use women as sexual or commercial objects."[24]

The analogy Norma Ramos mentioned between the fight against pornography to sex equality and the fight against segregation to race equality makes the analogy between the Indianapolis case and *Brown v. Board of Education*[25] evocative to me also. But I think we may be at an even prior point. The Supreme Court just told us that it is a constitutional right to traffic in our flesh, so long as it is done through pictures and words, and a legislature may not give us access to court to contest it. The Indianapolis case is the *Dred Scott*[26] of the women's movement. The Supreme Court told Dred Scott, to the Constitution, you are property. It told women, to the Constitution, you are speech. The struggle against pornography is an abolitionist struggle to establish that just as buying and selling human beings never was anyone's property right, buying and selling women and children is no one's civil liberty.

Afterword

Aplatform and a period of time and listeners who choose to be there create a threshold of mortality. If you never say anything else to them (you might not) and if you die right afterward (you could), what would have been worth this time? The chance to be heard always seems momentous. Each discourse in this collection was delivered, at some point, to a memorably responsive group—not one that arrived agreeing with me but one whose mental aliveness elicited these thoughts in this particular form. Audiences of every kind shaped these speeches. The audience is the material condition under which it suddenly becomes possible to want to say something, to know what one wants to say, to see a way to say the one thing that must be said. Specific audiences were, still are, the occasions, the life situations of these moments in consciousness. My part of the text is the interaction writ small; the audience is the interaction writ large, made world. To adapt what Lily Tomlin and Jane Wagner said of the relation between Andy Warhol's rendering of a Campbell's soup can and the soup can itself, the speech was soup, the audience was art.[1]

During a speech the audience is context. People listening in large numbers are highly communicative; it is unusual when they are not. They control how far and fast to go, how much of a raw nerve to expose without becoming intrusive, how deep to look into an open grave without widening a chasm that yawns there for the next three hours, when to risk the flight of an unfinished thought, when to use examples or analogies and which ones, and how idiomatic or specialized or imaged a vocabulary. Sometimes you feel someone think something specific and decide to address it. Speaking, for me, is always to a listener even more than writing is to a reader; it is at every moment "for the other." Spoken words carry the specific quality of their birth relation forever, even if they are later written down as one person's delivery. As a form, speaking remains dialogue.

After a presentation, the dialogue often becomes express, and the education of the speaker lasts as long as the janitor's shift. Then one can hear the pulse of hope, feel the texture of fear, see an evasion stumble, touch a perception as it moves, witness the gawky elegance

215

of an expressed experience finding its first legs. Notice, but remark as rarely as death is remarked to frame life, the silences that frame the speech.

From these exchanges I have learned that feminism—in the form of a tacit belief that women are human beings in truth but not in social reality—has gone deep into women and some younger men, becoming taken for granted, becoming part of the background. The feminism of women who do not identify as feminists, feminism delivered in the form of a self-respecting identity and a lived commitment to change for women, came to matter more than the identification. Women everywhere articulated their situations and analyzed their pain with confrontive realism, indominability, and solidarity—with, in short, more feminism than anything yet called feminism has exhausted or expressed. Those who have lived through or worked hands-on with violence against women displayed a more nuanced and systemic conceptual understanding than most published writing on the subject. Sometimes it seemed as though the more invisible the woman, the deeper the truth she possessed. More than any other group, former prostitutes were possessed by truth, haunted by truth, vivid with knowledge against a canon of credibility that has all but obliterated them. The professed feminism of many others, by contrast, began to seem tepid and removed, like heads talking, brittle and second hand, like upward mobility.

In the established abstract refuges of academia I often encountered a tendency to turn women into a field or an idea or a subspecialty, an artifact of one theoretical approach or another. Little deep challenge to existing approaches is happening in these places, less understanding of the lives of most women (or even, say, the sexual violence in academic women's own lives) and virtually no commitment to change. What is happening instead is frantic image management, with a lived accountability to the structure of power that has put these women where they are, and an apparent lack of awareness that their failure to question it helps keep most women out and down. Some of the women who are the most successful in existing terms, those who most exemplify the achievements feminism has fought to make possible to all—of whom, of course, there are very few—were, I found, the most likely to defend those abuses of women, such as prostitution and pornography, which keep their own value high, high at least among women. What does it mean when those few who have probably never had to sell their bodies on the street or for a camera defend as liberation the system of sex for survival that comprises the limits of the possible for so many? Who is Linda Marchiano to them? If I had ever been tempted to mistake the ghetto of the organized women's movement for women in movement, this ended it.

The intellectual defense of sexuality and gender as they are, couched in terms of more freedom having been achieved, while all aggregate indices show that the options available to most women have improved little, is epidemic. This suggests not only an independent stake in the belief in progress, not only a sentimentalist tendency to see things as actually being the way one wishes they were, but a vision of change for all having been traded for a better deal for some. One struggles to recall that there was a vision of change that meant more than the sum of individual advances. Perhaps the meaning for the women's movement of the national turn to the right is that more and more are settling for less and less, for things as they are, feminists included. Maybe this is one of the ways that initially brave movements for change come to settle for so little and turn into more of the same.

Take, for example, lawyers, a group whose radicals concededly tend to look radical only when compared with other lawyers during the best of times. Too many women lawyers seem comfortable seeing women as in need of help, as a perpetual client population. But when confronted with a serious risk of empowerment, many of them become remarkably system-identified and start talking about rights we all enjoy, as if legal neutrality were not a coverup for inequalities we do not all equally share. This is at once fertile self-reflection and familiarly treacherous ground. This system survives partly because such women give it a patina of legitimacy by functioning as the pads on its cells, softening its appearance of force. But they are not the other side. A political movement simply implodes when internal betrayals become the only other side it can see.

Audiences constantly expressed their desire for sexual connection undominated by dominance, unimplicated in the inequality of the sexes, a sexuality of one's own yet with another, both of whom are equally present because yes is meaningful because no is meaningful. Meaning in relation is understood to require much more than a scenario of sensation; pleasure is easy compared with connection, which is hard. The problem, it seems to me, is that many people want to believe they already have this more than they want to have it. Their questions suggested this in many forms: because sex feels good, this critique is bad; because I want sex to feel right, this critique is wrong; because I (want to) believe sex could feel true, this critique is false.

217

Afterword

Their questions come in many voices: since Freud, the derepression of sexuality has been part of the movement for human liberation, which, as I understand it, you seem to be questioning . . .; you mean, all these years with Claire . . . ? What we have had, what we do have, what we can have are deeply confounded here. The tenses and levels get mixed by an underlying biologism through which sexuality is part of the natural world first, the social world incidentally, the political world only when the state gets involved. Audiences want to affirm that the sexuality for which we need what we do not have—a society of sex equality—already exists and merely needs to be unearthed. They desperately want at least an account of its current possibility.

To put it mildly, people take sex personally. A woman has to feel bad about sex every minute, apparently, or a critique of sexuality as a realm of sex inequality is reductive or demeaning or incorrect. In serious political analyses, say marxism, a worker can sometimes have a good day or even a good job. That does not mean the worker has false consciousness or the work is not exploited labor, structurally speaking. Conceiving the sexual as a realm of the subjective, the final outpost of individual feeling, the touchstone for authentic emotion, is part of the way the sexual works as politics, so that sexual abuse can become what is called sex. Because sexism is basic and has been impervious to basic change, it makes sense that it would live in something socially considered basic, deceptively a part of the given, enshrouded with celebratory myth and ritual. Sex feeling good may mean that one is enjoying one's subordination; it would not be the first time. Or it may mean that one has glimpsed freedom, a rare and valuable and contradictory event. Under existing conditions, what else would freedom be? The point is, the possible varieties of interpersonal engagement, including the pleasure of sensation or the experience of intimacy, does not, things being as they are, make sex empowering for women. Frankly, this is not news, but it is apparently as tabooed and as subversive as the equally old public declaration that the emperor has no clothes. Which probably ruined his good time, too.

Many women in this country believe gender is a crushing reality from which no woman is exempt. They also believe, or rather act out a belief on a daily basis, that they are or can be exempt. If every tacit "present company excluded" exception I encountered on the road were excluded from the analysis, an analysis would remain that everyone accepts as generally true, but that almost no one—meaning nearly everyone—acknowledges applies to them in particular. Sexuality is like this with a vengeance. Sometimes I say that those who believe women can fuck our way to freedom have rather limited horizons. Sometimes I say that their denial of reality means that they don't like the same things we don't like and do want the same things we want. Sometimes I feel I am spitting in an ocean.

Audiences want to hear about the design of life after male supremacy. Or, after all this negative, what do I have to say positive. This requests a construction of a future in which the present does not exist, under existing conditions. It dreams that the mind were free and could, like Milton, make a heaven of hell or a hell of heaven. The procedure is: imagine the future you want, construct actions or legal rules or social practices *as if* we were already there, and that will get us from here to there. This magical approach to social change, which is methodologically liberal, lives entirely in the head, a head that is more determined by present reality than it is taking seriously, yet it is not sufficiently grounded in that reality to do anything about it. As one scholar (a man) said to one ACLU liberal (a woman) who told him if he didn't like the record albums (fill in television, convenience store, cable, newsstand, theater, or adult bookstore pornography), he didn't have to expose himself to them, "What world do you live in?" As a strategy for social change (as opposed to a narrative strategy for fiction, for instance), the "let's pretend" strategy is idealist and elitist both. How can its proponents not miss women's voices too much to proceed to imagine *for them* the world they should be part of building? Maybe one reason liberalism accomplishes so little is that it is designed to serve those who want to think or say or imagine they are doing good more than they want to do it.

Not to mention that to consider "no more rape" as only a negative, no more than an absence, shows a real failure of imagination. Why does "out now" contain a sufficiently positive vision of the future for Vietnam and Nicaragua but not for women? Is it perhaps because Vietnam and Nicaragua exist, can be imagined without incursions, while women are unimaginable without the violation and validation of the male touch?

Many of my listeners express anguish and embarrassment that women in positions of power behave just as badly as men. The question whether women would exercise power "differently" always smells faintly of the body, as if women might be congenitally nicer or would mother the country as head of state or would clean up corruption because of a genetic affinity for cleaning. From the left, this question usually stands in for whether women in power would change anything—meaning anything other than the powerlessness of women. I think that men are the way they are because they have power, more than that they have power because they are the way they are. If this is so, women who succeed to male forms of power will largely be that way too. This will seem inappropriate only to those who expected less and to those who expected more. Which includes nearly everybody.

I have to admit being among those who did expect more from Judge Ellen Bree Burns, who judged the first case of sexual harassment in education as her first major case on the federal bench. She decided that Pamela Price, a Black woman student at Yale, was not credible when she accused a white male Yale professor of sexually harassing her.[2] The case did establish that sexual harassment is a legal claim for sex discrimination in education. But the judge's findings of fact were so unsupported that they were unreviewable, hence irreversible.[3] In a true triumph of hope over experience, I continued to expect more from Judge Sarah Evans Barker who, in her first major case on the federal bench, decided that pornography, about which she had little good to say, was more important than women were. She misquoted and mischaracterized the ordinance under review, blamed the victims, and treated the law of sex discrimination as if it did not exist.[4] The demands of the judicial role did not require either decision, but ruling the other way surely would have compromised these women's protective coloration. Did we work to put them there so they could pass? There are, of course, counterexamples.[5] But most women in power are accountable to men in power, because those in power are men. When women in power are accountable to women, it is because they choose to be, just as some men do. This will be true as long as sex inequality exists.

Many questions I was repeatedly asked revolved about a tacit free will/determinism axis. For example, the parade of horrors demonstrating the systematic victimization of women often produces the criticism that for me to *say* women are victimized reinforces the stereotype that women "are" victims, which in turn contributes to their victimization. If this stereotype is a stereotype, it has already been accomplished, and I come after. To those who think "it isn't good for women to think of themselves as victims," and thus seek to deny the reality of their victimization, how can it be good for women to deny what is happening to them? Since when is politics therapy?

Two deeper notions of the function of speech are at work here, though. One is that whatever is authoritatively *said* creates reality.

The other involves a utopian conception of the task of political speech. From their vantage point, my purpose on that platform is not to capture and confront the truth, but to invent a desirable vision of the world for the audience to crawl into for a few hours. In this conception of politics as fantasy and entertainment, the speaker speaks as though what she wishes were true *is true* as a strategy for making it so. Speak as though women are not victimized and we will not be any more. Apparently it is the *image* of women as victims that comes first, then their treatment accordingly. Exposing the truth of women's victimization by speech thus becomes more dangerous than covering up the fact of women's victimization by silence. Speech has an almost mystical power here. This is so odd, coming as it always does from those who argue that pornography cannot be harmful because all it does is propagate false images of women, which are only images. I do understand one thing that those who believe this seem (unaccountably) not to: the experience of sex in pictures and words is an experience of sex. I have yet to understand why my critique of victimization through sex is part of victimization through sex.

I do understand that in the liberal mind, the worse and more systematic one's mistreatment is, the more it seems justified. Liberalism has a regard for power that never *sees* it, yet sees *only* it: it never sees power as power, yet can see as significant only that which power does. One example is the belief that sexual abuse is inevitable. The more we expose the extent of sexual abuse, the more we show it is common, pervasive, persistent, legitimate, and utterly random, the more we support its inevitability. A similar convergence of denial with despair forms a set of bedrock beliefs that most of my audiences do not believe they believe: they do not believe they believe rape is inevitable, but they do; they do not believe they believe the media, but they do; they do not believe they believe they are exempt from gender, but they do.[6] More than anything else I spoke about, these beliefs, which insinuate themselves into society on the level of a sneaky metaphysics, this deep structure of sex inequality rose and cracked like an iceberg when I spoke on pornography.

Speaking about pornography is not like speaking about anything else. It is crazier. It has logic by Escher. Things fall up. It makes grown men cry and smart people stupid. Those who speak as if they know everything there is to know about pornography often, it turns out, have never seen any. Those who, it turns out, know everything there is to know about pornography from rather intimate acquaintance often act as though they haven't the faintest idea what I am talking

221

about. Some say that doing something about pornography won't do anything real because it isn't real. Others are in a panic because they are convinced that doing anything about pornography will take something very real away from them. When I suggest that *they* go in a room and work this out like the Three Christs of Ypsilanti,[7] that seems to be the cue for those who will consider my critique if they like my solution to ask me about a future in which pornography has magically disappeared overnight. The epistemic situation is one in which, almost necessarily, the best are ignorant and the informed have lost all sensibility.

Some of the social theorists in my audiences are not convinced that pornography can be part of the subordination of women because the subordination of women happens in places where, they say, there is no pornography. So the theory is not historically specific enough. Pornography, they say, is effect and not cause because the oppression of women predates pornography, so anything done about pornography will do nothing about the oppression of women. It does not matter that racism happens in specific forms all over the world without ceasing to be racist. It does not matter that these people think something should be done about the Ku Klux Klan even though white racists in South Africa do not wear sheets and burn crosses. It does not matter that they know that the Holocaust was an anti-Semitic atrocity on a world-historic scale, even though it happened only in Germany and anti-Semitism predates the Third Reich. They do not say apartheid should be ignored as effect rather than cause because white racism predates it and happens elsewhere in different forms. They do not say the camps do not matter because Jews were also victims of pogroms in Russia and torture in Argentina, where there are no Nazis. It does not even matter that other social theorists are not persuaded that pornography is part of male supremacy because male supremacy is a cultural universal—so the theory is not universal enough. It does not worry any of them that women's situation fits none of their theories. Nothing matters except that the pornography stays. That is gravity.

Audiences of lawyers say it is politically naive to rely on courts to administer our pornography law our way. Then they say we should rely on existing law and existing courts for relief of any harms of pornography that they concede are real. Our civil rights law will produce a police state, they say. Then they recommend vigorous enforcement of criminal laws against rapists and batterers, whose victims are conceded to number well over half of all women.[8] When told that

222

they are, in effect, recommending reversing the numbers of those in and out of prisons, they say, do not rely on law at all. Now that we want a law against pornography, they say that law doesn't do anything significant anyway. Rely on the First Amendment—as if that is not a law. Forget law, educate—as if law is not educational. They say that the state is eager for the chance to suppress all sexually explicit materials. They have no explanation—these, the political sophisticates to our political naiveté—for the fact that with a tool as vague and discretionary as criminal obscenity statutes, this same state has stood by and watched the pornography industry double in the last ten years.[9] Some day try solving a legal problem that has vexed legal minds for decades only to find (or, perhaps, to prove) that many people do not want it solved. And that many of these people are lawyers.

Many in my audiences appear convinced that ads do a lot more damage to women than even the most violent pornography. This is because ads are more legitimate, more pervasive, more artistic, more subtle, and do not show recognizable violence . . . but *Playboy* is absolutely harmless. Some are so concerned about the larger evil of mass media as a whole—of which pornography is only a small part—that nothing should be done about any of it. (They want a law to regulate ads maybe?)

Pornography is ideas; ideas matter. Whatever goes on in the mind of pornography's consumer matters tremendously. The final horror of the astronauts plunging to their deaths was that they might have *known*, for a final series of seconds, what was about to happen to them. But whatever goes on in the minds of women hurt through pornography, or even all women, who live knowing what *will*, sooner or later, happen to them, and then it happens—that is trivial and does not matter at all. Understand, these are people who claim to understand what Derrida means when he says that speech is "always already" writing, but claim not to be able to grasp how sexuality could be always already pornography. Then there are the interpretation people, for whom social reality has no fixed, determinate reality. Society is all mental. Pornography, too, is just a fantasy. But if *it* is only mental, in a world in which *everything* is only mental, why isn't it as real as anything else?

Lawyers think this issue is all political, politicians think it is all legal, and the guardians of the First Amendment are telling me what I cannot *say:* to the Women and the Law Conference I cannot say what feminism means; to governmental bodies I cannot say I speak in the interest of women; on national news I cannot say that pornography makes all women into cunts, a status now, with the repudiation of a law guaranteeing women's rights against pornography, officially sanctioned by the U.S. Supreme Court. The republic will fall if anything is done for women who are hurt by these materials, but no damage is done by keeping us from speaking about it. Distributors are so intimidated by being asked, in words, if they sell pornography that they might choose not to sell it, therefore foregoing protected rights, but pornography itself intimidates no one, invades no protected rights, because it is only words.[10] And all the lies got there first: Linda loved it, we all do; feminist work against pornography is inherently right wing; the First Amendment is absolute and in constant danger; women are already legally inviolate and in no danger at all.

Speaking about pornography is also not like speaking about anything else because one is told that pornography is exactly like everything else. This contention is central to every intellectual defense of pornography—by which I mean central to those defenders of pornography who present their defenses in intellectual terms, and pornography has long had its intellectual defenders. They come to my speeches too. To them, pornography is the good, the true, and the beautiful. Good because it liberates sexuality, because it is sex, and sex is good. True because it reflects what happens, the empirically accurate, which (in an act of conceptual imperialism) they term reality. Beautiful because it embodies all that is valued in literature and art. Moving on from the good, its unfettered availability is just, therefore legal. Moving on from the true, it is scientific, because what it shows must have happened. (And happened, and happened, and happened.) And, moving on from the beautiful—believe me, *anything* has "an aesthetic." In this way, what is done to women is transformed into sex and speech, each defended by an absolutism: Freudian absolutism for sex, First Amendment absolutism for speech. To object that this is being done *to women* is to be told that one is too literal, too simple-minded, one mistakes the reality of women for the idea of women, a fantasy of a dead prostitute for her life.

Traditionalists, who do not like the way I talk about men and cannot understand why I am against obscenity law, take the opposite position. Instead of being the good, the true, and the beautiful, pornography is the bad, the false, and the ugly. To moralists from Lawrence to Falwell, pornography does dirt to sex, makes sex look bad. To the scientists, the ever-hopeful, the true social innocents, it

224

portrays sexuality inaccurately (don't we wish). And to the aesthetes, it is tasteless.

Maybe some day someone will explain to me why the feminist critique of pornography—clearly labeled a political argument for a redistribution and transformation in the terms of power—is taken by both pornography's traditional defenders and its traditional critics to be the secular equivalent of how to get into heaven, of how to live a more upright life, a so-American "how-to." But the strangest experience in this crowded field is simply, factually, to describe the pornography, only to have that description taken as a moral exhortation. I will never get used to this. I keep imagining that the question of whether it is a *good idea* systematically to torture and demean human beings is closed—even when it is done for pleasure and profit, even when it is done through pictures and words, even when it is called sex and done to women.

Recall that the feminist critique of pornography, which is not like anything else, is one in which pornography is presented as not like anything else. Pornography, in these talks, is not a question of good or bad, false or true, edifying or tawdry, but of power and powerlessness. It is first a political question, a question of sexual politics.[11] Those for whom left and right are like north and south and who cannot navigate political waters without these points of reference may never understand this. Everyone else does. Women who have rejected every idea of sex equality they have ever heard leave these speeches, and those of other feminists working against pornography, calling pornography sex discrimination and meaning that it is part of the violation and exploitation of women as a class. The women with the responsive faces who never say anything pass me notes: "I am a civil libertarian and a victim. I don't know how you are going to do it, but it needs to be done."

The most likely to speak are the women with the "I am not really defending pornography" defense of pornography. They will never have as much credibility again in their lives, like those conservative women who opposed the Equal Rights Amendment in this society's last major debate on the meaning of sex equality under law, whose arguments they replicate in every formal respect.[12] Then it was said that the status quo was fine and getting better all the time. Any problems could be solved by enforcing existing laws. It was said that advocates of the ERA demeaned full-time wives and mothers by suggesting that they were victims of restricted options on the basis of sex rather than free agents exercising positive choice. Government

225

should not get involved in these intimate issues at all. With a measure so vague and so broad, there was no telling what it would cover. Then followed all the heinous things it clearly would cover, like pregnant women in foxholes and mothers forced to work outside the home. Why should we run all these risks just when things are getting better? Enforce the basic bargain, don't change it.

I think that these women—much ridiculed by the liberals—feared the meaning of sex equality in their lives, because sex inequality gave them what little they had, so little that they felt they couldn't afford to lose it.[13] They hung onto their crumbs from experience, as if that was all they were ever going to get. Even more, I think they opposed ERA because they heard in it a judgment of existing possibilities that meant that they had lived their one and only life under conditions that were less than they might have been, which made *them* less than they might have been. So they defended the life they identified with: the domestic status quo.

Women who oppose the civil rights law against pornography are simply conservative about other things. When they defend the life they identify with, it is the sexual status quo they defend. It is fine and getting better all the time. Enforcing existing laws would solve any remaining problems. Acknowledging civil rights for women in pornography suggests that they are victims of restricted options on the basis of their sex and that some are directly coerced. This demeans as victims women who choose to survive through sexual sale through pure free will. Besides, the government should not get involved in intimate issues like the subordination of women because who knows how far it will go. The law is so vague and so broad, who can tell what it would cover. Clearly, it would cover *Barbarella* and *The Taming of the Shrew*. Why run all these risks when we are just beginning to get the benefit of the sexual revolution? These women sense a judgment on their lives: that they have gone along with and sometimes even enjoyed inequality in the sexual sphere. They would rather live that way forever, and make sure other women do too, than face what it means, in order to change it. They recommend appeasement. Enforce the bargain, the bargain with *their* men. They may one day explain why women and children must be tortured and abused or no one can freely think, write, or publish.

Why do so many of us put so much into trying to get the benefit of a bargain that is hopelessly stacked against us and so little, comparatively, into trying to change it? Some old behavioral experiments stick, emblematically, in my mind. In one on rewards, chickens were

226

divided into three groups: the first group got fed every time they pecked; the second, every other time; the third, at random. When the food was cut off, the first group stopped trying immediately. The second group stopped soon after. The third group *never stopped trying*. In another experiment, on punishments, rats were shocked every time they tried to get out of their cages. After not too long, their cage doors could be left open for long periods, and they never intentionally tried to leave again.

Women are randomly rewarded and systematically punished for being women. We are not rewarded systematically and punished at random, as is commonly supposed. We may or may not be rewarded if we go along with male supremacy. If we try to get out of its cage, it is virtually certain we will be punished. Actually, we are punished whether we try to get out or not, which is not even done to rats in experiments. So we peck forever for the occasional crumb that seems to reward our efforts and reinforces our hopes out of all proportion to reality, and we spend the rest of our time skulking in the corners of the cages we no longer try to leave. Not even when the door—as it occasionally is, through inadvertence or compassion or perversity or who knows what, or maybe even because some others of us bent the thing or picked the lock—is ajar.[14]

In spite of everything, I suspect those who are fond of pronouncing the women's movement dead of sharing the pornographers' love for dead women, especially dead feminists. To those for whom "no more of this" is an insufficiently affirmative goal, I recommend the only definition of a human being I can recall that didn't make me secretly glad I wasn't one. Bishop Desmond Tutu, speaking about something Blacks under apartheid want from white South Africans, said, "All we are asking you to do is to recognize that we are humans, too. When you scratch us, we bleed. When you tickle us, we laugh."[15] Women in pornography, when you tickle us, we get turned on; when you scratch us, we start to come; when you kill us, we orgasm until death. So long as this is how we are seen and loved, in law and in life, women will not inhabit the world, and it is the whole world we are entitled to. Some of us are determined, if not exactly hopeful, that we will have it, whether we live to see it or not. We live here. Now we want to live here.

Three years into the debate over the civil rights law against pornography that Andrea Dworkin and I conceived, this is what I have come to think. If you define what you want and have a right to have narrowly, you will be satisfied—even grateful—to be given a corner of your own, flattered to be permitted to grow through a crack in the cement, and you will never notice that you are alone with a bunch of men. Words like "autonomy" and "merit" and "agency," you believe, meaningfully apply to your experience. And deep down, you don't believe that the woman in the pornography is you. If it is inescapably clear to you that women have been and still are confined to a very narrow corner, constrained by strictures that don't disappear no matter what we think about them, and down is not up, you realize you are in the company of women, and the woman in the pornography is you.

The question then becomes not whether one trusts the law to behave in a feminist way. We do not trust medicine, yet we insist it respond to women's needs. We do not trust theology, but we claim spirituality as more than a male preserve. We do not abdicate the control of technology because it was not invented by women. We do not abandon the environment, the more it is taken over. We do not trust the media; we are more likely to pressure it to express our values than to let it go on as it is because it doesn't. If women are to restrict our demands for change to spheres we can trust, spheres we already control, there will not be any.

The question the civil rights law against pornography raises, then, is not only when will acts of violation stop being defended as fantasies of violation, not only when will acts of cruelty stop being defended as acts of love, but when will women occupy the world? Access to things as they are, yes; to be taken on our own terms, that too. But more: to participate in defining the terms that create the standards, to be a voice in drawing the lines. This has been at the heart of every women's initiative for civil equality from suffrage to the Equal Rights Amendment: the simple notion that law—only words, words that set conditions as well as express them, words that are their own kind of art, words in power, words of authority, words in life—respond to women as well as to men.

Notes
Acknowledgments
Index

Notes

Introduction

1. Harris v. McRae, 448 U.S. 297 (1980). Attempts to take away the abortion right have been rebuffed, ever precariously, in Akron v. Akron Center for Reproduction Rights, Inc., 462 U.S. 416 (1983) and Thornburgh v. American College of Obstetricians and Gynecologists, 106 S. Ct. 2169 (1986).

2. Comparing the median income of the sexes from twenty-five to fifty-four years of age, 1975 to 1983, the U.S. Department of Labor Women's Bureau reports that in 1975, women made $8,155.00 to men's $14,105.00; in 1983, women made $15,349.66 to men's $24,458.33. U.S. Department of Labor, Women's Bureau, *Time of Change: 1983 Handbook of Women Workers,* Bulletin 298, 456 (1983). The same publication notes that "among professionals in 1981, men earned 54% more than did women." Id. at 92. In 1981, men's overall earnings exceeded women's by 68.8 percent. Id. at 93. The Equal Pay Act was passed in 1963.

3. Phyllis Chesler, *Mothers on Trial* (1986).

4. Julia R. Schwendinger and Herman Schwendinger, *Rape and Inequality,* Sage Library of Social Research, 44 (1983); Kenneth Polk, "Rape Reform and Criminal Justice Processing," 31 *Crime and Delinquency* 191–205 (April 1985) ("What can be concluded about the achievement of the underlying goals of the rape reform movement? . . . If a major goal is to increase the probability of convictions, then the results are slight at best . . . or even negligible." At 199) (California data); *see also* P. Bart and P. O'Brien, *Stopping Rape: Successful Survival Strategies* 129–31 (1985).

5. An example would be Federal Rule of Evidence 412, the "rape shield law," and its state counterparts, which preclude inquiry into an alleged rape victim's sexual history, except that with the perpetrator.

6. California Federal Savings and Loan Assn. v. Guerra, 758 F.2d 390 (9th Cir. 1985), *cert. granted,* 54 U.S.L.W. 3460 (Jan. 13, 1986). See "Difference and Dominance," note 18.

7. After ten years of steady legal progress in the lower courts, sexual harassment was unanimously held to be sex discrimination by the U.S. Supreme Court in 1986. Meritor Savings Bank, FSB v. Vinson, 106 S. Ct. 2399 (1986). Progress in the area of marital rape is charted by Joanne Schulman, "State-By-State Information on Marital Rape Exemption Laws," in Diana E. H. Russell, *Rape in Marriage* 375–81 (1982).

8. I refer to Robin Morgan's elemental *Sisterhood Is Powerful: An Anthology of Writings from the Women's Liberation Movement* (Robin Morgan ed.) (1970).

9. "Desire and Power" in Part I particularly develops this theme.

10. In addition to the colloquialism, I refer to the influence of Jacques Derrida, *e.g.*, his 1968 lecture, "La différance" in *Marges* (1972), fully expounded in *Of Grammatology* (G. Spivak trans. 1977) and *Positions* (Alan Bass trans. 1981). "Différance" in his sense is a triple pun, referring to combined meanings of differing/deferring/detouring, so that which is "different" is characterized by a presence always under erasure and a self never quite there, radically latent, constituted by its lack of full recognition and realization. However, Derrida does not treat women's "différance" as a social criticism of women's position under male supremacy. *See, e.g.*, his *Spurs: Nietzsche's Styles* (Barbara Harlow trans.) (1981).

11. *See* "Difference and Dominance" in Part I for a fuller discussion and critique of the theory that sex is a "difference."

12. *See* "Francis Biddle's Sister" in Part III.

13. After being passed and signed into law in Indianapolis, the civil rights law against pornography was sued by a coalition of publishers and distributors, some pornographers and some not, known as "The Media Coalition." The ordinance was found unconstitutional in two decisions by two Reagan appointees, American Booksellers v. Hudnut, 598 F. Supp. 1316 (S.D. Ind. 1984) (Barker, J.); Hudnut v. American Booksellers, 771 F.2d 323 (7th Cir. 1985) (Easterbrook, J.). The U.S. Supreme Court summarily affirmed, 106 S. Ct. 1172 (1986). See "The Sexual Politics of the First Amendment" in Part III for further discussion.

14. "Liberal legalism" is a phrase from Karl Klare, "Law-Making as Praxis," 12 *Telos* 123 (1979).

15. "Sex and Violence: A Perspective" in Part II contains an early development of the criticism of the idea that what is sex cannot be violent, and what is violent cannot be sex. The argument is further developed in Part III, particularly in "Francis Biddle's Sister."

16. Theorists who most expressly exemplify this tendency include Nancy Chodorow, *The Reproduction of Mothering: Psychoanalysis and the Sociology of Gender* (1978), Dorothy Dinnerstein, *The Mermaid and the Minotaur: Sexual Arrangements and Human Malaise* (1977), and Carol Gilligan, *In a Different Voice: Psychological Theory and Women's Development* (1982). The law of sex discrimination, both mainsteam doctrine under existing law and the interpretation that dominated the debate over the Equal Rights Amendment, takes basically the same view. For discussion, see "Not By Law Alone: From a Debate with Phyllis Schlafly" and "Difference and Dominance."

17. Florence Rush, *The Best-Kept Secret: Sexual Abuse of Children* (1980), Judith Herman, *Father-Daughter Incest* (1981), and Jeffrey M. Masson, *The Assault on Truth: Freud's Suppression of the Seduction Theory* (1983), show the ideology and history of the specifically Freudian disbelief that young girls are sexually violated by older men.

18. Diana Russell produced this figure at my request from the random sample data base of 930 San Francisco households discussed in her *The Secret Trauma: Incest in the Lives of Girls and Women* 20–37 (1986) and *Rape in Marriage*

27–41 (1982). The figure includes all the forms of rape or other sexual abuse or harassment surveyed, noncontact as well as contact, from gang rape by strangers to obscene phone calls, unwanted sexual advances on the street, unwelcome requests to pose for pornography, and subjection to peeping Toms and sexual exhibitionists (flashers).

19. Susan Brownmiller, *Against Our Will: Men, Women and Rape* (1975), is the most widely recognized work conceptualizing rape as violence, not sex. This was a breakthrough at a time when labeling virtually any act sex was considered exonerating—as in fact it still is. We must confront the further problem, however, that the line between sex and violence is indistinct and mobile in a society in which violence means violation of that worthy of respect, and women are not. The fact is, anything that anybody with power experiences as sex is considered ipso facto not violence, because someone who matters enjoyed it. And power, of which violence is merely an extreme expression, is apparently very sexy. The point is to confront all of this in fact rather than to try to wish it out of existence through theory.

20. Diana Scully and Joseph Marolla, "'Riding the Bull at Gilley's': Convicted Rapists Describe the Rewards of Rape," 32 *Social Problems* 251 (1985). (The manuscript version of this paper was subtitled "Convicted Rapists Describe the Pleasure of Raping.")

21. Henry Lee Lucas, quoted in S. Cook, "Grisly Saga of a 'Recreational Killer,'" *San Francisco Examiner*, Oct. 28, 1984, A15. (Lucas said he murdered twenty-three women; he may or may not have.) He may be referring to having sex as part of the torture leading to murder, to the sexual thrill of the murder itself, to having sex with the body after death, or to all three. *See also* Gordon Burn, ". . . *Somebody's husband, somebody's son": The Story of Peter Sutcliffe* 258–65 (1984).

22. Arthur Goode, on death row in Florida for sexual molestation and murder of children, is here quoted in *City Pages* (Minneapolis, Minn.) Mar. 9–15, 1984, 4,10.

23. Annie McCombs, *off our backs*, October 1984, at 34 ("understand that violence *is* sex to those who practice it *as* sex") (letter).

24. *See* Jacobo Timerman, *Prisoner Without a Name, Cell Without a Number* (1981). *See also Torture in the Eighties*, An Amnesty International Report (1984). A lot more inquiry is needed into the collective political effect on people of knowing that a triage process of selection for torture or death is actively occurring around them. Agents of torture other than nation states should be included in such investigations.

25. This theme is developed in "Difference and Dominance," and, in its application to culture and ethnicity, in "Whose Culture?" both in Part I.

26. To get a sense of what this distinction looks like in application, consider the contrast between gender as women live it, which is as an unequal distribution of power, and gender as it is abstractly theorized, which is as a bivariate differentiation. Observe that women as a group typically share some behaviors and attitudes common to victims regardless of sex. If gender is a difference, this commonality means that women's responses to victimiza-

tion are not sex based; when women exhibit these qualities, it is not as women, but as a part of the larger class of all victims, gender neutral. If gender is instead a substantive process of inequality, to be victimized in certain ways may mean to be feminized, to partake of the low social status of the female, to be made into the girl regardless of biological sex. This does not mean that men experience or share the meaning of being a woman, because part of that meaning is that the inferiority is indelible and total until it is changed for all women. It does mean that gender is an outcome of a social process of subordination that is only ascriptively tied to body and doesn't lose its particularity of meaning when it shifts embodied form. Femininity is a lowering that is imposed; it can be done to anybody and still be what feminine means. It is just women to whom it is considered natural.

27. *See* Edward M. Levi, *An Introduction to Legal Reasoning* 2,6,8 (1949). Most nonlawyers have no idea why lawyers think so peculiarly. For example, why must they always bring up other matters in order to discuss the one at hand? Lawyers have been taught that law is general rules to be both discerned and devised out of particular instances. Thus, to talk legally is to talk of any particular instance in terms of its general rulelike qualities, and vice versa. So lawyers want to look at other particular instances to see if the general rule that accords with a particular example would be equally desirable under other conditions. This always gives the appearance of proceeding according to some preformulated but obscure agenda. Its mechanistic quality makes the relation of legal thinking to thinking a bit like that of military music to music. More formally put, this legal method combines a Kantian-type categorical imperative with a rough scientific method, effecting a loose synthesis between liberal moralism and primitive positivism beneath a gloss of frontier pragmatism.

28. Berkey v. Third Avenue Ry. Co., 244 N.Y. 84, 94, 155 N.E. 58, 61 (1926).

29. Linda Lovelace and Michael McGrady, *Ordeal* (1980). See also her account with Michael McGrady of her life after escape, including her attempts to be believed, *Out of Bondage* (1986).

30. Although some jurisdictions have held *Deep Throat* obscene, and some have held it not obscene, the reality is that *Deep Throat* is freely sold and exhibited nearly everywhere, including over the counter in video stores worldwide and through home cassette markets.

Examples, not obscene: United States v. Various Articles of Obscene Merchandise, Schedule No. 2102, No. 81 Civ. 5295 (S.D.N.Y. Nov. 4, 1981) (United States sought forfeiture and condemnation of materials including *Deep Throat*. The court found that they were not patently offensive to the average person in that community), *aff'd*, 709 F.2d 132 (2d Cir. 1983) (no abuse of discretion in finding the materials "not patently offensive under contemporary standards in the New York area"); State v. Aiuppa, 298 So. 2d 391 (Fla. 1974) ("Juries in Jacksonville and Key West, Florida, have rendered verdicts that the movie 'Deep Throat' does not offend local community standards"); Keller v. State, 606 S.W. 2d 931 (Tex. Cr. App. 1980) ("[*Deep Throat* testified to as] 'the longest playing motion picture in Houston motion picture theatre history' . . . widespread attendance indicates community acceptance . . ." at 932, 933). *See also* City of Sioux Falls v. Mini-Kota Art Theatres, Inc., 247 N.W. 2d 676, 678–79 (S.D. 1977).

Examples, obscene: United States v. Battista, 646 F.2d 237 (6th Cir. 1981) (conviction of conspiracy to violate obscenity statute by transporting *Deep Throat* in interstate commerce, affirmed on appeal); United States v. Peraino, 645 F.2d 548 (6th Cir. 1981) (conviction of conspiracy to violate federal obscenity statute by transporting *Deep Throat* in interstate commerce overturned for due process lack of venue); United States v. One Reel of Film, 360 F. Supp. 1067 (D. Mass. 1973) (forfeiture of *Deep Throat* under 18 U.S.C. §1305 ordered); Fairvilla Twin Cinema II v. State *ex rel.* Eagan, 353 So. 2d 909 (Fla. App. 1977) (injunction restraining showing of *Deep Throat* issued); State *ex rel.* Cahalan v. Diversified Theatrical Corporation, 59 Mich. App. 223, 229 N.W. 2d 389 (1975) (*Deep Throat* enjoined as lewd, public nuisance); Western Corp. v. Commonwealth, 558 S.W. 2d 605 (Ky. 1977) (agreeing with jury verdict that *Deep Throat* lacks any serious literary, political, artistic, or scientific value); Magnum v. State's Attorney for Baltimore City, 275 Md. 450, 341 A.2d 786 (1975) ("This case [on *Deep Throat*] is the first case in which the question of hard-core pornography has been considered by this Court since the *Miller* definition was formulated . . . The film is clearly within the *Miller* definition of obscenity or hard-core pornography"); People v. Mature Enterprises, 73 Misc. 2d 749, 343 N.Y.S. 2d 911 (1971) (defendant guilty of obscenity in promoting obscene material, *Deep Throat* "a nadir of decadence" at 778), *aff'd* 36 N.Y.S. 2d 520, 323 N.E.2d 704 (1974); Houston v. Hennessey, 534 S.W.2d 52 (Mo. App. 1975) (*Deep Throat* obscene, theater enjoined from showing it held in contempt for violating order); Commonwealth v. 707 Main Corp., 371 Mass. 374, 357 N.E. 2d 753 (1976) (defendant guilty of obscenity in exhibiting *Deep Throat*); Coleman v. Wilson, 123 N.J. Super. 310, 302 A.2d 555 (1973) (*Deep Throat* obscene); Inland Empire Enterprises, Inc. v. Morton, 365 F. Supp. 1014 (C.D. Cal. 1973) (complaint to enjoin further searches and seizures of *Deep Throat* dismissed with prejudice as violating abstention from interference with state obscenity prosecutions).

Ambiguous: United States v. Marks, 520 F.2d 913 (1975) (*Deep Throat* is "obscenity at its worst" at 918) *rev'd*, 430 U.S. 188 (1977) (court must apply *Memoirs* test—is material "utterly without redeeming social value"?—because conduct occurred prior to *Miller*); United States v. Pinkus, 579 F.2d 1174 (9th Cir. 1978) (on remand from U.S. Supreme Court, use of *Deep Throat* as standard for named film, meets test of comparability, no decision on acceptability to community).

31. Mandina v. Lovelace, et al., No. 81–14286 (CA05) (Dade County, Florida). This case was settled in 1986.

32. Deposition of C——— M———, Mandina v. Lovelace (Jan. 18, 1986) 212 (victim of Charles Traynor just prior to his capture of Linda Marchiano).

33. *Effect of Pornography on Women and Children: Hearings Before the Subcommittee on Juvenile Justice of the Senate Committee on the Judiciary*, 98th Cong., 2d Sess. 227–55 (1984) (testimony of Andrea Dworkin).

34. This is probably why women who take themselves seriously and reject traditional femininity—reject being had—are so often regarded as lesbian whether they are or not. This may also be part of the necessity to stigmatize the lesbian—possibly even part of the identification itself, for some.

35. A defense of this debased notion of equality is central in the argument presented by F.A.C.T. (Feminist Anti-Censorship Task Force) in opposition to the civil rights ordinance against pornography. The brief argues that pornography must not be actionable by its victims because, among other reasons, "The range of feminist imagination and expression in the realm of sexuality has barely begun to find voice. Women need the freedom and the socially recognized space to appropriate for themselves the robustness of what traditionally has been male language." Brief Amici Curiae of Feminist Anti-Censorship Task Force, et al. 31, Hudnut v. American Booksellers, 771 F.2d 323 (7th Cir. 1985). Thus, "Even pornography which is problematic for women can be experienced as affirming of women's desires and of women's equality: 'Pornography can be a psychic assault . . . but for women as for men it can also be a source of erotic pleasure . . . A woman who enjoys pornography (even if that means enjoying a rape fantasy) is in a sense a rebel, insisting on an aspect of her sexuality that has been defined as a male preserve'" (quoting Ellen Willis). Id. at 30. Equality here clearly means equal access to pornography for women, that is, equal access *by women* to the population *of women* that must be treated in the ways the ordinance prohibits so the pornography of them can be made available. The F.A.C.T. brief further objects that "[t]he ordinance . . . delegitimates and makes socially invisible women who find sexually explicit images of women 'in positions of display' or 'penetrated by objects' to be erotic, liberating or educational." Id. at 42. The fact that the materials which present women "in positions of display" are actionable under the Indianapolis ordinance only by women coerced to make them or assaulted because of them raises the question of who is making whom invisible.

36. Tolerance of systematic inequality has been liberalism's solution to the famous obsession with "the slippery slope" that its penchant for abstraction creates. *See, e.g.,* F. Schauer, "Slippery Slopes," 99 *Harvard Law Review* 361 (1985). As liberals see this problem they invented, the trouble with doing anything about anything is that if you do something for somebody, you might have to do everything for everybody. It follows that nothing gets done for anybody. No step for some people ever leads to another step for anyone like them, while everything gets done for some other people without the slope ever turning slippery under foot, but this fact never seems to catch up with this worry. Every time something is considered that would benefit a "discrete and insular minority," United States v. Carolene Products Co., 304 U.S. 144, 153 n.4 (1938), we hear that it cannot be done for anyone because it would have to be done for everyone. Never why it should or shouldn't be done for all. Or that it *won't* be "while this court sits." Panhandle Oil Company v. Knox, 277 U.S. 218, 223 (1928) ("[t]he power to tax is not the power to destroy while this Court sits") (Holmes, J., dissenting). And never that no

minority is more discrete and insular than the one that runs this country, Robert Dahl, *Who Governs?* (1961), and everything is done for them—and only for them.

37. Susan Rae Peterson, "Coercion and Rape: The State as a Male Protection Racket," in *Feminism and Philosophy* 360 (1977). See p. 239, note 16.

38. Norman Mailer, quoted in S. Griffin, *Pornography and Silence: Culture's Revenge against Nature* 206 (1981).

1. Not By Law Alone

1. Diana E. H. Russell, *The Secret Trauma: Incest in the Lives of Women and Girls* 217, 270 (1986). *See also* David Finkelhor, *Sexually Victimized Children* 83, 92 (1979); Judith Herman and Lisa Hirschman, "Father-Daughter Incest," 2 *Signs: Journal of Women in Culture and Society* 735 (1977).

2. Diana E. H. Russell and Nancy Howell, "The Prevalence of Rape in the United States Revisited," 4 *Signs: Journal of Women in Culture and Society* 688 (1983); Federal Bureau of Investigation, *Uniform Crime Reports* 1965, 1974, 1976; Federal Bureau of Investigation, *Uniform Crime Reports* 1980 at 6, 14, 15 (1981); M. Hindelang and B. Davis, "Forcible Rape: A Statistical Profile," in *Forcible Rape: The Crime, the Victim, and the Offender* 91–110 (Duncan Chapell, Robley Geis, and Gilbert Geis eds. 1977); Diana E. H. Russell, *Rape in Marriage* (1982).

3. For citation, see "Introduction," note 18.

4. R. Emerson Dobash and Russell Dobash, *Violence against Wives* 14–20 (1979); Roger Langley and Richard Levy, *Wife Beating* (1977); Harold R. Lentzner and Marshall M. DeBerry, Bureau of Justice Statistics, U.S. Department of Justice, *Intimate Victims: A Study of Violence among Friends and Relatives* (1980); Evan Stark, Anne Flitcraft, and William Frazier, "Medicine and Patriarchal Violence: The Social Construction of a Private Event," 9 *International Journal of Health Services* 461–93 (1979); Leonore Walker, *The Battered Woman* 19–20 (1979).

5. James Boudouris, "Homicide and the Family," 33 *Journal of Marriage and the Family* 667, 671 (1971); Evelyn Gibson and S. Klein, *Murder 1957 to 1968: A Home Office Statistical Division Report on Murder in England and Wales* (1969); Hans Von Hentig, *The Criminal and His Victim* 392 (1948); Arthur MacDonald, "Death Penalty and Homicide," 16 *American Journal of Sociology* 88, 96 (1911); Donald J. Mulvihill, Melvin M. Tumin, and Lynn A. Curtis, *Crimes of Violence*, XI Report of the National Commission on the Causes and Prevention of Violence (1969); data of the National Commission on the Causes and Prevention of Violence discussed in Lee H. Bowker, "The Criminal Victimization of Women," 4 *Victimology: An International Journal* 371, 384 (1979); Marvin E. Wolfgang, *Patterns in Criminal Homicide* 32, 50–67, 204, 213–14, 217 (1958); Margaret A. Zahn, "The Female Homicide Victim," 13 *Criminology* 400 (1975).

6. Joint Economic Committee, "Employment, Unemployment and Wages: Status of the Labor Force," *Economic Indicators: January 1982*, 97th Cong., 2d Sess. 11, 12.

7. Myra H. Strober, "Formal Extrafamily Child Care—Some Economic Observations," in *Sex, Discrimination and the Division of Labor* 346–75 (Cynthia B. Lloyd ed.) (1975).

8. Moira K. Griffin, "Wives, Hookers and the Law," *Student Lawyer* (Jan. 1982) at 18. Pimps probably receive most of this money.

9. Id. *See* esp. 18, quoting Priscilla Alexander, codirector of NOW National Task Force on Prostitution.

10. Id. *See also* Kathleen Barry, *Female Sexual Slavery* (1979).

11. U.S. Merit Systems Protection Board, Office of Merit Systems Review and Studies, *Sexual Harassment in the Federal Workplace: Is It a Problem?* (1981); on education, *see* National Advisory Council on Women's Education Programs, U.S. Department of Education, *Sexual Harassment: A Report on the Sexual Harassment of Students* (1980).

12. I have rendered "Black" in upper case. Black is conventionally, I am told, regarded as a color rather than a racial or national designation, and hence is not usually capitalized. I do not regard Black as merely a color of skin pigmentation, but as a heritage, an experience, a cultural and personal identity. It acquires its meaning under specific social conditions, one of which is racism, one of which is politically self-conscious struggle against racism. Black is thus as much socially created as, and at least in the American context is as meaningful and definitive as, any linguistic, tribal, or religious ethnicity, all of which are conventionally recognized by capitalization. While capitalizing "white" might expose it as equally contingent and political, perhaps even reveal the definitive unity of the privilege it confers, under current conditions of white supremacy it seems to me to require no underlining as an affirmative self-identification. Capitalizing both would also communicate an equality that is now false, and would take no side toward making the equality a true one.

Data and views on abortion come from National Center for Health Statistics, *United States, 1980,* Table 5: Legal abortions, abortion-related deaths and death rates, and relative risk of death, according to period of gestation: United States, 1973–75 and 1976–78 (1980); Mary Steichen Calderone (ed.), *Abortion in the United States* (1958), *see* esp. "Illegal Abortions in the United States" at 50–66; Andrea Dworkin, *Right-Wing Women* chap. 3 (1983); *Ethics, Religion and Abortion: Hearings on S. 158 before the Subcommittee on the Separation of Powers of the Senate Committee on the Judiciary,* 97th Cong., 1st Sess., 831 (1981) (statement of Rosemary Radford Ruether); Germaine Grisez, *Abortion: The Myths, the Realities and the Arguments* (1970) (a conservative critical work, *see* esp. chap. 2, "A Sociological View"); Westchester Coalition for Legal Abortion, *Legal Abortion: Arguments Pro and Con* (n.d.).

13. Monique Wittig, *Les Guérillères* 89 (1973).

14. Ellen E. Morgan, "The Erotization of Male Dominance/Female Submission," University of Michigan Papers in Women's Studies (1975).

15. Charles J. Anderson, *1981–82 Fact Book for Academic Administrators,* American Council on Education 119 (1981); R. Beazley, *Salaries, Tenure and*

Full Time Instructional Faculty in Institutions of Higher Education 1975–76 2; W. Vance Grant and Leo J. Eiden, National Center for Education Statistics, *Digest of Education Statistics* 107, 109, 119 (1981); W. Vance Grant and C. George Lind, National Center for Education Statistics, *Digest of Education Statistics* 100 (1979); Janet Mitchell (ed.), *Higher Education Exchange* 722 (1981).

16. Susan Rae Peterson, "Coercion and Rape: The State as a Male Protection Racket," *Feminism and Philosophy* 360 (Mary Vetterling-Bragin, Frederick A. Elliston, and Jane English eds.) (1977). *See also* Janet Rifkin, "Toward a Theory of Law and Patriarchy," 3 *Harvard Women's Law Journal* 83 (1980).

17. This debate occurred in the waning months of the most recent attempt to ratify a federal Equal Rights Amendment (ERA). I had not spoken on ERA before and had not been actively involved in the ratification effort. Because I did not want to hurt its chance for approval, its chance to do *something* for women, I had allowed myself to be persuaded to modify my criticism of its leading interpretation, Barbara Brown, Thomas I. Emerson, Gail Falk, and Ann E. Freedman, "The Equal Rights Amendment: A Constitutional Basis for Equal Rights for Women," 80 *Yale Law Journal* 871 (1971). For the criticism as modified see Catharine A. MacKinnon, *Sexual Harassment of Working Women* 114–15 and 264 n.55 (1979).

Now I do not think it was right to remain silent while the debate on the meaning of sex equality was defined in liberal terms, excluding most issues most crucial to most women and most central to their situations. I was told that pursuing an untried, if more true, analysis of sex equality risked losing something that, once gained, might be more meaningfully interpreted. Deference to this calculus overcame the sense, a sense that grew into a conviction with each setback, that ERA's leading interpretation and the strategies based on it would not only limit the value of the measure if it won but would ensure its loss. I felt that the reduction of the principle of equality of rights to empirical sameness between groups was somehow connected not only with the inability of the campaign to reach the hopes and touch the resentments of many women (for a feminist analysis of conservative women as women, *see* Andrea Dworkin, *Right Wing Women* [1983]), but also with the contempt many ERA proponents communicated for its female opponents, Mrs. Schlafly prominently included. By spring of 1982, there seemed little to lose, even from the truth. I was determined to have a real discussion with this formidable woman. *See* C. Felsenthal, *Sweetheart of the Silent Majority* (1981); Deborah Rhode, "Equal Rights in Retrospect," 1 *Law & Inequality: A Journal of Theory and Practice* 1 (1983).

ERA means women's equality, to those who urgently seek it, to those who abhor it, and to those who find saying it in law somewhat obvious if not yet redundant. That was true then and it is true now. The same ERA was reintroduced after its defeat on July 14, 1982, although it failed to secure the necessary votes. It remains important to say what the equality of women might mean and what is in its way.

2. Difference and Dominance

1. The Bona Fide Occupational Qualification (BFOQ) exception to Title VII of the Civil Rights Act of 1964, 42 U.S.C. § 2000 e-(2)(e), permits sex to be a job qualification when it is a valid one. The leading interpretation of the proposed federal Equal Rights Amendment would, pursuing a similar analytic structure, permit a "unique physical characteristic" exception to its otherwise absolute embargo on taking sex into account. Barbara Brown, Thomas I. Emerson, Gail Falk, and Ann E. Freedman, "The Equal Rights Amendment: A Constitutional Basis for Equal Rights for Women," 80 *Yale Law Journal* 893 (1971).

2. Title VII of the Civil Rights Act of 1964, 42 U.S.C. § 2000 e; Phillips v. Martin-Marietta, 400 U.S. 542 (1971). Frontiero v. Richardson, 411 U.S. 484 (1974) is the high-water mark of this approach. *See also* City of Los Angeles v. Manhart, 435 U.S. 702 (1978); Newport News Shipbuilding and Dry Dock Co. v. EEOC, 462 U.S. 669 (1983).

3. Title IX of the Education Amendments of 1972, 20 U.S.C.§1681; Cannon v. University of Chicago, 441 U.S. 677 (1981); Mississippi University for Women v. Hogan, 458 U.S. 718 (1982); *see also* De La Cruz v. Tormey, 582 F.2d 45 (9th Cir. 1978).

4. My impression is that women appear to lose most academic sex discrimination cases that go to trial, although I know of no systematic or statistical study on the subject. One case that won eventually, elevating the standard of proof in the process, is Sweeney v. Board of Trustees of Keene State College, 439 U.S. 29 (1979). The ruling for the plaintiff was affirmed on remand, 604 F.2d 106 (1st Cir. 1979).

5. Hishon v. King & Spalding, 467 U.S. 69 (1984).

6. *See, e.g.,* Vanguard Justice v. Hughes, 471 F. Supp. 670 (D. Md. 1979); Meyer v. Missouri State Highway Commission, 567 F.2d 804, 891 (8th Cir. 1977); Payne v. Travenol Laboratories Inc., 416 F. Supp. 248 (N.D. Mass. 1976). *See also* Dothard v. Rawlinson, 433 U.S. 321 (1977) (height and weight requirements invalidated for prison guard contact positions because of disparate impact on sex).

7. Frontiero v. Richardson, 411 U.S. 484 (1974); Schlesinger v. Ballard, 419 U.S. 498 (1975).

8. This situation is relatively complex. *See* Gomes v. R.I. Interscholastic League, 469 F. Supp. 659 (D. R.I. 1979); Brenden v. Independent School District, 477 F.2d 1292 (8th Cir. 1973); O'Connor v. Board of Education of School District No. 23, 645 F.2d 578 (7th Cir. 1981); Cape v. Tennessee Secondary School Athletic Association, 424 F. Supp. 732 (E.D. Tenn. 1976), *rev'd,* 563 F.2d 793 (6th Cir. 1977); Yellow Springs Exempted Village School District Board of Education v. Ohio High School Athletic Association, 443 F. Supp. 753 (S.D. Ohio 1978); Aiken v. Lieuallen, 593 P.2d 1243 (Or. App. 1979).

9. Rostker v. Goldberg, 453 U.S. 57 (1981). *See also* Lori S. Kornblum, "Women Warriors in a Men's World: The Combat Exclusion," 2 *Law and Inequality: A Journal of Theory and Practice* 353 (1984).

10. David Cole, "Strategies of Difference: Litigating for Women's Rights in a Man's World," 2 *Law & Inequality: A Journal of Theory and Practice* 34 n.4 (1984) (collecting cases).

11. Devine v. Devine, 398 So. 2d 686 (Ala. Sup. Ct. 1981); Danielson v. Board of Higher Education, 358 F. Supp. 22 (S.D.N.Y. 1972); Weinberger v. Wiesenfeld, 420 U.S. 636 (1975); Stanley v. Illinois, 405 U.S. 645 (1971); Caban v. Mohammed, 441 U.S. 380 (1979); Orr v. Orr, 440 U.S. 268 (1979).

12. Lenore Weitzman, "The Economics of Divorce: Social and Economic Consequences of Property, Alimony and Child Support Awards," 28 *U.C.L.A. Law Review* 1118, 1251 (1982), documents a decline in women's standard of living of 73 percent and an increase in men's of 42 percent within a year after divorce.

13. Equal Pay Act, 29 U.S.C. § 206(d)(1) (1976) guarantees pay equality, as does case law, *but cf.* data on pay gaps, "Introduction," note 2.

14. Examples include Christenson v. State of Iowa, 563 F.2d 353 (8th Cir. 1977); Gerlach v. Michigan Bell Tel. Co., 501 F. Supp. 1300 (E.D. Mich. 1980); Odomes v. Nucare, Inc., 653 F.2d 246 (6th Cir. 1981) (female nurse's aide denied Title VII remedy because her job duties were not substantially similar to those of better-paid male orderly); Power v. Barry County, Michigan, 539 F. Supp. 721 (W.D. Mich. 1982); Spaulding v. University of Washington, 740 F. 2d 686 (9th Cir. 1984).

15. County of Washington v. Gunther, 452 U.S. 161 (1981) permits a comparable worth–type challenge where pay inequality can be proven to be a correlate of intentional job segregation. *See also* Lemons v. City and County of Denver, 17 FEP Cases 910 (D. Colo. 1978), *aff'd,* 620 F.2d 228 (10th Cir. 1977), *cert. denied,* 449 U.S. 888 (1980); AFSCME v. State of Washington, 770 F.2d 1401 (9th Cir. 1985). *See generally* Carol Jean Pint, "Value, Work and Women," 1 *Law & Inequality: A Journal of Theory and Practice* 159 (1983).

16. Combine the result in Bob Jones University v. United States, 461 U.S. 547 (1983) with Mississippi University for Women v. Hogan, 458 U.S. 718 (1982), and the tax-exempt status of women-only schools is clearly threatened.

17. A particularly pungent example comes from a case in which the plaintiff sought to compete in boxing matches with men, since there were no matches sponsored by the defendant among women. A major reason that preventing the woman from competing was found not to violate her equality rights was that the "safety rules and precautions [were] developed, designed, and tested in the context of all-male competition." Lafler v. Athletic Board of Control, 536 F. Supp. 104, 107 (W.D. Mich. 1982). As the court put it: "In this case, the real differences between the male and female anatomy are relevant in considering whether men and women may be treated differently with regard to their participating in boxing. The plaintiff *admits* that she wears a protective covering for her breasts while boxing. Such a protective covering . . . would violate Rule Six, Article 9 of the Amateur Boxing Federation rules currently in effect. The same rule *requires* contestants to wear a protective

cup, a rule obviously designed for the unique anatomical characteristics of men." Id. at 106 (emphasis added). The rule is based on the male anatomy, therefore not a justification for the discrimination but an example of it. This is not considered in the opinion, nor does the judge discuss whether women might benefit from genital protection, and men from chest guards, as in some other sports.

18. This is a reference to the issues raised by several recent cases which consider whether states' attempts to compensate pregnancy leaves and to secure jobs on return constitute sex discrimination. California Federal Savings and Loan Assn. v. Guerra, 758 F.2d 390 (9th Cir. 1985), *cert. granted* 54 U.S.L.W. 3460 (U.S. Jan. 13, 1986); *see also* Miller-Wohl v. Commissioner of Labor, 515 F. Supp. 1264 (D. Montana 1981), *vacated and dismissed,* 685 F.2d 1088 (9th Cir. 1982). The position argued in "Difference and Dominance" here suggests that if these benefits are prohibited under Title VII, Title VII is unconstitutional under the equal protection clause.

This argument was not made directly in either case. The American Civil Liberties Union argued that the provisions requiring pregnancy to be compensated in employment, without comparable coverage for men, violated Title VII's prohibition on pregnancy-based classifications and on sex. Montana had made it illegal for an employer to "terminate a woman's employment because of her pregnancy" or to "refuse to grant to the employee a reasonable leave of absence for such pregnancy." Montana Maternity Leave Act § 49-2-310(1) and (2). According to the ACLU, this provision "grants pregnant workers certain employment rights not enjoyed by other workers . . . Legislation designed to benefit women has . . . perpetuated destructive stereotypes about their proper roles and operated to deny them rights and benefits enjoyed by men. The [Montana provision] deters employers from hiring women who are or may become pregnant, causes resentment and hostility in the workplace, and penalizes men." Brief of American Civil Liberties Union, et al. *amicus curiae,* Montana Supreme Court No. 84-172, at 7. The National Organization for Women argued that the California provision, which requires employers to give pregnant workers unpaid disability leave with job security for up to four months, would violate Title VII should Title VII be interpreted to permit it. Brief of National Organization for Women, et al., United States Court of Appeals for the Ninth Circuit, 685 F.2d 1088 (9th Cir. 1982).

When Congress passed the Pregnancy Discrimination Act, amending Title VII, 42 U.S.C. § 2000 e(k), it defined "because of sex" or "on the basis of sex" to include "because of or on the basis of pregnancy, childbirth, or related medical conditions; and women affected by pregnancy, childbirth, or related medical conditions shall be treated the same for all employment-related purposes." In so doing, Congress arguably decided that one did not have to be the same as a man to be treated without discrimination, since it guaranteed freedom from discriminatory treatment on the basis of a condition that is not the same for men as it is for women. It even used the word "women" in the statute.

Further, Congress made this decision expressly to overrule the Supreme Court decision in General Electric v. Gilbert, 429 U.S. 125 (1976), which had held that failure to cover pregnancy as a disability was not sex discrimination because the line between pregnant and nonpregnant was not the line between women and men. In rejecting this logic, as the Court found it did expressly in Newport News Shipbuilding and Dry Dock Co. v. EEOC, 462 U.S. 669, 678 (1983), Congress rejected the implicit measuring of women's entitlement to equality by a male standard. Nor need all women be the same, that is, pregnant or potentially so, to have pregnancy-based discrimination be sex-based discrimination.

Upholding the California pregnancy leave and job security law, the Ninth Circuit opinion did not require sameness for equality to be delivered: "The PDA does not require states to ignore pregnancy. It requires that women be treated equally . . .[E]quality under the PDA must be measured in employment opportunity, not necessarily in amounts of money expended—or in amounts of days of disability leave expended. Equality . . . compares coverage to actual need, not coverage to hypothetical identical needs." California Federal v. Guerra, 758 F.2d 390 (9th Cir. 1985) (Ferguson, J.). "We are not the first court to announce the goal of Title VII is equality of employment opportunity, not necessarily sameness of treatment." Id. at 396 n.7.

19. Most women work at jobs mostly women do, and most of those jobs are paid less than jobs that mostly men do. *See, e.g.*, Pint, note 15 above, at 162–63 nn.19, 20 (collecting studies). To the point that men may not meet the male standard themselves, one court found that a union did not fairly represent its women in the following terms: "As to the yard and driver jobs, defendants suggest not only enormous intellectual requirements, but that the physical demands of those jobs are so great as to be beyond the capacity of any female. Again, it is noted that plaintiffs' capacity to perform those jobs was never tested, despite innumerable requests therefor. It is also noted that defendants have never suggested *which* of the innumerable qualifications they list for these jobs (for the first time) the plaintiffs might fail to meet. The court, however, will accept without listing here the extraordinary catalogue of feats which defendants argue must be performed in the yard, and as a driver. That well may be. However, one learns from this record that one cannot be too weak, too sick, too old and infirm, or too ignorant to perform these jobs, *so long as one is a man.* The plaintiffs appear to the layperson's eye to be far more physically fit than many of the drivers who moved into the yard, over the years, according to the testimony of defense witnesses . . . In short, they were all at least as fit as the men with serious physical deficits and disabilities who held yard jobs." Jones v. Cassens Transport, 617 F. Supp. 869, 892 (1985) (emphasis in original).

20. Phillips v. Martin-Marietta, 400 U.S. 542 (1971).

21. Reed v. Reed, 404 U.S. 71 (1971) held that a statute barring women from administering estates is sex discrimination. If few women were taught to read and write, as used to be the case, the gender difference would not be

imaginary in this case, yet the social situation would be even more sex discriminatory than it is now. Compare City of Los Angeles v. Manhart, 434 U.S. 815 (1978), which held that requiring women to make larger contributions to their retirement plan was sex discrimination, in spite of the allegedly proven sex difference that women on the average outlive men.

22. Kahn v. Shevin, 416 U.S. 351, 353 (1974).

23. Schlesinger v. Ballard, 419 U.S. 498 (1975).

24. Dothard v. Rawlinson, 433 U.S. 321 (1977); *see also* Michael M. v. Sonoma County Superior Court, 450 U.S. 464 (1981).

25. Doerr v. B.F. Goodrich, 484 F. Supp. 320 (N.D. Ohio 1979). Wendy Webster Williams, "Firing the Woman to Protect the Fetus: The Reconciliation of Fetal Protection with Employment Opportunity Goals Under Title VII," 69 *Georgetown Law Journal* 641 (1981). *See also* Hayes v. Shelby Memorial Hospital, 546 F. Supp. 259 (N.D. Ala. 1982); Wright v. Olin Corp., 697 F.2d 1172 (4th Cir. 1982).

26. Congress requires the Air Force (10 U.S.C. § 8549 [1983]) and the Navy (10 U.S.C. § 6015 [1983]) to exclude women from combat, with some exceptions. Owens v. Brown, 455 F. Supp. 291 (D.D.C. 1978), had previously invalidated the prior Navy combat exclusion because it prohibited women from filling jobs they could perform and inhibited Navy's discretion to assign women on combat ships. The Army excludes women from combat based upon its own policies under congressional authorization to determine assignment (10 U.S.C. § 3012 [e] [1983]).

27. Carol Gilligan, *In a Different Voice* (1982).

28. Id.

29. I argued this in Appendix A of my *Sexual Harassment of Working Women: A Case of Sex Discrimination* (1979). That book ends with "Women want to be equal and different, too." I could have added "Men are." As a standard, this would have reduced women's aspirations for equality to some corresponding version of men's actualities. But as an observation, it would have been true.

30. Diana Russell and Nancy Howell, "The Prevalence of Rape in the United States Revisited," 8 *Signs: Journal of Women in Culture and Society* 689 (1983) (44 percent of women in 930 households were victims of rape or attempted rape at some time in their lives).

31. Diana Russell, "The Incidence and Prevalence of Intrafamilial and Extrafamilial Sexual Abuse of Female Children," 7 *Child Abuse & Neglect: The International Journal* 133 (1983).

32. R. Emerson Dobash and Russell Dobash, *Violence against Wives: A Case against the Patriarchy* (1979); Bruno v. Codd, 90 Misc. 2d 1047, 396 N.Y.S. 2d 974 (Sup. Ct. 1977), *rev'd,* 64 A.D. 2d 582, 407 N.Y.S. 2d 165 (1st Dep't 1978), *aff'd* 47 N.Y. 2d 582, 393 N.E. 2d 976, 419 N.Y.S. 2d 901 (1979).

33. Kathleen Barry, *Female Sexual Slavery* (1979); Moira K. Griffin, "Wives, Hookers and the Law: The Case for Decriminalizing Prostitution," 10 *Student Lawyer* 18 (1982); Report of Jean Fernand-Laurent, Special Rapporteur on the Suppression of the Traffic in Persons and the Exploitation of the Prostitution of Others (a United Nations report), in *International Feminism: Networking*

against Female Sexual Slavery 130 (Kathleen Barry, Charlotte Bunch, and Shirley Castley eds.) (Report of the Global Feminist Workshop to Organize against Traffic in Women, Rotterdam, Netherlands, Apr. 6–15, 1983 [1984]).

34. Galloway and Thornton, "Crackdown on Pornography—A No-Win Battle," *U.S. News and World Report*, June 4, 1984, at 84. *See also* "The Place of Pornography," *Harper's*, November 1984, at 31 (citing $7 billion per year).

35. Loving v. Virginia, 388 U.S. 1 (1967), first used the term "white supremacy" in invalidating an antimiscegenation law as a violation of equal protection. The law equally forbade whites and Blacks to intermarry. Although going nowhere near as far, courts in the athletics area have sometimes seen that "same" does not necessarily mean "equal" nor does "equal" require "same." In a context of sex inequality like that which has prevailed in athletic opportunity, allowing boys to compete on girls' teams may diminish overall sex equality. "Each position occupied by a male reduces the female participation and increases the overall disparity of athletic opportunity which generally exists." Petrie v. Illinois High School Association, 394 N.E. 2d 855, 865 (Ill. 1979). "We conclude that to furnish exactly the same athletic opportunities to boys as to girls would be most difficult and would be detrimental to the compelling governmental interest of equalizing general athletic opportunities between the sexes." Id.

36. The scholars Tussman and tenBroek first used the term "fit" to characterize the necessary relation between a valid equality rule and the world to which it refers. J. Tussman and J. tenBroek, "The Equal Protection of the Laws," 37 *California Law Review* 341 (1949).

37. Royster Guano Co. v. Virginia, 253 U.S. 412, 415 (1920): "[A classification] must be reasonable, not arbitrary, and must rest upon some ground of difference having a fair and substantial relation to the object of the legislation, so that all persons similarly circumstanced shall be treated alike." Reed v. Reed, 404 U.S. 71, 76 (1971): "Regardless of their sex, persons within any one of the enumerated classes . . . are similarly situated . . . By providing dissimilar treatment for men and women who are thus similarly situated, the challenged section violates the Equal Protection Clause."

38. Washington v. Davis, 426 U.S. 229 (1976) and Personnel Administrator of Massachusetts v. Feeney, 442 U.S. 256 (1979) require that intentional discrimination be shown for discrimination to be shown.

3. Desire and Power

1. Catharine A. MacKinnon, "Feminism, Marxism, Method and the State: An Agenda for Theory," 7 *Signs: Journal of Women in Culture and Society* 515 (1982).

2. Catharine A. MacKinnon, "Feminism, Marxism, Method and the State: Toward Feminist Jurisprudence," 8 *Signs: Journal of Women in Culture and Society* 635 (1983).

3. *See* "Not By Law Alone," note 2.

4. The following notes to "Not By Law Alone" document these data: on

incest, note 1; on battery, note 4; on murder, note 5. On pornography, Galloway and Thornton, "Crackdown on Pornography—A No-Win Battle," *U.S. News and World Report*, June 4, 1984, at 84; M. Langelan, "The Political Economy of Pornography," *Aegis: Magazine on Ending Violence against Women* 5–17 (1981); Andrea Dworkin, *Pornography: Men Possessing Women* (1981).

5. Nancy Chodorow, *The Reproduction of Mothering: Psychoanalysis and the Sociology of Gender* (1978); Dorothy Dinnerstein, *The Mermaid and the Minotaur: Sexual Arrangements and Human Malaise* (1977).

4. Whose Culture?

1. Washington v. Davis, 426 U.S. 229 (1976); Arlington Heights v. Metropolitan Housing Corp., 429 U.S. 252 (1977); Personnel Administrator of Mass. v. Feeney, 442 U.S. 256 (1979).

2. *See* David Cole, "Strategies of Difference: Litigating for Women's Rights in a Man's World," 2 *Law & Inequality: A Journal of Theory and Practice* 33 (1984).

3. Data at Catharine A. MacKinnon, *Sexual Harassment of Working Women: A Case of Sex Discrimination* 9–15 (1979). The patterns have not changed.

4. "We emphasize that the differentiating factor between de jure segregation and so-called de facto segregation" is *"purpose* or *intent* to segregate." Keyes v. School District No. 1, Denver, Colo., 413 U.S. 189, 208 (1973). Narrowing the scope of lawsuits through focus on fault (intent) is one of the ways effective segregation can be maintained society-wide in the face of legal mandates against it. The basic move is to shift the issue from whether or not a problem exists to whether or not it is the exclusive fault of the defendant, so that the original cause of the discrimination is always elsewhere. So long as racism is pervasive, such a defense will remain plausible. *See also* Milliken v. Bradley, 418 U.S. 717 (1974); Hazlewood School Dist. v. United States, 433 U.S. 299 (1977); Columbus Bd. of Educ. v. Penick, 443 U.S. 449 (1979); Dayton Bd. of Educ. v. Brinkman, 443 U.S. 526 (1979).

5. "Our Constitution is color-blind." Plessy v. Ferguson, 163 U.S. 537, 559 (1896) (Harlan, J., dissenting). *See also* Fullilove v. Klutznick, 448 U.S. 448, 482 (1980); United Steelworkers of America v. Weber, 443 U.S. 193 (1979); Regents of the University of California v. Bakke, 438 U.S. 256, 327 (1978).

6. Santa Clara Pueblo v. Martinez, 436 U.S. 49 (1978).

7. 436 U.S. at 71–72.

8. Tribal sovereignty includes rules of membership and inheritance, domestic relations and child custody or adoption, substantive criminal and civil laws and tribal court jurisdiction in internal matters. Tribes may levy taxes, allocate tribal property among members and regulate its uses, regulate hunting and fishing by its members, exclude persons from tribal territory, and exercise some civil regulatory and judicial jurisdiction over non-Indians. Tribes are not sovereign concerning alienation of tribal land. They may not have direct commercial or governmental relations with foreign nations and have no jurisdiction over non-Indian crimes on the reservation. Congress may grant leases and rights of way and even dispose of tribal property with-

out tribal consent, and may regulate, modify, or abrogate tribal hunting and fishing rights, although this is rarely done. *See* Felix S. Cohen, *Handbook of Federal Indian Law* (1982). The help of Jean Ramirez with this analysis is gratefully acknowledged.

9. 25 U.S.C. §§ 331–58 (General Allotment Act).

10. 436 U.S., at 54 (1978) (quoting Martinez v. Santa Clara Pueblo, 402 F. Supp. 5, 15 [D.N.M. 1975]).

11. The issue has also arisen in Canada. *See* Attorney-General of Canada v. Lavell, 38 D.L.R. 3d 481 (Can. 1973). Under the Indian Act, Can. Rev. Stat. ch. 1–6 (1970) § 12 (1)(b), Native women lose Indian status if they marry non-Indian men, while Native men do not if they marry non-Indian women. Further, section 11 (1)(f) confers Indian status upon non-Indian women who marry Indian men. Evidence exists that these discriminatory provisions are not indigenous to native peoples in Canada, some of whom had matrilineal traditions prior to contact, like some tribes in what is now the United States. Native Women's Association of Canada, "Statement by Native Women's Association of Canada on Native Women's Rights," in *Women and the Constitution in Canada* (Audrey Doerr and Micheline Carrier eds. 1981) 66–67. *See* Jennifer K. Bankier, "Equality, Affirmative Action, and the Charter: Reconciling 'Inconsistent' Sections" 1 *Canadian Journal of Women and Law* 134,150 (1985).

5. On Exceptionality

1. Oliver Wendell Holmes, *The Common Law* 5 (Mark D. Howe ed. 1881; 1963 edition).

2. Dothard v. Rawlinson, 433 U.S. 321, 335, 336 (1977).

3. Weinberger v. Wiesenfeld, 420 U.S. 636 (1975).

4. Virginia Woolf, *Three Guineas* 80 (1938; 1966 Harbinger edition).

5. "Introduction," note 18.

6. A Rally against Rape

1. For whites and Blacks, the National Commission on the Causes and Prevention of Violence finds that 90 percent of rapes are intraracial. *Final Report of the National Commission on the Causes and Prevention of Violence* 210 (1969). Menachim Amir, *Forcible Rape* 44 (1971), finds 95 percent. *See also* Diana E. H. Russell, *Sexual Exploitation* 90–93 (1984).

2. The rapist is a stranger in 55 percent of all rapes and attempted rapes reported to the police, but in only 17 percent of all incidents. Of actual rapes and attempts, 26 percent are by acquaintances, 18 percent by dates, 5 percent by boyfriends, 3 percent by family friends, 8 percent by authority figures, 9 percent by lovers or ex-lovers, 9 percent by friends of the victim, 5 percent by relatives (not husbands). Russell, note 1 above, at 96–97. Of all women who have ever been married, 14 percent report being raped by their husbands. Of all reported rapes in the Russell study, 38 percent were marital, as

were 10 percent of the rapists. Diana E. H. Russell, *Rape in Marriage* 66–67 (1982).

3. One study shows the rates for Black women are 50 percent, or one in two; for white women, 12 percent, or one in eight in a study in which the overall percentage probability of rape is found to be vastly lower than it is now known to be. Amir, note 1 above, at table 3.7.

4. This statement of reasons comes from my own work and from Linda Belden, "Why Women Do Not Report Sexual Assault," City of Portland Public Service Employment Program, Portland Women's Crisis Line, Portland, Ore., March 1979.

7. Sex and Violence

1. Gerald D. Robin, "Forcible Rape: Institutionalized Sexism in the Criminal Justice System," *Crime and Delinquency* (April 1977) 136–53. "Forcible rape is unique among crimes in the manner in which its victims are dealt with by the criminal justice system. Raped women are subjected to an institutionalized sexism that begins with the treatment by the police, continues through a male-dominated criminal justice system influenced by pseudo-scientific notions of victim precipitation, and ends with the systematic acquittal of many de facto rapists." Lorenne M. G. Clark and Debra Lewis, *Rape: The Price of Coercive Sexuality* 57 (1977).

2. Examples are particularly clear in England, Canada, and California. Director of Public Prosecutions v. Morgan, 2411 E.R.H.L. 347 (1975); Pappajohn v. The Queen, 11 D.L.R. 3d 1 (1980); People v. Mayberry, 15 Cal. 3d 143, 542 P. 2d 1337 (1975). *But cf.* People v. Barnes, 228 Cal. Rptr. 228 (Cal. 1986).

3. Jacobellis v. Ohio, 378 U.S. 184, 197 (1964) (Stewart, J., concurring).

4. R. Emerson Dobash and Russell Dobash, *Violence against Wives* (1979) at 14–21.

5. Susan Brownmiller, *Against Our Will: Men, Women and Rape* (1975).

8. Privacy v. Equality

1. Roe v. Wade, 410 U.S. 113 (1973).

2. Harris v. McRae, 448 U.S. 297 (1980). This is not to support the *Harris* ruling or to propose individual hearings to determine coercion prior to allowing abortions. Nor is it to criticize Justice Blackmun, author of the majority opinion in *Roe*, who undoubtedly saw legalizing abortion as a way to help women out of a desperate situation, which it has done.

3. D. H. Regan, "Rewriting *Roe v. Wade*," 77 *Michigan Law Review* 1569 (1979), in which the Good Samaritan happens upon the fetus.

4. As of 1973, ten states that had made abortion a crime had exceptions for rape and incest; at least three had exceptions for rape only. Many of these exceptions were based on Model Penal Code § 230.3 (Proposed Official Draft 1962), quoted in Doe v. Bolton, 410 U.S. 179, 205–07, App. B (1973), permit-

ting abortion, inter alia, in cases of "rape, incest, or other felonious intercourse." References to states with incest and rape exceptions can be found in Roe v. Wade, 410 U.S. 113 n.37 (1973). Some versions of the Hyde Amendment, which prohibits use of public money to fund abortions, have contained exceptions for cases of rape or incest. All require immediate reporting of the incident.

5. Kristin Luker, *Taking Chances: Abortion and the Decision Not to Contracept* (1976).

6. Roe v. Wade, 410 U.S. 113 (1973).

7. Griswold v. Connecticut, 381 U.S. 479 (1965).

8. Eisenstadt v. Baird, 405 U.S. 438 (1972).

9. Harris v. McRae, 448 U.S. 297 (1980).

10. T. Gerety, "Redefining Privacy," 12 *Harvard Civil Rights–Civil Liberties Law Review* 233, 236 (1977).

11. Kenneth I. Karst, "The Freedom of Intimate Association," 89 *Yale Law Journal* 624 (1980); "Developments—The Family," 93 *Harvard Law Review* 1157 (1980); Doe v. Commonwealth Atty, 403 F. Supp. 1199 (E.D. Va. 1975), *aff'd without opinion*, 425 U.S. 901 (1976), *but cf.* People v. Onofre, 51 N.Y.2d 476 (1980), *cert. denied* 451 U.S. 987 (1981). The issue was finally decided, for the time, in Bowers v. Hardwick, 106 S. Ct. 2841 (1986) (statute criminalizing consensual sodomy does not violate right to privacy).

12. Tom Grey, "Eros, Civilization and the Burger Court," 43 *Law and Contemporary Problems* 83 (1980).

13. Susan Sontag, "The Third World of Women," 40 *Partisan Review* 188 (1973).

14. *See* Adrienne Rich, *Of Woman Born: Motherhood as Experience and Institution* chap. 3 (1977), esp. 47, 48: "The child that I carry for nine months can be defined *neither* as me or as not-me" (emphasis in the original).

15. Kristin Booth Glen, "Abortion in the Courts: A Lay Woman's Historical Guide to the New Disaster Area," 4 *Feminist Studies* 1 (1978).

16. Judith Jarvis Thomson, "A Defense of Abortion," 1 *Philosophy and Public Affairs* 47 (1971).

17. Andrea Dworkin, *Right Wing Women* (1983). You must read this book. See also Friedrich Engels arguing on removing private housekeeping into social industry, *Origin of the Family, Private Property and the State* (1884).

18. H. L. v. Matheson, 450 U.S. 398 (1981); Bellotti v. Baird, 443 U.S. 622 (1979); *but cf.* Planned Parenthood of Central Missouri v. Danforth, 428 U.S. 52 (1976). *See also* "Introduction," note 1.

19. *See* Dworkin, note 17 above, at 98–99.

20. S. Warren and L. Brandeis, "The Right to Privacy," 4 *Harvard Law Review* 190, 205 (1890); but note that the right of privacy under some *state* constitutions has been held to *include* funding for abortions: Committee to Defend Reproductive Rights v. Meyers, 29 Cal. 3d 252 (1981); Moe v. Secretary of Admin. and Finance, 417 N.E.2d 387 (Mass. 1981).

21. As Andrea Dworkin once said to me, women may identify with the fetus not only because what happens to it, happens to them, but also be-

cause, like them, it is powerless and invisible. The vicissitudes of abortion law and policy have vividly expressed that commonality while purporting to relieve it. The discussion in this speech is a beginning attempt to recast the abortion issue toward a new legal approach and political strategy: sex equality.

Examination of the legal record in these two cases reveals little attempt, other than in one amicus brief, to argue that state action against abortions is a practice of sex discrimination. The original complaint in Roe v. Wade contained a cause of action for denial of equal protection of the laws, First Amended Complaint CA-3-3690-B (N.D. Tex., Apr. 22, 1970) IV, 5. But the inequality complained of did not, as it developed, refer to inequality on the basis of sex, and oral argument in the district court appears to have been confined largely to the right to privacy. "Aside from their Ninth Amendment and vagueness arguments, plaintiffs have presented an array of constitutional arguments. However, as plaintiffs conceded in oral argument, these additional arguments *are peripheral to the main issues.* Consequently, they will not be passed upon." Opinion of the District Court, Civil Action No. CA-3-3690-B and 3-3691-C (June 17, 1970) 116 n.7 (emphasis added). In the U.S. Supreme Court, the Center for Constitutional Rights filed an amicus brief arguing that criminal abortion statutes like those of Texas and Georgia "violate the most basic Constitutional rights of women." "[It] is the woman who bears the disproportionate share of the de jure and de facto burdens and penalties of pregnancy, child birth and child rearing. Thus, any statute which denies a woman the right to determine whether she will bear those burdens denies her the equal protection of the laws." Brief *Amicus Curiae* on behalf of New Women Lawyers, Women's Health and Abortion Project, Inc., National Abortion Action Coalition 6 (Aug. 2, 1971). However, the brief assumes that sex is equal and voluntary, even if preganancy is not: "Man and woman have equal responsibility for the act of sexual intercourse. Should the woman accidentally become pregnant, against her will, however, she endures in many instances the entire burden or 'punishment.'" Id. at 26. "And it is not sufficient to say that the woman 'chose' to have sexual intercourse, for she did not choose to become pregnant." Id. at 31.

A brief to the Supreme Court for Planned Parenthood by Harriet Pilpel, now general counsel for the American Civil Liberties Union, argued *amicus curiae* that the same privacy that protected the possession of pornography in the home should protect the abortion right. In so doing she suggested that abortion may, indeed, be an issue of sexuality: "A wide range of private individual activity in the areas of marriage, the family and sex has thus been safeguarded against governmental interference. The right to procreate, described by this Court as 'one of the basic civil rights of man' led the Court to invalidate as a violation of equal protection an Oklahoma statute which imposed sterilization upon persons convicted two or more times of larceny but not upon similarly situated persons convicted of embezzlement . . . Similarly, the right to marry, the right to direct the education of one's children, the right to have possession of pornography in the privacy of one's own home, have all been held to be fundamental rights under the Constitution." Brief for Planned Parenthood Federation of America, Inc. and American Association of Planned Parenthood Physicians as *Amici Curiae*, Sept. 15, 1972, at 33. Other vigorous briefs argued that the criminal abortion statutes discriminated against poor and nonwhite women—never women, period. In a brief of Women for the Unborn et al. in support of opponents of the abortion right, the unborn are argued to be a class deserving of equal protection. Thus, proponents of the abortion right failed to make an equality claim for women—other than the lone amicus brief which argued women's rights and equal protection but based it on gender not *sexual* inequality—while opponents of the abortion right made equality claims for the fetuses the women were carrying.

The complaint in Harris v. McRae alleged discrimination "based on poverty, race and minority status, which deprives and punishes the plaintiff class of women in violation of due process and equal protection of the law." Plaintiffs' and Proposed Intervenors' Amended Complaint, McRae v. Califano, 74 Civ. 1804 (JFD) Jan. 5, 1977, para. 74. No discrimination on the basis of sex. Only one brief argues sex discrimination, and that is not to make the *legal* argument that not paying for abortions, a state act that hurts only women, *is* sex discrimination. It is to argue that since women are *socially* discriminated against on the basis of sex, denying them abortions is an additional hardship: "The plight of indigent women denied medically necessary abortions is exacerbated by the pervasive sex discrimination that impacts especially hard on women in poverty." Brief *Amici Curiae* for NOW et al., No. 79–1268 (U.S. Supreme Court, filed Mar. 18, 1980) 44.

As a whole, virtually every kind of social discrimination against women other than sexual, and every illegal discrimination against women other than gender, has been used to try to support the abortion right. With the partial exception of the CCR brief—an effort both made audacious and weakened by the fact that sex discrimination as a constitutional doctrine had just been recognized—burdens on abortion have never been legally argued as simple sex discrimination.

9. Sexual Harassment

1. The first case to hold this was Williams v. Saxbe, 413 F. Supp. 654 (D. D.C. 1976), followed by Barnes v. Costle, 561 F.2d 983 (D.C. Cir. 1977).

2. Alexander v. Yale University, 459 F. Supp. 1 (D. Conn. 1977), *aff'd,* 631 F.2d 178 (2d Cir. 1980).

3. Rabidue v. Osceola Refining, 584 F. Supp. 419, 427 n.29 (E.D. Mich. 1984).

4. See data at "Rally against Rape," notes 1–3.

5. U.S. Merit System Protection Board, *Sexual Harassment in the Federal Workplace: Is It a Problem?* (1981).

6. National Advisory Council on Women's Education Programs, Department of Education, *Sexual Harassment: A Report on the Sexual Harassment of*

Students (1980); Joseph DiNunzio and Christina Spaulding, Radcliffe Union of Students, *Sexual Harassment Survey (Harvard/Radcliffe)* 20–29 (1984): 32 percent of tenured female faculty, 49 percent of nontenured female faculty, 42 percent of female graduate students, and 34 percent of female undergraduate students report some incident of sexual harassment from a person with authority over them; one-fifth of undergraduate women report being forced into unwanted sexual activity at some point in their lives. The Sexual Harassment Survey Committee, *A Survey of Sexual Harassment at UCLA* (185), finds 11 percent of female faculty (N = 86), 7 percent of female staff (N = 650), and 7 percent of female students (N = 933) report being sexually harassed at UCLA.

7. If a superior sexually harasses a subordinate, the company and the supervisor are responsible if the victim can prove it happened. 29 C.F.R. 1604.11(c). With coworkers, if the employer can be shown to have known about it or should have known about it, the employer can be held responsible. 29 C.F.R. 1604.11(d). Sexual harassment by clients or other third parties is decided on the specific facts. *See* 29 C.F.R. 1604.11(e).

8. The EEOC's requirement that the employer must receive notice in co-worker cases suggests that they do not understand this point. 29 C.F.R. 1604.11(d). One reasonable rationale for such a rule, however, is that a co-worker situation does not become hierarchical, hence actionable as *employment* discrimination, until it is reported to the workplace hierarchy and condoned through adverse action or inaction.

In one inferior-to-superior case, staff was alleged to have sexually harassed a woman manager because of an interracial relationship. Moffett v. Gene B. Glick Co., Inc., 621 F. Supp. 244 (D. Ind. 1985). An example of a third-party case that failed of "positive proof" involved a nurse bringing a sex discrimination claim alleging she was denied a promotion that went to a less qualified female nurse because that other nurse had a sexual relationship with the doctor who promoted her. King v. Palmer, 598 F. Supp. 65, 69 (D.D.C. 1984). The difficulty of proving "an explicit sexual relationship between [plaintiff] and [defendant], each of whom vigorously deny it exists or even occurred," id., is obvious.

9. Catharine A. MacKinnon, *Sexual Harassment of Working Women* 203 (1979).

10. Dissenters from the denial of rehearing en banc in Vinson v. Taylor attempted a revival, however. *Vinson v. Taylor*, 760 F.2d 1330, 1333 n.7 (Circuit Judges Bork, Scalia, and Starr).

11. Scott v. Sears & Roebuck, 605 F. Supp. 1047, 1051, 1055 (N.D. Ill. 1985).

12. Coley v. Consolidated Rail, 561 F. Supp. 647, 648 (1982).

13. Meritor Savings Bank, FSB v. Vinson, 106 S.Ct. 2399 (1986); Horn v. Duke Homes, 755 F.2d 599 (7th Cir. 1985); Crimm v. Missouri Pacific R.R. Co., 750 F.2d 703 (8th Cir. 1984); Simmons v. Lyons, 746 F.2d 265 (5th Cir. 1984); Craig v. Y & Y Snacks, 721 F.2d 77 (3d Cir. 1983); Katz v. Dole, 709 F.2d 251 (4th Cir. 1983); Miller v. Bank of America, 600 F.2d 211 (9th Cir. 1979); Tomkins v. Public Service Electric & Gas Co., 568 F.2d 1044 (3d Cir. 1977); Barnes v. Costle, 561 F.2d 983 (D.C. Cir. 1977); Bundy v. Jackson, 641

F.2d 934 (D.C. Cir. 1981); Henson v. City of Dundee, 682 F.2d 897 (11th Cir. 1982) (sexual harassment, whether quid pro quo or condition of work, is sex discrimination under Title VII). The court in *Rabidue* was particularly explicit on the rootedness of sexual harassment in the text of Title VII. Rabidue v. Osceola Refining, 584 F. Supp. 419, 427–29 (E.D. Mich. 1984). Woerner v. Brzeczek, 519 F. Supp. 517 (E.D. Ill. 1981) exemplifies the same view under the equal protection clause. Gender has also been found to create a class for a 42 U.S.C. § 1985(3) claim if the injury is covered by the Fourteenth Amendment. Scott v. City of Overland Park, 595 F. Supp. 520, 527–529 (D. Kansas 1984). *See also* Skadegaard v. Farrell, 578 F. Supp. 1209 (D.N.J. 1984). An additional question has been whether sexual harassment is intentional discrimination. Courts have been unimpressed with intent-related defenses like, he did it but "it was his way of communicating." French v. Mead Corporation, 333 FEP Cases 635, 638 (1983). Or, I did all of those things, but I am just a touchy person. Professor Sid Peck, in connection with the sexual harassment action brought against him by Ximena Bunster and other women at Clark University, reportedly stated that he exchanged embraces and kisses as greetings and to establish a feeling of safety and equality. *Worcester Magazine*, Dec. 3, 1980, at 3; *Boston Phoenix*, Feb. 24, 1981, at 6. *But see* Norton v. Vartanian, where Judge Zobel finds, inter alia, that the overtures were never sexually intended, so no sexual harassment occurred. 31 FEP Cases 1260 (D. Mass. 1983). The implicit view, I guess, is that the perpetrator's intent is beside the point of the harm, that so long as the allegations meet other requirements, the perpetrator does not need to intend that the sexual advances be discriminatory or even sex-based for them to constitute sex discrimination. Katz v. Dole holds that a showing of "sustained verbal sexual abuse" is sufficient to prove "the intentional nature of the harassment." 709 F. 2d, 255–56 esp. 256 n.7. As I understand it, this means that so long as the harassment is not credibly inadvertent, acts of this nature are facially discriminatory. Intentionality is inferred from the acts; the acts themselves, repeated after indications of disinclination and nonreceptivity, show the mental animus of bias. In short, the acts may not be intentionally discriminatory, yet still constitute intentional discrimination. The upshot seems to be that sexual harassment allegations are essentially treated as facial discrimination.

14. Zabkowicz v. West Bend Co., 589 F. Supp. 780, 782–83 (E.D. Wisc. 1984).

15. 589 F. Supp., 784.

16. Henson v. City of Dundee, 29 FEP Cases 787, 793 (11th Cir. 1983). In Huebschen v. Dept. of Health, 32 FEP Cases 1582 (7th Cir. 1983), the facts were found not gender-based on a doctrinally dubious rationale. There a man was found to have been sexually harassed by his female superior. This result was reversed on the partial basis that it did not present a valid gender claim. Basically the court said that the case wasn't gender-based because it was individual. I remember this argument: the events were individual, not gender-based, because there was no employment problem until the relationship went sour. In my view, if the defendant is a hierarchical superior and the

plaintiff is damaged in employment for reasons of sexual pressure vis à vis that superior, especially if they are a woman and a man, a claim is stated. It is one thing to recognize that men as a gender have more power in sexual relations in ways that may cross-cut employment hierarchies. This is not what the court said here. This case may have been, on its facts, a personal relationship that went bad, having nothing to do with gender. But these are not the facts as found at trial. The Court of Appeals did suggest that this plaintiff was hurt as an individual, not as a man, because the employment situation was fine so long as the sexual situation was fine—that is, until it wasn't. After which, because of which, the man was fired. Maybe men always stay individuals, even when women retaliate against them through their jobs for sexual refusals. But, doctrinally, I do not understand why this treatment does not state a gender-based claim. Not to, seems to allow employment opportunities to be conditional on the *continuing* existence of an undesired sexual relationship, where those opportunities would never be allowed to be conditioned on such a relationship's *initial* existence. Women have at times been gender female personally: "As Walter Scott acknowledges, he 'was attracted to her as a woman, on a personal basis. Her femaleness was a matter of attraction.'" Estate of Scott v. deLeon, 37 FEP Cases 563, 566 (1985).

17. *Barnes v. Costle* is the classic case. All of the cases in note 13 above are quid pro cases except *Vinson, Katz, Bundy,* and *Henson.* Note that the distinction is actually two poles of a continuum. A constructive discharge, in which a woman leaves the job because of a constant condition of sexual harassment, is an environmental situation that becomes quid pro quo.

18. In Vinson v. Taylor, 23 FEP Cases 37 (D.D.C. 1980), plaintiff accused defendant supervisor of forced sex; the trial court found, "If the plaintiff and Taylor did engage in an intimate or sexual relationship . . .[it] was a voluntary one by plaintiff." At 42. Vinson won a right to a new trial for environmental sexual harassment. Meritor Savings Bank, FSB v. Vinson, 106 S. Ct. 2399 (1986). *See also* Cummings v. Walsh Construction Co., 561 F. Supp. 872 (S.D. Ga. 1983) (victim accused perpetrator of consummated sex); Micari v. Mann, 481 N.Y.S.2d 967 (Sup. Ct. 1984) (students accused professor of forced sex as part of acting training; won and awarded damages).

19. Vinson v. Taylor, 753 F.2d 141 (D.C. Cir. 1985), *aff'd* 106 S. Ct. 2399 (1983).

20. Micari v. Mann, 481 N.Y.S.2d 967 (Sup. Ct. 1984).

21. Cummings v. Walsh Construction Co., 31 FEP Cases 930, 938 (S. D. Ga. 1983).

22. *Bundy* and *Henson,* note 13 above, establish environmental sexual harassment as a legal claim. Both that claim and the plaintiff's credibility in asserting it, since she was abused for such a long time, were raised in Vinson v. Taylor before the U.S. Supreme Court.

23. Huebschen v. Department of Health, 547 F. Supp. 1168 (W.D. Wisc. 1982).

24. Heelan v. Johns-Manville, 451 F. Supp. 1382 (D. Colo. 1978). *See also* Sensibello v. Globe Security Systems, 34 FEP Cases 1357 (E.D. Pa. 1964).

25. Katz v. Dole, 709 F.2d 251, 254 n.3 (4th Cir. 1983) ("A person's private and consensual sexual activities do not constitute a waiver of his or her legal protections against unwelcome and unsolicited sexual harassment").

26. An attorney discussed this case with me in a confidential conversation.

27. Gan v. Kepro Circuit Systems, 28 FEP Cases 639, 641 (E.D. Mo. 1982). *See also* Reichman v. Bureau of Affirmative Action, 536 F. Supp. 1149, 1177 (M.D. Penn. 1982).

28. Morgan v. Hertz Corp., 542 F. Supp. 123, 128 (W.D. Tenn. 1981).

29. EEOC v. Sage Realty, 507 F. Supp. 599 (S.D.N.Y. 1981).

30. Pryor v. U.S. Gypsum Co., 585 F. Supp. 311, 316 n.3 (W.D. Mo. 1984). The issue here was whether the injuries could be brought under worker's compensation. The suggestion is that women who work in adult entertainment might be covered under that law for sexual harassment on their jobs.

31. EEOC Decision 82-13, 29 FEP Cases 1855 (1982).

32. Commission Decision 83-1, EEOC Decisions (CCH) 6834 (1983).

33. Koster v. Chase Manhattan, 93 F.R.D. 471 (S.D.N.Y. 1982).

34. Priest v. Rotary, 32 FEP Cases 1065 (N.D. Cal. 1983) is consistent with congressional actions in criminal rape, Fed. R. Evid., Rule 412, 124 *Cong. Rec.* H11944–11945 (daily ed. Oct. 10, 1978) and 124 *Cong. Rec.* S18580 (daily ed. Oct. 12, 1978) (evidence of prior consensual sex, unless with defendant, is inadmissible in rape cases) and with developments in civil rape cases. Fults v. Superior Court, 88 Cal. App. 3d 899 (1979).

35. Vinson v. Superior Court, Calif. Sup. SF 24932 (rev. granted, Sept. 1985).

36. A further possibility—more political fantasy than practical—might be to insist that if the plaintiff's entire sexual history is open to inspection, the defendant's should be also: all the rapes, peeping at his sister, patronizing of prostitutes, locker-room jokes, use of pornography, masturbation fantasies, adolescent experimentation with boyfriends, fetishes, and so on.

37. *See, e.g.,* U.S. v. Kasto, 584 F.2d 268, 271–72 (8th Cir. 1978), *cert. denied,* 440 U.S. 930 (1979); State v. Bernier, 491 A.2d 1000, 1004 (R.I. 1985).

38. Another reason women do not bring claims is fear of countersuit. The relationship between sexual harassment and defamation is currently unsettled on many fronts. *See, e.g.,* Walker v. Gibson, 604 F. Supp. 916 (N.D. Ill. 1985) (action for violation of First Amendment will not lie against employer Army for hearing on unwarranted sexual harassment charge); Spisak v. McDole, 472 N.E.2d 347 (Ohio 1984) (defamation claim can be added to sexual harassment claim); Equal Employment Opportunity Commission v. Levi Strauss & Co., 515 F. Supp. 640 (N.D. Ill. 1981) (defamation action brought allegedly in response to employee allegation of sexual harassment is not necessarily retaliatory, if brought in good faith to vindicate reputation); Arenas v. Ladish Co., 619 F. Supp. 1304 (E.D. Wisc. 1985) (defamation claim may be brought for sexual harassment in the presence of others, not barred by exclusivity provision of worker's compensation law); Ross v. Comsat, 34 FEP Cases 261 (D. Md. 1984) (man sues company for retaliation in discharge following his complaint against woman at company for sexual harassment).

Educational institutions have been sued for acting when, after investigation, they find the complaints to be true. Barnes v. Oody, 28 FEP Cases 816 (E.D. Tenn. 1981) (summary judgment granted that arbitrators' holding for women who brought sexual harassment claim collaterally estops defamation action by sexual harassment defendant; immunity applies to statements in official investigation). Although it is much more difficult to prove defamation than to defeat a sexual harassment claim, threats of countersuit have intimidated many victims.

39. Rabidue v. Osceola Refining, 584 F. Supp. 423 (E.D. Mich. 1984).

40. Cobb v. Dufresne-Henry, 603 F. Supp. 1048, 1050 (D. Vt. 1985).

41. McNabb v. Cub Foods, 352 N.W. 2d 378, 381 (Minn. 1984).

42. Morgan v. Hertz Corp., 27 FEP Cases at 994.

43. Seratis v. Lane, 30 FEP 423, 425 (Cal. Super. 1980).

44. Rabidue v. Osceola Refining, 584 F. Supp. 419, 435 (E.D. Mich. 1984). This went to whether the treatment was sex-based. Note that the plaintiff did not say that she was offended but that she was discriminated against.

45. Women students at MIT filed a sexual harassment claim under Title IX, which was dismissed for lack of jurisdiction. Baker v. M.I.T., U.S. Dept. Education Office of Civil Rights #01-85-2013 (Sept. 20, 1985).

46. Particularly given the formative contribution to the women's movement of the struggles against racial and religious stigma, persecution, and violence, it is heartening to find a Jewish man and a Black man recovering for religious and racial harassment, respectively, based on sexual harassment precedents. Weiss v. U.S., 595 F. Supp. 1050 (E.D. Va. 1984) (pattern of anti-Semitic verbal abuse actionable based on *Katz* and *Henson*); Taylor v. Jones, 653 F.2d 1193, 1199 (8th Cir. 1981) (*Bundy* cited as basis for actionability of environmental racial harassment under Title VII).

10. Women, Self-Possession, and Sport

1. The attempt of a male athletic association to take over a women's athletics association is documented in the women's unsuccessful antitrust action, Association for Intercollegiate Athletics for Women v. National Collegiate Athletics Association, 558 F. Supp. 487 (D.D.C. 1983), *aff'd* 735 F.2d 577 (D.C. Cir. 1984). *Playboy* has begun sexualizing athletic women.

2. As to the law of this issue, American courts have not often considered the legality of institutions or programs that disadvantaged groups such as women have organized to promote their equality, such as separate sex athletic teams or organizations. Existing law on single-sex institutions is dominated by members of advantaged groups seeking the further advantage of access to the few resources previously available exclusively to disadvantaged groups. For instance, the U.S. Supreme Court found sex discrimination in the exclusion of a man from a public all-women's nursing school. Mississippi University for Women v. Hogan, 458 U.S. 718, 725 (1982). However, it was important that no institution of comparable convenience and quality existed at which the plaintiff could study.

Separate associations, activities, or programs of or for the disadvantaged have sometimes been permitted when equal treatment is thereby promoted by compensating for disadvantages. Mississippi University for Women v. Hogan, 458 U.S. 718, 730 n.16; Califano v. Webster, 430 U.S. 313, 318–20 (1977) (per curiam); Schlesinger v. Ballard, 419 U.S. 498, 508 (1975); *see also* Orr v. Orr, 440 U.S. 268, 283 (1979). Scholars have found the compensatory rationale even more appropriate when applied to women's membership organizations that seek sex equality than when applied to economic benefits, C. Feldblum, N. Krent, and V. Watkin, "Legal Challenges to All-Female Organizations," 21 *Harvard Civil Rights–Civil Liberties Law Review* 171, 215 (Winter, 1986). It would seem that where a women's organization with sex equality goals is a power base and leadership laboratory, is activist or service-oriented or a support system rather than a ghetto, such an organization may be seen to counteract and undermine the inferiority of women that compulsory sex segregation is based upon.

In a context in which women are socially unequal to men, all-women affiliations and activities are often not seen to run the same risks of perpetuating sex inequality that all-male affiliations can. The area of athletics provides examples of all-women groupings seen to further equality goals. By federal and constitutional law, teams for girls must be provided or girls must be given opportunities to compete in athletics programs formerly for boys, with some modifications for contact sports. The Title IX guidelines permit separate-sex teams where "athletic opportunities for members of that sex have previously been limited." 45 C.F.R. 86.41. *See* Yellow Springs Exempted Village School District Board of Education v. Ohio High School Athletic Association, 647 F.2d 651 (6th Cir. 1981); Leffel v. Wisconsin Interscholastic Athletic Association, 444 F. Supp. 1117 (D. Wisc. 1978). Women-only sports have been preserved against sex equality attacks both by exceptional girls seeking to compete on boys' teams when girls' teams were available, O'Connor v. Board of Education of School District 23, 545 F. Supp 376 (N.D. Ill. 1982) and by boys seeking to compete on girls' teams when boys' teams were not available. Petrie v. Illinois High School Association, 394 N.E.2d 855 (Ill. App. 1979). *But cf. Darrin v. Gould*, 85 Wash. 2d 859, 540 P.2d 882 (Wash. 1975).

In this context, courts have concluded that women-only teams are consistent with the sex-equality goal of precluding "a male dominance" of a sport. 394 N.E.2d 857; Ritacco v. Norwin School District, 361 F. Supp. 931 (D. Pa. 1973). "Overall" equality considerations for all girls often justify such results. Forte v. Board of Education, North Babylon Union Free School District, 431 N.Y.S. 2d 321 (Sup. 1980); Hoover v. Meiklejohn, 430 F. Supp. 164 (D. Colo. 1979), even in individual cases of boys who have no comparable opportunities. Mularadelis v. Haldane Central School Board, 427 N.Y.S. 2d 458 (Sup. Ct. 1980). The Ninth Circuit Court of Appeals has similarly held that a boy who was denied admission to a girls' volleyball team was not discriminated against on grounds of sex because girls-only sports further the social interest in sex equality, an interest which admitting boys to the girls' team would undermine. Clark v. Arizona Interscholastic Association, 695 F.2d 1126 (9th

Cir. 1982), *cert. denied*, 464 U.S. 818 (1983). Even though there was no boys' volleyball team, girls were seen to retain their equality interest in the single-sex team in the absence of a symmetry of opportunity for boys.

11. Linda's Life and Andrea's Work

1. See, e.g., Henry Krystal, ed., *Massive Psychic Trauma* 28 (1968). In that collection, Dr. Niederland described survivors of the Nazi concentration camps: "Most had to deny the reality of their condition ("it cannot be true") . . . all feelings ceased to be, on the surface, because one could not exist and at the same time live with such feelings of abhorrence, disgust, and terror. Simultaneous with the isolation of affects, there was an automatization of the ego which produced a robotlike numbness, giving the inmates a sordid-looking, emaciated, puppetlike appearance." Id. at 67 (discussing Robert Lifton's concept of "psychological closure," observed in survivors of Hiroshima). It is striking that Dr. Niederland distinguishes this denial "from what we see in civilian life," id., yet Dr. Krystal introduces the volume as follows: "It is hoped that the study of these aftereffects and problems may help us to understand, treat, and prevent traumatization in the milieu where it occurs most commonly: the home." Id. at 7. See also Sydney S. Furst, ed., *Psychic Trauma* (1967).

2. "Introduction," note 30.

3. Linda Lovelace and Michael McGrady, *Ordeal* (1980).

12. "More Than Simply a Magazine"

1. This is the subtitle of *Playboy* Magazine. Of course, it is questionable that this sexuality is "women's" in the sense that we own or possess it, or even that it accurately characterizes us. It *is*, however, the sexuality that is *attributed to* women by pornographers. Women, under conditions of sex inequality, then may come to exhibit it or even claim and embrace it as their own.

2. Examples include: Center for Women Policy Studies, Community Action for Legal Services (Litigation for Battered Women), Wider Opportunities for Women, NOW Legal Defense and Education Fund, Women's Action Alliance, Working Women United Institute, National Institute for Working Women, National Women's Political Caucus, National Gay Task Force, ACLU Women's Rights Project, ERA Strike Force, Federation of Women Lawyers' Judicial Screening Panel, National Organization for Women (benefit). Some of these groups have later repudiated, returned, or stopped receiving Playboy's money. Some have not.

3. "I would be a feminist whatever I did." Interview by Dave Newhouse with Christie Hefner, Playboy vice president, 1 *Event* 38 (Fall 1980); Bella

Stumbo, "Believes Playboy Liberates Women—Hefner on Hefner: 'Real Guy' Is a Very Moral Man," *Los Angeles Times*, Dec. 28, 1984, at 1, 17, 18. "I am a feminist." Hefner quoted in *Newsweek*, Aug. 4, 1986, at 54.

4. Hugh M. Hefner, "For some few, a photograph of the female figure—no matter how attractively posed—is embarrassing, objectionable and even downright sinful. In fact, one sometimes gets the feeling that the more attractively posed—and therefore appealing—the female is, the more objectionable and sinful she becomes to the critical. In order to react in this way, of course, one must believe that sex itself is objectionable and sinful—especially as typified by a beautiful woman." Hugh M. Hefner "The Playboy Philosophy," 1 *Playboy* 41 (Jan. 1963). Notice how "a photograph of the female figure" and "the female" become equated with "sex itself" in this passage. Actually, Playboy has very precise object standards for their Bunnies. Playboy's evaluation scale for "Bunny Image" is:

1. a *flawless* beauty (face, figure *and* grooming)

2. an exceptionally beautiful girl

3. marginal (is aging or has developed a correctible appearance problem)

4. has lost Bunny Image (either through aging or an *incorrectible* appearance problem)

Weber v. Playboy Club of N.Y., Playboy Clubs International, Inc., Hugh Hefner, App. No. 774, Case No. CSF-22619-70 (Human Rts. App. Bd., N.Y., N.Y., Dec. 17, 1971) at 2 (emphasis in original). This was a complaint for sex discrimination in a discharge occasioned by "loss of Bunny Image." She lost; the board said "complainant's services were terminated . . . because of her loss of weight and because she did not meet acceptable standards in reference to physical proportions," not because of her sex.

5. Miller v. California, 413 U.S. 15, 24 (1973).

6. Paris Adult Theatre I v. Slaton, 413 U.S. 49, 67 (1973).

7. Penthouse International v. McAuliffe, 610 F.2d 1353, 1362–73 (5th Cir. 1980). Perhaps it is this feature of *Playboy* that caused Justice Marshall to label it a "pretentious girlie magazine." California v. LaRue, 409 U.S. 109, 127–28 (1972).

8. "To encourage new research, the Foundation provides funds to Professor Edward Donnerstein of the University of Wisconsin to complete his work on the possible relationships between violent pornography and violence against women." *The Playboy Foundation* (pamphlet, n.d., at 6). Professor Donnerstein told me he did not apply for the funding but resisted an impulse to return it, on the view that refusing it would call into question the neutrality of his research.

9. Hugh M. Hefner, "The Playboy Philosophy" pt. II, *Playboy*, February 1963, at 41. Note how "passive" is supposed to be the antithesis of "brutality." *See also* Peter Bogdanovich's account of Hugh Hefner forcing sex on

Dorothy Stratten, Playmate of the Year in 1980, murdered by her pimp husband the same year. Bogdanovich, *The Killing of the Unicorn: Dorothy Stratten, 1960–1980* (1984). Hefner has denied this charge.

10. One woman who worked inside Playboy for ten years stated, "I want the public to recognize that *Playboy* magazine is not the coffee table literature that Hugh Hefner says it is, but rather a pornographic magazine." She detailed "the detrimental effects" Playboy had on the lives of the women she supervised as director of Playmate Promotions: "alienation from family, friends and religious practices, sexual exploitation and harassment, job discrimination, rape, mental—date rape, too, by the way—mental and physical abuse, murder and attempted murder, illegal drug abuse, attempted suicide, prostitution, unwanted pregnancies, abortions, venereal diseases, unnecessary cosmetic surgery." Miki Garcia, Hearings of the National Commission on Pornography 116 (Los Angeles, Oct. 17, 1985). *Penthouse* and *Hustler*, with which *Playboy* competes, tend to be more, and increasingly, violent. Neil Malamuth and Barry Spinner, "A Longitudinal Content Analysis of Sexual Violence in the Best-Selling Erotic Magazines," 17 *Journal of Sex Research* 226–37 (1981), find significant increases in pictorial violent sex. *Playboy* will lose its market if it doesn't get even more overtly violent. This is because it, with the rest of the pornography market, is creating a population of increasingly desensitized consumers. Explicit sex, after a while, puts men to sleep. It takes increasingly explicit violation, meaning violence, to wake them up, *erotically* speaking.

11. Abrams v. U.S., 250 U.S. 616, 630 (1919) (Holmes, J., joined by Brandeis, J., dissenting).

12. The Weimar Republic, the liberal democracy that preceded the Third Reich, had a rigorous legal tradition of abstract rights.

13. Letter from six student organizations to Charles Nesson, Feb. 24, 1982, protested his role as a possible judge in the First Amendment Awards in light of his otherwise sensitive response to issues of sexism: "Despite its arguably worthy journalism and fiction, [*Playboy*] persists through its cartoons, photographs and philosophy in perpetuating an image of women as sex objects ultimately subservient to macho masculinity . . . Women here have felt [their] contempt quite personally when Playboy cartoons insulting 'lady lawyers' have been anonymously placed in our mailbox." These were also frightening cartoons; one is about raping a lady lawyer. The letter continues, "We believe that by refusing to take part as a judge you would not be expressing a judgment on the censorship question, but that by consenting to be a judge you undoubtedly would be contributing to an impression of the legitimacy of these proceedings and of Playboy's treatment of women . . . We believe that far from being a worthy cause and a genuine statement of our First Amendment freedom, [the ceremony] is merely an attempt by Playboy to bolster its sagging image and justify its existence."

14. Information from contemporaneous discussions with students and "Nesson Resigns from Playboy Panel," *Harvard Crimson*, Mar. 22, 1982, at 1: "I did not owe it to anybody to participate in an activity that could possibly

lend credence to something I disapprove of—sexism in *Playboy* magazine." Playboy lists this professor as a judge of the First Amendment Awards in 1981.

15. The Vitullo kit, prepared by Citizen's Committee for Victim Assistance. (Chicago). See also *The Playboy Foundation*, note 8 above, at 9.

16. "Most Playboy Foundation grants are under $10,000.00. The proposal should highlight a special project that would benefit [*sic*] a grant of this size." *The Playboy Foundation*, note 8 above, at 19.

17. Playboy's revenue is shrinking. I am told by a person at the Ford Foundation that Playboy considers itself in a short-term cash "crunch." They are divesting themselves of some holdings, some voluntarily, some with regret. (The regrets apparently include their gambling operations.) Playboy is apparently not in wonderful financial condition at the moment. *Newsweek*, Aug. 4, 1986, at 54.

18. Grants (January 1968) to the Institute for Reproductive Biology "assisted researchers William Masters and Virginia Johnson in developing a comprehensive program for the training of health care professionals in treatment of sexual dysfunction." *The Playboy Foundation*, note 8 above, at 3. "Masters and Johnson received a total of at least $300,250.00 from Playboy by November, 1979." Interview by Laura Lederer with M. Bailey, "Questionable Partnership: Sexologists and the Pornography Industry" *OASIS* (Organized against Sexism in Sex) *Newsletter of Feminists against Pornography*, (Washington, D.C.) (Jan./Feb. 1982).

19. "During the past decade, the pornography industry appears to have acquired a nearly monopolistic influence over sex information . . . I have come to strongly suspect that the pornography industry is shaping our national forums of sex information by its grants-giving programs. I further suspect that such gifts are encouraging sexologists to study certain questions and ignore others. If this is correct, then what pornographers in effect have attained is a nearly monopolistic influence over sexology." M. Bailey in Lederer, note 18 above.

20. "July 1967: The Foundation provides the first of several major grants to the Sex Information and Education Council of the United States (SIECUS)," *The Playboy Foundation*, note 8 above, at 3. They also funded Dr. Mary Calderone.

21. "December, 1965: Playboy becomes the first major national magazine to advocate legal abortion—on the grounds that women have *the same rights as men* to control their own bodies." *The Playboy Foundation*, note 8 above, at 2 (emphasis added).

22. This is a male notion of what abortion involves. *See* 93–102 above.

23. Fortunately, this was more true in 1982 than it is in 1986. Even in 1982, legions of feminists at all levels of grassroots organizations were probably entirely clear about the role of pornography in the victimization of women. But this is not the same as a self-conscious direct confrontation with the industry and its hold over sexuality and women, as is now being built, even as Playboy's money is being widely turned down.

24. Conference on the Discrimination and Harassment of Women in Employment, Center for Women Policy Studies, July 7–9, 1981.

25. At least *some* women are paying for it. *See, e.g.,* Bogdanovich, note 9 above, at 25; Linda Lovelace and Michael McGrady, *Ordeal* (1980).

13. Not a Moral Issue

Many of the ideas in this essay were developed and refined in close collaboration with Andrea Dworkin. It is difficult at times to distinguish the contribution of each of us to a body of work that—through shared teaching, writing, speaking, organizing, and political action on every level—has been created together. I have tried to credit specific contributions that I am aware are distinctly hers. This text is mine; she does not necessarily agree with everything in it.

1. This speech as a whole is intended to communicate what I mean by pornography. The key work on the subject is Andrea Dworkin, *Pornography: Men Possessing Women* (1981). No definition can convey the meaning of a word as well as its use in context can. However, what Andrea Dworkin and I mean by pornography is rather well captured in our legal definition: "Pornography is the graphic sexually explicit subordination of women, whether in pictures or in words, that also includes one or more of the following: (i) women are presented dehumanized as sexual objects, things or commodities; or (ii) women are presented as sexual objects who enjoy pain or humiliation; or (iii) women are presented as sexual objects who experience sexual pleasure in being raped; or (iv) women are presented as sexual objects tied up or cut up or mutilated or bruised or physically hurt; or (v) women are presented in postures of sexual submission, servility or display; or (vi) women's body parts—including but not limited to vaginas, breasts, and buttocks—are exhibited, such that women are reduced to those parts; or (vii) women are presented as whores by nature; or (viii) women are presented being penetrated by objects or animals; or (ix) women are presented in scenarios of degradation, injury, torture, shown as filthy or inferior, bleeding, bruised, or hurt in a context that makes these conditions sexual." Pornography also includes "the use of men, children or transsexuals in the place of women." Pornography, thus defined, is discrimination on the basis of sex and, as such, a civil rights violation. This definition is a slightly modified version of the one passed by the Minneapolis City Council on December 30, 1983. Minneapolis, Minn., Ordinance amending tit. 7, chs. 139 and 141, Minneapolis Code of Ordinances Relating to Civil Rights (Dec. 30, 1983). The ordinance was vetoed by the mayor, reintroduced, passed again, and vetoed again in 1984. *See* "Francis Biddle's Sister" for subsequent developments.

2. "Congress shall make no law . . . abridging the freedom of speech, or of the press . . ." U.S. Const. amend. I.

3. Justice Black, at times joined by Justice Douglas, took the position that the Bill of Rights, including the First Amendment, was "absolute." Hugo Black, "The Bill of Rights," 35 *New York University Law Review* 865, 867 (1960);

Edmund Cahn, "Justice Black and First Amendment 'Absolutes': A Public Interview," 37 *New York University Law Review* 549 (1962). For a discussion, see Harry Kalven, "Upon Rereading Mr. Justice Black on the First Amendment," 14 *UCLA Law Review* 428 (1967). For one exchange in the controversy surrounding the "absolute" approach to the First Amendment, as opposed to the "balancing" approach, *see, e.g.*, W. Mendelson, "On the Meaning of the First Amendment: Absolutes in the Balance," 50 *California Law Review* 821 (1962); L. Frantz, "The First Amendment in the Balance," 71 *Yale Law Journal* 1424 (1962); Frantz, "Is the First Amendment Law?—A Reply to Professor Mendelson," 51 *California Law Review* 729 (1963); Mendelson, "The First Amendment and the Judicial Process: A Reply to Mr. Frantz," 17 *Vanderbilt Law Review* 479 (1964). In the pornography context, *see e.g.*, Roth v. United States, 354 U.S. 476, 514 (1957) (Douglas, J., joined by Black, J., dissenting); Smith v. California, 361 U.S. 147, 155 (1959) (Black, J., concurring); Miller v. California, 413 U.S. 15, 37 (1973) (Douglas, J., dissenting). The purpose of this discourse is not to present a critique of absolutism as such, but rather to identify and criticize some widely and deeply shared implicit beliefs that underlie both the absolutist view and the more mainstream flexible approaches.

4. The history of obscenity law can be read as a failed attempt to make this separation, with the failure becoming ever more apparent from the *Redrup* decision forward. Redrup v. New York, 386 U.S. 767 (1967). For a summary of cases exemplifying such a trend, see the dissent by Justice Brennan in Paris Adult Theatre I v. Slaton, 413 U.S. 49, 73 (1973).

5. Much has been made of the distinction between sex and gender. Sex is thought the more biological, gender the more social. The relation of sexuality to each varies. *See, e.g.*, Robert Stoller, *Sex and Gender* 9–10 (1974). Since I think that the importance of biology to the condition of women is the social meaning attributed to it, biology *is* its social meaning for purposes of analyzing the inequality of the sexes, a political condition. I therefore tend to use sex and gender relatively interchangeably.

6. The sense in which I mean women's perspective as different from men's is like that of Virginia Woolf's reference to "the difference of view, the difference of standard" in her "George Eliot," 1 *Collected Essays* 204 (1966). Neither of us uses the notion of a gender difference to refer to something biological or natural or transcendental or existential. Perspective parallels standards because the social experience of gender is confined by gender. *See* Catharine A. MacKinnon, *Sexual Harassment of Working Women* 107–41 (1979), and the articles mentioned in note 11, below; Virginia Woolf, *Three Guineas* (1938); *see also* Andrea Dworkin, "The Root Cause," in *Our Blood: Essays and Discourses on Sexual Politics* 96 (1976). I do not refer to the gender difference here descriptively, leaving its roots and implications unspecified, so they could be biological, existential, transcendental, in any sense inherent, or social but necessary. I mean "point of view" as a view, hence a standard, that is imposed on women by force of sex inequality, which is a political condition. "Male," which is an adjective here, is a social and political concept, not

a biological attribute; it is a status socially conferred upon a person because of a condition of birth. As I use "male," it has nothing whatever to do with inherency, preexistence, nature, inevitability, or body as such. Because it is in the interest of men to be male in the system we live under (male being powerful as well as human), they seldom question its rewards or even see it as a status at all.

7. Criminal Code, Can. Rev. Stat. chap. c-34, § 159(2)(c) and (d) (1970). People v. Sanger, 222 N.Y. 192, 118 N.E. 637 (1918).

8. *The Report of the Commission on Obscenity and Pornography* (1970) (majority report). The accuracy of the commission's findings is called into question by: (1) widespread criticism of the commission's methodology from a variety of perspectives, *e.g.*, L. Sunderland, *Obscenity—The Court, the Congress and the President's Commission* (1975); Edward Donnerstein, "Pornography Commission Revisited: Aggression—Erotica and Violence against Women," 39 *Journal of Personality and Social Psychology* 269 (1980); Ann Garry, "Pornography and Respect for Women," 4 *Social Theory and Practice* 395 (Summer 1978); Irene Diamond, "Pornography and Repression," 5 *Signs: A Journal of Women in Culture and Society* 686 (1980); Victor Cline, "Another View: Pornography Effects, the State of the Art," in *Where Do You Draw the Line?* (V. B. Cline ed. 1974); Pauline Bart and Margaret Jozsa, "Dirty Books, Dirty Films, and Dirty Data," in *Take Back the Night: Women on Pornography* 204 (Laura Lederer ed. 1982); (2) the commission's tendency to minimize the significance of its own findings, *e.g.*, those by Donald Mosher on the differential effects of exposure by gender; and (3) the design of the commission's research. The commission did not focus on questions about gender, did its best to eliminate "violence" from its materials (so as not to overlap with the Violence Commission), and propounded unscientific theories such as Puritan guilt to explain women's negative responses to the materials.

Further, scientific causality is unnecessary to legally validate an obscenity regulation: "But, it is argued, there is no scientific data which conclusively demonstrate that exposure to obscene materials adversely affects men and women or their society. It is [urged] that, absent such a demonstration, any kind of state regulation is 'impermissible.' *We reject this argument.* It is not for us to resolve empirical uncertainties underlying state legislation, save in the exceptional case where that legislation plainly impinges upon rights protected by the Constitution itself . . . Although there is no conclusive proof of a connection between antisocial behavior and obscene material, the legislature of Georgia could quite reasonably determine that such a connection does or might exist." Paris Adult Theatre I v. Slaton, 413 U.S. 49, 60–61 (1973) (Burger, J., for the majority) (emphasis added); see also Roth v. U.S., 354 U.S. 476, 501 (1957).

9. Some of the harm of pornography to women, as defined in note 1 above, and as discussed in this talk, has been documented in empirical studies. Recent studies have found that exposure to pornography increases the willingness of normal men to aggress against women under laboratory conditions; makes both women and men substantially less able to perceive ac-

counts of rape as accounts of rape; makes normal men more closely resemble convicted rapists psychologically; increases attitudinal measures that are known to correlate with rape, such as hostility toward women, propensity to rape, condoning rape, and predictions that one would rape or force sex on a woman if one knew one would not get caught; and produces other attitude changes in men, such as increasing the extent of their trivialization, dehumanization, and objectification of women. Diana E. H. Russell, "Pornography and Violence: What Does the New Research Say?" in Lederer, note 8 above, at 216; Neil M. Malamuth and Edward Donnerstein (eds.), *Pornography and Sexual Aggression* (1984); Dolph Zillman, *The Connection between Sex and Aggression* (1984); J. V. P. Check, N. Malamuth, and R. Stille, "Hostility to Women Scale" (1983) (unpublished manuscript); Edward Donnerstein, "Pornography: Its Effects on Violence against Women," in Malamuth and Donnerstein, eds., *Pornography and Sexual Aggression* (1984); Neil M. Malamuth and J. V. P. Check, "The Effects of Mass Media Exposure on Acceptance of Violence against Women: A Field Experiment," 15 *Journal of Research in Personality* 436 (1981); Neil M. Malamuth, "Rape Proclivities among Males," 37 *Journal of Social Issues* 138 (1981); Neil M. Malamuth and Barry Spinner, "A Longitudinal Content Analysis of Sexual Violence in the Best-Selling Erotic Magazines," 16 *Journal of Sex Research* 226 (1980); Mosher, "Sex Callousness Towards Women," in 8 *Technical Report of the Commission on Obscenity and Pornography* 313 (1971); Dolph Zillman and J. Bryant, "Effects of Massive Exposure to Pornography," in Malamuth and Donnerstein, eds., *Pornography and Sexual Aggression* (1984).

10. The following are illustrative, not exhaustive, of the body of work I term the "feminist critique of pornography." Andrea Dworkin, note 1 above; Dorchen Leidholdt, "Where Pornography Meets Fascism," *Win*, Mar. 15, 1983, at 18; George Steiner, "Night Words," in *The Case Against Pornography* 227 (D. Holbrook ed. 1973); Susan Brownmiller, *Against Our Will: Men, Women and Rape* 394 (1975); Robin Morgan, "Pornography and Rape: Theory and Practice," in *Going Too Far* 165 (Robin Morgan ed. 1977); Kathleen Barry, *Female Sexual Slavery* (1979); *Against Sado-Masochism: A Radical Feminist Analysis* (R. R. Linden, D. R. Pagano, D. E. H. Russell, and S. L. Star eds. 1982), especially chapters by Ti-Grace Atkinson, Judy Butler, Andrea Dworkin, Alice Walker, John Stoltenberg, Audre Lorde, and Susan Leigh Star; Alice Walker, "Coming Apart," in Lederer, *Take Back the Night*, note 8 above, and other articles in that volume with the exception of the legal ones; Gore Vidal, "Women's Liberation Meets the Miller-Mailer-Manson Man," in *Homage to Daniel Shays: Collected Essays 1952–1972* 389 (1972); Linda Lovelace and Michael McGrady, *Ordeal* (1980). Works basic to the perspective taken here are Kate Millett, *Sexual Politics* (1969) and Florence Rush, *The Best-Kept Secret: Sexual Abuse of Children* (1980). "Violent Pornography: Degradation of Women versus Right of Free Speech," 8 *New York University Review of Law and Social Change* 181 (1978) contains both feminist and nonfeminist arguments.

11. For more extensive discussions of this subject, *see* my prior work, especially "Feminism, Marxism, Method and the State: An Agenda for Theory,"

7 *Signs: Journal of Women in Culture and Society* 515 (1982) [hereinafter cited as *Signs* I]; "Feminism, Marxism, Method and the State: Toward Feminist Jurisprudence," 8 *Signs: Journal of Women in Culture and Society* 635 (1983) [hereinafter cited as *Signs* II].

12. Jacobellis v. Ohio, 378 U.S. 184, 197 (1964) (Stewart, J., concurring).

13. Justice Stewart is said to have complained that this single line was more quoted and remembered than anything else he ever said.

14. *See Signs* I, note 11 above.

15. Susan Griffin, *Pornography and Silence: Culture's Revenge Against Nature* 2–4, 251–65 (1981).

16. Dworkin, note 1 above.

17. *See also* Dworkin, note 6 above.

18. The position that pornography is sex—that whatever you think of sex you think of pornography—underlies nearly every treatment of the subject. In particular, nearly every nonfeminist treatment proceeds on the implicit or explicit assumption, argument, criticism, or suspicion that pornography is sexually liberating in some way, a position unifying an otherwise diverse literature. *See, e.g.,* D. H. Lawrence, "Pornography and Obscenity," in his *Sex, Literature and Censorship* 64 (1959); Hugh Hefner, "The Playboy Philosophy," *Playboy,* December 1962, at 73, and *Playboy,* February 1963, at 43; Henry Miller, "Obscenity and the Law of Reflection," in his *Remember to Remember* 274, 286 (1947); Deirdre English, "The Politics of Porn: Can Feminists Walk the Line?" *Mother Jones,* Apr. 1980, at 20; Jean Bethke Elshtain, "The Victim Syndrome: A Troubling Turn in Feminism," *The Progressive,* June 1982, at 42. To choose an example at random: "In opposition to the Victorian view that narrowly defines proper sexual function in a rigid way that is analogous to ideas of excremental regularity and moderation, pornography builds a model of plastic variety and joyful excess in sexuality. In opposition to the sorrowing Catholic dismissal of sexuality as an unfortunate and spiritually superficial concomitant of propagation, pornography affords the alternative idea of the independent status of sexuality as a profound and shattering ecstasy." David Richards, "Free Speech and Obscenity Law: Toward a Moral Theory of the First Amendment," 123 *University of Pennsylvania Law Review* 45, 81 (1974) (footnotes omitted). *See also* F. Schauer, "Response: Pornography and the First Amendment," 40 *University of Pittsburgh Law Review* 605, 616 (1979).

19. Spending time around adult bookstores, attending pornographic movies, and talking with pornographers (who, like all smart pimps, do some form of market research), as well as analyzing the pornography itself in sex/gender terms, all confirm that pornography is for men. That women may attend or otherwise consume it does not make it any less for men, any more than the observation that mostly men consume pornography means that pornography does not harm women. *See* Martha Langelan, "The Political Economy of Pornography," *Aegis: Magazine on Ending Violence against Women,* Autumn 1981, at 5; J. Cook, "The X-Rated Economy," *Forbes,* Sept. 18, 1978, at 60. Personal observation reveals that most women tend to avoid pornography as much as possible—which is not very much, as it turns out.

20. The "fantasy" and "catharsis" hypotheses, together, assert that pornography cathects sexuality on the level of fantasy fulfillment. The work of Edward Donnerstein, particularly, shows that the opposite is true. The more pornography is viewed, the *more* pornography—and the more brutal pornography—is both wanted and required for sexual arousal. What occurs is not catharsis, but desensitization, requiring progressively more potent stimulation. See works cited note 9 above; Murray Straus, "Leveling, Civility, and Violence in the Family," 36 *Journal of Marriage & The Family* 13 (1974).

21. Lovelace and McGrady, note 10 above, provides an account by one coerced pornography model. *See also* Andrea Dworkin, "Pornography's 'Exquisite Volunteers,'" *Ms.*, March 1981, at 65.

22. However, for one such inquiry, see Russell, note 9 above, at 228: a random sample of 930 San Francisco households found that 10 percent of women had at least once "been upset by anyone trying to get you to do what they'd seen in pornographic pictures, movies or books." Obviously, this figure could only include those who knew that the pornography was the source of the sex, so this finding is conservative. *See also* Diana E. H. Russell, *Rape in Marriage* 27–41 (1983) (discussing the data base). The hearings Andrea Dworkin and I held for the Minneapolis City Council on the ordinance cited in note 1 produced many accounts of the use of pornography to force sex on women and children. *Public Hearings on Ordinances to Add Pornography as Discrimination against Women*, Committee on Government Operations, City Council, Minneapolis, Minn., Dec. 12–13, 1983. (Hereinafter cited as *Hearings*).

23. *See Signs* I; *see also* Susan Sontag, "The Pornographic Imagination," 34 *Partisan Review* 181 (1977).

24. "Explicitness" of accounts is a central issue in both obscenity adjudications and audience access standards adopted voluntarily by self-regulated industries or by boards of censor. *See, e.g.,* Grove Press v. Christenberry, 175 F. Supp. 488, 489 (S.D.N.Y. 1959) (discussion of "candor" and "realism"); Grove Press v. Christenberry, 276 F.2d 433, 438 (2d Cir. 1960) ("directness"); Mitchum v. State, 251 So.2d 298, 302 (Fla. Dist. Ct. App. 1971) ("show it all"); Kaplan v. California, 413 U.S. 115, 118 (1973). How *much* sex the depiction shows is implicitly thereby correlated with how *sexual* (that is, how sexually arousing to the male) the material is. *See, e.g.,* Memoirs v. Massachusetts, 383 U.S. 413, 460 (1966) (White, J., dissenting); Richard Heffner, "What G, PG, R and X Really Means," 126 *Cong. Rec.* 172 (daily ed. Dec. 8, 1980); *Report of the Committee on Obscenity and Film Censorship* (the Williams Report) (1981). Andrea Dworkin brilliantly gives the reader the experience of this aesthetic in her account of the pornography. Dworkin, note 1 above, at 25–47.

25. To the body of law ably encompassed and footnoted by William Lockhart and Robert McClure, "Literature, the Law of Obscenity and the Constitution," 38 *Minnesota Law Review* 295 (1954) and "Censorship of Obscenity," 45 *Minnesota Law Review* 5 (1960), I add only the most important cases since then: Stanley v. Georgia, 394 U.S. 557 (1969); U.S. v. Reidel, 402 U.S. 351 (1970); Miller v. California, 413 U.S. 15 (1973); Paris Adult Theatre I v. Slaton,

413 U.S. 49 (1973); Hamling v. U.S., 418 U.S. 87 (1973); Jenkins v. Georgia, 418 U.S. 153 (1973); U.S. v. 12 200-Ft. Reels of Super 8mm Film, 413 U.S. 123 (1973); Erznoznik v. City of Jacksonville, 422 U.S. 205 (1975); Splawn v. California, 431 U.S. 595 (1976); Ward v. Illinois, 431 U.S. 767 (1976); Lovisi v. Slayton, 539 F.2d 349 (4th Cir. 1976). *See also* New York v. Ferber, 458 U.S. 747 (1982).

26. For a discussion of the role of the law of privacy in supporting the existence of pornography, see Ruth Colker, "Pornography and Privacy: Towards the Development of a Group Based Theory for Sex Based Intrusions of Privacy," 1 *Law and Inequality: A Journal of Theory and Practice* 191 (1983).

27. Louis Henkin, "Morals and the Constitution: The Sin of Obscenity," 63 *Columbia Law Review* 391, 395 (1963).

28. These parallels are discussed more fully in *Signs* II. It may seem odd to denominate "moral" as *female* here, since this article discusses male morality. Under male supremacy, men define things; I am describing that. Men define women *as* "moral." This is the male view of women. My analysis, a feminist critique of the male standpoint, terms "moral" the concept that pornography is about good and evil. This is *my* analysis of *them,* as contrasted with their attributions to women.

29. A reading of case law supports the reports in Robert Woodward and Scott Armstrong, *The Brethren* 194 (1979), to the effect that this is a "bottom line" criterion for at least some justices. The interesting question becomes why the tactics of male supremacy would change from keeping the penis hidden, covertly glorified, to having it everywhere on display, overtly glorified. This suggests at least that a major shift from private terrorism to public terrorism has occurred. What used to be perceived as a danger to male power, the exposure of the penis, has now become a strategy in maintaining it.

30. One possible reading of Lockhart and McClure, note 25 above, is that this was their agenda, and that their approach was substantially adopted in the third prong of the *Miller* doctrine. For the law's leading attempt to grapple with this issue, *see* Memoirs v. Massachusetts, 383 U.S. 413 (1966), *overruled in part,* Miller v. California, 413 U.S. 15 (1973). *See also* U.S. v. Ulysses, 5 F. Supp. 182 (S.D.N.Y. 1933), *aff'd* 72 F.2d 705 (2d Cir. 1934).

31. Andrea Dworkin and I developed this analysis in our class "Pornography" at the University of Minnesota Law School, Fall 1983. *See also* Dworkin, "Why So-Called Radical Men Love and Need Pornography," in Lederer, note 8 above, at 141 (the issue of pornography is an issue of sexual access to women, hence involves a fight among men).

32. Those termed "fathers" and "sons" in Dworkin's article, note 31 above, we came to call "the old boys," whose strategy for male dominance involves keeping pornography and the abuse of women private, and "the new boys," whose strategy for male dominance involves making pornography and the abuse of women public. In my view Freud and the popularization of his derepression hypothesis figure centrally in "the new boys'" approach and success. To conclude, as some have, that women have benefited from the public

availability of pornography and hence should be grateful for and have a stake in its continuing availability is to say that the merits of open condoned oppression relative to covert condoned oppression warrant its continuation. This reasoning obscures the possibility of *ending* the oppression. The benefit of pornography's open availability, it seems to me, is that women can know who and what we are dealing with in order to end it. How, is the question.

33. Miller v. California, 413 U.S. 15, 24 (1973).

34. Paris Adult Theatre I v. Slaton, 413 U.S. 49, 67 (1973). *See also* Miller v. California, 413 U.S. 15, 25 n.7 ("A quotation from Voltaire in the flyleaf of a book will not constitutionally redeem an otherwise obscene publication," quoting Kois v. Wisconsin, 408 U.S. 229, 231 [1972]).

35. Penthouse International v. McAuliffe, 610 F.2d 1353, 1362–73 (5th Cir. 1980). For a study in enforcement, *see* Coble v. City of Birmingham, 389 So.2d 527 (Ala. Ct. App. 1980).

36. Malamuth and Spinner, note 9 above (". . . the portrayal of sexual aggression within such 'legitimate' magazines as *Playboy* and *Penthouse* may have a greater impact than similar portrayals in hard-core pornography"); Neil M. Malamuth and Edward Donnerstein, "The Effects of Aggressive-Pornographic Mass Media Stimuli," 15 *Advances in Experimental Social Psychology* 103, 130 (1982).

37. Some courts, under the obscenity rubric, seem to have understood that the quality of artistry does not undo the damage. People v. Mature Enterprises, 343 N.Y.S.2d 911, 925 n.14 (N.Y. Sup. 1973) ("This court will not adopt a rule of law which states that obscenity is suppressible but that well-written or technically well produced obscenity is not," quoting, in part, People v. Fritch, 13 N.Y.2d 119, 126, 243 N.Y.S.2d 1, 7, 192 N.E.2d 713 [1963]). More to the point of my argument here is Justice O'Connor's observation that "[t]he compelling interests identified in today's opinion . . . suggest that the Constitution might in fact permit New York to ban knowing distribution of works depicting minors engaged in explicit sexual conduct, regardless of the social value of the depictions. For example, a 12-year-old child photographed while masturbating surely suffers the same psychological harm whether the community labels the photograph 'edifying' or 'tasteless.' The audience's appreciation of the depiction is simply irrelevant to New York's asserted interest in protecting children from psychological, emotional, and mental harm." New York v. Ferber, 458 U.S. 747, 774–75 (1982) (concurring). Put another way, how does it make a harmed child *not harmed* that what was produced by harming him is great art?

38. Women typically get mentioned in obscenity law only in the phrase, "women and men," used as a synonym for "people." At the same time, exactly who the victim of pornography is, has long been a great mystery. The few references to "exploitation" in obscenity litigation do not evoke a woman victim. For example, one reference to "a system of commercial exploitation of people with sadomasochistic sexual aberrations" concerned the customers of women dominatrixes, all of whom were men. State v. Von Cleef, 102 N.J. Super. 104, 245 A.2d 495, 505 (1968). The children at issue in *Ferber* were boys.

Similarly, Justice Frankfurter invoked the "sordid exploitation of man's nature and impulses" in discussing his conception of pornography in Kingsley Pictures Corp. v. Regents, 360 U.S. 684, 692 (1958).

39. Miller v. California, 413 U.S. 15, 24 (1973).

40. *See, e.g.*, Miller v. California, id. at 40–41 (Douglas, J., dissenting) ("What shocks me may be sustenance for my neighbors"); U.S. v. 12 200-Ft. Reels of Super 8mm Film, 413 U.S. 123, 137 (1972) (Douglas, J., dissenting) ("[W]hat may be trash to me may be prized by others"); Cohen v. California, 403 U.S. 15, 25 (1970) (Harlan, J.) ("One man's vulgarity is another's lyric"); Winters v. New York, 333 U.S. 507, 510 (1947) ("What is one man's amusement, teaches another's doctrine"); Lawrence, note 18 above, at 195 ("What is pornography to one man is the laughter of genius to another"); Ginzburg v. United States, 383 U.S. 463, 489 (1966) (Douglas, J., dissenting) ("Some like Chopin, others like 'rock and roll'"). As one man, the pimp who forced Linda Lovelace into pornography, said to another: "I don't tell you how to write your column. Don't tell me how to treat my broads." (Quoted in Gloria Steinem, "The Real Linda Lovelace," in *Outrageous Acts and Everyday Rebellions* 243, 252 [1983].)

41. For the resolution of this issue for nonconventional sexuality, *see* Mishkin v. New York, 383 U.S. 502, 508 (1966).

42. None of this is intended as a comment about the personal sexuality or principles of any judicial individual; it is rather a series of analytic observations that emerge from a feminist attempt to interpret the deep social structure of a vast body of case law on the basis of a critique of gender. Further research should systematically analyze the contents of the pornography involved in the cases. For instance, with respect to the last hypothesis in the text above, is it just chance that the first film to be found obscene by a state supreme court depicts male masturbation? Landau v. Fording, 245 C.A.2d 820, 54 Cal. Rptr. 177 (1966). Given the ubiquity of the infantilization of women and the sexualization of little girls, would *Ferber* have been decided the same way if it had shown twelve-year-old girls masturbating? Did works like *Lady Chatterley's Lover* and *Tropic of Cancer* get in trouble because male sexuality is depicted in a way that men think is dangerous for women and children to see?

43. Roth v. U.S., 354 U.S. 476 (1957), *but cf.* Stanley v. Georgia, 394 U.S. 557 (1969), in which the right to private possession of obscene materials is protected as a First Amendment *speech* right. *See* 67 *Landmark Briefs and Arguments of the Supreme Court of the United States: Constitutional Law* 850 (P. Kurland and G. Casper eds. 1975).

44. *E.g.*, *The Report of the Commission on Obscenity and Pornography*, note 8 above, at 1, charges the commission to study "[t]he effect of obscenity and pornography upon the public and particularly minors and its relation to crime and other antisocial behavior."

45. Naomi Scheman, "Making It All Up," transcript of speech, January 1982, at 7.

46. This body of work is usually taken to be diverse. Thomas I. Emerson,

Toward a General Theory of the First Amendment (1966); Emerson, *The System of Freedom of Expression* (1970); Alexander Meiklejohn, *Free Speech and Its Relation to Self-Government* (1948); Whitney v. California, 274 U.S. 357, 375 (1927) (Brandeis, J., concurring, joined by Holmes, J.); T. Scanlon, "A Theory of Free Expression," 1 *Philosophy and Public Affairs* 204 (1972); John Hart Ely, "Flag Desecration: A Case Study in the Roles of Categorization and Balancing in First Amendment Analysis," 88 *Harvard Law Review* 1482 (1975); Zechariah Chafee, *Free Speech in the United States* 245 (1948). This literature is ably summarized and anatomized by Ed Baker, who proposes an interpretative theory that goes far toward responding to my objections here, without really altering the basic assumptions I criticize. *See* C. E. Baker, "Scope of the First Amendment Freedom of Speech," 25 *UCLA Law Review* 964 (1978) and "The Process of Change and the Liberty Theory of the First Amendment," 55 *Southern California Law Review* 293 (1982).

47. Emerson, *Toward a General Theory of the First Amendment*, note 46 above, at 28.

48. *See* Erznoznik v. City of Jacksonville, 422 U.S. 205 (1975); Breard v. Alexandria, 341 U.S. 622, 641–45 (1951); Kovacs v. Cooper, 336 U.S. 77, 87–89 (1949).

49. Stanley v. Georgia, 394 U.S. 557 (1969).

50. *See* Walker, "Coming Apart," in Lederer, note 8 above, at 85; Russell, note 9 above; *Hearings. Cf.* Paris Adult Theatre I v. Slaton, 413 U.S. 49, 71 (1973) (Douglas, J., dissenting) ("[In] a life that has not been short, I have yet to be trapped into seeing or reading something that would offend me"). He probably hadn't.

51. *See* "Privacy v. Equality" in Part II for a fuller discussion of this point.

52. Emerson, *Toward a General Theory of the First Amendment*, note 46 above, at 16–25. *See also* Emerson, *The System of Freedom of Expression*, note 46 above, at 17.

53. The essentially scientific notion of causality did not *first* appear in this law at this time, however. *See, e.g.*, U.S. v. Roth, 237 F.2d 796, 812–17 (2d Cir. 1956) (Frank, J., concurring) ("According to Judge Bok, an obscenity statute may be validly enforced when there is proof of a causal relation between a particular book and undesirable conduct. Almost surely, such proof cannot ever be adduced." Id., 826 n.70).

Werner Heisenberg, criticizing old ideas of atomic physics in light of Einstein's theory of relativity, states what conditions must exist for a causal relation to make sense: "To coordinate a definite cause to a definite effect has sense only when both can be observed without introducing a foreign element disturbing their interrelation. The law of causality, because of its very nature, can only be defined for isolated systems." Werner Heisenberg, *The Physical Principles of the Quantum Theory* 63 (1930). Among the influences that disturb the isolation of systems are observers. Underlying the adoption of a causality standard in obscenity law is a rather hasty analogy between the regularities of physical and of social systems, an analogy that has seldom been explicitly justified or even updated as the physical sciences have questioned their own epistemological foundations. This kind of scientific causality may not be readily susceptible to measurement in social systems for the simple reason that social systems are not isolated systems; experimental research (which is where it *has* been shown that pornography causes harm) can only minimize the influence of what will always be "foreign elements." Pornography and harm may not be two definite events anyway; perhaps pornography *is* a harm. Moreover, if the effects of pornography are systematic, they may not be isolable from the system in which they exist. This would not mean that no harm exists. Rather, it would mean that because the harm is so pervasive, it cannot be sufficiently isolated to be *perceived* as existing according to this causal model. In other words, if pornography is seen as harmful only if it causes harm by this model, and if it exists socially only in ways that cannot be isolated from society itself, its harm will not be perceived to exist. I think this describes the conceptual situation in which we find ourselves.

54. Morton Horowitz, "The Doctrine of Objective Causation," in *The Politics of Law* 201 (David Kairys ed. 1982). The pervasiveness of the objectification of women has been treated as a reason why pandering should not be constitutionally restricted: "The advertisements of our best magazines are chock-full of thighs, ankles, calves, bosoms, eyes, and hair, to draw the potential buyer's attention to lotions, tires, food, liquor, clothing, autos, and even insurance policies." Ginzburg v. U.S., 383 U.S. 463, 482 (1966) (Douglas, J., dissenting). Justice Douglas thereby illustrated, apparently without noticing, that *somebody* knows that associating sex, that is, women's bodies, with things causes people to *act* on that association.

55. *See* Lovelace and McGrady, note 10 above.

56. Two boys masturbating with no showing of explicit force demonstrates the harm of child pornography in New York v. Ferber, 458 U.S. 747 (1982), while shoving money up a woman's vagina, among other acts, raises serious questions of "regulation of 'conduct' having a communicative element" in live sex adjudications, California v. LaRue, 409 U.S. 109, 113 (1972) (live sex can be regulated by a state in connection with serving alcoholic beverages). "Snuff" films, in which a woman is actually murdered to produce a film for sexual entertainment, are known to exist. People v. Douglas and Hernandez, Felony Complaint No. NF8300382, Municipal Court, North Judicial District, Orange County, Calif., Aug. 5, 1983, alleges the murder of two young girls to make a pornographic film. Hernandez turned state's evidence; Douglas was convicted of first-degree murder in November 1984. No snuff film was found. (Conversation with Tony Rackackaus, district attorney, Sept. 3, 1986.)

57. Both Griffin, note 15 above, and the oldest Anglo-Saxon obscenity cases locate the harm of pornography in the mind of the consumer. *See, e.g.,* Regina v. Hicklin, 3 L.R-Q.B. 360, 371 (1868) ("tendency . . . to deprave and corrupt those whose minds are open to such immoral influences and into whose hands a publication of this sort may fall"). The data of John Court and Berl Kutchinsky, both correlational, reach contrary conclusions on the relation of pornography's availability to crime statistics. Kutchinsky, "Towards

an Explanation of the Decrease in Registered Sex Crimes in Copenhagen," 7 *Technical Report of the Commission on Obscenity and Pornography* 263 (1971); Kutchinsky, "The Effect of Easy Availability of Pornography on the Incidence of Sex Crimes: The Danish Experience," 29 *Journal of Social Issues* 163 (1973); *cf.* Court, "Pornography and Sex Crimes: A Re-Evaluation in the Light of Recent Trends around the World," 5 *International Journal of Criminology and Penology* 129 (1977). More recent investigations into correlations focused on rape in the United States have reached still other conclusions. Larry Baron and Murray Straus have found a strong correlation between state-to-state variations in the rate of reported rape and the aggregate circulation rate of popular men's sex magazines, including *Playboy* and *Hustler.* "Sexual Stratification, Pornography, and Rape," Family Research Laboratory and Department of Sociology, University of New Hampshire, Durham, N.H., Nov. 18, 1983 (manuscript). The authors conclude that "the findings suggest that the combination of a society which is characterized by a struggle to secure equal rights for women, by a high readership of sex magazines which depict women in ways which may legitimize violence, and by a context in which there is a high level of non-sexual violence, constitutes a mix of societal characteristics which precipitate rape" at 16. *See also* the "Williams Report," note 24 above, and the opinions of Justice Harlan on the injury to "society" as a permissible basis for legislative judgments in this area. Roth v. U.S., 354 U.S. 476, 501–02 (1957) (concurring in companion case, Alberts v. California).

58. Laurence Tribe, *American Constitutional Law* 662 (1978).

59. I am conceiving rape as *sexual* aggression. On the connection between pornography and rape, *see* Neil M. Malamuth, "Rape Proclivity among Men," 37 *Journal of Social Issues* 138 (1981); Neil M. Malamuth, "Rape Fantasies as a Function of Exposure to Violent Sexual Stimuli," 10 *Archives of Sexual Behavior* 33 (1981); Scott Haber and Seymour Feshbach, "Testing Hypotheses Regarding Rape: Exposure to Sexual Violence, Sex Differences, and the 'Normality' of Rapists," 14 *Journal of Research in Personality* 121 (1980); Maggie Heim and Seymour Feshbach, "Sexual Responsiveness of College Students to Rape Depictions: Inhibitory and Disinhibitory Effects," 38 *Journal of Personality and Social Psychology* 399 (1980). *See also* works by Malamuth, note 9 above. Of course, there are difficulties in measuring rape as a direct consequence of laboratory experiments, difficulties that have led researchers to substitute other measures of willingness to aggress, such as electric shocks.

60. Apparently, it may be impossible to *make* a film for experimental purposes that portrays violence or aggression by a man against a woman that a substantial number of male experimental subjects do not perceive as sexual. *See Hearings,* at 31 (testimony of Edward Donnerstein).

61. *See* works of Zillman, note 9 above.

62. Immanuel Kant, *Fundamental Principles of the Metaphysics of Morals* (T. Abbott trans. 1969); Arthur Danto, "Persons," in 6 *Encyclopedia of Philosophy* 10 (P. Edwards ed. 1967); Margaret Radin, "Property and Personhood," 34 *Stanford Law Review* 957 (1982).

63. *See* Kant, note 62 above; Danto, note 62 above; Radin, note 62 above.

See also the "original position" of John Rawls, *A Theory of Justice* (1971), and Rawls, "Kantian Constructivism in Moral Theory," 9 *Journal of Philosophy* 515, 533–35 (1980).

64. Ludwig Wittgenstein, *Philosophical Investigations* 178 (G. Anscombe trans. 3d ed. 1958).

65. Karl Marx's critique of capitalist society is epitomized in *Capital* chap. 1 (1867). His concept of the "fetishism of commodities" in which "relations between men [assume], *in their eyes*, the fantastic form of a relation between things" (emphasis added) is presented in the 1970 edition at 72.

66. David Hume, "Of Personal Identity," in *A Treatise of Human Nature* bk. I, pt. IV, § VI (1888).

67. Bernard Williams, "Are Persons Bodies? Personal Identity and Individualization" and "Bodily Continuity and Personal Identity," in his *Problems of the Self* 1, 64 (1973). Bernard Williams was principal author of the "Williams Report," note 24 above, Britain's equivalent of the U.S. Commission on Obscenity and Pornography, in which none of his values of "persons" were noticed lacking in, or women deprived of them by, pornography.

68. *See Signs* I and II.

69. I have come to this conclusion from my analysis of all the empirical data available to date, the pornography itself, and personal observations.

70. Brownmiller, note 10 above, is widely considered to present the view that rape is an act of violence, not sex. Women Against Pornography, a New York based antipornography group, has argued that pornography is violence against women, not sex. This has been almost universally taken as *the* feminist position on the issue. For an indication of possible change, *see* 4 *NCASA News* 19–21 (May 1984).

71. This, again, does not mean that it is an *idea*. A new theory of ideology, prefigured in Dworkin, note 1 above, will be needed to conceptualize the role of pornography in constructing the condition of women.

72. Dworkin, note 1 above, at 115.

73. "Echoing Macaulay, 'Jimmy' Walker remarked that he had never heard of a woman seduced by a book." U.S. v. Roth, 237 F.2d 796, 812 (1956) (appendix to concurrence of Frank, J.) What is classically called seduction, I expect feminists might interpret as rape or forced sex.

14. Francis Biddle's Sister

1. We define pornography as in "Not a Moral Issue," note 1. The Indianapolis City and County Council passed a version of it eliminating subsections (i), (v), (vi), and (vii), and substituting instead as (vi) "women are presented as sexual objects for domination, conquest, violation, exploitation, possession, or use, or through postures or positions of servility or submission or display." Indianapolis, Ind., City-County General Ordinance No. 35 (June 11, 1984) (adding inter alia, ch. 16, § 16-3(q)(6) to the Code of Indianapolis and Marion County) [hereinafter cited as Indianapolis Ordinance]. It was signed by the mayor, and a suit immediately followed in federal court,

see American Booksellers, Inc. v. Hudnut, 598 F. Supp. 1316 (S.D. Ind. 1984), 771 F.2d 323 (7th Cir. 1985) *aff'd* 106 S.Ct. 1172 (1986).

2. *See Public Hearings on Ordinances to Add Pornography as Discrimination Against Women*, Committee on Government Operations, City Council, Minneapolis, Minn. (Dec. 12–13, 1983) [hereinafter cited as *Hearings*]. All those who testified in these hearings were fully identified to the City Council. Some are identified here only by their last initials for purposes of privacy.

3. I treat these themes more fully in "Feminism, Marxism, Method and the State: Toward Feminist Jurisprudence," 8 *Signs: Journal of Women in Culture and Society* 635 (1983); "Feminism, Marxism, Method and the State: An Agenda for Theory," 7 *Signs: Journal of Women in Culture and Society* 515 (1982).

4. Jacobellis v. Ohio, 378 U.S. 184, 197 (1964) (Stewart, J., concurring).

5. For my use of upper-case "Black" *see* "Not By Law Alone," note 12.

6. The classic enunciation of the meaning of neutrality as the principled approach to constitutional adjudication is Herbert Wechsler, "Toward Neutral Principles of Constitutional Law," 73 *Harvard Law Review* 1 (1959). The doctrine of gender neutrality applies this approach to the area of sex, which goes far toward explaining the predominance of male plaintiffs in the Supreme Court's leading gender discrimination cases, especially among successful plaintiffs. *See* cases collected at David Cole, "Strategies of Difference: Litigating for Women's Rights in a Man's World," 2 *Law & Inequality: Journal of Theory and Practice* 33, 34 n.4 (1984) ("The only area in which male plaintiffs do not dominate constitutional gender discrimination cases involves treatment of pregnancy").

7. For judicial discussions of the color-blindness of the law, *see* Fullilove v. Klutznick, 448 U.S. 448, 482 (1980); United Steelworkers of America v. Weber, 443 U.S. 193 (1979); Regents of the University of California v. Bakke, 438 U.S. 265, 327 (1978) (Brennan, White, Marshall, and Blackmun, JJ., concurring in part and dissenting in part); Swann v. Charlotte-Mecklenburg Bd. of Educ., 402 U.S. 1, 19 (1971); Plessy v. Ferguson, 163 U.S. 537, 559 (1896) ("Our Constitution is color-blind, and neither knows nor tolerates classes among citizens") (Harlan, J., dissenting). The view that the Constitution should also be sex-blind also animates the leading interpretation of the proposed federal Equal Rights Amendment. Barbara Brown, Thomas I. Emerson, Gail Falk, and Ann Freedman, "The Equal Rights Amendment: A Constitutional Basis for Equal Rights for Women," 80 *Yale Law Journal* 871 (1971).

8. The absolutist position on the entire Constitution was urged by Justice Black; *see, e.g.*, Hugo Black, "The Bill of Rights," 35 *New York University Law Review* 865, 867 (1960), focusing at times on the First Amendment; *see, e.g.*, E. Cahn, "Justice Black and First Amendment 'Absolutes': A Public Interview," 37 *New York University Law Review* 549 (1962). Justice Douglas as well as Justice Black emphatically articulated the absolutist position in the obscenity context. *See, e.g.*, Miller v. California, 413 U.S. 15, 37 (1973) (Douglas, J., dissenting); Smith v. California, 361 U.S. 147, 155 (1959) (Black, J., concurring); Roth v. United States, 354 U.S. 476, 514 (1957) (Douglas, J., joined by Black, J., dissenting). Absolutist-influenced discontent with obscenity law is

clear in Justice Brennan's dissent in Paris Adult Theatre I v. Slaton, 413 U.S. 49, 73 (1973).

9. The image of the First Amendment as guaranteeing the "free trade in ideas," in which the "best test of truth is the power of the thought to get itself accepted in the competition of the market," originated with Justice Holmes, dissenting in Abrams v. United States, 250 U.S. 616, 630 (1919) (joined by Brandeis, J.). Some possible shortcomings in this model are noticed in Laurence Tribe, *American Constitutional Law* 576–77 (1978).

10. *See* Wechsler, note 6, above.

11. Plessy v. Ferguson, 163 U.S. 537 (1896).

12. 347 U.S. 483 (1954) (*Brown I*); Brown v. Bd. of Educ., 349 U.S. 294 (1955) (*Brown II*).

13. *See* Lochner v. New York, 198 U.S. 45 (1905); Allgeyer v. Louisiana, 165 U.S. 578 (1897) (invalidating maximum hours restrictions on the ground of liberty to freely contract). For the rest of the tradition and its demise, see note 14 below.

14. *See, e.g.*, Muller v. Oregon, 208 U.S. 412 (1908) (sustaining women's hours restrictions). Adkins v. Children's Hospital, 261 U.S. 525 (1923) (legislation mandating minimum wages for women violated due process) was overruled in West Coast Hotel v. Parrish, 300 U.S. 379 (1937) (minimum wage laws for women may be legislated). *Parrish* followed Bunting v. Oregon, 243 U.S. 426 (1917) (upholding state law limiting hours). *See also* Stettler v. O'Hara, 243 U.S. 629 (1909) (upholding state minimum wage requirements for women factory workers). It is not that women as such were invisible to the judges who decided these cases. Indeed, it was their conception of women's distinctive (mostly physical) vulnerabilities as well as family place that justified the rulings upholding these laws, while laws protecting all workers, as in *Lochner*, were disallowed. Because this substantive view of women was so demeaning as well as so destructive, and because it became part of the critique of substantivity in adjudication as such, which was necessary to establish if social welfare legislation was to be allowed, the possibility was obscured that there might be a substantive analysis of the situation of women that was adequate to women's distinctive social exploitation, which could ground a claim to equality, and which did not license any more wholesale judicial discretion in the direction and to the degree it already existed. If one wants to claim no more for a powerless group than what can be extracted under an established system of power—if only the lines between that group and the powerful can be blurred as much as possible—one strategy is to try to claim that the powerless are entitled to what "everybody" is entitled to: in short, *abstract*. If, however, one's claim is against the distribution of power itself, one needs a critique not so much of the substantivity of the *Lochner*-era approach per se, but of its substance, with a critique of the tradition that replaced it, in which part of the strategy for hegemony is to present substance as substancelessness.

15. *See, e.g.*, Regents of the University of California v. Bakke, 438 U.S. 265 (1978); John Ely, *Democracy and Distrust: A Theory of Judicial Review* 54–55

(1981). *But see* Laurence Tribe, "Speech as Power: Swastikas, Spending, and the Mask of Neutral Principles," in *Constitutional Choices* (1985).

16. *See* Edward Levi, "An Introduction to Legal Reasoning," 15 *University of Chicago Law Review* 501 (1948).

17. *See, e.g.,* Derrick Bell, *Race, Racism and American Law* 1–85 (1972).

18. 347 U.S. 483 (1954).

19. On my analysis, the combined effect of Texas Dep't of Community Affairs v. Burdine, 450 U.S. 248 (1981) and Furnco Constr. Corp. v. Waters, 438 U.S. 567 (1978), both purporting to follow the standard first announced in McDonnell Douglas Corp. v. Green, 411 U.S. 792 (1973), is that anyone who has been discriminated against is assumed exceptional and living in that sex-discrimination-free universe that the burdens of proof are allocated to presuppose. The difficulty arises in the attempt to assume that discrimination because of sex neither exists nor does not exist in assessing facts such as those in *Burdine*, in which two persons are equally qualified, the man gets the job, and the woman sues. The Fifth Circuit in *Burdine* had required the employer to prove that the man who got the job was more qualified, but its decision was reversed. Facing the impossibility of neutrality here makes one wonder if there is any difference between nondiscrimination and affirmative action.

20. Selected publications are listed from the large body of work that exists.

On rape: Susan Brownmiller, *Against Our Will: Men, Women and Rape* (1975); L. Clark and D. Lewis, *Rape: The Price of Coercive Sexuality* (1977); N. Gager and C. Schurr, *Sexual Assault: Confronting Rape in America* (1976); A. Medea and K. Thompson, *Against Rape* (1974); Diana Russell, *Rape in Marriage* (1982); Diana Russell, *The Politics of Rape* (1975); Martha R. Burt, "Cultural Myths and Supports for Rape," 38 *Journal of Personality and Social Psychology* 219 (1980); Irene Frieze, "Investigating the Causes and Consequences of Marital Rape," 8 *Signs: Journal of Women in Culture and Society* 532 (1983); Gary LaFree, "Male Power and Female Victimization: Towards a Theory of Interracial Rape," 88 *American Journal of Sociology* 311 (1982); Diana Russell and Nancy Howell, "The Prevalence of Rape in the United States Revisited," 8 *Signs: Journal of Women in Culture and Society* 688 (1983).

On battery: R. Emerson Dobash and Russell Dobash, *Violence against Wives: A Case against the Patriarchy* (1979); R. Langley and R. Levy, *Wife Beating: The Silent Crisis* (1977); D. Martin, *Battered Wives* (rev. ed. 1981); S. Steinmetz, *The Cycle of Violence: Assertive, Aggressive, and Abusive Family Interaction* (1977) (referenced in E. Stanko, below, at 73); L. Walker, *The Battered Woman* (1979); Evan Stark, Ann Flitcraft, and William Frazier, "Medicine and Patriarchal Violence: The Social Construction of a 'Private' Event," 3 *International Journal of Health Services* 461 (1979).

On sexual harassment: Catharine A. MacKinnon, *Sexual Harassment of Working Women: A Case of Sex Discrimination* (1979); Donna J. Benson and Gregg E. Thompson, "Sexual Harassment on a University Campus: The Confluence of Authority Relations, Sexual Interest and Gender Stratification," 29 *Social Problems* 236 (1982); Phyllis Crocker and Anne E. Simon, "Sexual

Harassment in Education," 10 *Capital University Law Review* 3 (1981); U.S. Merit Systems Protection Board, *Sexual Harassment in the Federal Workplace: Is It a Problem?* (1981).

On incest and child sexual abuse: L. Armstrong, *Kiss Daddy Goodnight* (1978); Kathleen Brady, *Father's Days: A True Story of Incest* (1979); A. Burgess, N. Groth, L. Holmstrom, and S. Sgroi, *Sexual Assault of Children and Adolescents* (1978); S. Butler, *Conspiracy of Silence: The Trauma of Incest* (1978); D. Finkelhor, *Child Sexual Abuse: New Theory and Research* (1984); D. Finkelhor, *Sexually Victimized Children* (1979); J. Herman, *Father-Daughter Incest* (1981); Florence Rush, *The Best-Kept Secret: Sexual Abuse of Children* (1980); Diana Russell, *The Secret Trauma: Incest in the Lives of Girls and Women* (1986); Arthur C. Jaffe, Lucille Dynneson, and Robert TenBensel, "Sexual Abuse: An Epidemiological Study," 6 *American Journal of Diseases of Children* 689 (1975); Diana Russell, "The Prevalence and Seriousness of Incestuous Abuse: Stepfathers vs. Biological Fathers," 8 *Child Abuse and Neglect: The International Journal* 15 (1984); Diana Russell, "The Incidence and Prevalence of Intrafamilial and Extrafamilial Sexual Abuse of Female Children," 7 *Child Abuse and Neglect: The International Journal* 2 (1983).

On prostitution: Kathleen Barry, *Female Sexual Slavery* (1979); Jennifer James, *The Politics of Prostitution* (2d ed. 1975); Moira Griffin, "Wives, Hookers and the Law: The Case for Decriminalizing Prostitution," 10 *Student Lawyer* 13 (1982); Jennifer James and Jane Meyerding, "Early Sexual Experience as a Factor in Prostitution," 7 *Archives of Sexual Behavior* 31 (1977); "Report of Jean Fernand-Laurent, Special Rapporteur on the Suppression of the Traffic in Persons and the Exploitation of the Prostitution of Others" (a United Nations report), in *International Feminism: Networking against Female Sexual Slavery* 130 (K. Barry, C.Bunch, S. Castley eds. 1984) (Report of the Global Feminist Workshop to Organize Against Traffic in Women, Rotterdam, Netherlands, Apr. 6–15, 1983).

On pornography: Andrea Dworkin, *Pornography: Men Possessing Women* (1981); Linda Lovelace and Michael McGrady, *Ordeal* (1980); P. Bogdanovich, *The Killing of the Unicorn: Dorothy Stratten, 1960–1980* (1984); *Take Back the Night: Women on Pornography* (L. Lederer ed. 1980); Edward Donnerstein, "Pornography: Its Effects on Violence against Women," in *Pornography and Sexual Aggression* (N. Malamuth and E. Donnerstein eds. 1984); Martha Langelan, "The Political Economy of Pornography," *Aegis: Magazine on Ending Violence against Women* 5 (1981); Dorchen Leidholdt, "Where Pornography Meets Fascism," *Women's International News* (WIN), Mar. 15, 1983, at 18; Daniel Linz, Edward Donnerstein, and Steven Penrod, "The Effects of Long-Term Exposure to Filmed Violence against Women" (Mar. 22, 1984) (unpublished manuscript).

See generally: J. Long and P. Schwartz, *Sexual Scripts: The Social Construction of Female Sexuality* (1976); E. Morgan, *The Erotization of Male Dominance/Female Submission* (1975); Diana Russell, *Sexual Exploitation: Rape, Child Sexual Abuse and Workplace Harassment* (1984); D. Russell and N. Van de Ven, *Crimes against*

Women: Proceedings of the International Tribunal (1976); E. Schur, *Labeling Women Deviant: Gender, Stigma, and Social Control* (1984); Edith Phelps, "Female Sexual Alienation," in *Women: A Feminist Perspective* 16 (J. Freeman ed. 1975); Adrienne Rich, "Compulsory Heterosexuality and Lesbian Existence," 5 *Signs: Journal of Women in Culture and Society* 4 (1980); E. Stanko, *Intimate Intrusions* (1985) (called "No Complaints: Silencing Male Violence to Women" in manuscript).

21. *See* Menachem Amir, *Patterns in Forcible Rape* 229–52 (1971); *see also* N. Gager and C. Schurr, *Sexual Assault: Confronting Rape in America* (1976); Russell, *Sexual Exploitation*, note 20 above.

22. *See* Diana Russell, "The Prevalence of Rape in United States Revisited," 8 *Signs: Journal of Women in Culture and Society* 689 (1983).

23. *See* sexual harassment references, note 20 above.

24. U.S. Merit Systems Protection Board, note 20 above.

25. *See* battery references, note 20 above.

26. *See* child sexual abuse references, note 20 above, especially Diana Russell, "Incidence and Prevalence of Intrafamilial and Extrafamilial Sexual Abuse of Female Children."

27. Adrienne Rich, "Cartographies of Silence," in *The Dream of a Common Language* 16, 17 (1978).

28. *See* Florence Rush, *The Best-Kept Secret: Sexual Abuse of Children* (1980). *See also* Jeffrey Masson, *The Assault on Truth: Freud's Suppression of the Seduction Theory* (1983).

29. *See* D. Finkelhor, *Child Sexual Abuse: Theory and Research* (1984); D. Lockwood, *Prison Sexual Violence* 117 (1980): "For the player [the pimp-type prison rapist] to operate his game, however, he must 'feminize' his object of interest. We must remember that prisoners consider queens to be women, not men. As a consequence, the one who dominates the queen is a 'man.' Players live according to norms that place men who play female roles in submissive positions . . . The happy conclusion . . . is for the target to become a 'girl' under his domination, a receptacle for his penis, and a female companion to accentuate his masculinity." *See also* Jacobo Timmerman, *Prisoner without a Name, Cell without a Number* (1981).

30. *See* Employment Standards Administration, U.S. Department of Labor, *Handbook on Women Workers* (1975); U.S. Department of Labor, *Women's Bureau Bulletin* 297 (1975 and 1982 update).

31. "Introduction," note 18.

32. Foucault, "The West and the Truth of Sex," 20 *Sub-Stance* 5 (1978).

33. This became a lot clearer to me after reading Margaret Baldwin, "The Sexuality of Inequality: The Minneapolis Pornography Ordinance," 2 *Law and Inequality: Journal of Theory and Practice* 629 (1984). This paragraph is directly indebted to her insight and language there.

34. Andrea Dworkin, *Pornography: Men Possessing Women* (1981).

35. For a fuller development of this critique, *see* "Not a Moral Issue."

36. Miller v. California, 413 U.S. 15, 24 (1973).

37. *See The Report of the Presidential Commission on Obscenity and Pornography* (1970).

38. For the specific statutory language, *see* "Not a Moral Issue," note 1, and note 1 above.

39. *See, e.g.*, Gloria Steinem, "Erotica v. Pornography," in *Outrageous Acts and Everyday Rebellions* 219 (1983).

40. *See* Indianapolis Ordinance, "Not a Moral Issue," note 1.

41. *See* Catharine A. MacKinnon, *Sexual Harassment of Working Women* 101–41 (1979).

42. For a lucid discussion of subordination, *see* Andrea Dworkin, "Against the Male Flood: Censorship, Pornography, and Equality," 8 *Harvard Women's Law Journal* 1 (1985).

43. If this part stood alone, it would, along with its support, among other things, have to be equally imposed—an interesting requirement for an equality law, but arguably met by this one. *See* Carey v. Brown, 447 U.S. 455 (1980); Police Department of Chicago v. Mosley, 408 U.S. 92 (1972); Kenneth Karst, "Equality as a Central Principle in the First Amendment," 43 *University of Chicago Law Review* 20 (1975).

44. *See* KPNX Broadcasting Co. v. Arizona Superior Court, 459 U.S. 1302 (1982) (Rehnquist as Circuit Justice denied application to stay Arizona judge's order that those involved with heavily covered criminal trial avoid direct contact with press; mere potential confusion from unrestrained contact with press is held to justify order); New York v. Ferber, 458 U.S. 747 (1982) (child pornography, defined as promoting sexual performance by a child, can be criminally banned as a form of child abuse); F.C.C. v. Pacifica Found., 438 U.S. 726 (1978) ("indecent" but not obscene radio broadcasts may be regulated by F.C.C. through licensing); Young v. American Mini Theatres, Inc., 427 U.S. 50 (1976) (exhibition of sexually explicit "adult movies" may be restricted through zoning ordinances); Gertz v. Robert Welch, Inc., 418 U.S. 323, 347 (1974) (state statute may allow private persons to recover for libel without proving actual malice so long as liability is not found without fault); Pittsburgh Press Co. v. Human Relations Comm'n, 413 U.S. 376 (1973) (sex-designated help-wanted columns conceived as commercial speech may be prohibited under local sex discrimination ordinance); Miller v. California, 413 U.S. 15, 18 (1973) (obscenity unprotected by First Amendment in case in which it was "thrust by aggressive sales action upon unwilling [viewers]. . . ."); Red Lion Broadcasting Co. v. F.C.C., 395 U.S. 367, 387 (1969) (F.C.C. may require broadcasters to allow reply time to vindicate speech interests of the public: "The right of free speech of a broadcaster, the user of a sound truck, or any other individual does not embrace a right to snuff out the free speech of others."); Ginzburg v. United States, 383 U.S. 463, 470 (1966) (upholding conviction for mailing obscene material on "pandering" theory: "[T]he purveyor's sole emphasis [is] on the sexually provocative aspects of his publications."); Roth v. United States, 354 U.S. 476, 487 (1957) (federal obscenity statute is found valid; obscene defined as "material which

deals with sex in a manner appealing to prurient interest"); Beauharnais v. Illinois, 343 U.S. 250 (1952) (upholding group libel statute); Chaplinsky v. New Hampshire, 315 U.S. 568 (1942) (a state statute outlawing "fighting words" likely to cause a breach of peace is not unconstitutional under the First Amendment); Near v. Minnesota, 283 U.S. 697 (1931) (Minnesota statute permitting prior restraint of publishers who regularly engage in publication of defamatory material is held unconstitutional; press freedom outweighs prior restraints in all but exceptional cases, such as national security or obscenity); for one such exceptional case, *see* United States v. Progressive, Inc., 486 F. Supp. 5 (W.D. Wis. 1979) (prior restraint is allowed against publication of information on how to make a hydrogen bomb, partially under "troop movements" exception); Schenck v. United States, 249 U.S. 47, 52 (1919) ("clear and present dangers" excepted from the First Amendment: "The most stringent protection of free speech would not protect a man in falsely shouting fire in a theatre and causing a panic").

45. *See* Young v. American Mini Theatres, Inc., 427 U.S. 50 (1976); Pittsburgh Press Co. v. Human Relations Comm'n, 413 U.S. 376 (1973); Konigsberg v. State Bar of California, 366 U.S. 36, 49–51 (1961).

46. After the delivery of the Biddle Lecture, an Indiana federal court declared the ordinance unconstitutional in a facial challenge brought by the "Media Coalition," an association of publishers and distributors. The ordinance is repeatedly misquoted, and the misquotations are underscored to illustrate its legal errors. Arguments not made in support of the law are invented and attributed to the city and found legally inadequate. Evidence of harm before the legislature is given no weight at all, while purportedly being undisturbed, as an absolutist approach is implicitly adopted, unlike any existing Supreme Court precedent. To the extent that existing law, such as obscenity law, overlaps with the ordinance, even it would be invalidated under this ruling. And clear law on sex equality is flatly misstated. The opinion permits a ludicrous suit by mostly legitimate trade publishers, parties whose interests are at most tenuously and remotely implicated under the ordinance, to test a law that directly and importantly would affect others, such as pornographers and their victims. The decision also seems far more permissive toward racism than would be allowed in a concrete case even under existing law, and displays blame-the-victim misogyny: "Adult women generally have the capacity to protect themselves from participating in and being personally victimized by pornography . . ." American Booksellers v. Hudnut, 598 F. Supp. 1316, 1334 (S.D. Ind. 1984). For subsequent developments, *see* "The Sexual Politics of the First Amendment."

47. *See, e.g.,* Title IX of the Educ. Amends. of 1972, 20 U.S.C. §§ 1681–1686 (1972); Equal Pay Act, 29 U.S.C. § 206(d) (1963); Title VII of the Civil Rights Act of 1964, 42 U.S.C. §§ 2000e to 2000e–17 (1976). Many states have equal rights amendments to their constitutions, *see* Barbara Brown and Ann Freedman, "Equal Rights Amendment: Growing Impact on the States," 1 *Women's Rights Law Reporter* 1.63, 1.63–1.64 (1974); many states and cities, including Minneapolis and Indianapolis, prohibit discrimination on the basis of sex.

See also Roberts v. United States Jaycees, 468 U.S. 609 (1984) (recently recognizing that sex equality is a compelling state interest); Frontiero v. Richardson, 411 U.S. 677 (1973); Reed v. Reed, 404 U.S. 71 (1971); U.S. Const. amend. XIV.

48. *See* City of Los Angeles v. Manhart, 435 U.S. 702, 711 (1978) (City water department's pension plan was found discriminatory in its "treatment of a person in a manner which but for that person's sex would be different"). *See also* Orr v. Orr, 440 U.S. 268 (1979); Barnes v. Costle, 561 F.2d 983 (D.C. Cir. 1977).

49. *See* Plessy v. Ferguson, 163 U.S. at 551; Wechsler, note 6 above, at 33.

50. In each case cited in note 44 above (except *Near*), a recognized harm was held to be more important than the speech interest also at stake. The Supreme Court has also recognized, if not always in holdings, that the right to privacy or fair trial can outweigh the right to freedom of the press. *See* Zacchini v. Scripps-Howard Broadcasting Co., 433 U.S. 562 (1977) (performer has a proprietary interest in his act that outweighs press interest in publishing it); Nebraska Press Ass'n v. Stuart, 427 U.S. 539 (1976) (restraint on press is unconstitutional); Cox Broadcasting Corp. v. Cohn, 420 U.S. 469, 491 (1975) (no civil liability for privacy violations against broadcaster for truthfully publishing court records in which daughter of plaintiff was rape victim, but: "In this sphere of collision between claims of privacy and those of the free press, the interests on both sides are plainly rooted in the traditions and significant concerns of our society"); Time, Inc. v. Hill, 385 U.S. 374 (1967) (magazine has no liability for inaccurate portrayal of private life unless knowingly or recklessly false). *But see* KPNX Broadcasting Co., 459 U.S. 1302 (1982). *See also* Globe Newspaper Co. v. Superior Court, 457 U.S. 596 (1982) (state may not require exclusion of press and public from courtroom during testimony of minor victim of sex offense); Richmond Newspapers, Inc. v. Virginia, 448 U.S. 555 (1980).

The harm of defamatory speech to personal reputation is also the reason libel is actionable notwithstanding First Amendment protections of speech. *See, e.g.*, Gertz v. Robert Welch, Inc., 418 U.S. 323 (1974); "[D]efamation has long been regarded as a form of 'psychic mayhem,' not very different in kind, and in some ways more wounding, than physical mutilation." Tribe, note 9 above, at 649 (discussing issues raised by *Gertz*). In Los Angeles v. Taxpayers for Vincent, 466 U.S. 789 (1984), the City of Los Angeles' *aesthetic* interests outweighed a political candidate's speech right to post signs on public property.

51. Under the standard in *Miller*, 413 U.S. 15 (1973), obscenity prohibits materials that, inter alia, are "patently offensive" and appeal to the "prurient interest," id. at 24, terms with no apparent determinate meaning. Offensiveness is subjective. Prurience is a code word for that which produces sexual arousal. *See* F. Schauer, "Response: Pornography and the First Amendment," 40 *University of Pittsburgh Law Review* 605, 607 (1979). *See also* Justice Brennan's discussion of the vagueness of terms like "lewd" and "ultimate," in Paris Adult Theatre I, 413 U.S. at 86 (Brennan, J., dissenting). "Community stan-

dards," also part of the *Miller* test, is a standard that is open-ended by design. In F.C.C. v. Pacifica Found., 438 U.S. 726 (1978), the Supreme Court allowed a regulatory body to construe the meaning of the term "indecent," which represents a social value judgment. In *Ferber*, 458 U.S. 747 (1982), the Supreme Court did not seem at all bothered by the fact that "lewd," as in "lewd exhibition of the genitals" in the statute's definition of sexual performance, was statutorily undefined, 458 U.S. at 765. *Beauharnais*, 343 U.S. 250, 251 (1952), sustained a law that prohibited the publishing, selling, or exhibiting in any public place of any publication that "portrays depravity, criminality, unchastity, or lack of virtue of a class of citizens of any race, color, creed or religion." 343 U.S. at 251. Although doubt has been cast on the vitality of *Beauharnais*—see, *e.g.,* Collin v. Smith, 578 F.2d 1197, 1205 (7th Cir. 1978)—"*Beauharnais* has never been overruled or formally limited in any way." Smith v. Collin, 436 U.S. 953 (1978) (Blackmun, J., joined by Rehnquist, J., dissenting from denial of stay of Court of Appeals order).

52. Most obscenity laws provide criminal sanctions, with the appropriate procedural requirements. *Roth*, 354 U.S. at 478 n.1; *Miller*, 413 U.S. at 16 n.1. However, the injunction proceeding in *Paris Adult Theatre I*, 413 U.S. 49 (1973), was civil, and the statutory scheme discussed in Freedman v. Maryland, 380 U.S. 51 (1964) (under which prior restraints imposed by a censorship board were legal only if certain procedural requirements were met) was noncriminal. Of course, all a civil injunction can do under our ordinance is stop future profit-making or assault. A potential award of civil damages under our ordinance is not a negligible sanction; it is designed to deter victimization, but differently than potential incarceration does. A major purpose of pornography is to make money. Depriving the pornographers of profits by empowering those whom they exploit to make them, directly counteracts one reason pornographers engage in the exploitation at all, in a way that potential incarceration does not. Another not inconsiderable benefit of a civil rather than criminal approach to pornography is that criminal prohibitions, as well as eroticizing that which they prohibit, tend to create underground markets wherein the prohibited commodity is sold at inflated prices, passed hand to hand in secret settings, and elevated in value. If it were not possible to make or use pornography as it now is without exploiting its victims as they are exploited now, a civil prohibition would create no underground. This approach does not solve the problems of terror and intimidation that keep victims from suing, nor does it give them resources for suit. It does define who is hurt directly (versus the amorphous "community" that is considered hurt on the criminal side), gives victims (and lawyers) the incentive of a potential civil recovery, and leaves control over the legal actions as much as possible in the hands of the victims rather than the state. For further views on civil as opposed to criminal approaches to this area, see the opinions of Justice Stevens in F.C.C. v. Pacifica Found., 438 U.S. 726 (1978); Young v. American Mini Theatres, Inc., 427 U.S. 50 (1976); and, most fully, his dissent in Smith v. United States, 431 U.S. 291, 317 (1977) (criticizing community standards in a criminal context, but approving their "flexibility [as] a desir-

able feature of a civil rule designed to protect the individual's right to select the kind of environment in which he wants to live"). Some who oppose or are critical of obscenity restrictions have found it preferable to first adjudicate pornographic materials obscene in a civil or administrative proceeding. *See* Miller v. California, 413 U.S. 15, 41 (1973) (Douglas, J., dissenting); Z. Chafee, 1 *Government and Mass Communications* 228–31 (1947); William Lockhart, "Escape from the Chill of Uncertainty: Explicit Sex and the First Amendment," 9 *Georgia Law Review* 533, 569–86 (1975); William Lockhart and Robert McClure, "Censorship of Obscenity," 45 *Minnesota Law Review* 5, 105–07 (1960); American Civil Liberties Union, Policy No. 4(c) (2) (Feb. 14, 1970) (civil proceeding seen as the least restrictive method of censorship).

53. The harm of obscenity recognized in *Miller*, 413 U.S. 15 (1973), was the "danger of offending the sensibilities of unwilling recipients or of exposure to juveniles." Id. at 19. This statement was adduced from the Presidential Commission on Obscenity finding that it could not be concluded that obscenity causes harm. "[The] Commission cannot conclude that exposure to erotic materials is a factor in the causation of sex crime or sex delinquency." *Report of the Presidential Commission on Obscenity and Pornography* 27 (1970). The harm in F.C.C. v. Pacifica Found., 438 U.S. 726 (1978), was the possible overhearing of indecent speech by children, since radio intrudes into the home. Id. at 748–50. In United States v. Orito, 413 U.S. 139, 143 (1973), a federal ban on interstate transportation of obscene materials for private use was sustained on "a legislatively determined risk of ultimate exposure to juveniles or to the public." Throughout, exposure of juveniles to obscenity is assumed to be a risk, but the harm that exposure does per se is unspecified, not to say unsubstantiated and not in evidence. The harm recognized in *Ferber*, 458 U.S. 747 (1982), appears to be that done to a minor male by being seen having sex. The film depicted two boys masturbating; the Court concluded that this was "a permanent record of children's participation and the harm to the child is exacerbated by [its] circulation." Id. at 759. This same harm is at times characterized by the Court as "psychological," id. at 759 n.10, but is otherwise unspecified and in evidence only in the form of the film. In *Chaplinsky*, 315 U.S. 568 (1942), the harm apparently was a combination of the offense given by the speech itself with the risk of imminent breach of the peace occasioned by its utterance. As to group libel, the harm of the racist leaflet to the group as a whole recognized in *Beauharnais*, 343 U.S. 250 (1952), was *inferred* from observed racial inequality and racial unrest. Id. at 258–61.

54. *See* Galloway and Thornton, "Crackdown on Pornography—A No-Win Battle," *U.S. News and World Report*, June 4, 1984, at 84; *see also* J. Cook, "The X-Rated Economy," *Forbes*, Sept. 18, 1978, at 81 ($4 billion per year); Martha Langelan, "The Political Economy of Pornography," *Aegis: Magazine on Ending Violence against Women* 5 (1981) ($7 billion per year); "The Place of Pornography," *Harper's*, Nov. 1984, at 31 ($7 billion per year).

55. Flags, seen as symbols for the nation rather than mere pieces of brightly colored cloth or even as personal property, receive special solicitude by legislatures and courts, as to both the patriotic value of their protection

and the expressive value of their desecration. *See, e.g.,* Spence v. Washington, 418 U.S. 405 (1974); Street v. New York, 394 U.S. 576 (1969). I have not considered the applicability of this line of cases here, in light of my view that women in pornography are not simply symbols of all women but also *are* women. Of course, under male supremacy, each woman represents all women to one degree or another, whether in pornography or in bed or walking down the street, because of the stereotyping intrinsic to gender inequality. But that does not mean that, in a feminist perspective, each woman, including those in pornography, can be treated solely in terms of her representative or symbolic qualities, as if she is not at the same time alive and human. An underlying issue has to do with the extent to which women's bodies must be freely available as vocabulary and imagery for the expression of others, such that once they are so converted, whatever the means, women retain no rights in their use or abuse, in the face of evidence of the harm from such expropriation and exposure ranging from the individual so used to anonymous women subsequently used or treated or seen in light of their availability for such use. (Given the extent to which women now must be men's speech, one might rather be a flag.)

56. *Ferber*, 458 U.S. 747 (1982).

57. II *Hearings* 75 (testimony of a named former prostitute).

58. Linda Lovelace and Michael McGrady, *Ordeal* (1980).

59. As of September, 1978, *Deep Throat* had grossed a known $50 million worldwide. *See* Cook, note 54 above. Many of its profits are untraceable. The film has also recently been made into a home video cassette.

60. Priscilla Alexander, coordinator for the National Organization for Women's Task Force on Prostitution, said she was told this by a woman pornography model. Panel on Pornography, National Association of Women and the Law, Los Angeles, Apr. 1, 1984.

61. "In the movies known as snuff films, victims sometimes are actually murdered." 130 *Cong. Rec.* S13192 (daily ed. Oct. 3, 1984) (statement of Senator Specter introducing the Pornography Victims Protection Act). Information on the subject is understandably hard to get. *See* People v. Douglas, Felony Complaint No. NF 8300382 (Municipal Court, Orange County, Cal., Aug. 5, 1983); "Slain Teens Needed Jobs, Tried Porn" and "Two Accused of Murder in 'Snuff' Films," *Oakland Tribune,* Aug. 6, 1983, see "Not A Moral Issue," note 56; L. Smith, "The Chicken Hawks" (1975) (unpublished manuscript).

62. "[W]e were all introduced to prostitution through pornography, there were no exceptions in our group, and we were all under 18 . . . There were stacks of films all over the house, which my pimp used to blackmail people with." II *Hearings* 70, 79 (testimony of a named former prostitute). Kathleen Barry, author of *Female Sexual Slavery* (1979), refers to "season[ing]" to prostitution by "blackmailing the victim by threatening to send [photographs of coerced sex] to her family, and selling them to the pornographers for mass production." I *Hearings* 59 (letter of Kathleen Barry). A worker with adolescent prostitutes reports: "These rapes are often either taped or have photographs taken of the event. The young woman when she tries to escape or

leaves is told that either she continues in her involvement in prostitution or those pictures will be sent to her parents, will be sent to the juvenile court, will be used against her. And out of fear she will continue her involvement in prostitution." III *Hearings* 77 (testimony of Sue Santa).

63. Speech by Andrea Dworkin, in Toronto, Feb. 1984 (account told to Dworkin), reprinted in *Healthsharing*, Summer 1984, at 25.

64. Linda Marchiano, Panel on Pornography, Stanford University, Apr. 2, 1982.

65. "When *Deep Throat* was released, we [prostitutes] experienced men joking and demanding oral sex." II *Hearings* 74 (testimony of a named former prostitute). Increasing reports of throat rape in emergency rooms followed the exhibition of *Deep Throat*. One woman told Flora Colao, C.S.W., an emergency room nurse in New York City at the time, that the men who raped her said, as she was becoming unconscious, "Let's deep-throat her before she passes out." I *Hearings* 60 (Exhibit 13 [letter], Nov. 10, 1983). She also reported women dead of suffocation from rape of the throat. One woman wrote the Minneapolis City Council the day after Marchiano's testimony before it, in a letter typical of the accounts received by Marchiano since the publication of *Ordeal:* "I read about Linda Lovelace in our morning paper which said that she testified for women's civil rights. I only hope that she is able to undo some of the terrible damage that was done by making her movie. Those years started days of misery for me and a lot of my friends. Linda was so convincing that she enjoyed what she was doing that our husbands began to think they were cheated in life with us upper middle class wives. 'I'm not satisfied!' 'You don't know how to be a woman.' And every young girl in town was brainwashed to show our husbands that they could be a better 'Linda Lovelace' than the wife they had at home. I saw a lot of heartbreaks, nervous breakdowns to women that were being coerced in sex—many tranquilizers taken because they had to keep up with the times or else. Being forced to do something they don't enjoy or 'someone else will gladly go out with me!' I even saw a business fail because the husband was so preoccupied with this type of sex. Why do you think women's lib evolved—women became tired of being exploited, brainwashed and now Linda says she didn't enjoy it. It's too late for us 50 year olds, but help the young girls not to wreck their lives by letting boyfriends and husbands force them to be recepticals [sic] instead of cherished wives." Letter from "a bitter wife" to the Minneapolis City Council (Dec. 14, 1983).

66. The credibility of the pornography, as compared with that of the women in it, is underlined by the following: Vanessa Williams, formerly Miss America, lost her title when pornographic pictures of her were published by *Penthouse*. Williams says she posed for the sexually explicit pictures under the representation that they were for private use, at most for silhouettes, and that she did not consent to their publication. Brian DePalma, director of *Dressed to Kill* and *Body Double*, both "splatter" films of sexualized violence against women, who should know what it takes for a director to create an image of an interaction so that it *looks* like sex, was interviewed concerning

the Williams episode. Asked about her version of the events, DePalma said: "I believed her until I saw the pictures." "'Double' Trouble: Brian DePalma Interviewed by Marcia Pally," 20 *Film Comment*, Sept.-Oct. 1984, at 13, 16.

67. I am indebted for this argument's development to Margaret Baldwin, "Pornography: More Than a Fantasy," *The Hennepin Lawyer*, Mar.-Apr. 1984, at 8, 25.

68. This question and the paragraph that follows draw directly on Andrea Dworkin's speech, note 63 above.

69. I *Hearings* 56.

70. National Task Force on Child Pornography, "Let's Protect Our Children" 17 (1983).

71. 458 U.S. 747 (1982).

72. Id. at 759.

73. Id. at 747.

74. Id. at 761.

75. Id.

76. Id. at 763–64.

77. The harm of child pornography cannot be stopped effectively without also addressing the pornography of adult women. Adult pornography has been found commonly used "to show, teach or induce the children into the sexual activity or pornographic modeling" by child sex rings. *See* A. Burgess, C. Hartman, M. McCausland, and P. Powers, "Response Patterns in Children and Adolescents Exploited through Sex Rings and Pornography," 141 *American Journal of Psychiatry* 656, 657–58 (1984). Given what is done in pornography, it is even more difficult than usual to distinguish between adults and children. Adult women are infantilized in pornography; children are dressed and used as if they were adult women. The resulting materials are then used against both, and target both for abuse relatively interchangeably. For instance, the "shaved pussy" genre, in which adult women's genitals are made to resemble those of young girls, converges with the "Lolita" or "cherry tarts" genre, in which young girls are presented resembling the pornographers' image of adult female sexuality. It also seems worth observing that a law that has the abuse disappear legally when its victims get one day older is difficult to administer effectively.

78. "The forcing of pornography on any woman, man, child, or transsexual in any place of employment, in education, in a home, or in any public place." Code of Indianapolis and Marion County, note 1 above.

Section 16–17(a) states: "A complaint charging that any person has engaged in or is engaging in a discriminatory practice . . . may be filed . . . in any of the following circumstances: . . . (7) in the case of forcing pornography on a person, against the perpetrator(s) and/or institution."

79. III *Hearings* 71, 76 (testimony of Charlotte K. and Sue Santa).

80. II *Hearings* 85–90 (testimony of Jackie B.).

81. Along with events like those described in the text accompanying note 80, above, these often arise under the rubric of sexual harassment. *See, e.g.,* MacKinnon, *Sexual Harassment of Working Women*, note 20 above, at 29. Al-

though not providing the same range of relief, sexual harassment cases recognize concerns related to those underlying the Minneapolis ordinance: "The . . . workplace was pervaded with sexual slur, insult and innuendo, and [the plaintiff] Katz was personally the object of verbal sexual harassment by her fellow controllers. This harassment took the form of extremely vulgar and offensive sexually related epithets addressed to and employed about Katz by supervisory personnel as well as by other controllers. The words used were ones widely recognized as not only improper but as intensely degrading, deriving their power to wound not only from their meaning but also from 'the disgust and violence they express phonetically.'" Katz v. Dole, 709 F.2d 251, 254 (4th Cir. 1983) (quoting C. Miller and K. Swift eds., *Words and Women* 109 [1977]).

Do such words become *not* injurious by virtue of appearing in print? To an extent, Tribe's observation about the words whose regulation was allowed in *Chaplinsky* applies here: "[S]uch provocations are not part of human discourse but weapons hurled in anger to inflict injury or invite retaliation." Tribe, note 9 above, at 605. The fact that in the case of pornography, the projectiles hurled at women are other women, or constructions of one's own gendered anatomy, puts them on a slightly different plane and also helps to explain why pornography's injury has neither been seen by its perpetrators nor retaliated against by its victims: the injury it inflicts, it inflicts in such a humiliating and undermining way that it disables retaliation. Silence has been the usual response.

82. "Women were forced constantly to enact specific scenes that men had witnessed in pornography. They would direct women to copy postures and poses of things they had seen in magazines." II *Hearings* 73 (testimony of a named former prostitute).

83. Letter from Marvin Lewis to Catharine MacKinnon (Dec. 7, 1983). Attorney Lewis described to me situations in which therapists had women patients act out scenes from *The Story of O*.

84. "The pornographic view of women is one that is prevalent within the medical community unfortunately. This is expressed by the kinds of jokes that are made about women and their bodies, especially when they are under anesthesia and undergoing surgical procedures. This view includes seeing women as not worthy of respect and also seeing them primarily in terms of their sexual functioning. Several years ago when I was teaching at the Rutgers Medical School there was a week long sexuality program planned annually for students. The first day of this program consisted of all-day viewing of pornographic movies. The intent was to "de-sensitize" the students to sex." Letter from Michelle Harrison, M.D., to the Minneapolis City Council (Dec. 9, 1983).

See also P. Bart, "From Those Wonderful People Who Brought You the Vaginal Orgasm: Sex Education for Medical Students" 2 (1976) (paper presented at the meetings of the American Sociological Association, New York). "When I was asked to participate in the sex education program at the University of Illinois 6 years ago it was a joint venture of Gynecology and Psychiatry and its primary purpose was to 'desensitize' the medical students. My first thought was, 'Aren't they insensitive enough as it is?' The term, however, has a technical meaning. It means that the subject will not react emotionally when presented with certain stimuli that previously she/he had such reactions to . . . In order to achieve this purpose the students were shown porno films." The specifics in the text are drawn from examples many people have recounted to me as a standard part of the program customarily used in medical schools.

85. Students and clients reported this to me in the course of my research into sexual harassment in education.

86. *See* III *Hearings* 13–16 (testimony of Susan G.) (discussing sexual abuse of an adult woman with whom she lived).

87. *See, e.g.,* III *Hearings* 69–74 (testimony of Charlotte K.). Now tell me no girl was ever ruined by a book. *See also* United States v. Roth, 237 F.2d 796, 812 (2d Cir. 1956) (Frank, J., appendix to concurring opinion) ("Echoing Macaulay, Jimmy Walker remarked that he had never heard of a woman seduced by a book.") Seduction here is the term that attributes consent or acquiescence or enjoyment of rape to the rape victim.

88. *See* II *Hearings* 90–100. A woman who lived in a neighborhood into which pornography had been zoned said, if you think pornography is harmless, "you move into my neighborhood and I will move into yours." Testimony of Shannon M., id. at 99.

89. Averting one's eyes is supposed to be an alternative to the injury, as it may well have been in Cohen v. California, 403 U.S. 15, 21 (1971) ("Those in the Los Angeles courthouse could effectively avoid further bombardment of their sensibilities simply by averting their eyes"). Or, less so but still arguably, in Erznoznik v. City of Jacksonville, 422 U.S. 205, 212 (1975) (the screen was not "so obtrusive as to make it impossible for an unwilling individual to avoid exposure to it") (quoting Redrup v. New York, 386 U.S. 767, 769 [1967]). The situations that our ordinance is premised upon and is designed to address directly are more like that of the woman who was tied to a chair in front of a video screen in her home and forced to watch pornography; *see, e.g.,* III *Hearings* 24.

90. *See* Stanley v. Georgia, 394 U.S. 557 (1969) (right to privacy protects possession of obscenity at home). The Court seems to assume that Mr. Stanley is at home *alone.*

91. Many Jewish citizens, survivors of the Nazi extermination, live in Skokie, Illinois. The town's attempts to keep Nazis from demonstrating there produced years of local ordinances, all ultimately held unconstitutional. Dissenting from a denial of certiorari, Justice Blackmun said: "On the one hand, we have precious First Amendment rights vigorously asserted . . . On the other hand, we are presented with evidence of a potentially explosive and dangerous situation, inflamed by unforgettable recollections of traumatic experiences in the second world conflict." Smith v. Collin, 439 U.S. 916, 918 (1968). Observing that citizens had asserted "that the proposed demonstration is scheduled at a place and in a manner that is taunting and overwhelm-

ingly offensive to the citizens of that place," he thought their claim deserved to be heard, "for 'the character of every act depends upon the circumstances in which it is done.'" Id. at 919 (quoting Schenck v. United States, 249 U.S. 47, 52 [1919]).

92. II *Hearings* 112 (testimony of Mags D.).

93. Code of Indianapolis and Marion County, ch. 16, § 16–3(g) (as amended, June 11, 1984) provides: "Assault or physical attack due to pornography: The assault, physical attack, or injury of any woman, man, child, or transsexual in a way that is directly caused by specific pornography." No damages or compensation for loss is recoverable from traffickers under this section "unless the complainant proves that the respondent knew or had reason to know that the materials were pornography." Id. at § 16–3(g)(8). Pornography that caused the acts can be reached under this provision, although it would be very difficult to prove "direct cause."

94. "The First Amendment demands more than a horrible example or two of the perpetrator of a crime of sexual violence, in whose pocket is found a pornographic book, before it allows the Nation to be saddled with a regime of censorship." Memoirs v. Massachusetts, 383 U.S. 413, 432 (1966) (Douglas, J., concurring). One wonders how many bodies must pile up before individual victims will be allowed to enjoin the proven cause, simply because that cause is a book. *See also* id. at 452 (Clark, J., dissenting) (noting repeated reports "that pornography is associated with an overwhelmingly large number of sex crimes").

95. II *Hearings* 43 (testimony of Rita M.).

96. III *Hearings* 18–19 (testimony of Carol L.).

97. Ongoing research on sex offenders in Hennepin County, Minn., that documents these similarities was presented by Candace Kruttschnitt to the City of Minneapolis Task Force on Pornography, Mar. 13, 1984. The data are consistent with that of all researchers who find it difficult to document differences between sex offenders and populations of normal men on virtually any dimension. *See* note 118 below. My analysis is that the few measurable differences between these populations involve the likelihood of getting caught for sex offenses more than the likelihood of committing them.

98. Only 9.5 percent of all rapes and rape attempts are reported. Diana Russell, *Sexual Exploitation* 31 (1984). The reporting rate of most sexual violations is as low or lower. Six percent of extrafamilial child sexual assault and 2 percent of incestuous assault are reported to authorities. Id. at 172. *See also* Judith Herman, *Father-Daughter Incest* 12–15 (1981). Another study estimates that only 1 of every 270 incidents of wife abuse is ever reported to authorities. *See* S. Steinmetz, *The Cycle of Violence: Assertive, Aggressive, and Abusive Family Interaction* (1977) (referenced in E. Stanko, note 20 above, at 73). This is probably a low figure. Although 42 percent of federal employees had been subjected to sexual harassment in the two years prior to one survey, 29 percent in severe forms, most had not reported the behavior. U.S. Merit Systems Protection Board, note 20 above, at 35, 71.

99. III *Hearings* 36 (testimony of Barbara Chester, director of the Rape and Sexual Assault Center, Hennepin County, Minn.).

100. III *Hearings* 44–45 (testimony of Bill Seals, director of Sexual Assault Services, Center for Behavior Therapy, Minneapolis, Minn.).

101. III *Hearings* 64 (testimony of Nancy Steele, therapist with sex offenders).

102. Id.

103. III *Hearings* 88 (testimony of Michael Laslett, reading statement by Floyd Winecoff, psychotherapist specializing in services for men).

104. Id. at 86.

105. III *Hearings* 44 (testimony of Bill Seals).

106. III *Hearings* 59 (testimony of Gerry Kaplan, executive director of Alpha Human Services, an inpatient program for sex offenders).

107. Examples range from the seemingly correlational to the integral to the causal. *See, e.g.,* Hoggard v. State, 277 Ark. 117, 640 S.W.2d 102 (1982), *cert. denied,* 460 U.S. 1022 (1983), in which the court, in ruling on a challenge that the prejudicial effect of pornography outweighed its probative value in allegation of the rape of a six-year-old boy, stated: "We readily agree the material was prejudicial, it could hardly be otherwise. But the argument that its probative value was lacking fades under scrutiny. This pornography and the offense being tried had a clear correlation: the pornography depicted deviate sexual acts by young males and the crime charged was deviate sexual acts of a forty-two-year-old man and a six-year-old boy. More importantly, the pornography was used as the instrument by which the crime itself was solicited—the child was encouraged to look at the pictures and then encouraged to engage in it. The value of the evidence as proof of the crime is obvious." 277 Ark. at 124–25, 640 S.W.2d at 106.

In an action for statutory rape, the defendant cared for two children, seven and six, "and while they were there had the children perform various sexual acts with him and each other while he took photographs, some of which he sent to foreign publishers of pornographic magazines." Qualle v. State, 652 P.2d 481, 483 (Alaska Ct. App. 1982). As to his own children: "Documents, photographs, and films seized from Qualle's home in 1979 showed that he had taken sexually explicit films and photographs of his children and had tried to sell at least two rolls of such pictures to European companies. He asked for money or pornographic magazines in exchange for his pictures. One magazine ("Lolita") published a series of pictures of one of his daughters." Id. at 484. In State v. Natzke, 25 Ariz. App. 520, 522, 544 P.2d 1121, 1123 (1976), pornography was admissible in a rape case in which the defendant's daughter "expressed a reluctance to perform the requested sexual acts . . . appellant told her that these acts were all right and that 'everybody does it,' and that as proof of this fact, appellant showed his daughter pictures and magazines showing sexual activities." In People v. Reynolds, 55 Cal. App. 3d 357, 127 Cal. Rptr. 561 (1976), the defendant sought to suppress pornographic pictures of victims in a prosecution for kidnapping and rape. "According to Tracy, the suspect forced her to take some yellow capsules with a can of cola, and she became groggy; he gave her pornography to read, and at one point stopped the car to make a telephone call and she heard him say: 'I have got the girl' . . . When the officers searched his room they discovered pornographic negatives and photographs, some of which depicted the Konoske girls . . . More photographs were [later] found which were pornographic." 55 Cal. App. 3d at 362, 365, 127 Cal. Rptr. at 564, 566. In another case the defendant was charged, inter alia, with encouraging minors to participate in pornographic films and to engage in sexual intercourse with him: "Defendant showed pornographic films to two boys, and defendant was an actor in one of them. He also showed a pornographic film to two of the girls . . . He suggested to two of the girls that they become prostitutes. Defendant had a movie camera set up to photograph his bed so that, 'in case some of these young girls tried to say that he raped them, he would have this as proof that he did not.'" State v. Dobbs, 665 P.2d 1151, 1155, 1159 (N.M. Ct. App. 1983). In one case, the defendant was an Episcopal priest who ran a boy's farm, which was supposedly for the benefit of wayward and homeless boys, but was "maintained largely from funds raised . . . from the sale of photographs and slides of the children to some 200 or more 'sponsors.' These photographs depicted the boys (most of whom were eleven to sixteen years of age when photographed) posed in the nude and engaged in various acts of simulated or actual fellatio and sodomy." Vermilye v. State, 584 S.W.2d 226, 228 (Tenn. Crim. App. 1979).

See also People v. Cramer, 67 Cal. 2d 126, 127, 429 P.2d 582, 583, 60 Cal. Rptr. 230, 231 (1967) ("At the house, they swam, and defendant served Phillip vodka and 7-Up and showed him some Playboy magazines"); People v. Hunt, 72 Cal. App. 3d 190, 195–196, 139 Cal. Rptr. 675, 677 (1977) (rape case in which the "[d]efendant told her his name was John and that he was a 'porno' photographer . . . This time the defendant took a polaroid picture of Chris (the victim) performing the act [oral copulation]"); People v. Mendoza, 37 Cal. App. 3d 717, 721, 112 Cal. Rptr. 565, 567 (1974) ("He then invited Tad and Jim into his apartment, where he gave the boys candy and pointed out a Playboy magazine centerfold photograph of a nude girl on the wall"); Whiteman v. State, 343 So. 2d 1340 (Fla. Dist. Ct. App.) (admissibility of pornography in sexual battery of niece), cert. denied, 353 So. 2d 681 (Fla. 1977); Brames v. State, 273 Ind. 565, 406 N.E.2d 252 (1980) (attempt to introduce evidence of rape defendant's prior visit to pornographic movie house rejected as part of insanity plea); Allan v. State, 92 Nev. 318, 321, 549 P.2d 1402, 1404 (1976) (minor's testimony concerning defendant's past advances admissible as "tending to show proof of a motive . . . wherein minors were lured to appellant's quarters and, after being 'conditioned' by the showing of his pornographic movies, subjected to his sexual desires"); Stein v. Beta Rho Alumni Ass'n, 49 Or. App. 965, 968, 621 P.2d 632, 634 (1980) (personal injury suffered to a burlesque dancer who performed for a fraternity after "a pornographic movie had been shown"). Finally, in Padgett v. State, 49 Ala. App. 130, 133, 269 So. 2d 147, 149 (Crim.), cert. denied, 289 Ala. 749, 269 So. 2d 154

(1972), a husband was convicted for shooting his wife, allegedly accidentally, after he admittedly "'nagged' [her] about the girls in the Playboy magazine 'to try to irritate her.'"

California's new spousal rape law, effective January 1980, has made many reports of sexual violence in intimate contexts visible for the first time. "Beglin was watching an X-rated movie [on cable TV] in the family room. Beglin allegedly entered the bedroom, threw her [his wife] on the bed and bound her. Beglin also ripped off her clothing and began taking nude photos of her, [Prosecutor Alphonsus C.] Novick said. He then sexually assaulted her." Brown, "Man on Trial Again on Wife Rape Count," *Los Angeles Times*, May 19, 1981. The husband was acquitted after claiming his wife consented. *See* Kutzmann, "Beglin Innocent of Wife Rape," *Costa Mesa Daily Pilot*, May 29, 1981. Evidence included testimony of crisis center workers and an emergency room doctor and photos of her wrists and ankles, "allegedly marked from being tied to a bed with ropes." The prosecutor said, "The case couldn't have been any better . . . Unfortunately, we may have to wait until some wife is severely mutilated or murdered until they'll see." LaGuire, "Spousal-Rape Trial: Husband Cleared, Prosecutor Angered," *Los Angeles Herald Examiner*, May 30, 1981, at A-1. In Merced, California, Victor Burnham was convicted of spousal rape for forcing his wife to have sex with neighbors and strangers (a total of sixty-eight; see Wharton, "Sex Torture Charges Unveiled in Burnham Trial," *Sun-Star* [Merced, Calif.], May 29, 1981) while he took photographs. She was also forced, through assault and holding their child hostage, to stand on the corner and invite men in for sex, and to have sex with a dog. See "Burnham Pleads No Contest on Charge of Possession of Automatic Rifle," *Sun-Star* (Merced, Calif.), May 27, 1981; "Man Found Guilty of Spousal Rape," *Times-Delta* (Tulare County, Calif.), June 6, 1981. She testified to "episodes of torture with a battery-charged cattle prod and an electric egg beater." Wharton, "Sex Torture Charges," above. The defense attorney, "attempting to show the jury there was no force used by the defendant, quizzed Mrs. Burnham about photographs in the albums showing her smiling during the sexual encounters. Mrs. Burnham said her husband threatened her with violence if she did not smile when the pictures were taken." "Wife Testifies in Burnham Sex Case," *Sun-Star* (Merced, Calif.), May 28, 1981. Two of Burnham's previous wives testified that he had forced them to commit similar acts. Id. Burnham said Mrs. Burnham agreed to the acts; his lawyer showed the photos to the jury to "see for themselves that the pictures were in complete conformity with Becky's morals." *See* Wharton, "Guilty Verdict in Sex Trial," *Sun-Star* (Merced, Calif.), June 5, 1981. Burnham's conviction was overturned for failure to instruct *sua sponte* that he might have believed she consented. People v. Burnham, 222 Cal. Rptr. 630 (Ct. App. 1986), (*rev. denied*, May 22, 1986).

My general impression from rape and sexual harassment cases is that it takes a minimum of three women testifying to the same or similar treatment to create a chance of overcoming the man's credibility when he defends against an accusation of sexual force by saying that the woman consented to the act. (For example, some educational institutions have a covert policy of not moving to investigate claims of sexual harassment of students by teachers until they receive complaints from three different women about the same man. They also do not keep reports over time except by memory.) In another such case, "the woman testified that her husband tortured her on several occasions, including sewing her to the bed, burning her with a lamp until she blistered, cutting her with a razor blade and raping her with objects ranging from a coat hanger to a hair brush . . . [He] used duct tape to keep her from screaming . . . When Deputy Attorney Lela Henke asked the woman where her husband got the idea to rape her with a coat hanger, the woman replied they had seen it in a movie on cable television." "Wife Tells of Assault, Torture," *Press Courier* (Oxnard, Calif.), May 9, 1984. Similarly, a woman told of her husband "sewing her sexual organs with needle and yarn." Green, "Wife Describes Brutal Attacks by Mate as He Listens in Court," *Star Free Press* (Ventura, Calif.), May 10, 1984.

Apparently 500 to 1,000 deaths occur each year from "autoerotic asphyxia," in which young men asphyxiate, usually from a noose around the neck, something presented in pornography as producing intense erections. Usually "pornographic material is nearby." Brody, "'Autoerotic Death' of Youths Causes Widening Concern," *New York Times*, Mar. 27, 1984, at C3.

108. State v. Herberg, 324 N.W.2d 346, 347 (Minn. 1982).

109. Code of Indianapolis and Marion County, note 1 above, § 16–3(4) states: "Trafficking in pornography: the production, sale, exhibition, or distribution of pornography.

(A) City, state, and federally funded public libraries or private and public university and college libraries in which pornography is available for study, including on open shelves, shall not be construed to be trafficking in pornography, but special display presentations of pornography in said places is sex discrimination.

(B) The formation of private clubs or associations for purposes of trafficking in pornography is illegal and shall be considered a conspiracy to violate the civil rights of women.

(C) This paragraph (4) shall not be construed to make isolated passages or isolated parts actionable." Section 16–17(b) states: "In the case of trafficking in pornography, any woman may file a complaint as a woman acting against the subordination of women and any man, child, or transsexual may file a complaint but must prove injury in the same way that a woman is injured in order to obtain relief under this chapter."

110. *See, e.g.*, U.S. Commission on Obscenity and Pornography, *Commission Report* (1970); Commission on Obscenity and Film Censorship, *Report*, Cmd. No. 7772 (1979) (United Kingdom).

111. Regina v. Hicklin, 3 L.R.-Q.B. 360, 370 (1868) (obscene meaning "calculated to produce a pernicious effect in depraving and debauching the minds of the persons into whose hands it might come").

112. Roth v. United States, 354 U.S. 476, 501–02 (1956) (Harlan, J., concurring in companion case of Alberts v. California); *see also* Jacobellis v. Ohio,

378 U.S. 184, 202 (1964) (Warren, C.J., dissenting) ("[p]rotection of society's right to maintain its moral fiber").

113. The data of John H. Court and of Berl Kutchinsky, both correlational, reach contradictory conclusions on the relation between the availability of pornography and the level of crime. *Compare* Kutchinsky, "The Effect of Easy Availability of Pornography on the Incidence of Sex Crimes: The Danish Experience," 29 *Journal of Social Issues* 163 (1973); Kutchinsky, "Towards an Explanation of the Decrease in Registered Sex Crimes in Copenhagen," 7 *Technical Report of the Commission on Obscenity and Pornography* 263 (1971) with Court, "Pornography and Sex-Crimes: A Re-Evaluation in the Light of Recent Trends around the World," 5 *International Journal of Criminology and Penology* 129 (1977). More recent investigations into the relationship between the circulation rates of popular men's sex magazines and the rate of reported rape establish a correlation between them in the United States. Larry Baron and Murray Straus, "Sexual Stratification, Pornography, and Rape in the United States" in *Pornography and Sexual Aggression* 185 (N. Malamuth and E. Donnerstein eds. 1984).

114. Roth v. United States, 354 U.S. 476, 485 (1957) (quoting Chaplinsky v. New Hampshire, 315 U.S. 568, 572 [1942]). *See also* Paris Adult Theatre I v. Slaton, 413 U.S. 49, 57–58 (1973) ("[T]here are legitimate state interests at stake . . .[T]hese include the interest of the public in the quality of life").

115. Positivistic causality—linear, exclusive, unidirectional—has become the implicit standard for the validity of connection between pornography and harm. This standard requires the kind of control that can be achieved only, if at all, in laboratory settings. When it is found there, as it has been, that pornography causes harm (*see* note 117 below), the objection is heard that laboratory settings are artificial. But their artificiality is what makes a conclusion about causality possible under this causal model. In real-world settings, a relation of linear consequentiality between pornography and harm is seldom sufficiently isolable or uncontaminated—indeed, seldom even sufficiently separable, the pornography and its impact being so pervasive and interwined—to satisfy this standard. I am suggesting that the positivistic model of causation may be inappropriate to the social reality of pornography. *See also* Werner Heisenberg, *The Physical Principles of Quantum Theory* 63 (1930); Morton Horowitz, "The Doctrine of Objective Causation," in *The Politics of Law* 201 (David Kairys ed. 1982).

116. Major sources are Malamuth and Donnerstein, *Pornography and Sexual Aggression*, note 113 above; Dolph Zillman, *Connections Between Sex and Aggression* (1984); Edward Donnerstein and Leonard Berkowitz, "Victim Reactions in Aggressive Erotic Films as a Factor in Violence against Women," 41 *Journal of Personality and Social Psychology* 710–24 (1981); Neil M. Malamuth and John H. Check, "The Effects of Mass Media Exposure on Acceptance of Violence against Women: A Field Experiment," 15 *Journal of Research on Personality* 436–46 (1981); Neil M. Malamuth and Edward Donnerstein, "The Effects of Aggressive-Pornographic Mass Media Stimuli," 15 *Advances in Experimental Social Psychology* 103 (1982); Diana Russell, "Pornography and

Violence: What Does the New Research Say?" in *Take Back the Night* 216 (L. Lederer ed. 1983); Dolph Zillman and Jennings Bryant, "Pornography, Sexual Callousness, and the Trivialization of Rape," 32 *Journal of Communication* 16–18 (1982); I *Hearings* 13–45 (testimony of Edward Donnerstein); Daniel Linz, Edward Donnerstein, and Steven Penrod, "The Effects of Long-Term Exposure to Filmed Violence against Women" *Journal of Personality and Social Psychology* (forthcoming).

117. In addition to the references listed in note 116 above, *see* E. Donnerstein and J. Hallam, "The Facilitating Effects of Erotica on Aggression Toward Females," *Journal of Personality and Social Psychology* 1270 (1978); R. Geen, D. Stonner, and G. Shope, "The Facilitation of Aggression by Aggression: Evidence against the Catharsis Hypothesis," 31 *Journal of Personality and Social Psychology* 721 (1975); B. S. Sapolsky and Dolph Zillman, "The Effect of Soft-Core and Hard-Core Erotica on Provoked and Unprovoked Hostile Behavior," 17 *Journal of Sex Research* 319 (1981); Dolph Zillman, J. L. Hoyt, and K. B. Day, "Strength and Duration of the Effect of Aggressive, Violent, and Erotic Communications on Subsequent Aggressive Behavior," 1 *Communication Research* 286 (1974). *See also* N. Malamuth, "Factors Associated with Rape as Predictors of Laboratory Aggression against Women," 45 *Journal of Personality and Social Psychology* 432 (1983) (valid relation between factors associated with real-world aggression against women and laboratory aggression).

118. Neil M. Malamuth and John Check, "Penile Tumescence and Perceptual Responses to Rape as a Function of Victim's Perceived Reactions," 10 *Journal of Applied Social Psychology* 528 (1980); Neil M. Malamuth, Scott Haber, and Seymour Feshbach, "Testing Hypotheses Regarding Rape: Exposure to Sexual Violence, Sex Difference, and the 'Normality' of Rapists," 14 *Journal of Research in Personality* 121 (1980). The lack of distinction between reactions of convicted rapists and of control groups may be the reason many people have concluded that pornography does not do anything. When all the unreported, undetected, not to mention unconscious or potential, rapists in the control groups are considered, this conclusion stops being mysterious. See text accompanying note 98, above. *See also* Gene Abel, Judith Becker, and L. Skinner, "Aggressive Behavior and Sex," 3 *Psychiatric Clinics of North America* 133, 140 (1980) (fewer than 5 percent of rapists are psychotic while raping); N. Malamuth, "Rape Proclivity among Males," 37 *Journal of Social Issues* 4 (1981); Malamuth and Check, note 116 above; N. Malamuth, J. Heim, and S. Feshbach, "Sexual Responsiveness of College Students to Rape Depictions: Inhibitory and Disinhibitory Effects," 38 *Social Psychology* 399 (1980).

On the general subject of men's attitudes toward rape, *see* T. Beneke, *Men on Rape* (1982); P. Burt, "Cultural Myths and Supports for Rape," 38 *Journal of Personality & Social Psychology* 217 (1980); "Introduction," note 20; S. D. Smithyman, "The Undetected Rapist" (Ph.D. diss., Claremont Graduate School 1978). A currently unknown number of incidents originally reported as rapes are now considered by police to be unfounded, meaning "the police established that no forcible rape offense or attempt occurred." In 1976, the last year the FBI reported its "unfounding" rate, it was 19 percent of reports. Federal Bureau of Investigation, *Crime in America* 16 (1976).

On the supposition that it was not the truth of the statement that they were protesting, I dedicate this footnote to those members of the Biddle Lecture audience who hissed when I made the statement in the text.

119. *See* notes 116 and 118 above. It is perhaps worth noting that there is no experimental research to the contrary.

120. *See* John Briere and Neil M. Malamuth, "Self-Reported Likelihood of Sexually Aggressive Behavior: Attitudinal versus Sexual Explanations," 37 *Journal of Research in Personality* 315, 318 (1983) (58 percent of college males in survey reported some likelihood of forcing sex on a woman if they knew they would not get caught). *See also* Mary Koss and Cheryl J. Oros, "Sexual Experiences Survey: A Research Instrument Investigating Sexual Aggression and Victimization," 50 *Journal of Consulting and Clinical Psychology* 455 (1982).

121. *See* I *Hearings* 21–38 (testimony of E. Donnerstein discussing supporting data submitted in the record). *See also* Zillman and Bryant, note 116 above (normal males exposed to films like *Debbie Does Dallas* see rape victims as many times more worthless than men who had not seen the films, and also saw less than half the amount of injury to the victim). In spite of this factual support, it is likely that the Indianapolis version of the ordinance would not apply to trafficking in such materials. *See* § 16–3(8) of the Indianapolis Ordinance, which states: "Defenses: It shall be a defense to a complaint under paragraph (g)(4) . . . that the materials complained of are those covered only by paragraph (q)(6)."

122. *See* note 121 above. *See also* Linz, Donnerstein and Penrod, note 116 above. On female subjects, see Carol Krafka, "Sexually Explicit, Sexually Violent, and Violent Media: Effects of Multiple Naturalistic Exposures and Debriefing on Female Viewers" (Ph.D. diss., University of Wisconsin, 1985).

123. *See* I *Hearings* 37–38 (testimony of E. Donnerstein) ("subjects who have seen violent material or X-rated material see less injury to a rape victim than people who haven't seen these films. Furthermore, they consider the woman to be more worthless"); *see also* Zillman and Bryant, note 116 above.

124. Dr. Donnerstein says this in most of his talks.

125. Russell, *Rape in Marriage* 228 (1984).

126. Id. at 84.

127. *See* II *Hearings* 68 (testimony of Ruth M.).

128. II *Hearings* 55 (testimony of Nancy C.).

129. III *Hearings* 29 (testimony of Sharon Rice Vaughn, reading statement by Donna Dunn of Women's Shelter, Inc., in Rochester, Minn., which describes events reported by a woman at the shelter).

130. Id.

131. III *Hearings* 83 (testimony of Sue Schafer).

132. II *Hearings* 74 (testimony of a named former prostitute). The use of pornography in sexual abuse of prostitutes, and its use in getting them into prostitution, is documented by Mimi Silbert and Ayala Pines, "Pornography

and Sexual Abuse of Women," 10 *Sex Roles: Journal of Research* 857 (1984). Even though no specific questions were asked about pornography, 24 percent of the subjects (current and former prostitutes) mentioned references to pornography by the men who raped them, often references to specific materials in which prostitutes were presented as loving and wanting violent abuse and death. Ten percent mentioned being used as children in pornography, again in unsolicited open-ended accounts of their lives. Had they been directly asked, "it is assumed that the actual response to this question would be notably higher." Id. at 865.

133. II *Hearings* 74–75 (testimony of a named former prostitute).

134. I *Hearings* 56 (testimony of Gordon C.).

135. Id.

136. III *Hearings* 94–95 (testimony of Omar J.).

137. Id. at 95.

138. *See* Dworkin, "The Bruise That Doesn't Heal," 3 *Mother Jones* 31, 35 (1978) ("Reality is when something is happening to you and you know it and you say it and when you say it, other people understand what you mean and believe you").

139. *See* Dworkin, *Pornography: Men Possessing Women* 149 (1981) ("She wants it, they all do").

140. I think it is important that when the *actual object*, for example the pornography, is present, finding facts about it is thought to become *more* rather than less difficult—compared, for example, with finding facts about a rape. This suggests that the usual process of proof amounts to a credibility contest between conflicting stories, which come to court in personae. Pornography has pervasively written women's side of the story as not a rape. When there is no story about reality to provide a proxy for simplifying it to a question of whose version one believes, but the reality itself is there, perhaps—if it is measured against standards devised to describe it—women will have a chance.

141. *See* Miller v. California, 413 U.S. 15, 19 (1973).

142. *See* Kaplan v. California, 413 U.S. 115, 120 (1973); Paris Adult Theatre I v. Slaton, 413 U.S. 49, 60 (1973); Roth v. United States, 354 U.S. 476, 501 (1957) (Harlan, J., concurring).

143. New York v. Ferber, 458 U.S. 742, 757 (1982).

144. *See* consideration of civil as opposed to criminal procedures and remedies, note 52 above. It does seem to me that criminal civil rights legislation might be worth considering at the federal level, but only in addition to providing access to court to private civil claimants.

145. III *Hearings* 53 (testimony of Cheryl Champion, member, Sexual Abuse Unit, Washington County, Minn., Human Services).

146. 315 U.S. 568, 572 (1941).

147. Actually, some have. See Ann Hansen, "Direct Action: Sentencing Statements," 17 *Open Road*, Winter 1984 (Vancouver, B.C.), at 11–12 (on receiving a life sentence for firebombing the Red Hot Video store, among other actions). Nikki Craft, with the Preying Mantis Women's Brigade, engages in

disruptive and exemplary acts against pornography, from staging the Myth California Pageant (in opposition to the Miss California Pageant) to destroying copies of *Hustler*, for which she served time. *See* Linda Hooper, "Preying on Porn Propaganda," *City on a Hill* 5–7 (Apr. 5, 1984) (Santa Cruz, Calif.). Women in Europe have also engaged in destruction of property to express their dissent against pornography, and to attempt to destroy some of it. *See* Dworan, "Review," *off our backs*, May 6, 1984, at 18–19 (reviewing *Breaching the Peace: a Collection of Radical Feminist Papers* [1983]).

148. *See* Beauharnais v. Illinois, 343 U.S. 250, 263 (1952) ("[T]he dignity accorded him may depend as much on the reputation of the racial and religious group to which he willy-nilly belongs as on his own merits").

149. *See* Whitney v. California, 274 U.S. 357, 377 (1927) (Brandeis, J., concurring).

150. *See* Tribe, note 9 above, at 731.

151. *See* T. Emerson, "Toward a General Theory of the First Amendment," 72 *Yale Law Journal* 877, 879–81 (1963); C. E. Baker, "Scope of the First Amendment Freedom of Speech," 25 *UCLA Law Review* 964, 990–1005 (1978).

152. *See* A. Meiklejohn, *Political Freedom* 24–28 (1960). The importance of participation in civic life is also recognized by Emerson: "[M]an in his capacity as a member of society has a right to share in the common decisions that affect him." T. Emerson, *The System of Freedom of Expression* 6 (1970).

153. *See* T. Emerson, note 152 above. Emerson is entirely aware that some groups lack power in a way that the political process does not accommodate, but simply considers this a risk posed principally to "the nonbelonging individual," id. at 37, rather than advancing any substantive analysis of who does and does not have power and thus access to the means of speech. In the absence of such a substantive analysis, pornographers can cast themselves as outsiders when they are actually paradigmatic. *See also* Clark, "Liberalism and Pornography," in *Pornography and Censorship* 57 (D. Copp and S. Wendell eds. 1983).

154. One case has squarely balanced a municipal ordinance prohibiting sex discrimination in advertising against the First Amendment. Noting that commercial speech is not the highest order of speech—a position with strong parallels to the plurality's treatment of the "sexually explicit" in Young v. American Mini Theatres, 427 U.S. 50 (1976)—the *presumptive* connection between sex segregation in job advertisements and sex segregation in the workplace stated a harm that outweighed freedom of the press. Further, the Supreme Court recently held that the compelling state interest in eradicating discrimination against women justified the impact of Minnesota's Human Rights Act on First Amendment rights of expressive association. *See* Roberts v. United States Jaycees, 468 U.S. 609 (1984). Holding that the state's interest in sex equality outweighed the First Amendment interests implicated, the Court stated that the equality interest is not "limited to the provision of purely tangible goods and services," but also includes steps to remove "the barriers to economic advancement and political and social integration that have historically plagued certain disadvantaged groups, including women."

Id. at 626. In a formulation strikingly apposite to the antipornography ordinance, the Court said: "[A]cts of invidious discrimination in the distribution of publicly available goods, services, and other advantages cause unique evils that government has a compelling interest to prevent—wholly apart from the point of view such conduct may transmit. Accordingly, like violence or other types of potentially expressive activities that produce special harms distinct from their communicative impact, such practices are entitled to no constitutional protection." Id. at 628.

155. In one obscenity case the Supreme Court stated: "Appellant was not prosecuted here for anything he said or believed, but for what he did, for his dominant role in several enterprises engaged in producing and selling allegedly obscene books." Mishkin v. New York, 383 U.S. 502, 504–05 (1966). The statute upheld in *Ferber*, 458 U.S. 747 (1982), defined publication of child pornography as "promoting a sexual performance by a child," N.Y. Penal Law § 263 (McKinney 1980), logic that extended to support the law against the pornography's distribution. It is arguable that a major reason obscenity was defined as "nonspeech" is because speech was considered to communicate ideas, and obscenity was understood to function physically rather than ideationally. For some further thoughts on this subject, see "Not a Moral Issue." To state the obvious, I do not argue that pornography is "conduct" in the First Amendment doctrinal sense.

156. Ginsberg v. New York, 390 U.S. 629, 649 (1968) (Stewart, J., concurring in result) (emphasis added).

157. Roth v. United States, 354 U.S. 476, 514 (Douglas, J., dissenting) (citing Giboney v. Empire Storage & Ice Co., 336 U.S. 490, 498 [1949]); Labor Board v. Virginia Power Co., 314 U.S. 469, 477–78 (1941). *See also* Memoirs v. Massachusetts, 383 U.S. 413, 426 (1966) (Douglas, J., concurring) (First Amendment does not permit the censorship of expression not brigaded with illegal action); Pittsburgh Press Co. v. Human Relations Comm'n, 413 U.S. 376, 398 (1973) (Douglas, J., dissenting) (speech and action not so closely brigaded as to be one).

158. Rape, battery, assault, kidnaping, and prostitution are all crimes, and they are absolutely integral to pornography as we define and make it actionable. Compare with *Ferber*, 458 U.S. 747 (1982): masturbating is not a crime, nor is watching it; yet making and distributing a film of two boys masturbating is.

159. Speech by Dworkin, note 63 above.

160. This example is from an interview with a victim done in preparation for the Minneapolis Hearings.

161. *See* Foucault, note 32 above.

162. "He [her husband] told me if I loved him I would do this. And that, as I could see from the things he read me in the magazines initially, a lot of times women didn't like it but if I tried it enough I would probably like it and I would learn to like it. And he would read me stories where women learned to like it." II *Hearings* 63 (testimony of Ruth M.).

163. *See* Rennie Simson, "The Afro-American Female: The Historical Context of the Construction of Sexual Identity," in *Powers of Desire: The Politics of Sexuality* 231 (A. Snitow, C. Stansell and S. Thompson eds. 1983) (quoting a Black slave, Harriet Jacobs, who speaks for many women under circumstances of compulsion when she writes of her rape by her white master: "It seems less demeaning to give one's self, than to submit to compulsion." Jacobs subsequently resisted by hiding in an attic cubbyhole, "almost deprived of light and air, and with no space to move my limbs, for nearly seven years" to avoid him.

164. This paraphrases a portion of Andrea Dworkin's speech, note 63 above.

165. *See* U.S. Const. amend. I.

166. Francis Biddle, *A Casual Past* (1961); *see also* Biddle, *In Brief Authority* (1962).

167. A. Fisher, "Francis Biddle," 9 *Harvard Civil Rights–Civil Liberties Law Review* 423, 424 (1974) (foreword to Herbert Wechsler, "The Francis Biddle Lectures," 9 *Harvard Civil Rights–Civil Liberties Law Review* 426 [1974]). It was also said that "Mr. Biddle deeply shared what Justice Brandeis called the 'conviction' of Justice Holmes, that 'man should be free in a large way.'" Id. at 426. So, it seems to me, should woman.

168. Andrea Dworkin, "The Bruise That Doesn't Heal," 3 *Mother Jones* 31, 36 (July 1978).

169. V. Woolf, *A Room of One's Own* 48–50 (1929) inspired the form of this vision.

15. On Collaboration

1. LEXIS is a computerized service for legal research that allows random searches of random phrases as well as of concepts and cases.

2. Brown v. Board of Education, 347 U.S. 483, 494 (1954) (". . . a feeling of inferiority as to their status in the community that may affect their hearts and minds in a way unlikely ever to be undone").

3. American Booksellers Association v. Hudnut, 598 F. Supp. 1316 (S.D. Ind. 1984) (Sarah Evans Barker, J.). For subsequent history, *see* "Francis Biddle's Sister," notes 1, 46.

16. The Sexual Politics of the First Amendment

1. Isaiah Berlin distinguishes negative from positive freedom. Negative freedom asks the question, "what is the area within which the subject—a person or group of persons—is or should be left to do or be what [he] is able to do or be, without interference from other persons?" Positive freedom asks the question, "what, or who, is the source of control or interference that can determine someone to do, or be, this rather than that?" "Two Concepts of Liberty," in *Four Essays on Liberty* 121–22 (1970). Is it not obvious that if one group is granted the positive freedom to do whatever they want to another

group, to determine that the second group will be and do this rather than that, that no amount of negative freedom guaranteed to the second group will make it the equal of the first? The negative state is thus incapable of effective guarantees of rights in any but a just society, which is the society in which they are needed the least.

2. The analysis here is indebted to Andrea Dworkin, "For Men, Freedom of Speech, For Women, Silence Please" in *Take Back the Night: Women on Pornography* 255–58 (Laura Lederer ed. 1982).

3. *But cf.* the words of framer William Livingston, who said, "Liberty of the press means promoting the common good of society, it does not mean unrestraint in writing." Livingston, "Of the Use, Abuse and Liberty of the Press," *Independent Reflector* (1754), quoted in Richard Buel, *The Press and the American Revolution* 69 (1980). Livingston's press was founded "to oppose superstition, bigotry, priestcraft, tyranny, servitude, public mismanagement and dishonesty in office." Quoted in Leonard W. Levy, *Emergence of a Free Press* 138 (1985). Levy, an absolutist, finds the theory that gave rise to the *Independent Reflector* "in fact reactionary if not vicious . . . That a Framer could ever have held such views surprises" at 138.

4. There is a major controversy about the intent of the framers in relation to existing law and values of the colonial period. The controversy is discussed in T. Terrar, "The New Social History and Colonial America's Press Legacy: Tyranny or Freedom?" (1986) (unpublished manuscript).

5. Red Lion Broadcasting Co. v. F.C.C., 395 U.S. 367 (1969). In F.C.C. v. League of Women Voters, 468 U.S. 364 (1984), the Supreme Court hints that it would be receptive to a challenge to the fairness doctrine on the basis that it impedes rather than furthers the values of the First Amendment, 376 n.11, 378 n.12.

6. Schneider v. State, 308 U.S. 147 (1939) (restricting street circulars because of litter is invalid if it is possible to clean them up).

7. Slave codes prohibited teaching slaves or free Blacks to read, write, or spell and giving them reading materials and permitting meetings for schooling. Punishments for Blacks included whipping; whites caught in the act could be fined and imprisoned but never whipped. Alabama: *Clay's Digest* 543, Act of 1832, § 10 (crime to teach Black to spell, read, or write); North Carolina: *Revised Statutes* ch. 3, § 74 (1836–7) (crime to teach slave to read or write, except figures, to give or sell to slave a book or pamphlet); ch. 3, § 27 (slave who receives instruction receives thirty-nine lashes); Georgia: 2 *Cobb's Digest* 1001 (1829) (crime to teach Black to read or write); Virginia: "Every assemblage of Negroes for the purpose of instruction in reading or writing shall be an unlawful assembly." *Virginia Code*, §§ 747–48 (1849); South Carolina: meetings including even one person of color "for the purpose of mental instruction in a confined or secret place are declared to be an unlawful meeting." Police can "break doors" and may lash participants sufficiently to deter them from future such acts. 7 *Statutes of South Carolina* 440 (1800). *See generally* George M. Stroud, *Sketch of the Laws Relating to Slavery* 58–63 (1856, 1968 ed.).

The slaves understood that literacy was as fundamental to effective expression as it was to every other benefit of equality: "It seemed to me that if I could learn to read and write, the learning might—nay I really thought it would, point out to me the way to freedom, influence, and real, secure, happiness." Slave narrative quoted in Thomas L. Webber, *Deep Like the Rivers: Education in the Slave Quarter Community* 144 (1978). The Statutes of Louisiana 208 (1852) state: "Whosoever shall make use of language in any public discourse from the bar, the bench, the stage, the pulpit, or in any place whatsoever, or whoever shall make use of language in private discourses or conversations, or shall make use of signs or actions, having a tendency to produce discontent among the free colored population of this state, or to excite insubordination among the slaves, or whosoever shall knowingly be instrumental in bringing into this state any paper, pamphlet or book having such tendency as aforesaid, shall, on conviction thereof before any court of competent jurisdiction, suffer imprisonment at hard labour not less than three years nor more than twenty-one years, or DEATH, at the discretion of the court" at 208.

8. The best examples are the laws against treason, bribery, conspiracy, threats, blackmail, and libel. Acts can also be expression, but are not necessarily protected as such. *See, e.g.,* Giboney v. Empire Storage & Ins. Co., 336 U.S. 490 (1946) (labor picketing can be enjoined on the ground the First Amendment does not cover "speech or writing used as an integral part of conduct in violation of a valid criminal statute"). Action "is often a method of expression and within the protection of the First Amendment . . ." but "picketing [is] 'free speech plus' [and] can be regulated when it comes to the 'plus' or 'action' side of the protest." Brandenburg v. Ohio, 395 U.S. 444, 455 (1969) (Douglas, J., concurring). *See also* United States v. O'Brien, 391 U.S. 367 (1968) (burning draft card not protected speech as symbolic protest); Street v. New York, 394 U.S. 576 (1969) (burning flag while speaking not punishable because speech is protected even though burning is crime); Spence v. Washington, 418 U.S. 407 (1974) (altering flag is protected speech despite flag desecration statute); Clark v. Committee for Creative Non-Violence, 468 U.S. 288 (1984) (sleeping in park to protest homelessness not protected as expressive conduct when it violates regulation against camping).

9. Roth v. U.S., 354 U.S. 476, 508–14 ("The first amendment, in prohibitions in terms absolute" at 514); Memoirs v. Massachusetts, 383 U.S. 413, 424–33 (concurring); Miller v. California, 413 U.S. 15, 37–47; Paris Adult Theatres v. Slaton, 413 U.S. 49, 70–73 (1973).

10. 106 S. Ct. 1172 (1986).

11. American Booksellers v. Hudnut, 771 F.2d 323 (7th Cir. 1985), *aff'd* 106 S. Ct. 1172 (1986).

12. 771 F.2d at 329.

13. Renton v. Playtime Theatres, 106 S.Ct. 925 (1986).

14. *E.g.,* Miller v. California, 413 U.S. 15 (1973).

15. *E.g.,* New York v. Ferber, 458 U.S. 747 (1982).

16. 106 S.Ct. at 933 n.1 (Brennan, J., dissenting).

17. Laws against rape also express the view that sexual subordination is impermissible, and this is not considered repressive of thought, although presumably some thought is involved.

18. An erection is not a thought, either, unless one thinks with one's penis.

19. The most celebrated and equivocal example is the prosecution of unionist McNamara brothers for blowing up the virulently anti-union *Los Angeles Times*. The McNamaras pleaded guilty but doubt remains whether they did it. Although the bombing was criticized as inhumane (many people died), needlessly destructive, and instrategic, I found no argument within the movement that the *Times* should not have been attacked because it was "speech." *See* P. Foner, *History of the Labor Movement in the United States*, vol. 5: *The AFL in the Progressive Era, 1910–1915* ch. 1 (1980).

20. Abraham Lincoln ordered "copperhead" (northern pro-slavery) newspapers closed and editors jailed during the Civil War. The postmaster general barred some "copperhead" newspapers from the mail. Abolitionists "threatened, manhandled, or tarred editors, required changes in editorial policy, [and] burned print shops" of pro-slavery presses. Harold L. Nelson, *Freedom of the Press from Hamilton to the Warren Court* xxvi–xxvii, 236–237 (1967).

21. For example, the Sons of Liberty in 1775 issued the following ultimatum to New York printers: "Sir, if you print, or suffer to be printed in your press anything against the rights and liberties of America, or in favor of our inveterate foes, the King, the Ministry and Parliament of Great Britain, death and destruction, ruin and perdition shall be your portion. Signed by Order of the Committee of Tarring and Feathering." Thomas Jones, *History of New York During the Revolutionary War* (E. F. DeLancey ed. 1879), quoted in Levy, note 3 above, at 175.

22. Beauharnais v. Illinois, 343 U.S. 250 (1952).

23. This was particularly true of the American-occupied zone. German publishers were licensed, and those who published materials inconsistent with the American objectives had their licenses revoked. They were kept under surveillance. Americans also imposed school reform and curriculum changes to reeducate German youth against the Nazi ideology. John Gimbel, *The American Occupation of Germany: Politics and the Military (1945–1949)* 246–47 (1968). Positive steps were also taken. American propaganda efforts included radio and television campaigns against the harm of Nazism and attacks on neo-Nazis. Kurt P. Tauber, *Beyond Eagle and Swastika* 434 (1967). The British and American forces denied that they practiced censorship, but destructive criticism of the occupying powers was forbidden. Clara Menck, *A Struggle for Democracy in Germany* 298–99 (Gabriel L. Almon ed. 1965).

24. *La Gaceta-Diario Oficial* 73–75 (Sept. 13, 1979), Ley General Provisional Sobre los Medios de Comunicacion Arto. 3o prohibits materials "que utilicen a la mujer como objeto sexual o comercial" ("that uses women as sexual or commercial objects") Decree No. 48, Aug. 17, 1979, at 74. I make this reference not to hold up this language or this effort as an ideal to be strictly followed, but rather to remind leftists in particular that some efforts that they

otherwise take as admirable do (even under conditions very different from those in the United States) consider that the use of women to sell things, as well as prostitution itself, is the opposite of the liberation of women as intended by their revolutions. It is also instructive to notice that an otherwise hard-headed revolutionary government with a lot to worry about does not regard the issue of sexual sale of women as either too unimportant to address or too moralistic for political concern.

25. Brown v. Board of Education, 347 U.S. 483 (1954).

26. Dred Scott v. Sanford, 60 U.S. (19 How.) 393 (1856).

Afterword

1. In the closing line of Lily Tomlin and Jane Wagner's Broadway play *The Search for Signs of Intelligent Life in the Universe,* the bag lady who has been instructing her "little friends" from other planets in the distinction between Campbell's soup and Warhol's art reports that when they attended a play, they found the audience more entertaining than the play: "The play was soup; the audience was art."

2. Alexander v. Yale University, 459 F. Supp. 1 (1977).

3. Alexander v. Yale University, 631 F.2d 178 (2d Cir. 1980).

4. American Booksellers v. Hudnut, 598 F. Supp. 1316 (S.D. Ind. 1984) *aff'd* 771 F.2d 323 (7th Cir. 1985) *aff'd* 106 S.Ct. 1172 (1986) (summary affirmance).

5. Judge Veronica Simmons McBeth sentenced a slumlord to thirty days in his own building for failure to bring it up to the housing code. People v. Milton Avol, Docket No. 31334373 (Mun. Ct. Los Angeles, Calif. 1986). Judge LaDoris Cordell found an ordinance an unconstitutional violation of freedom of expression under which Nikki Craft, an anti-pornography activist, had been jailed for protesting the Miss Nude America pageant by spilling the blood of raped women across the entrance. People v. Spray a/k/a Craft, Case C8284675 (Mun. Ct. San Jose, Calif. Jan. 5, 1983). Burns and Barker are white; McBeth and Cordell are Black.

6. A stunning example of the denial of gender occurred in a dialogue in which I participated at Buffalo Law School. In apparent response to a version of my "Difference and Dominance," Mary Dunlap, a feminist attorney, said: "I am speaking out of turn. I am also standing, which I am told by some is a male thing to do. But I am still a woman—standing. I am not subordinate to any man! I find myself very often contesting efforts at my subordination—both standing and lying down and sitting and in various other positions—but I am not subordinate to any man! And I have been told by Kitty MacKinnon that women have never *not* been subordinate to men. So I stand here an exception and invite all other women here to be an exception and stand. Everyone who believes it is true that we have never *not* been subordinate to men, remain seated. Everyone who believes that you do not have to be subordinate to men, stand if you can." A version of this exchange was later published in "Feminist Discourse, Moral Values, and the Law—a Conversation,"

305

34 *Buffalo Law Review* 11, 76 (1985). This statement turns a critique of a structural condition into a statement of individual inevitability, an indictment of oppression into a reason for passivity and despair. An empirical indictment of what is becomes opposed by a rallying cry of what does not have to be—surely a misplaced opposition. And any woman's victory over sexism becomes a source of proud disidentification from the rest of her sex and proud denial of the rest of her life. If subordination had to be, it would surely be a waste of time to fight for women's rights. But under existing conditions, asking women to single themselves out as exceptions to the condition of women amounts to saying, "all women who are exempt from the condition of women, all women who are not women, stand with me." I was encouraged that only about a quarter of an audience of predominantly female law students fell for it. And I understood with new clarity what conservative women have been trying to tell us about feminists.

7. This is a reference to a study of the attempted psychiatric treatment of three men, each of whom believed he was Christ. The doctors attempted to get them to work it out together, with the result that one became the Father, one the Son, and one the Holy Spirit. Milton Rokeach, *The Three Christs of Ypsilanti: A Psychological Study* (1964).

8. The figures on rape and attempted rape alone are 44 percent of all women. "Not By Law Alone," note 2.

9. Compare the 1973 figure of $4 billion per year, J. Cook, "The X-Rated Economy," *Forbes*, Sept. 18, 1978, 81, with the 1983 figure of $8 billion per year, Galloway and Thornton, "Crackdown on Pornography—A No-Win Battle," *U.S. News & World Report*, June 4, 1984, 84.

10. Playboy and others sued the Attorney General's Commission on Pornography to keep the commission from *publishing information* testified to before the commission concerning retail outlets for pornography and information secured through a follow-up letter, asking the retailers if they did, indeed, sell pornography and if so why. Securing this information *by letter* was regarded as intimidating (recall that pornography intimidates no one). Playboy Enterprises, Inc. et al. v. Meese, Docket No. 86-1346 and Magazine Publishers Association v. Meese, Docket No. 86-1447 (D.D.C. 1986). They obtained an *injunction.* Playboy Enterprises, Inc. v. Meese, 639 F. Supp. 581 (D.D.C. 1986).

11. Andrea Dworkin, *Pornography: Men Possessing Women* (1981), a work of genius, originated this analysis.

12. This parallel is brilliantly developed by Twiss Butler in a letter to *off our backs*, October 1985, 28.

13. *See* the lucid discussion in Andrea Dworkin, *Right Wing Women* (1983).

14. As Dr. Meerloo observed of Holocaust survivors, "There are certain psychic wounds that prevent the utilization of new-found freedom," in Henry Krystal, ed., *Massive Psychic Trauma* 73 (1968).

15. Bishop Tutu, quoted in Alan Cowell, "Fight Apartheid, Tutu Tells Investors," *New York Times*, Jan 3, 1985, 3. This locution derives from Shylock's speech in Shakespeare's *The Merchant of Venice*, which ends "and if you wrong us, shall we not revenge?"

Acknowledgments

In a very real sense, these speeches are a collective effort of my friends, students, clients, co-workers, and colleagues, as well as of my audiences. Individuals who were particularly generous in discussing ideas, criticizing manuscript, and doing work are legion. I am especially indebted to all those who testified for the civil rights ordinance against pornography in Minneapolis, and to Roni Alexander, Gloria Allred, Meg Baldwin, Jeanne Barkey, Kathy Barry, Pauline Bart, Peter Bogdanovich, Paul Brest, Sally Burns, Twiss Butler, Pat Butler, Michelle Campbell, Lu Ann Carter, Iris Chester, Susan Cole, Ruth Colker, Beulah Coughenour, Mark Dall, Deborah Daniels, Karen Davis, Thelma Dekker, Andrea Dworkin, Mary Eberts, Tom Emerson, Ruth Emerson, Susan Geiger, Steve Goldsmith, Gerry Gunther, Karen Haney, Michelle Harrison, Kent Harvey, Valerie Heller, Florence Henderson, Louise B. Hoogstratten, Charlee Hoyt, Steve Jevning, Evelina Kane, Kathleen Lahey, Dorchen Leidholdt, Chris Littleton, Linda Marchiano, Jeff Masson, Annie McCombs, Sheila McIntyre, Frank Michelman, Martha Minow, Glenn Morris, Helen Neally, Fran Olsen, Lorelei Pettigrew, Aric Press, Pamela Price, Norma Ramos, David Rayson, Deborah Rhode, Myra Riddell, Betty Rosenstein, Diana Russell, Betsy Sahlkind, Naomi Scheman, Alan Sears, Steve Shiffrin, Reva Siegal, Anne Simon, Janet Spector, Therese Stanton, Bob Stein, Wendy Stock, John Stoltenberg, Kathleen Sullivan, Cass Sunstein, Gerald Torres, Larry Tribe, Elaine Valadez, Kathy Watson, Rosalie Wahl, Mary Whisner, Van White, Jack Winkler, and Susan Williams. Thank you all. I thank William B. Hudnut for changing the course of history.

Lindsay Waters invented this book. Without the support of Dean Robert A. Stein, virtually none of it would have happened. Others who helped in material ways include my brothers Jim MacKinnon and Leonard MacKinnon, Jeanne Barkey, Karen Davis (whom Andrea Dworkin dubbed "The New Woman" for good reason), John Ely, Annie McCombs, John Kerwin, Marjorie Resnick, Twiss and Pat Butler, Dorothy Monica, Valerie Harper, David Satz, Penelope Seator, and Elsa Gidlow. Anne Simon backstopped me on the footnotes yet again, and Kent Harvey simply made life possible in ways great and small. But for all this help, I might have thought these thoughts, but no one else would have heard them.

Some speeches in this volume were previously published in whole or in part. Permission to use the following previously published material is gratefully acknowledged: "Excerpts from a Debate with Phyllis Schlafly," 1 *Law & Inequality: A Journal of Theory and Practice* 341 (1983); "Desire and Power," in

Acknowledgments

Cary Nelson and Lawrence Grossberg, eds., *Marxism and the Interpretation of Culture* (Champaign-Urbana, Ill.: University of Illinois Press, 1987); "Difference and Dominance: On Sex Discrimination," in Robert K. Fullinwider and Claudia Mills, eds., *The Moral Foundations of Civil Rights* (Totowa, N.J.: Rowman and Littlefield, 1986); "Feminist Discourse, Moral Values, and the Law— a Conversation" (with Carol Gilligan, Mary Dunlap, Ellen Dubois, and Carrie Menkel-Meadow), 34 *Buffalo Law Review* 11, 20–36, 69–77 (1985); "A Rally against Rape," *Stanford Daily*, Nov. 16, 1981; "Violence against Women: A Feminist Perspective," 33 *Aegis: Magazine on Ending Violence against Women* 51 (Winter 1982) (Box 21033, Washington, D.C. 20009); "The Male Ideology of Privacy: A Feminist Perspective on the Right to Abortion," 17 *Radical America* (July-August 1983); "Roe v. Wade: A Study in Male Ideology," in J. Garfield and P. Hennessey, eds., *Abortion: Moral and Legal Perspectives* (Amherst, Mass.: University of Massachusetts Press, 1984); "Not a Moral Issue," 2 *Yale Law and Policy Review* 321 (1984); and "Pornography, Civil Rights, and Speech," 20 *Harvard Civil Rights–Civil Liberties Law Review* 1 (1985).

Index

Abortion, 1, 26, 28, 93–102; and incest, 94, 99; illegal, 25; Medicaid funding of, 93, 96; *Playboy* funding of, 144–145; and rape, 248n4; and sex discrimination, 249n21

Abstract categories, and justice under law, 65, 71, 73, 164–166, 167, 168, 170

Advertising, sex in, 27, 223, 272n54; sex discrimination in, 299n154

Aesthetics, and pornography, 4, 61, 150, 224

Affirmative action, 33, 36, 166

Alimony, 76; and gender neutrality, 35

Allende, Isabel, 10

American Booksellers v. Hudnut, 210–212, 281n46

American Civil Liberties Union, 202, 209, 242n18

Androgyny, 118

Anti-Semitism, 55, 140, 222, 289n91

Aronowitz, Stanley, 50, 58

Asian women, depicted in pornography, 200

Athletics: women in, 36, 74, 117–124, 241n17, 255n2; separate for women, 256n2

Autoerotic asphyxia, 291n107

Barker, Sarah Evans, 220

Barrett, Michelle, 54

Battery, 5; domestic, 1, 24, 28, 41, 52, 170; erotization of, 85, 92; rate, 169; and pornography, 171, 184, 199; and rape, 182

Beauharnais v. Illinois, 192

Berlin, Isaiah, 301n1

Biddle, Francis, 195

Bisexual defense, 107–108

Black, Hugo, 262n3

Black, meaning of, 238n12

Black men, and rape, 81

Black slavery, 55, 167–168, 208, 302n7

Black women, 76; death from illegal abortions, 25; rape of, 7, 82, 248n3; invisibility of, 81–82; depicted in pornography, 199–200

Blackmail, sexual, 15

Bona Fide Occupational Qualification, 33, 240n1

Brandeis, Louis, 193

Brant, Beth, 63

Brennan, William, 212

Brown v. Board of Education, 165, 168, 202, 213

Brownmiller, Susan, 92, 233n19

Burns, Ellen Bree, 220

California Federal v. Guerra, 243n18

Cardozo, Benjamin, 9

Cartesian doubt, 57–58

Catton, Bruce, 206

Censorship, 140, 143–144, 154, 195; Feminist Anti-Censorship Task Force, 236n35

Chaplinsky v. New Hampshire, 192

Child care responsibilities, 37

Child custody, 1; and gender neutrality, 35

Children: sexual abuse of, 5, 6, 23, 41, 51, 169, 170, 184; and pornography, 157, 171, 172, 179–181, 182, 184, 189, 212, 287n77, 291n107; coerced into prostitution, 180–181

Choice, 14; and pornography, 172

Civil rights: pornography as violation of, 3–4, 14, 163, 175–195, 199–205, 210–213, 222–223, 226; of individuals, 13; of Indian women, 66–69, 247n11

Class: and gender, 2, 8, 25; marxist theory of, 48–49

Collaboration, and consent, 7

Community standards, 174

Consent, 100; and collaboration, 7; in sex, 11; and pornography, 172, 180–183

309

Index

Contraception, 25, 28, 95

Control, 48–50; over reproduction, 94, 95, 97–98, 100; over sexuality, 94, 97–98

Cordell, LaDoris, 211

Coyne, Mary Jean, 70, 77

Credibility of women, 110–113, 133, 191

Cultural values, 63, 65–66, 68

de Beauvoir, Simone, 55

Deep Throat, 10–11, 13, 128–129, 180, 181, 234n30

Defamation, 11, 192–193; countersuits to rape charges, 255n38

Desexualization of women, 97

Desire, 49, 54, 61, 149, 174

Difference, 51, 118, 175; and gender, 3, 8–9, 23, 32–45, 175, 233n26; theory of sex equality, 23, 32–45; and sex discrimination, 41–44; social meaning of, 51; in liberalism, 137

Divorced women: standard of living of, 24; alimony, 35, 76

Dominance and submission: erotization of, 3, 6–7, 29, 50–51, 53–54, 149, 152, 160–161; and pornography, 3, 173, 222; in sex discrimination, 40–41, 42–43

Donnerstein, Ed, 188

Dothard v. Rawlinson, 73

Douglas, William O., 194, 208, 209

Dred Scott v. Sanford, 213

Dunlap, Mary, 305n6

Dworkin, Andrea, 5, 13, 79, 99, 127, 129–133, 149, 163, 173, 175, 194, 196, 199–200, 207, 210, 226

Easterbrook, Frank, 210, 211

Education, access to, 131

Educational institutions: sexual harassment in, 107, 110, 220, 251n6; pornography in, 116, 183, 288n84; women in, 216; sex discrimination in, 240n4

El Saadawi, Nawal, 5

Epistemology, 50, 178; and power, 147, 163–164, 169; and politics, 166

Equal Rights Amendment, 1, 28, 239n17; conservative attack on, 1, 21, 26–27, 225–226; and gay marriages, 27; and military draft, 27

Equality, 37, 63, 175; abstract v. substantive, 14, 71, 73, 164–166; as sameness, 22, 23, 32–45; and distribution of power, 40; and neutrality under law, 65, 71, 73, 164–166, 167, 168, 170; and freedom, 166, 177, 205; meaning for women, 171, 177, 207. *See also* Sex equality

Erotica, 175

Ethnic discrimination, 2, 63, 64, 65

Family, 49, 96; conservative defense of, 24, 30

Femininity, 6, 122; and women lawyers, 74–75

Feminism, 9–10, 169, 216, 217; failure to change women's status, 1–2; second wave of, 1; and politics, 3; applied to law, 4–5; and sexual abuse, 5–6; liberal, 15–16, 60, 118–120, 136–137; conservative attack on, 21, 26, 30–31; goals of, 21–31; critique of gender hierarchy, 22–23; and uses of power, 23, 26, 50–51; meaning of, 48–50, 137; and sexuality, 48–50; postmarxist, 60–61, 135; radical, 60, 119, 120, 137; socialist, 60; critique of pornography, 147, 149, 151, 225; critique of First Amendment, 206–213, 281n46

Ferrenbacher, Don E., 206

First Amendment, 138, 165, 169; and pornography, 4, 129–132, 140–141, 146–162, 177–178, 181, 191–193, 195, 203–204, 223–224; absolutism, 146, 156, 157, 208–209, 212, 224; feminist critique of, 206–213, 281n46

Fisher, A., 196

Frankfurter, Felix, 192

Freedom, and equality, 166

Freud, Sigmund, 51, 85, 143, 144, 151, 170

Frigidity, 97, 143

Gender, 218; and race and class attributes, 2; difference gender makes, 3, 8–9, 23, 32–45, 175, 233n26; imposition of, 3; as sexualization of inequality, 6–7, 8, 14, 40, 43–44, 51, 53, 90; social meaning of, 3, 23, 49, 54–55, 88, 90, 149; and status, 8, 169; hierarchy, 22–23, 118, 137, 178–179; and moral reasoning, 38–39; and pornography, 172–173; in sex discrimination law, 175; and sex, 263n5

Gender inequality. *See* Sex inequality
Gender neutrality, 33–34, 37, 71–73, 152,
  175; in custody and divorce, 35; and
  abortion, 98
General Electric v. Gilbert, 243n18
Genocide, 55, 65, 67, 222
Gilligan, Carol, 38–39
Ginsburg v. New York, 194
Griffin, Susan, 148
Grossberg, Larry, 55

Harrington, Edward, 79
Harris v. McRae, 93, 96–97, 100–101,
  249n21
Harris, Jean, 8
Hefner, Christie, 135, 258n3
Hefner, Hugh, 135, 258n4
Hermeneutics, 53
Heterosexuality, 7, 49, 60, 87, 122; glorifi-
  cation of, 29
Hierarchy, 37, 40, 52, 88, 107, 118; gender
  hierarchy, 22–23, 118, 137, 178–179
Holmes, Nancy, 182
Holmes, Oliver Wendell, 71
Horowitz, Morton, 157
Housework, wages for, 24, 28
Huebschen v. Dept. of Health, 253n16
Humanism, 11, 169
Hume, David, 159
Hyde Amendment, 94

Idealism, 137
Incest, 23, 51, 82; and abortion rights, 94,
  99; and rape, 248n4
Indian Civil Rights Act, 66
Indian tribal rights, 66, 246n8
Indian women, 65–69, 184, 247n11
Individualism, 137
Inequality, 3, 8, 169, 172. *See also* Sex in-
  equality
Insurance coverage, 36

Jews, and anti-Semitism, 55, 140, 222,
  289n91
Jones v. Cassens Transport, 243n19
Joseph, Burton, 127, 129, 130, 131, 133
Judges, women, 70, 77
Justice, as neutrality between abstract
  categories, 65, 71, 73, 164–166, 167

Kant, Immanuel, 158

Katz v. Dole, 287n81
Kennedy, David, 55

LaDuke, Winona, 210
Lafler v. Athletic Board of Control, 242n17
Language: politics of, 47, 55; in sexual
  harassment cases, 112, 115, 287n81
Law: feminism applied to, 4–5; and liber-
  alism, 164–165
Lawyers: women, 70, 71, 74–77, 199,
  200–205, 217, 305n6; as power role, 74
Legal reasoning, 9, 234n27
Legal system, 64; and sexual abuse, 12–
  13; and women's rights, 26, 104–105,
  167, 169, 195; and abortion cases, 93–
  102; and sexual harassment, 103–115
Legalism, hegemony of, 129
Lesbians, 86, 122; and sadomasochism,
  15; and sex in pornography, 199; stigmatization of, 236n34
Levi, Edward M., 234n27
Libel, 11, 192–193
Liberalism, 14; how legitimized, 2; and
  feminism, 15–16, 60, 118–120, 136–137;
  misogyny of, 15, 140–141, 205; and tolerance, 15; conservative attack on, 21;
  on equality as sameness, 22, 36; and
  abortion, 94; and pornography, 136,
  140, 148–149, 154–157; and male supremacy, 151; and law, 164–165; and
  equality-freedom dilemma, 166; and
  power, 221
Literacy, 47, 208, 302n7
Literary criticism, and pornography, 4
Lochner v. New York, 165
Lovelace, Linda. *see* Marchiano, Linda
Loving v. Virginia, 245n35

Mailer, Norman, 16
Male supremacy, 3, 31, 43, 53, 118, 164;
  and pornography, 3, 130, 148, 154,
  172–174; as politics, 3; and sexual access to women, 14; and sex equality,
  39–40; and sexualized objectification,
  50, 54–55, 119, 139; and Indian tribal
  rules, 67–68; and liberalism, 151
Maleness, as entitlement, 37
Mann, Paul, 110
Manners, and politics, 46
Marchiano, Linda, 10–14, 125, 127–129,
  130, 132, 133, 180, 181, 182

Index

Marital rape, 1, 26, 76, 170, 247n2, 291n107
Marriage, 96; gay, 27
Martial arts, 83–84
Martinez v. Santa Clara Pueblo, 65–69
Marxist theory, 48, 58–60, 158–159; and feminism, 60–61, 135
Masculinity, 52, 122; of money as power, 2; and sex discrimination, 71
Medicaid funding of abortions, 93, 96
Meiklejohn, Alexander, 193
Military draft and service, 27, 35, 38, 244n26
Miller v. California, 191
Misogyny: and sex inequality, 5; and sexual sadism, 5; in liberalism, 15, 140–141, 205; and sexual harassment, 114
Money: as power, 2; *Playboy*'s money, 134–135, 137, 141–142, 145
Monroe, Marilyn, 16
Moralism, 137
Morality, and obscenity, 147, 150–151, 152, 162, 175, 186
Moral reasoning, gender differences in, 38–39
Morals legislation, 91
Mother-child relation, 52–53
Murder, 6, 24, 52; depicted in pornography, 172, 180, 199, 200, 272n56

Native tribal sovereignty, 66, 246n8
Native women, 65–69, 184, 247n11
Natural law, 12, 13
Naturalism, 137
Nesson, Charles, 260nn13, 14
Neutral principles in constitutional law, 65, 71, 73, 164–166, 167, 168, 170
Newport News Shipbuilding and Dry Dock Co. v. EEOC, 243n18
New York v. Ferber, 182, 269n37

Objectification, 118, 119, 139; in pornography, 174, 175, 182, 199
Objectivity, 50, 54–55, 86, 146–162, 174–175
Obscenity, 90, 91, 97, 139, 140, 191, 192; and morality, 147, 150–151, 152, 162, 175, 186; social value standard in, 152–153 and First Amendment absolutism, 208–209; *Report of the Commission on*

Obscenity and Pornography, 264n8, 284n53
Occupational health hazards, 38
Orgasms, female: faking, 58, 129
Orgasms, male: from pornography, 190
Orwell, George, 146

Paternalism, institutional, 104–105
Pay inequality, 1, 24, 25, 28, 41, 171, 243n19; comparable worth doctrine, 36, 64, 198; median income of men and women, 231n2
Penis: in fellatio, 10, 11, 128, 286n65; as a weapon, 130; exposure of, 151, 268n29
Penthouse magazine, 189, 286n66
Pimps, 10, 145; violence of, 11
Playboy Foundation, 99, 133
Playboy magazine, 134–145, 152, 158, 189, 209, 223, 260n10
Plessy v. Ferguson, 165
Political philosophy, 166
Politics: and feminism, 3; of sex inequality, 3, 7, 34, 41–42; of pornography, 12; and manners, 46; of language, 47, 55; and epistemology, 166; of First Amendment, 206–213, 281n46
Pornography, 2, 5, 27, 41, 52, 221–222; as civil rights violation, 3–4, 14, 163, 175–195, 199, 200–205, 210–213, 222–223, 226; and male supremacy, 3, 130, 148, 154, 172–174, 222; and sex inequality, 3, 148, 172–174, 193–195, 204, 205; as "speech," 3, 11, 15, 28, 129–132, 154–158, 161–162, 193, 195, 200, 204, 209–213; and aesthetics, 4, 61, 150, 224; and First Amendment, 4, 129–132, 140–141, 146–162, 177–178, 181, 191, 192, 195, 203, 204, 223–224; and literary criticism, 4; and power, 4, 175; as sex, 4, 53–54, 148, 266n18; trafficking, 4, 179, 186, 190, 191, 198, 203–204, 210, 212, 294n109; and Linda Marchiano ("Linda Lovelace"), 10–14, 128–129, 130, 180, 181, 182; and violence, 11, 85–87, 90, 91, 139, 148, 160, 171–172, 174, 185, 187–190, 192, 194, 199, 202, 203, 210; politics of, 12; and sexual access to women, 14, 138, 140, 149, 150, 153, 173, 190, 199; and women's silence, 15, 16, 130, 140, 181, 188–189,

190, 193, 194–195, 209; in workplace, 115, 183; in educational institutions, 116, 183, 288n84; as terrorism, 130, 140, 149, 151, 183, 188, 203; liberal defense of, 136, 140, 148–149, 154–157; ideological defense of, 137, 224–225; feminist critique of, 147, 149, 151, 225; harm caused by, 155, 156, 212, 264n9, 295n115; and children, 157, 171–172, 179–181, 182, 184, 189, 212, 287n77, 291n107; dehumanizing effects of, 158–161, 175; defined, 160, 175, 262n1, 274n1; women defined by, 166, 171–172, 178, 181, 190, 284n55; and battery, 171, 184, 199; and prostitution, 171, 285n62, 297n132; and rape, 171, 172, 182, 184–189, 194, 198, 272n57, 291n107; and sexual harassment, 171, 183, 198–199; consent and coercion in, 172, 180–183; killing depicted in, 172, 180, 199, 200, 272n56; objectification in, 174, 175, 182, 199; as sex discrimination, 175–195, 199–205, 210–213; criminal v. civil approach, 179, 203, 283n52; racism in, 199–200, 213; *Report of the Commission on Obscenity and Pornography,* 264n8, 284n53

Poverty, 55, 64, 73, 132

Power, 57, 164; money as masculine form of, 2; and gender, 8, 14, 40, 43–44, 90; feminist theory of, 23, 26, 50–51; hierarchy of, 37, 40, 52, 88, 107, 172; equality and distribution of power, 40, 43–44; exercise of male power, 52, 53, 58, 130, 219–220; female power, 53; lawyers as power role, 74; sexual harassment as abuse of, 85–88, 90–91; and legitimacy, 135, 137, 138, 141, 142; and epistemology, 147, 163–164, 169; and powerlessness, 164, 165, 171, 220; and social reality, 166; and maleness, 171; and pornography, 175; and liberalism, 221

Pregnancy, 36; and maternity benefits, 1, 242n18

Price, Pamela, 220

Prisons: employment in, 38, 73; abuse of prisoners, 170, 279n29; women compared to prisoners, 170

Privacy: and abortion, 1, 93, 96–102; a

feminist view of, 100–102; and pornography, 155, 211

Prostitution, 5, 24–25, 52, 61, 169; and pornography, 171, 285n62, 297n132; children coerced into, 180–181

Prurient interest standard, 153–154, 174, 182

Puerto Rican women: death from illegal abortions, 25

Race: and gender, 2; and death from illegal abortions, 25

Racial discrimination, 64, 65, 167; legal treatment of, 9, 42, 44; and social hierarchy, 88

Racism, 2, 55, 154, 164, 167–168, 222; and sexism, 66–67; and rape, 81–82; in pornography, 199–200, 213

Ramos, Norma, 213

Rape, 5, 6; convictions, 1, 88, 231n4; marital, 1, 26, 76, 170, 247n2, 291n107; rate, 1, 23, 41, 51, 169; of black women, 7, 248n3; as sex, 11; normalization of, 61; New Bedford gang rape, 79, 194; publicizing, 81; reporting, 81–83, 88, 290n98; and racism, 81–82; as crime of violence, 82–83, 85–87, 88–89, 92, 160, 233n19; acquaintance rape, 83, 95, 247n2; defense against, 83–84; prosecutions, 83, 248n1; defined, 87; and sexuality, 87–88; victim's view of, 87–88; rapist's view of, 88; and abortion rights, 94, 99, 248n4; and sexual harassment, 110, 112; victim's sexual history, 113, 231n5; and pornography, 171, 172, 182, 184–186, 187, 188–189, 194, 198, 272n57, 291n107; and battery, 182; and incest, 248n4; and defamation countersuits, 255n38

Red Lion Broadcasting Co. v. F.C.C., 208

Renton v. Playtime Theaters, 211, 212

Reproduction, control over, 94, 95, 97–98, 100

Rich, Adrienne, 93, 170

Roberts v. United States Jaycees, 299n154

Roe v Wade, 93, 96, 97, 100, 101, 249n21

Sadomasochism, 161; and misogyny, 5; lesbian, 15

Sartre, Jean Paul, 19

Index

Scheman, Naomi, 154–155

Schlafly, Phyllis, 21, 22, 24, 25, 27, 29, 30, 31, 76

Segregation, 64, 165, 178, 193–194, 202, 208, 213

Self-interest, 15

Self-possession, 121, 159

Self-respect, 121, 122, 159, 160

Separatism, 123

Sex, 217–218; and male-female relations, 3; dominance and submission as, 3, 6–7, 29, 50, 53, 54, 149, 152, 160–161; pornography as, 4, 53–54, 148, 266n18; and violence, 5–6, 85–92, 151, 184, 187; being anti-sex, 7–8; consent in, 11; rape as, 11; in advertising, 27, 223, 272n54; as continuum, 44; battery as, 85, 92; and gender, 263n5

Sex discrimination, 32–45, 64–65, 71–74, 168; benign discrimination, 71; sexual harassment as, 103, 109, 231n7, 252n13; and gender, 175; pornography as, 175–195, 199–205, 210–213; in educational institutions, 240n4; and anti-abortion laws, 249n21; in advertising, 299n154

Sex equality: and abortion, 1, 93, 96–102; and maternity benefits, 1, 242n18; and pay, 1; sameness/difference theory of, 23, 32–45; politics of, 34; and male supremacy, 39–40; as governmental interest, 178

Sex inequality, 2, 9; and pornography, 3, 148, 195, 204, 205; and misogyny, 5; erotization of, 6–7, 14, 172–174; legal treatment of, 9, 42; and politics, 41–42; and speech, 129

Sexism, 7, 30, 118, 131, 154, 164, 170, 218; and racism, 66–67

Sex objects, women as, 50, 173

Sex specificity, 55–56, 57, 71, 72, 76, 166–167, 175

Sexual abuse, 5, 7, 171; of children, 5, 6, 23, 41, 51, 169, 170; and feminism, 5–6; and legal system, 12–13; and pornography, 171, 172, 184, 185–186; reporting, 191

Sexual access: and male supremacy, 14; coercive and unwanted, 83, 86; and pornography, 138, 140, 149–150, 153, 173, 190, 199; and freedom of speech, 140, 144

Sexual blackmail, 15

Sexual harassment, 1, 5, 6, 26, 61, 73, 103–116, 198, 252n8; conservative views on, 25; rate, 25, 51–52, 106, 169; as abuse of power, 85–88, 90–91; as sex discrimination, 103, 109, 231n7, 252n13; in educational institutions, 107, 110, 220, 251n6; and rape, 110, 112; reporting, 111, 114–115, 255n38; and language, 112, 115, 287n81; and sexual misogyny, 114; *Playboy*'s funding of conferences on, 145; and pornography, 171, 183, 198–199

Sexuality, 218–219; and sex inequality, 6–7, 14; and women's status, 6; and feminism, 48–50; social meaning of, 49–52, 60–61; feminist theory of, 53–54; and rape, 87–88; control over, 94, 97–98; Freudian theory of, 143–144, 151; *Playboy*'s definition of, 143

Silence, of women, 15, 16, 55–56, 104, 130, 140, 144, 169–170, 181, 188–189, 190, 193, 194–195, 209

Skokie-type injuries, 184, 289n91

Slavery, 55, 167–168, 208, 302n7

"Slippery slope" problem, 236n36

Social reality, and power, 166

Social relations: and gender, 3, 23, 54–55, 88, 90, 149; and sexuality, 49–51, 60–61; and racial discrimination, 88

Sontag, Susan, 98

Special protection (special benefits) rule, 33, 38, 71–73

Speech: pornography as, 3, 11, 15, 28, 129–132, 154–158, 161–162, 193, 195, 200, 204, 209–213; and sex inequality, 129; conduct distinguished from, 130; and sexual access to women, 140, 144; and First Amendment absolutism, 146, 156, 157, 212, 224; protection of, 207–213; high-value and low-value, 211; functions of, 220–221

Spivak, Gayatri, 54, 55, 58

Sports, women in, 36, 74, 117–124, 241n17, 255n2

State, women's relation to, 26–27, 104–105

Status, 2, 25, 55; effect of feminism on,

1–2; and sexuality, 6; and gender, 8, 169

Stereotyping, 118–119

Stewart, Potter, 90, 148, 194

Subordination, 144; of women to men, 2, 147, 152, 175, 201, 210, 222, 305n6

Suspect classification theory, 44

Terrorism, 7; pornography as, 130, 140, 149, 151, 183, 188, 203

Thomson, Judith Jarvis, 98

Tomlin, Lily, 215

Traynor, Charles, 10, 132

Tribe, Laurence, 193

Tutu, Desmond, 226

Uncertainty principle, 58

Victim: use of term, 13

Victimization of women, 64, 104, 149, 174, 220, 221, 226

Violence, 41, 57; and sex, 5–6, 85–92, 151, 184, 187; of pimps, 11; and pornography, 11, 87, 90–91, 139, 148, 160, 171–172, 174, 185, 187–190, 192, 194, 199, 202, 203, 210; domestic, 24, 28, 41, 52, 170; rape as, 82–83, 85–87, 88–89, 92, 160, 233n19

Voluntarism, 137

Wagner, Jane, 215

Wahl, Rosalie, 70, 77

Wechsler, Herbert, 165

White supremacy, 164–165, 167, 245n35

Williams, Bernard, 159

Williams, Vanessa, 286n66

Wittgenstein, Ludwig, 158

Wittig, Monique, 28

Women: opposition to ERA, 1; class status of, 2; comparative privileges of, 2, 12, 37–38, 76–77; silence of, 15, 16, 130, 140, 181, 188–189, 190, 193, 194–195, 209; conservative views on, 22; feminist views on, 22; in work force, 24, 243n19; and legal system, 26, 104–105, 165, 167, 169, 195; history of, 39; as sex objects, 50, 173; sexual desire in, 54; as objects, 55; "to be" women, 58–59; victimization of, 64, 104, 149, 174, 220, 221, 226; as judges, 70, 77; as lawyers, 70, 71, 74–77, 199, 200–205, 217, 305n6; as and for women, 71, 73–74, 77; as abstract persons, 72; survival tactics of, 94, 135; desexualization of, 97; as uses to which men put them, 98; credibility of, 110–113, 133, 191; as whores, 112, 128, 132; defined by pornography, 166, 171–172, 178, 181, 190, 284n55; and equality-freedom issue, 166, 177, 205; compared to prisoners, 170; in academia, 216; reward and punishment for being, 226

Woolf, Virginia, 74, 125, 196

Work: Marxist theory of, 48; sexualization of, 112–113, 115

Workplace, pornography in, 115, 183. *See also* Sexual harassment

Yale University, 220

Young v. American Mini Theatres, 299n154